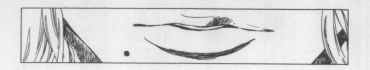

It is not frightening
To know misfortune.
What is frightening
Is to know lost happiness
Will never come back again.

BLEACH46 BACK FROM BLIND

Shonen Jump Manga

STARS AND

黒崎一護

Ichigo Kurosaki

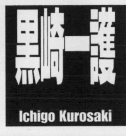

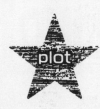
plot

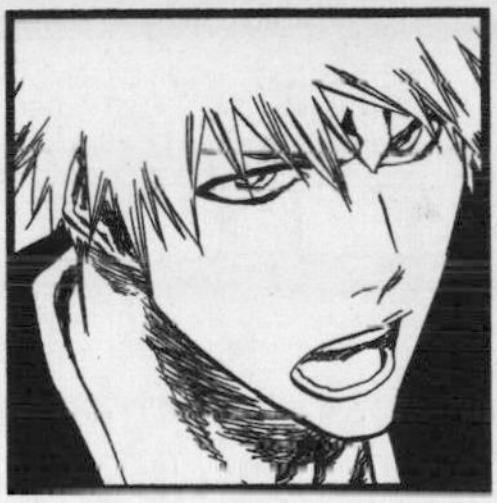

When high school student Ichigo Kurosaki meets Soul Reaper Rukia Kuchiki his life is changed forever. Soon Ichigo is a soul-cleansing Soul Reaper too, and he finds himself having adventures, as well as problems, that he never would have imagined. Now Ichigo and his friends must stop renegade Soul Reaper Aizen and his army of Arrancars from destroying the Soul Society and wiping out Karakura as well.

After a fierce battle in Las Noches to save Orihime, Ichigo heads to Karakura Town for the final battle! But a coalition of the Thirteen Court Guard Companies and the Visoreds seem unable to defeat Aizen. Now the only thing standing between Aizen and total victory is Ichigo Kurosaki!

BLEACH ALL

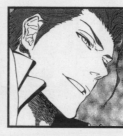
市丸ギン

Gin Ichimaru

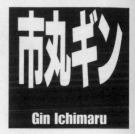

Sôsuke Aizen

藍染惣右介
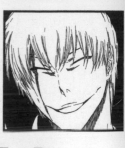

STORIES

BLEACH46

BACK FROM BLIND

Contents

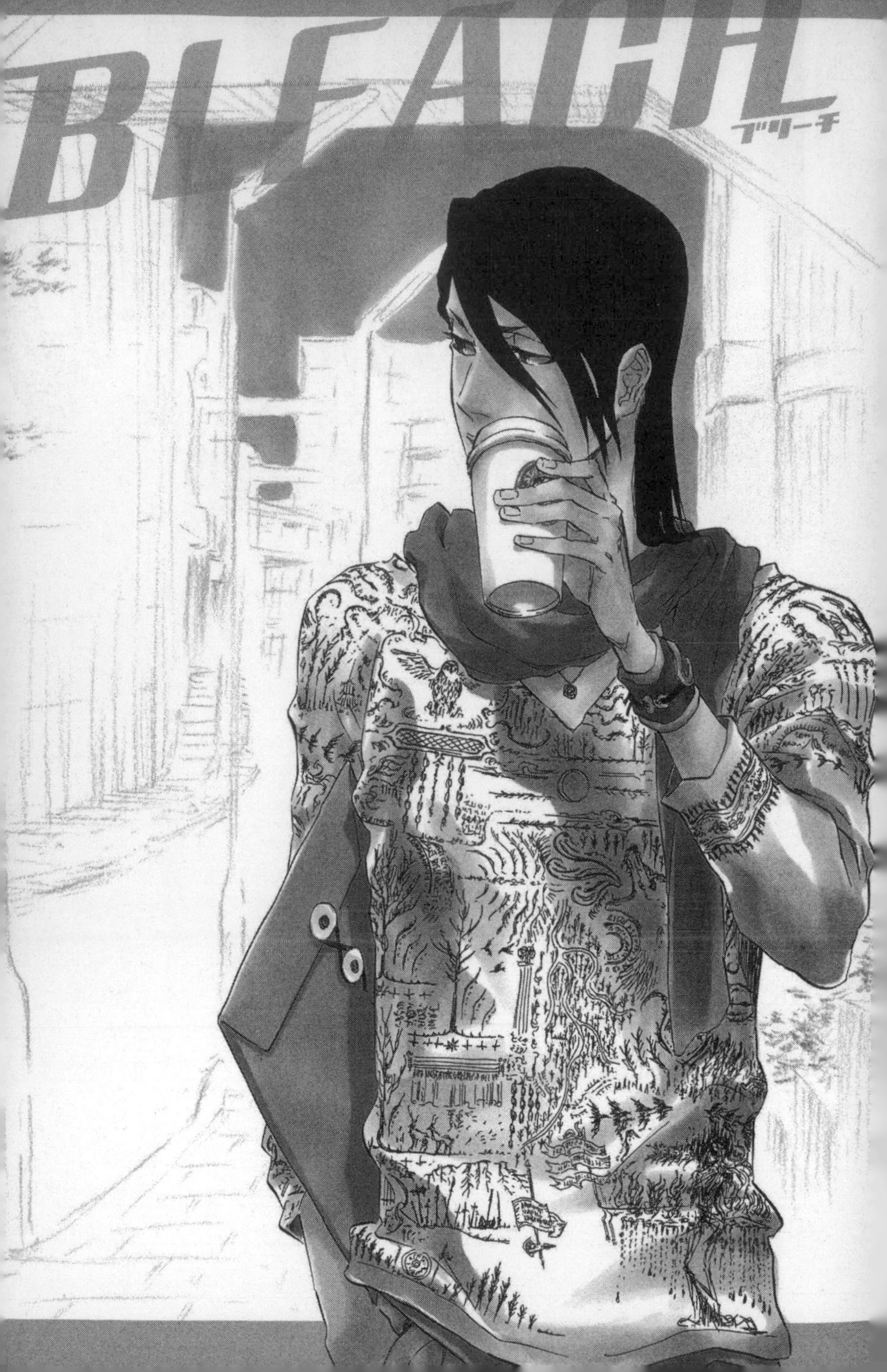
BLEACH
ブリーチ

BLEACH

ブリーチ

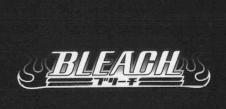

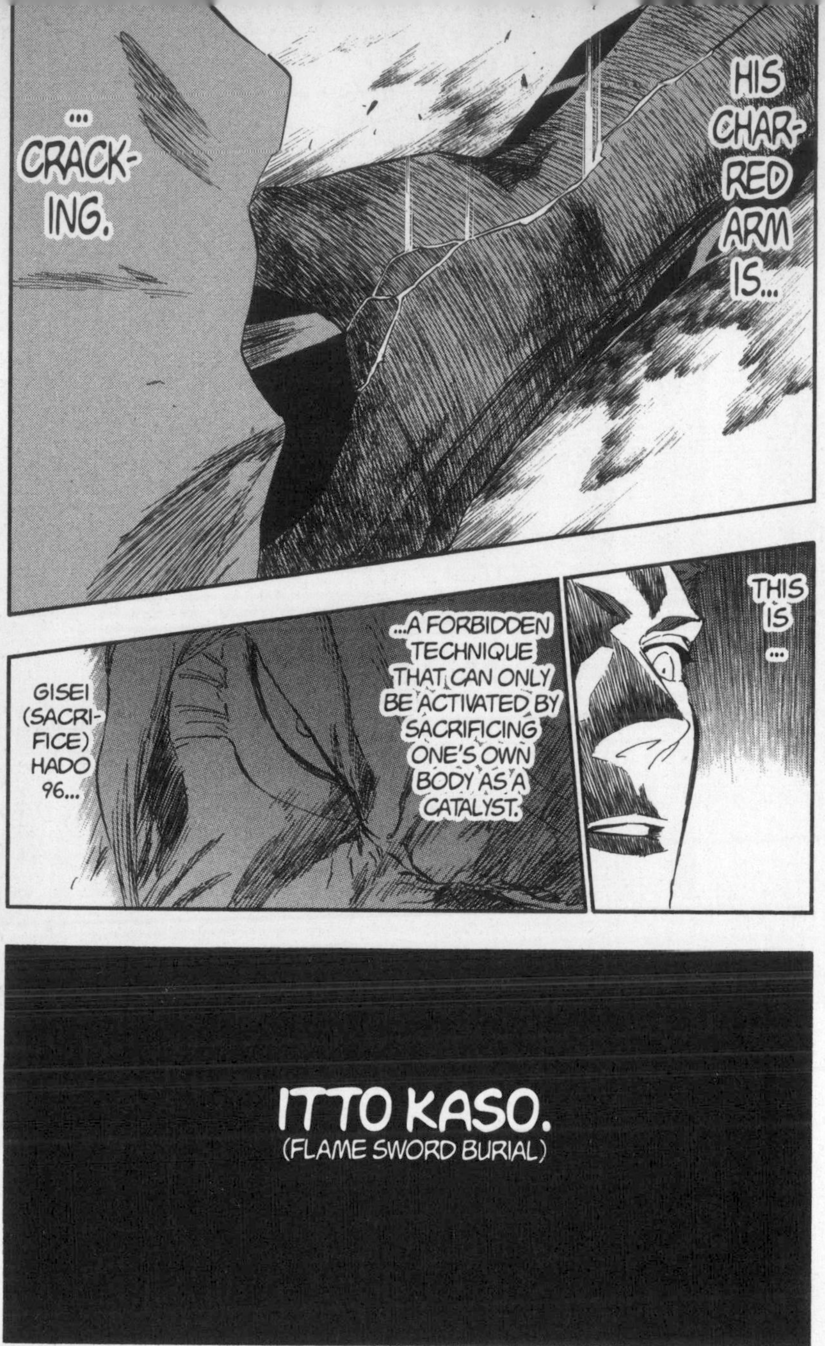

HIS CHARRED ARM IS...
... CRACKING.
THIS IS ...
...A FORBIDDEN TECHNIQUE THAT CAN ONLY BE ACTIVATED BY SACRIFICING ONE'S OWN BODY AS A CATALYST.
GISEI (SACRIFICE) HADO 96...
ITTO KASO.
(FLAME SWORD BURIAL)

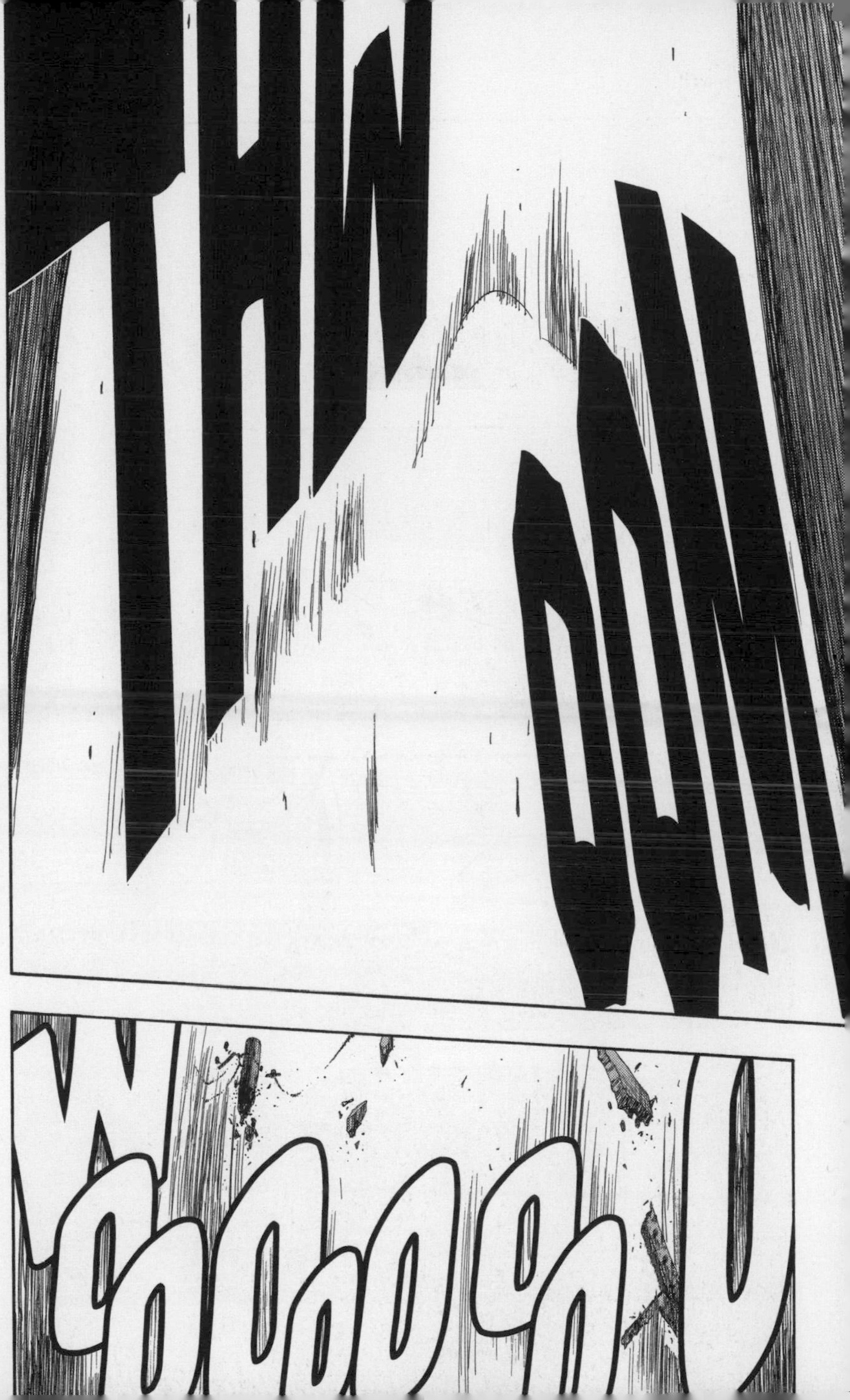

READ THIS WAY

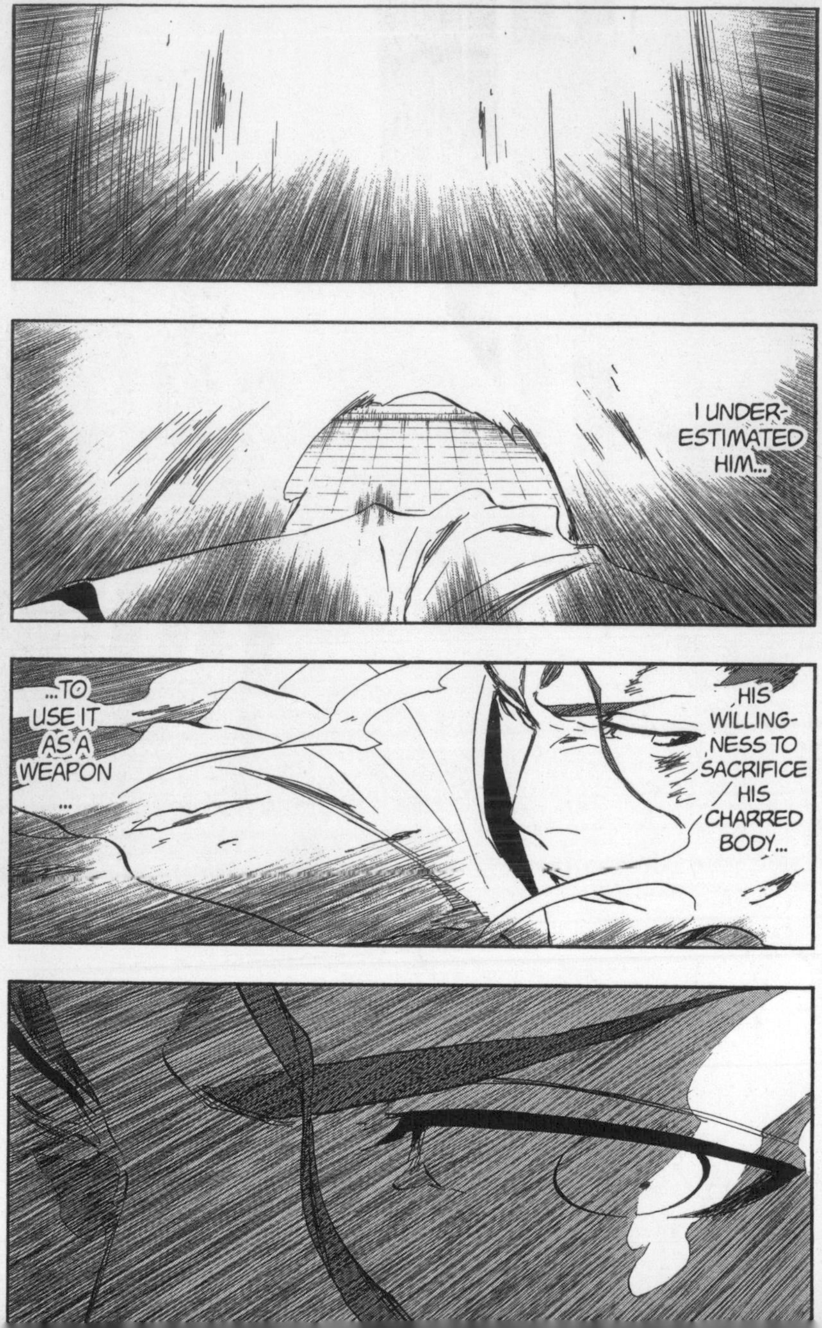
I UNDER-ESTIMATED HIM...
HIS WILLINGNESS TO SACRIFICE HIS CHARRED BODY...
...TO USE IT AS A WEAPON...

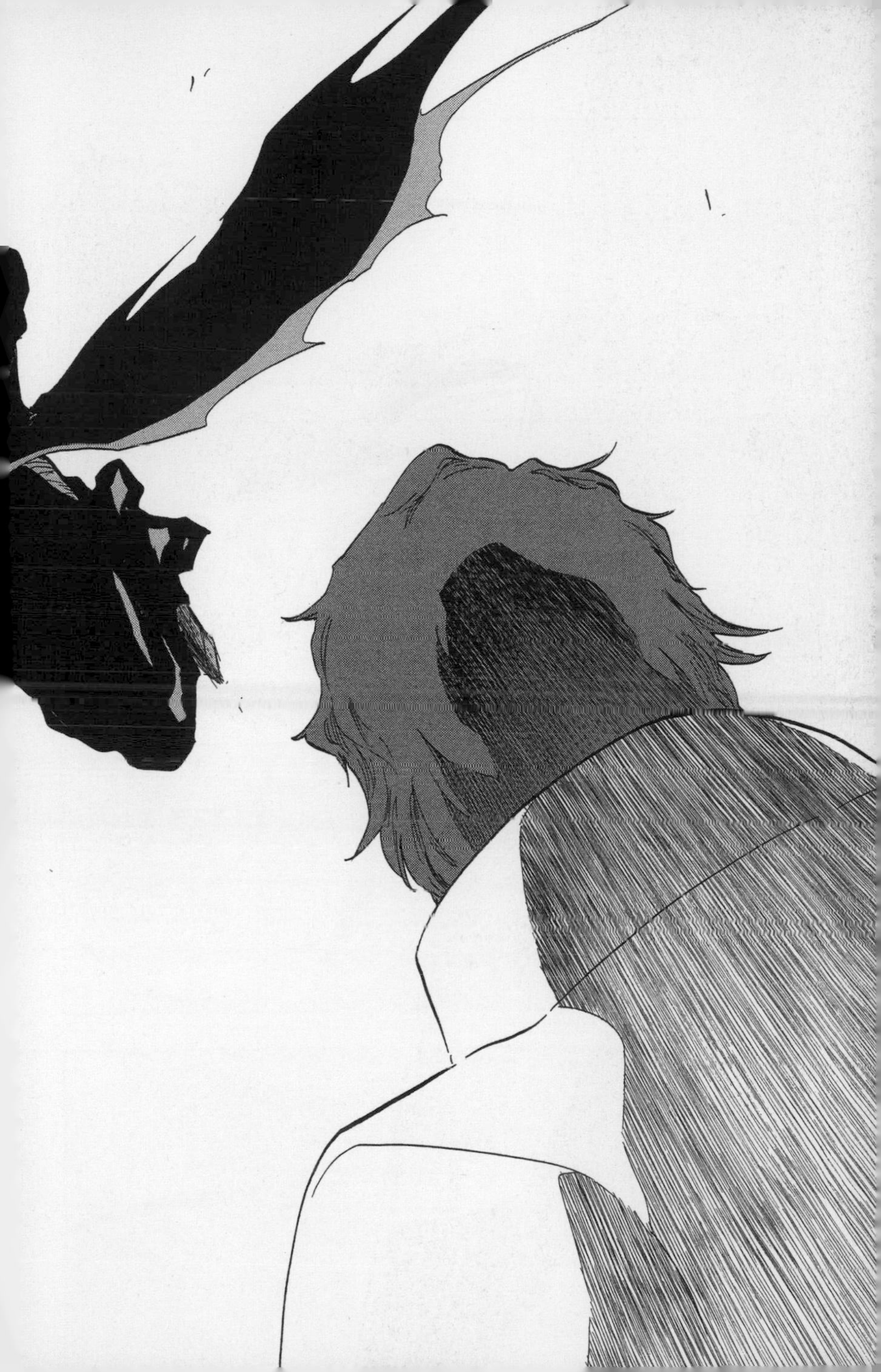

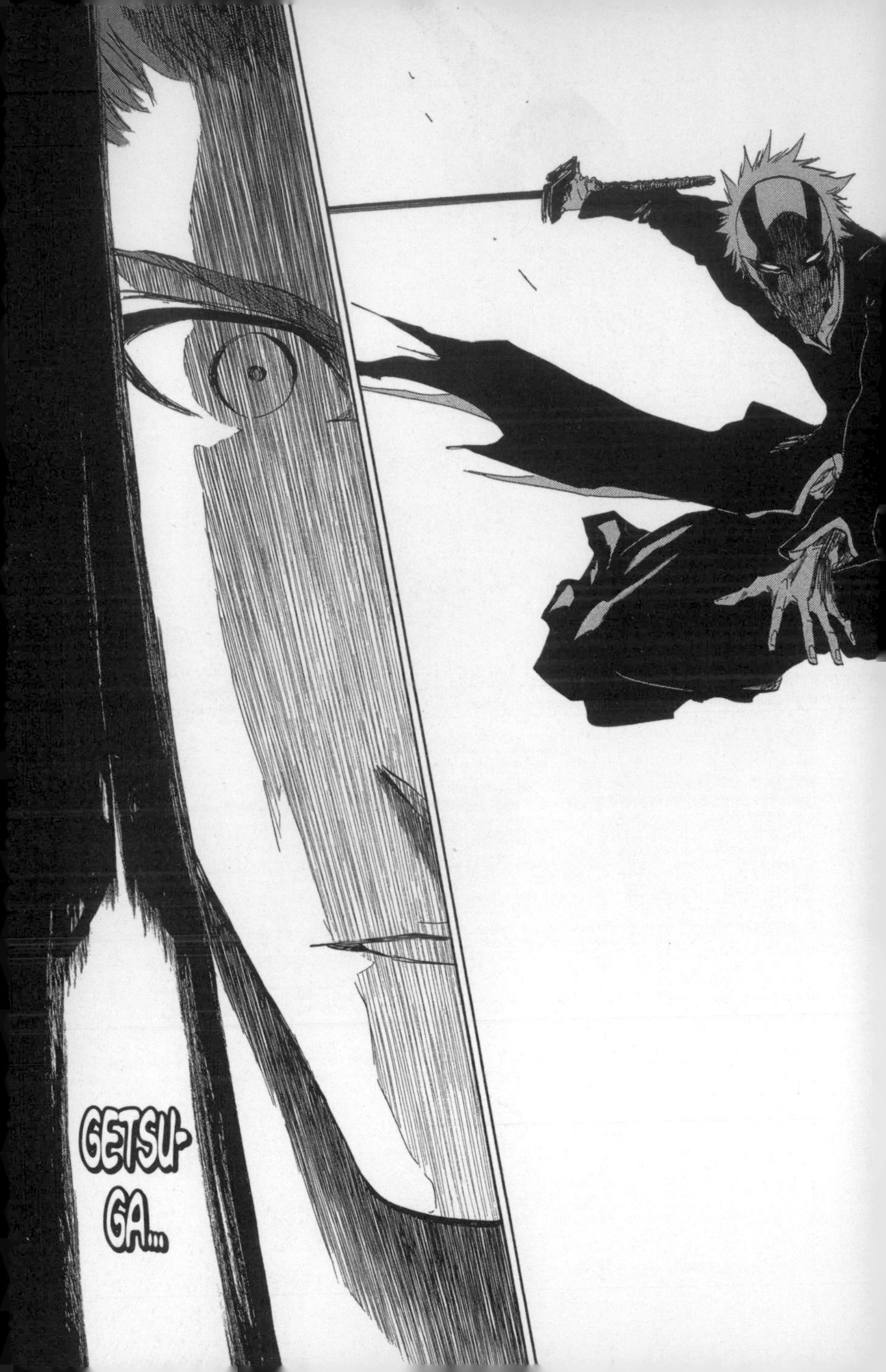
GETSU-
GA...

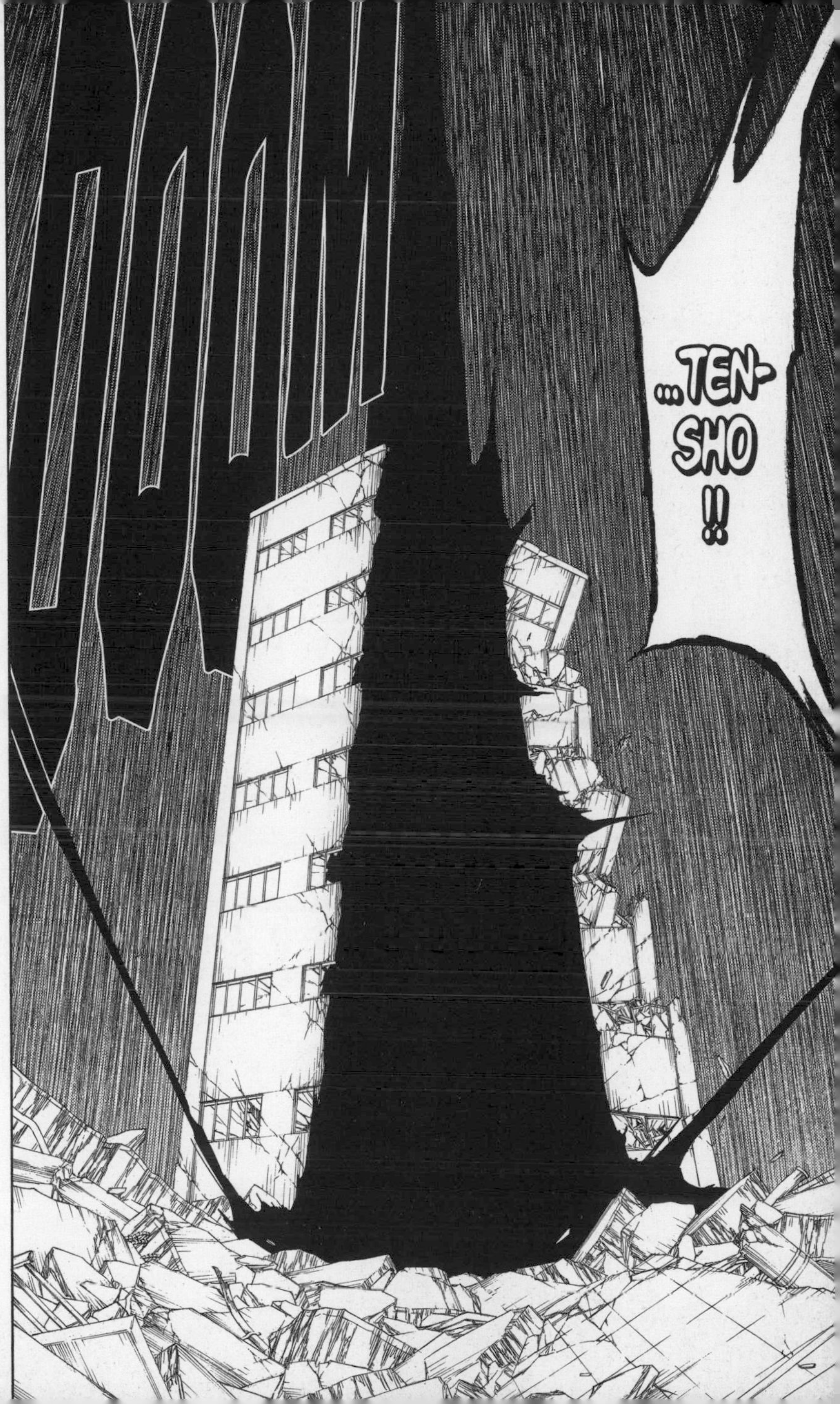
...TEN-SHO!!

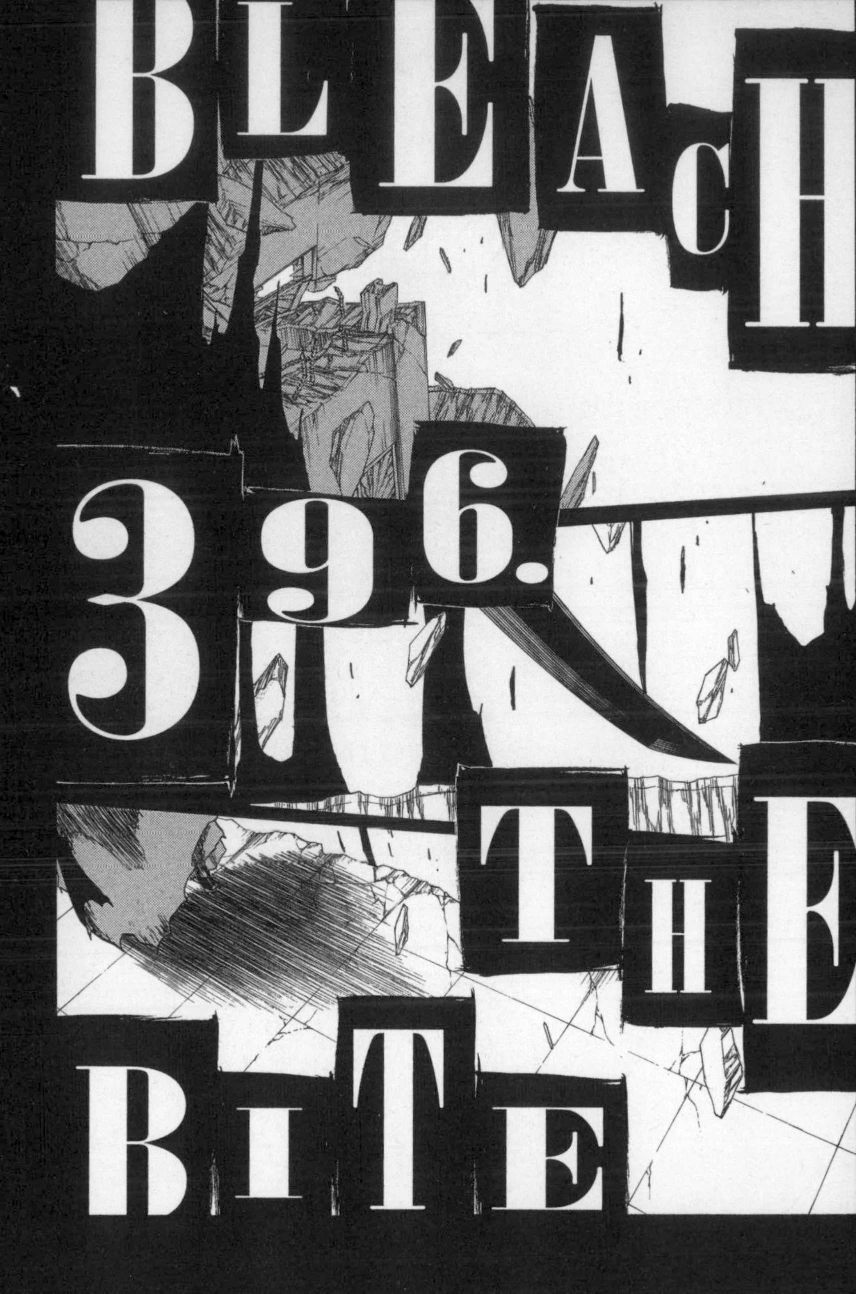
BLEACH
396.
THE BITE

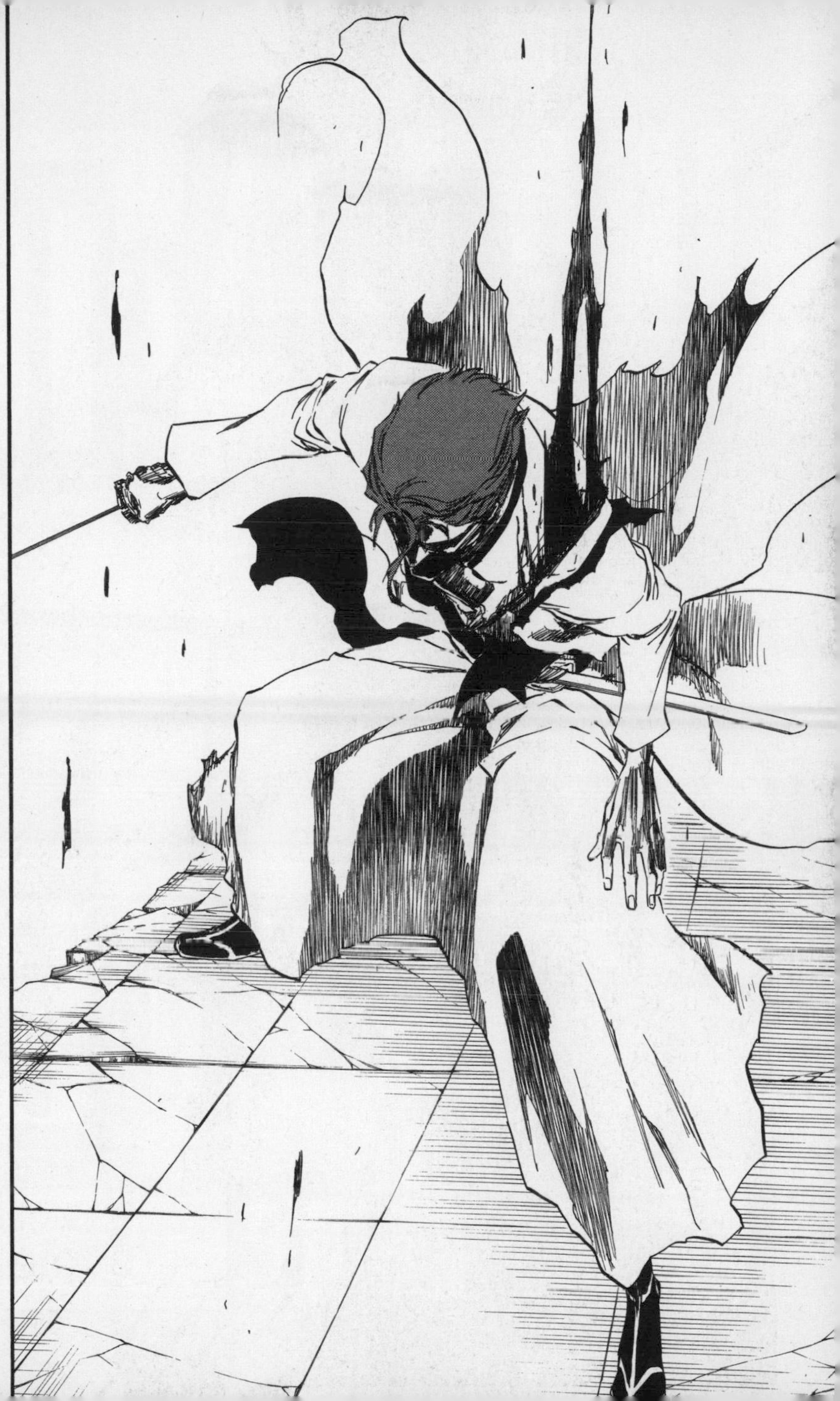

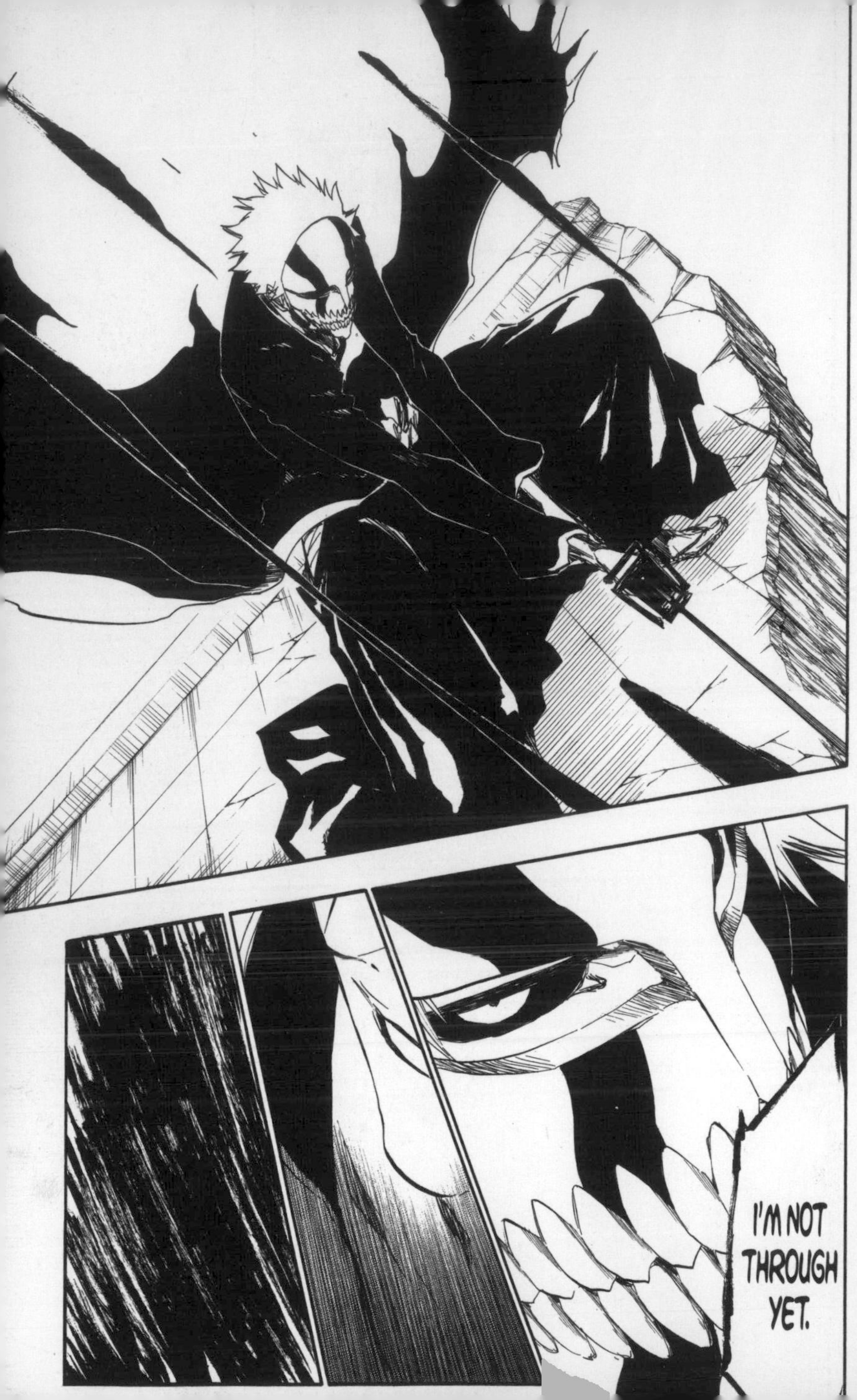
I'M NOT THROUGH YET.

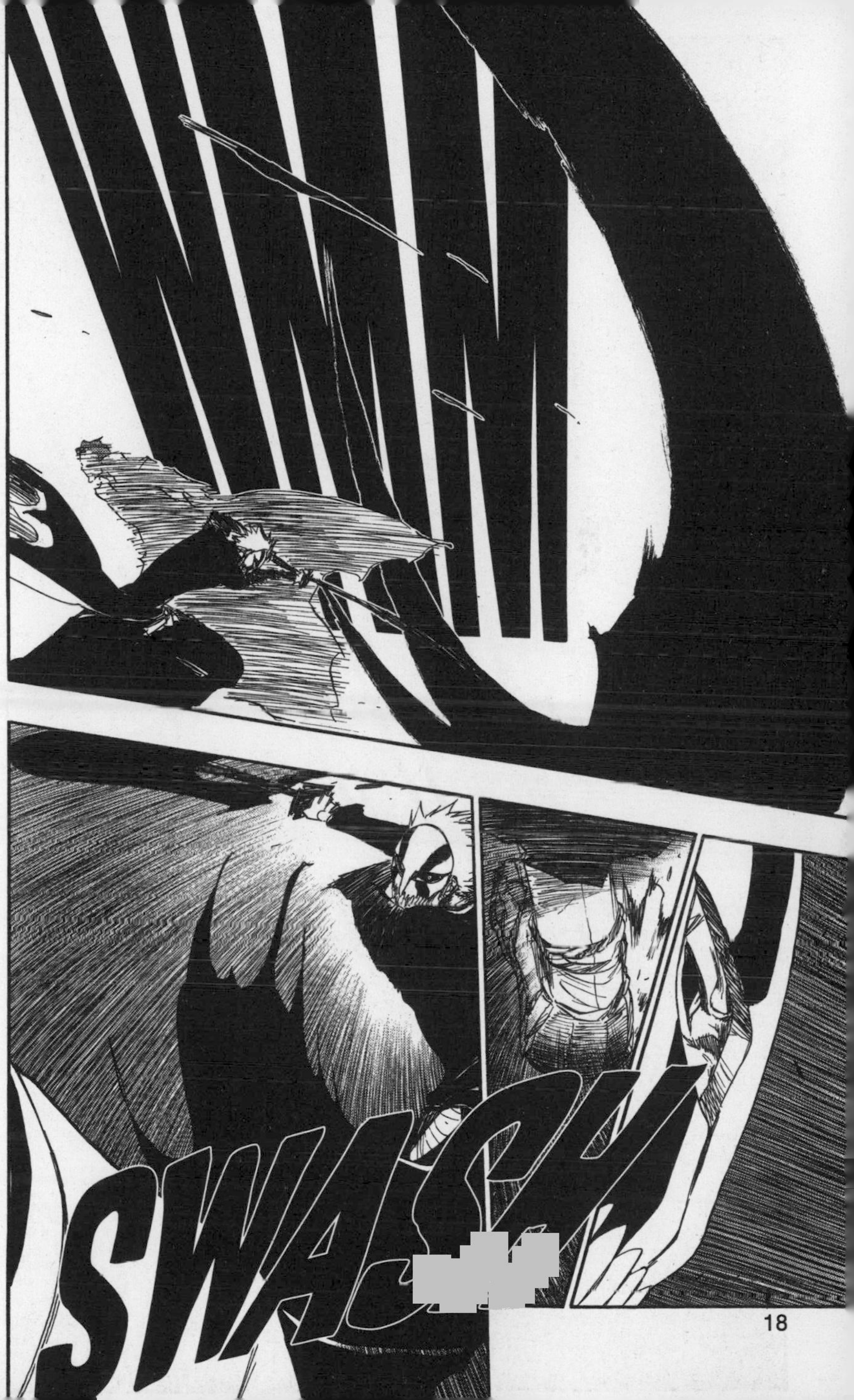
SWASH

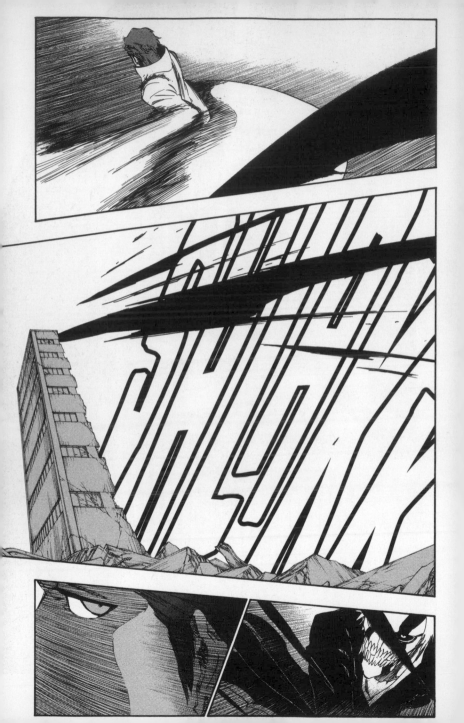

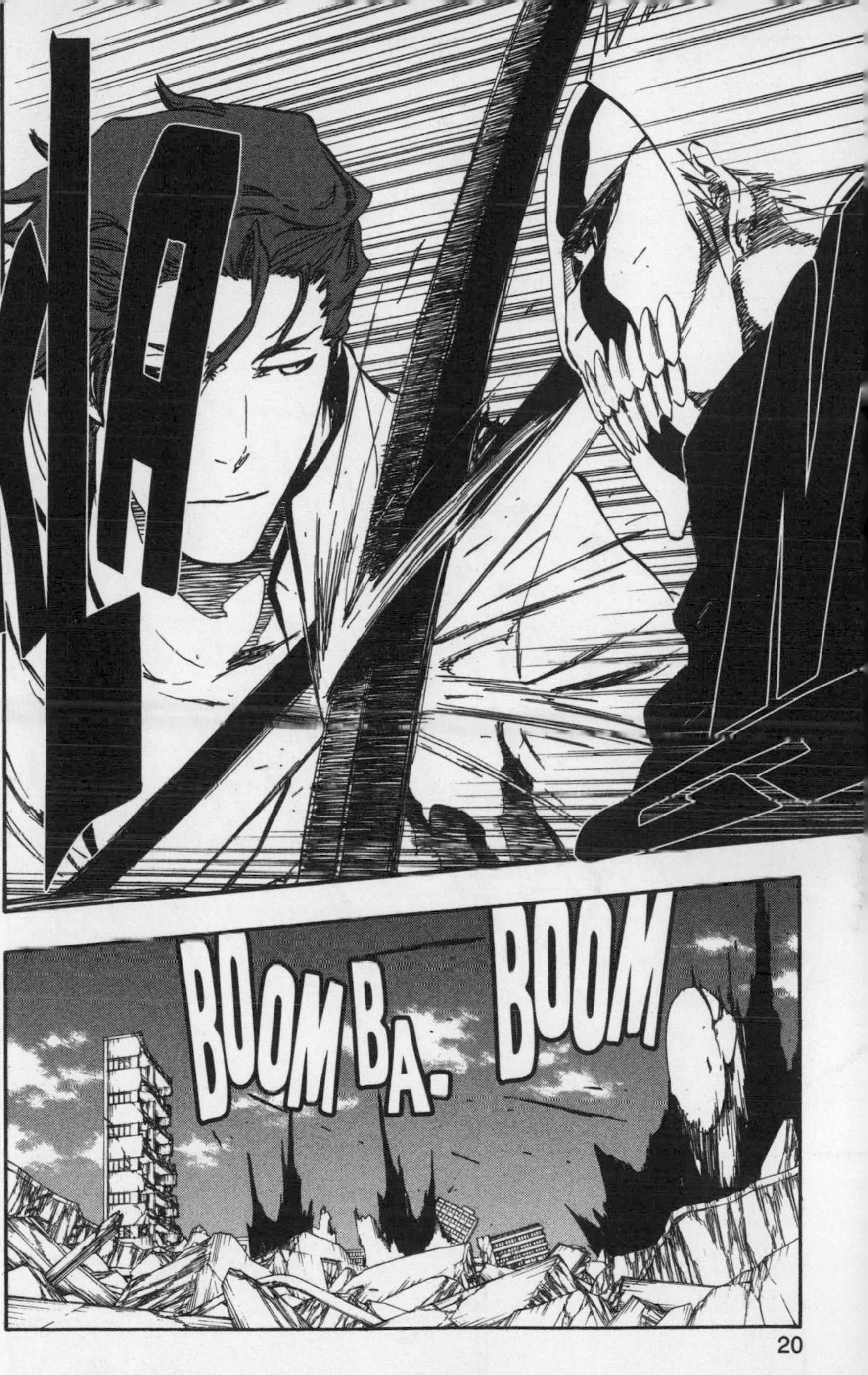
BOOM BA. BOOM

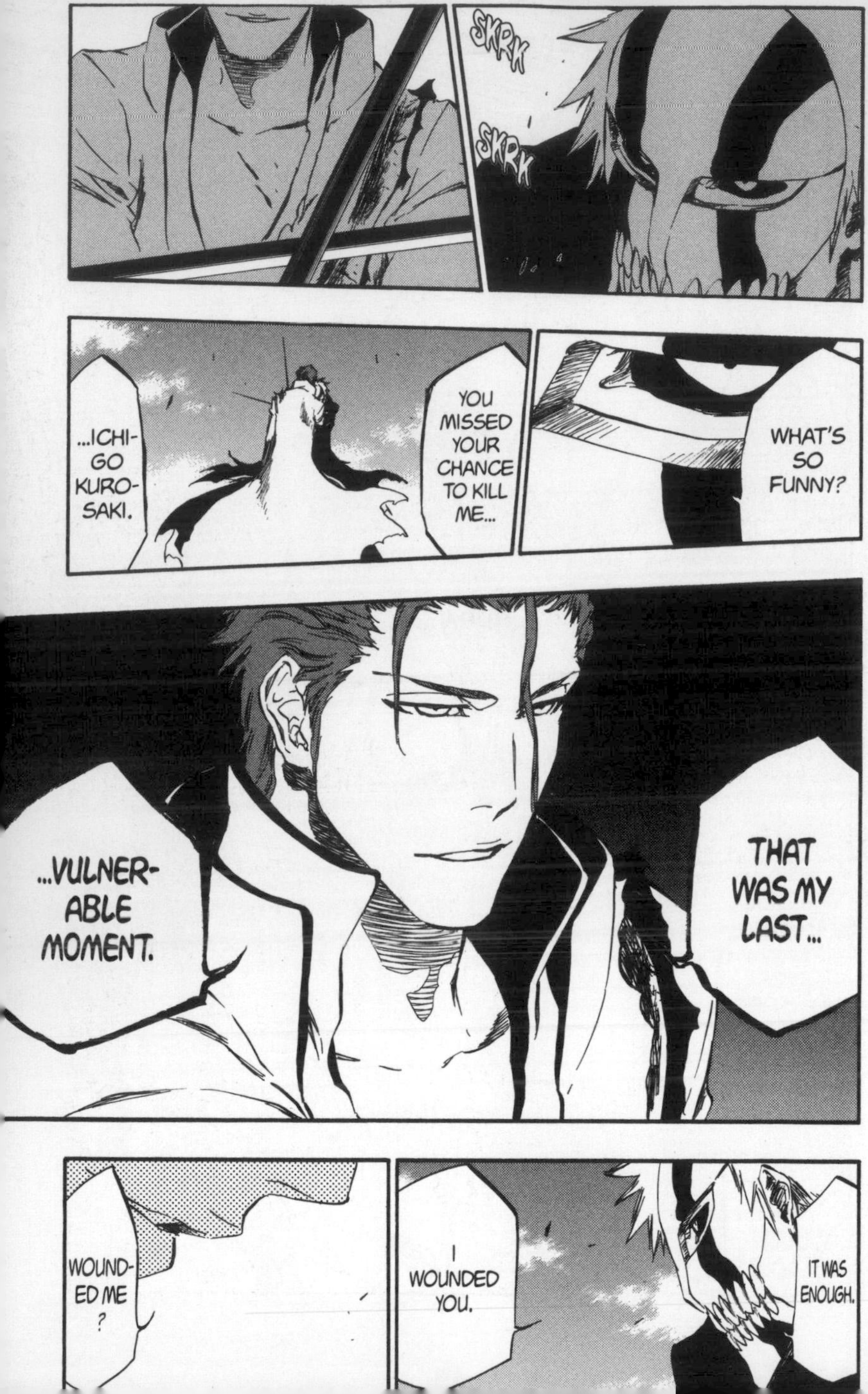
SKRK
SKRK
WHAT'S SO FUNNY?
YOU MISSED YOUR CHANCE TO KILL ME...
...ICHIGO KUROSAKI.
THAT WAS MY LAST...
...VULNERABLE MOMENT.
IT WAS ENOUGH.
I WOUNDED YOU.
WOUNDED ME?

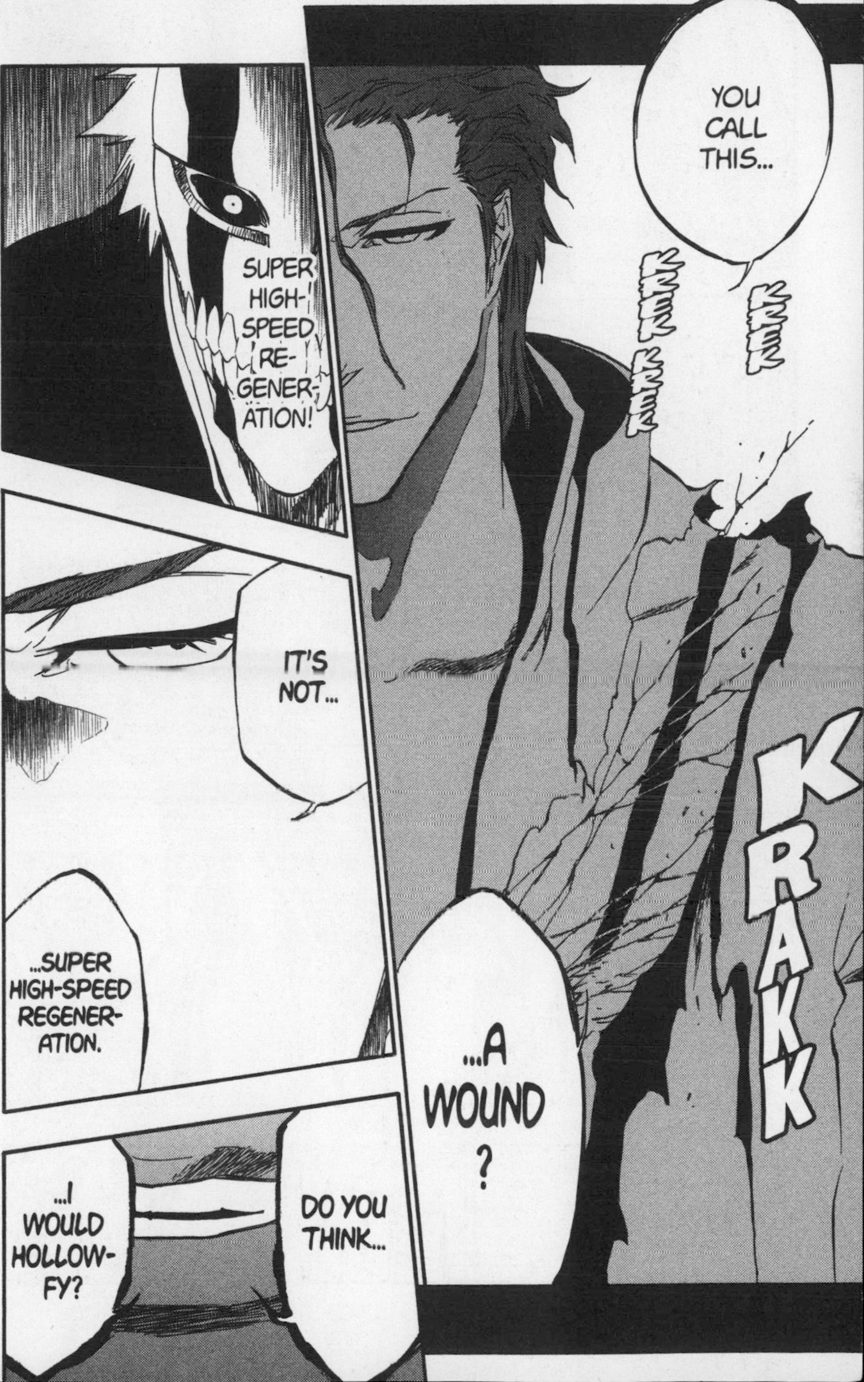
YOU CALL THIS...
KREK KREK KREK
KRAKK
...A WOUND?
SUPER HIGH-SPEED REGENERATION!
IT'S NOT...
...SUPER HIGH-SPEED REGENERATION.
DO YOU THINK...
...I WOULD HOLLOWFY?

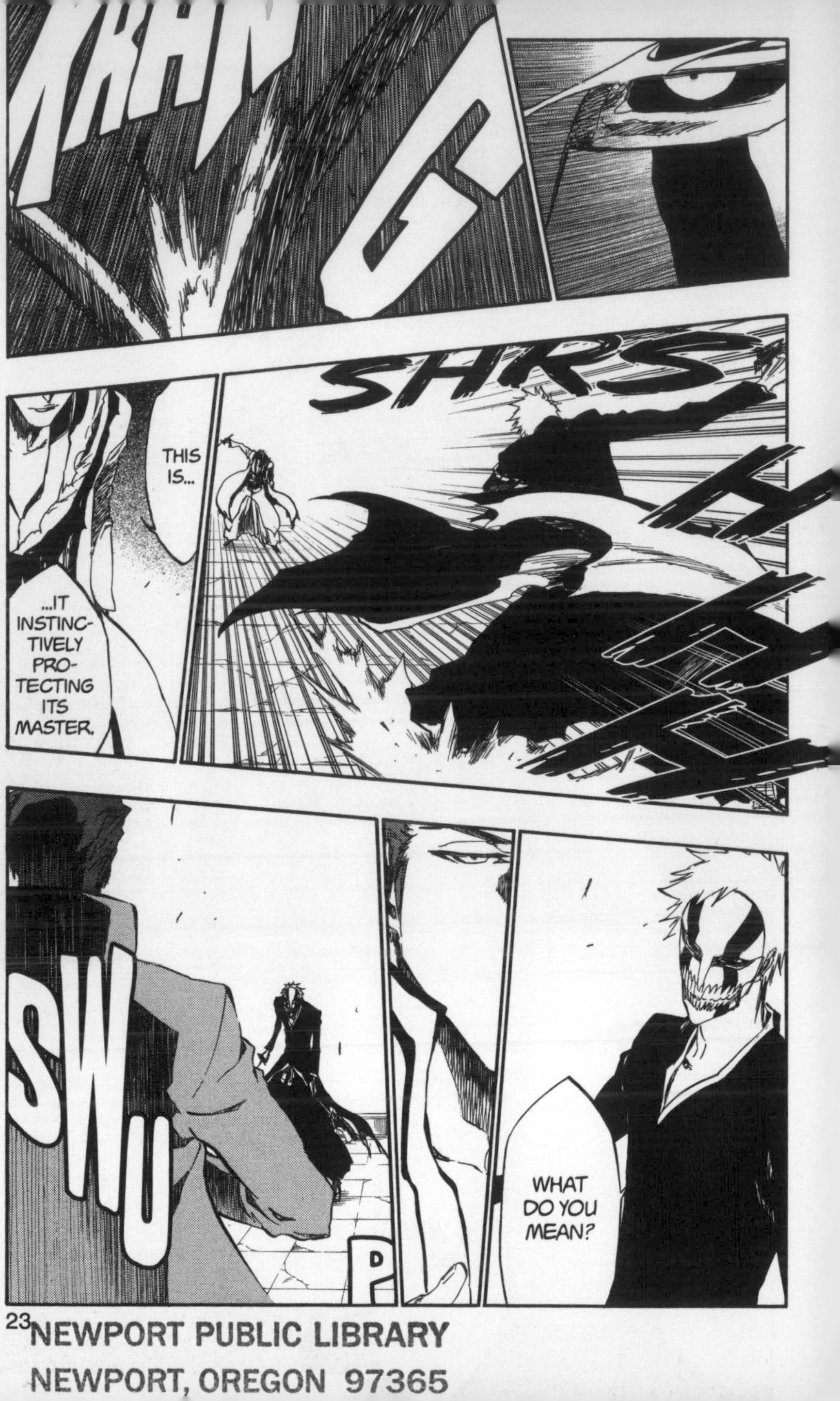
SHRS
THIS IS...
...IT INSTINCTIVELY PROTECTING ITS MASTER.
WHAT DO YOU MEAN?
SWUP

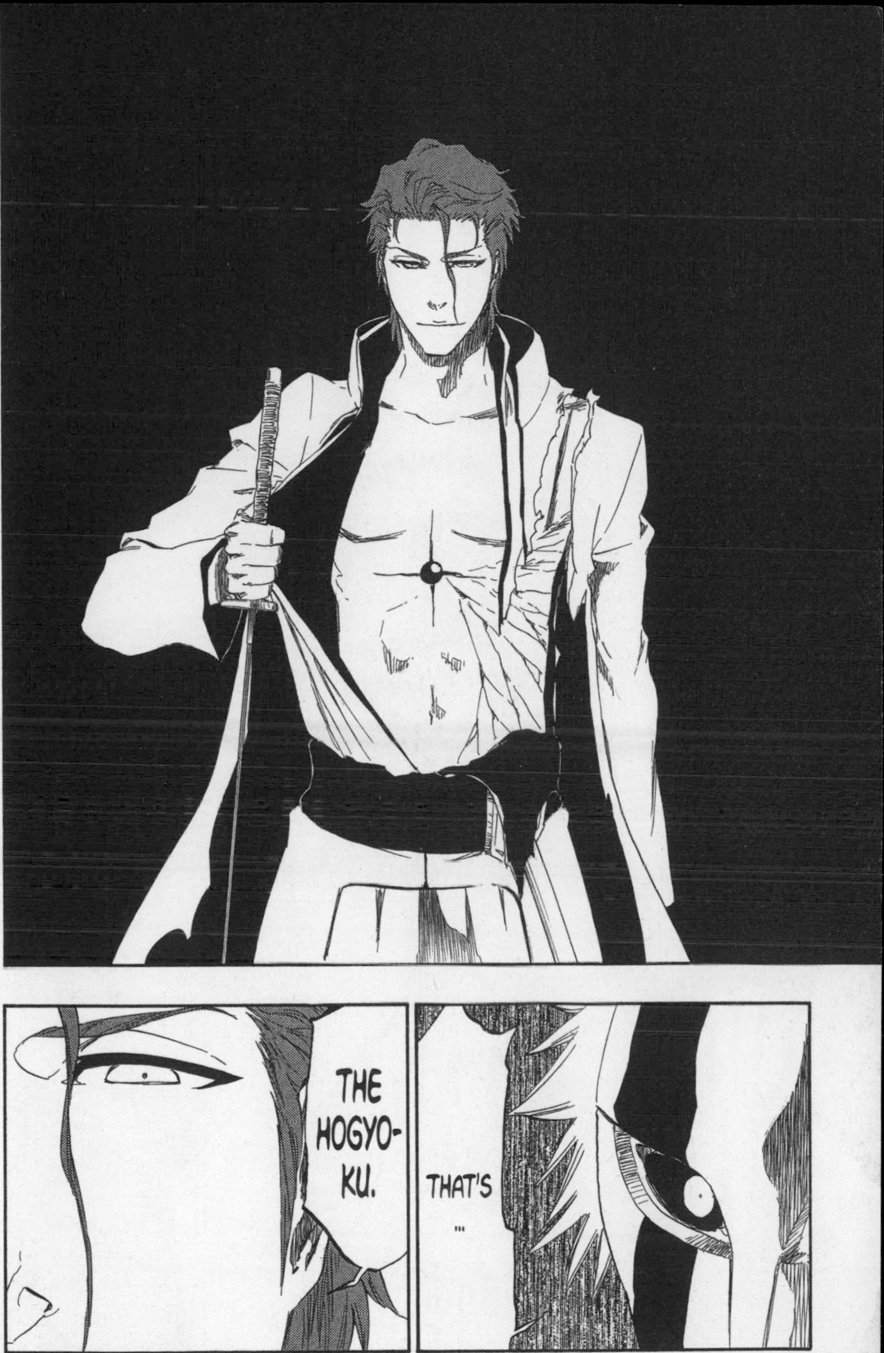
THAT'S …
THE HOGYO-KU.

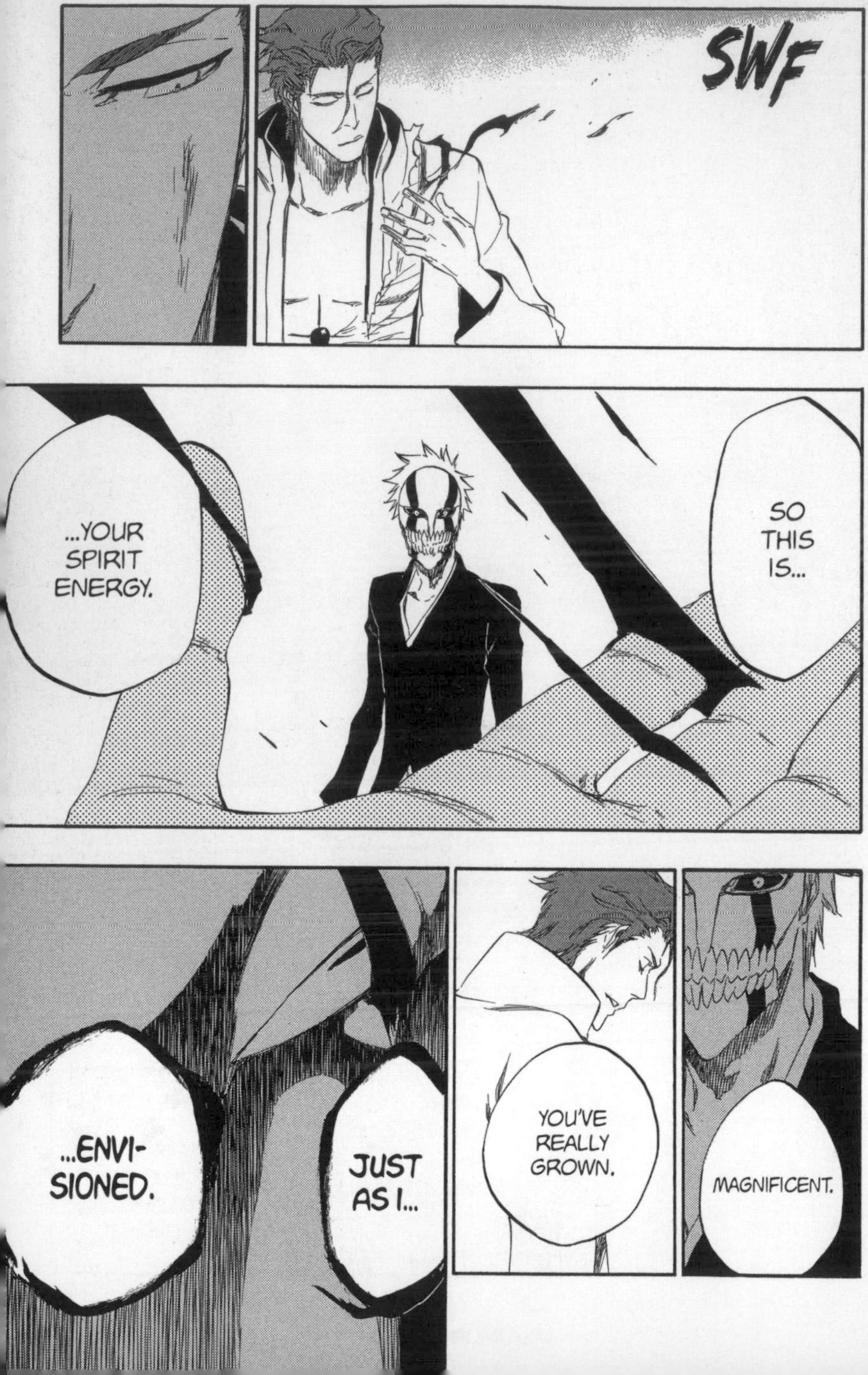
SWF
SO THIS IS...
...YOUR SPIRIT ENERGY.
MAGNIFICENT.
YOU'VE REALLY GROWN.
JUST AS I...
...ENVI-SIONED.

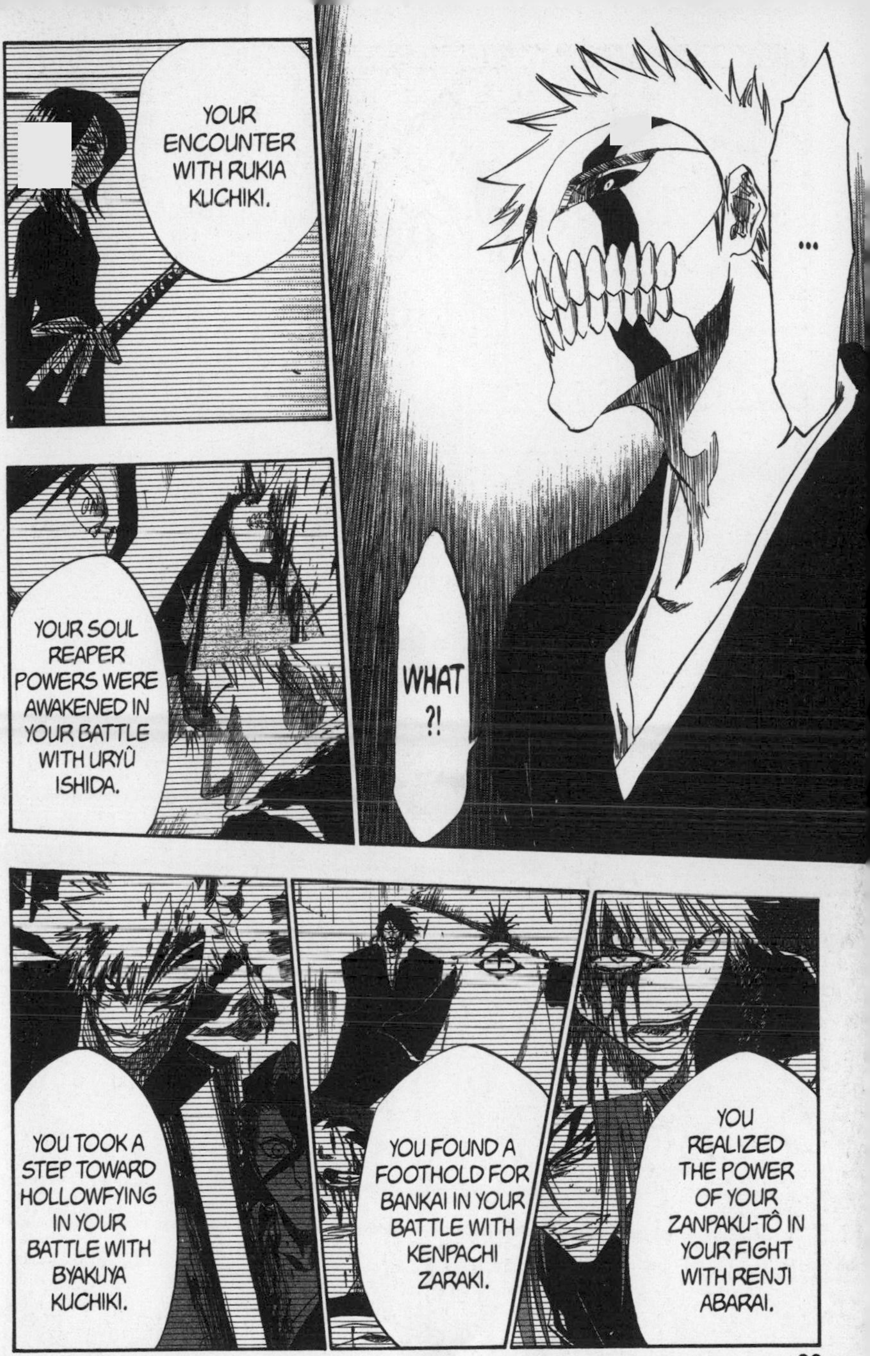
...
WHAT ?!
YOUR ENCOUNTER WITH RUKIA KUCHIKI.
YOUR SOUL REAPER POWERS WERE AWAKENED IN YOUR BATTLE WITH URYÛ ISHIDA.
YOU REALIZED THE POWER OF YOUR ZANPAKU-TÔ IN YOUR FIGHT WITH RENJI ABARAI.
YOU FOUND A FOOTHOLD FOR BANKAI IN YOUR BATTLE WITH KENPACHI ZARAKI.
YOU TOOK A STEP TOWARD HOLLOWFYING IN YOUR BATTLE WITH BYAKUYA KUCHIKI.

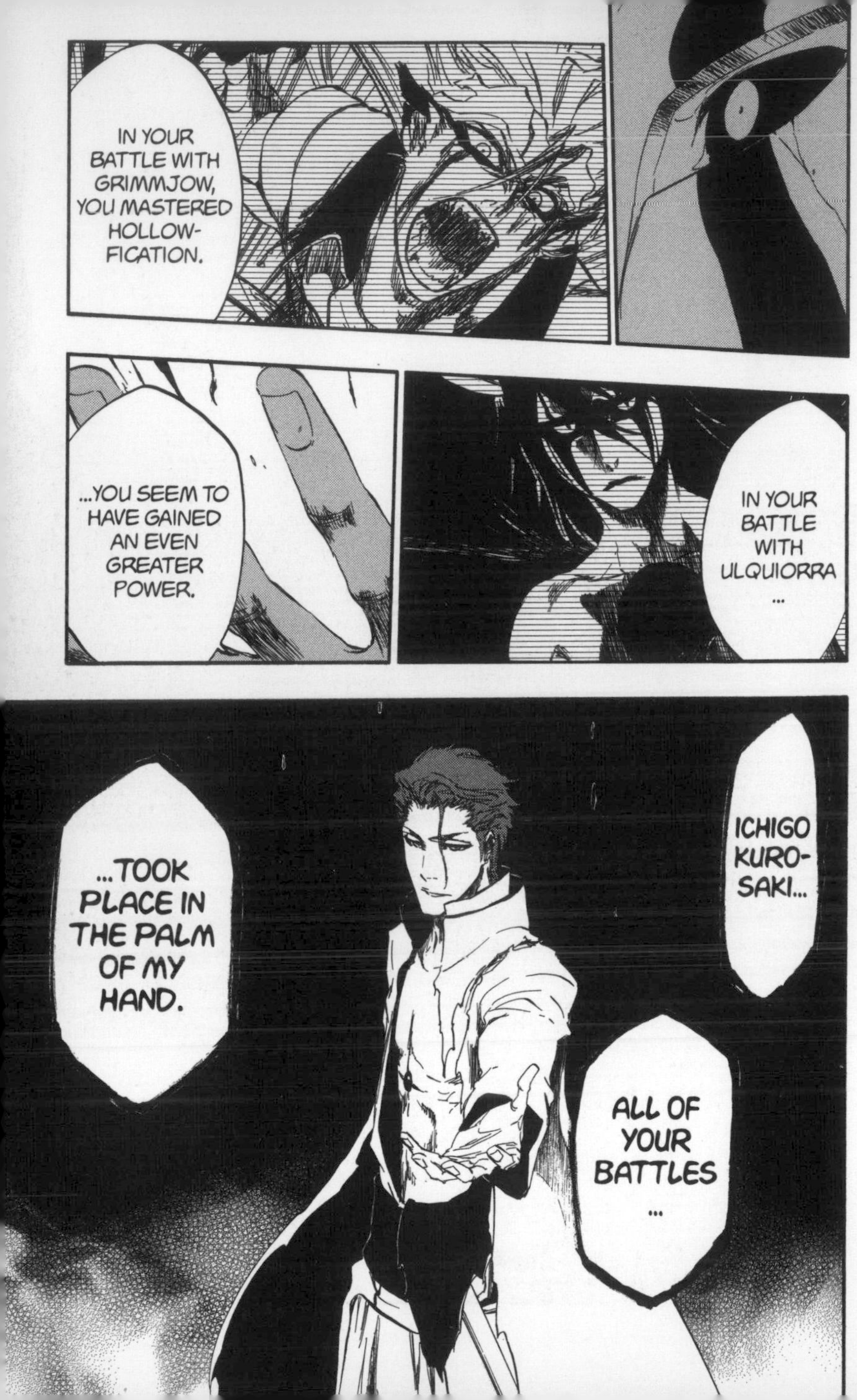
IN YOUR BATTLE WITH GRIMMJOW, YOU MASTERED HOLLOW-FICATION.
IN YOUR BATTLE WITH ULQUIORRA ...
...YOU SEEM TO HAVE GAINED AN EVEN GREATER POWER.
ICHIGO KURO-SAKI...
ALL OF YOUR BATTLES ...
...TOOK PLACE IN THE PALM OF MY HAND.

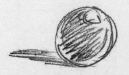

397. Edge of the Silence

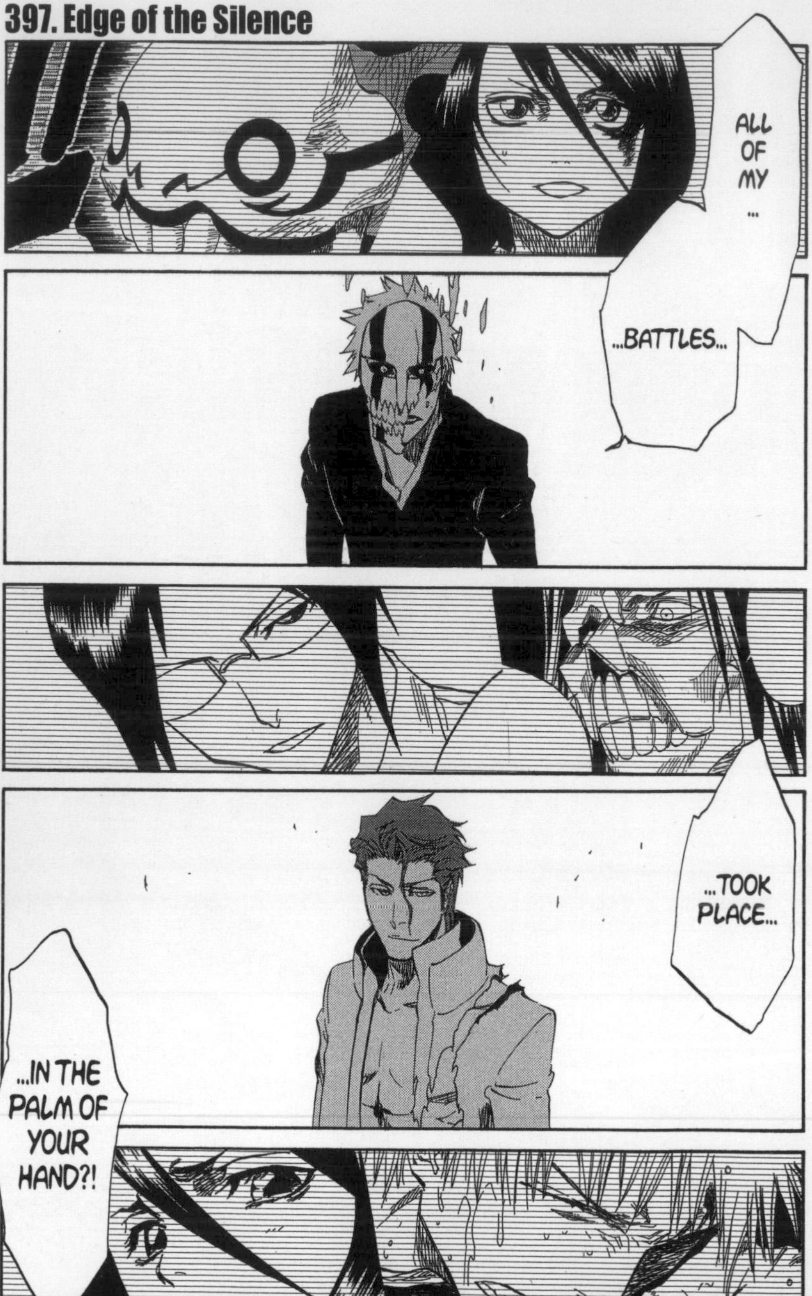
ALL OF MY ...
...BATTLES...
...TOOK PLACE...
...IN THE PALM OF YOUR HAND?!

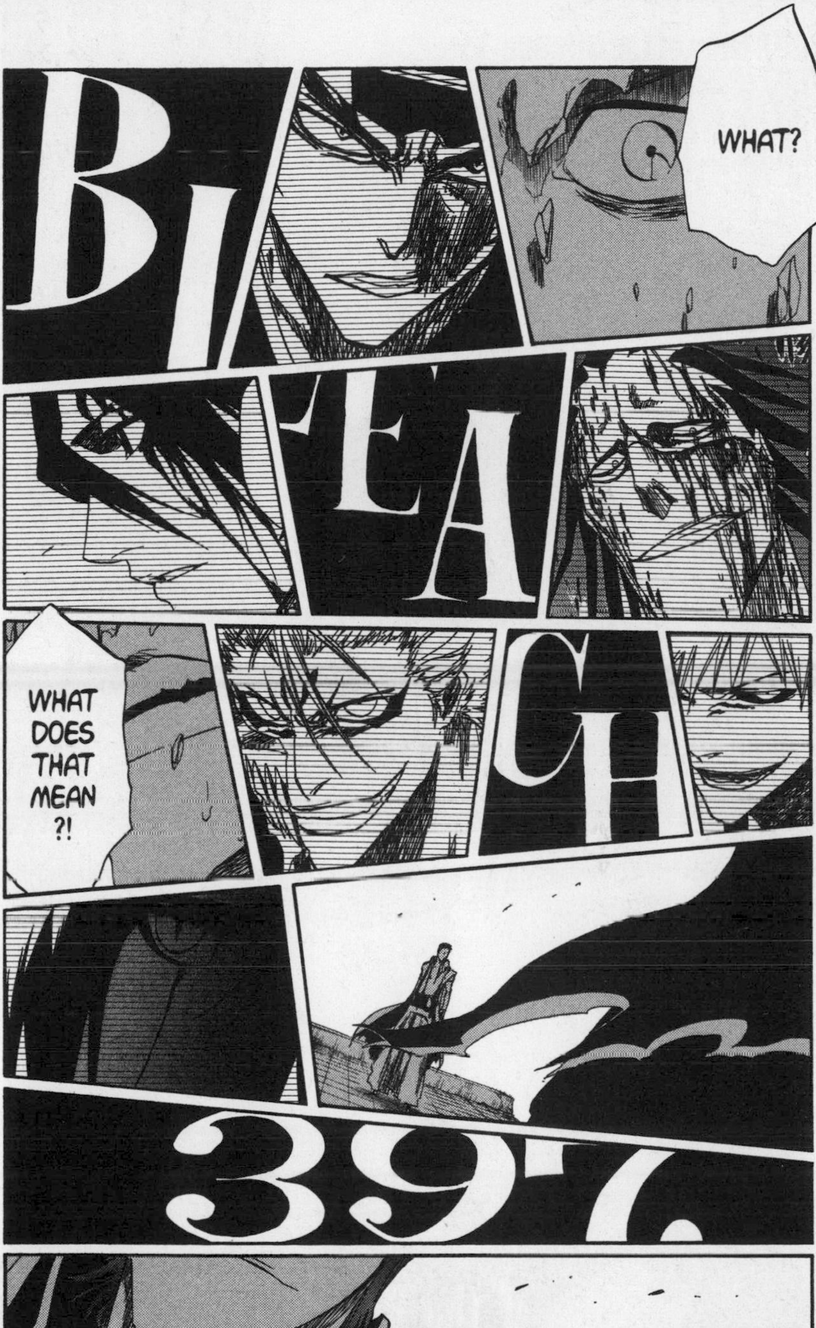
WHAT?
BLEACH
WHAT DOES THAT MEAN ?!
397.

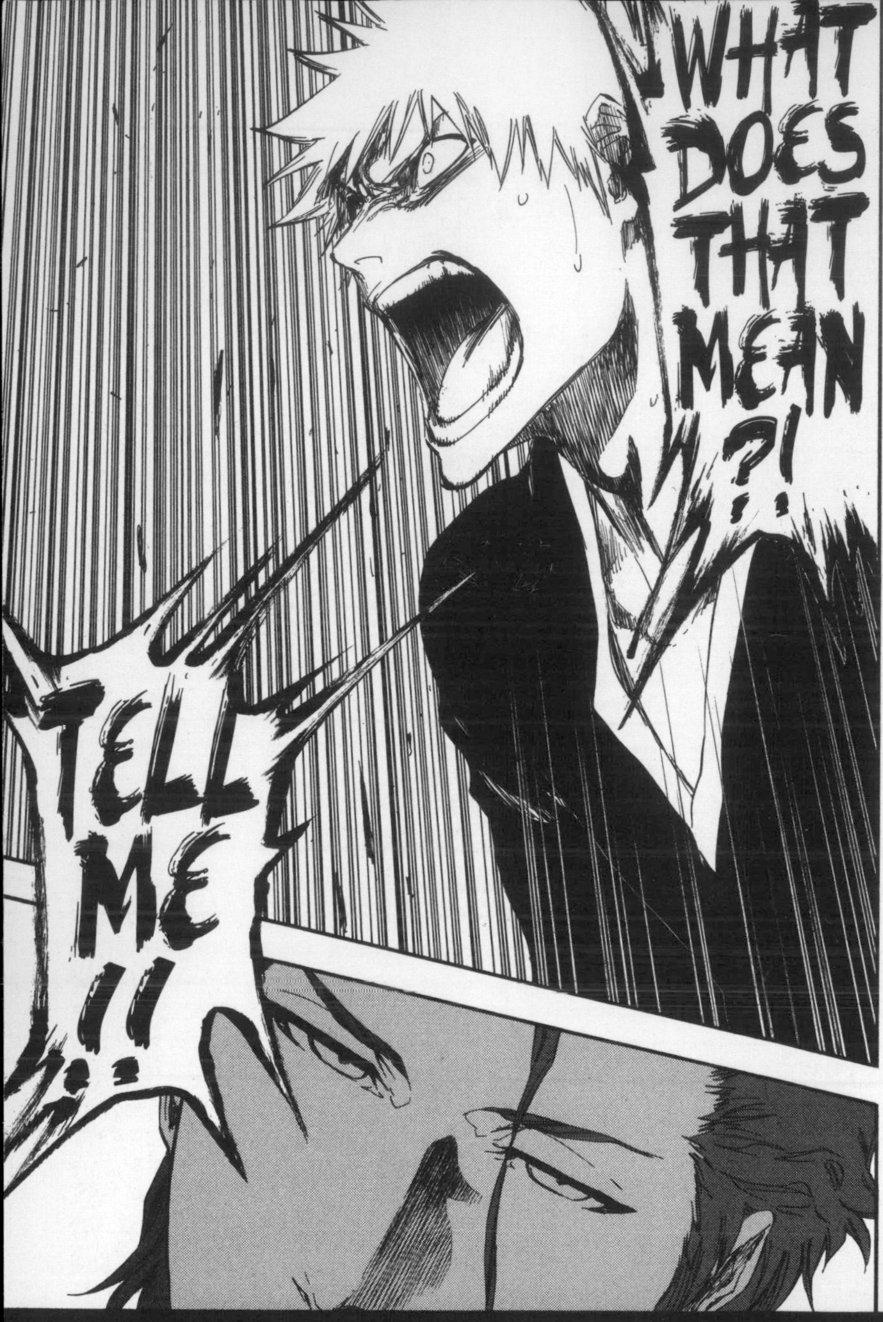
WHAT DOES THAT MEAN ?!
TELL ME !!

Edge of the Silence

DON'T...

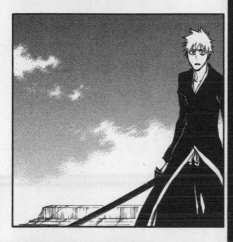

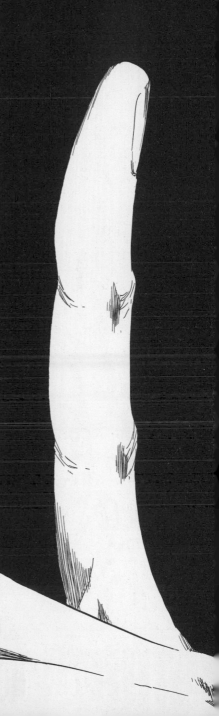

...RAISE YOUR VOICE...

...ICHIGO KURO-SAKI.

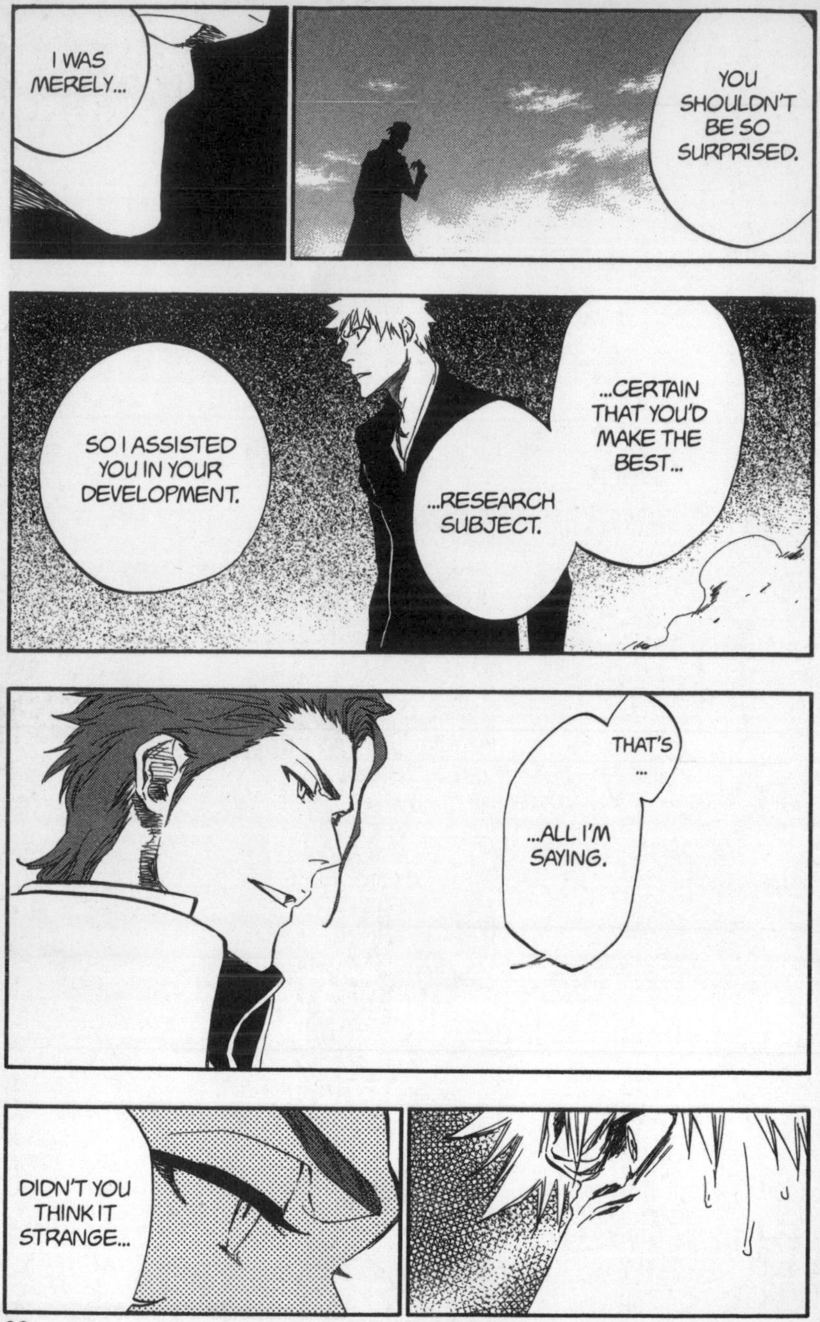
YOU SHOULDN'T BE SO SURPRISED.
I WAS MERELY...
...CERTAIN THAT YOU'D MAKE THE BEST...
...RESEARCH SUBJECT.
SO I ASSISTED YOU IN YOUR DEVELOPMENT.
THAT'S ...
...ALL I'M SAYING.
DIDN'T YOU THINK IT STRANGE...

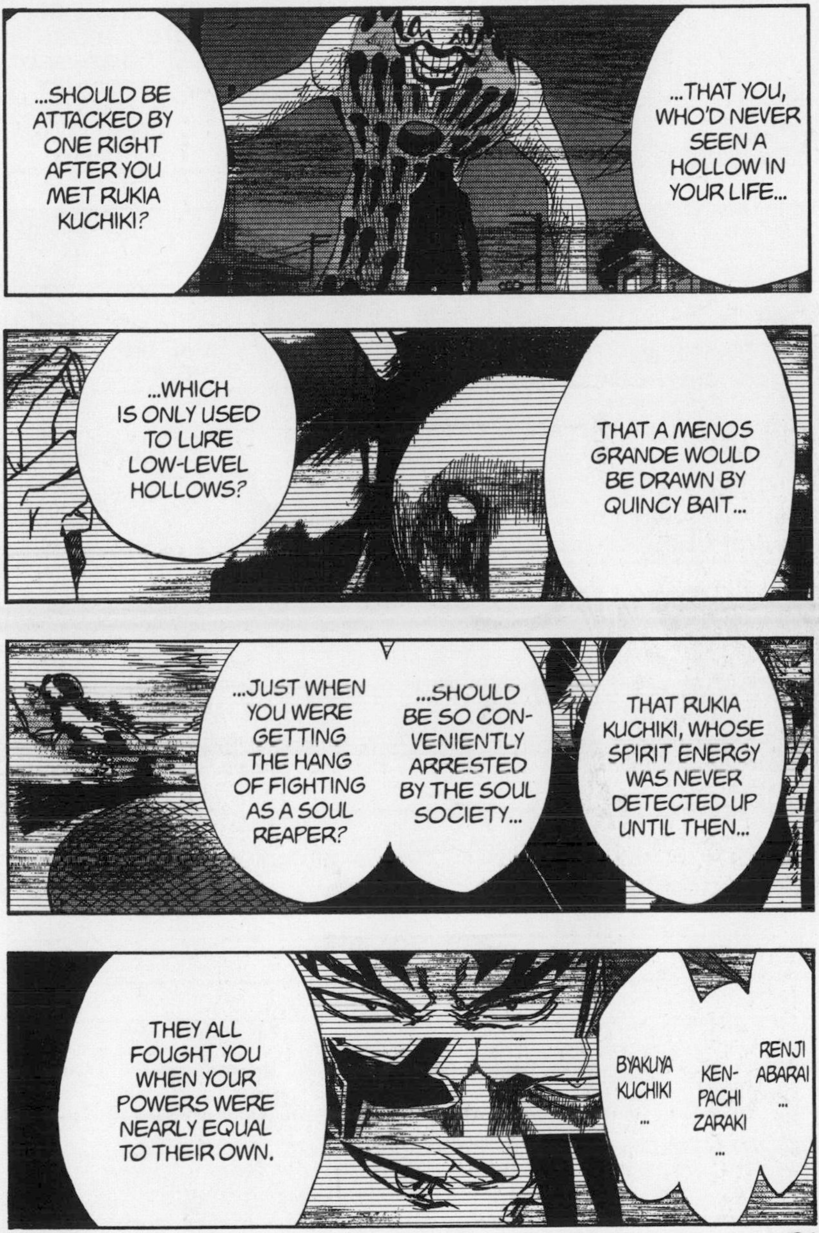
...THAT YOU, WHO'D NEVER SEEN A HOLLOW IN YOUR LIFE...
...SHOULD BE ATTACKED BY ONE RIGHT AFTER YOU MET RUKIA KUCHIKI?
THAT A MENOS GRANDE WOULD BE DRAWN BY QUINCY BAIT...
...WHICH IS ONLY USED TO LURE LOW-LEVEL HOLLOWS?
THAT RUKIA KUCHIKI, WHOSE SPIRIT ENERGY WAS NEVER DETECTED UP UNTIL THEN...
...SHOULD BE SO CON-VENIENTLY ARRESTED BY THE SOUL SOCIETY...
...JUST WHEN YOU WERE GETTING THE HANG OF FIGHTING AS A SOUL REAPER?
RENJI ABARAI...
KEN-PACHI ZARAKI...
BYAKUYA KUCHIKI...
THEY ALL FOUGHT YOU WHEN YOUR POWERS WERE NEARLY EQUAL TO THEIR OWN.

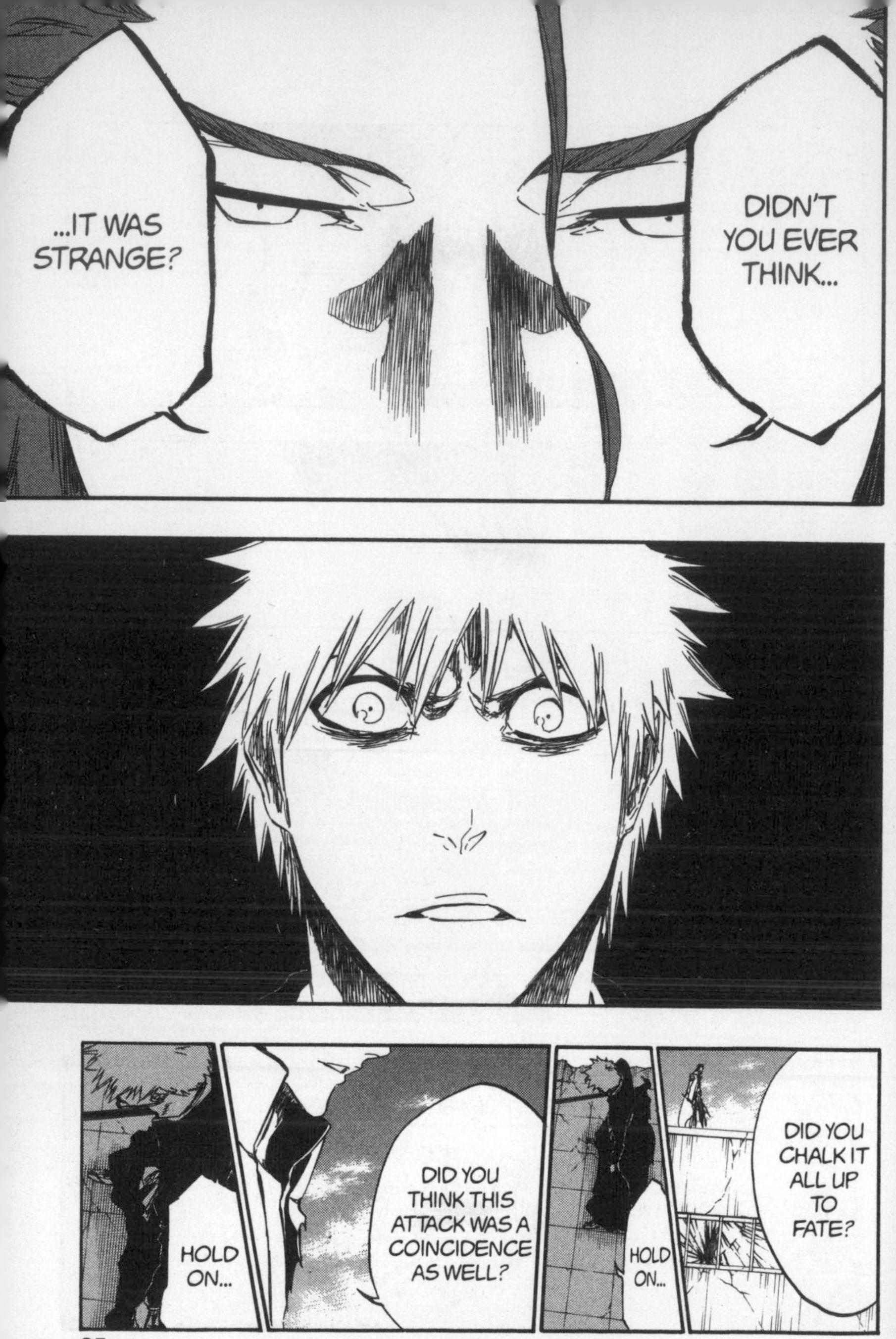
DIDN'T YOU EVER THINK...
...IT WAS STRANGE?
DID YOU CHALK IT ALL UP TO FATE?
HOLD ON...
DID YOU THINK THIS ATTACK WAS A COINCIDENCE AS WELL?
HOLD ON...

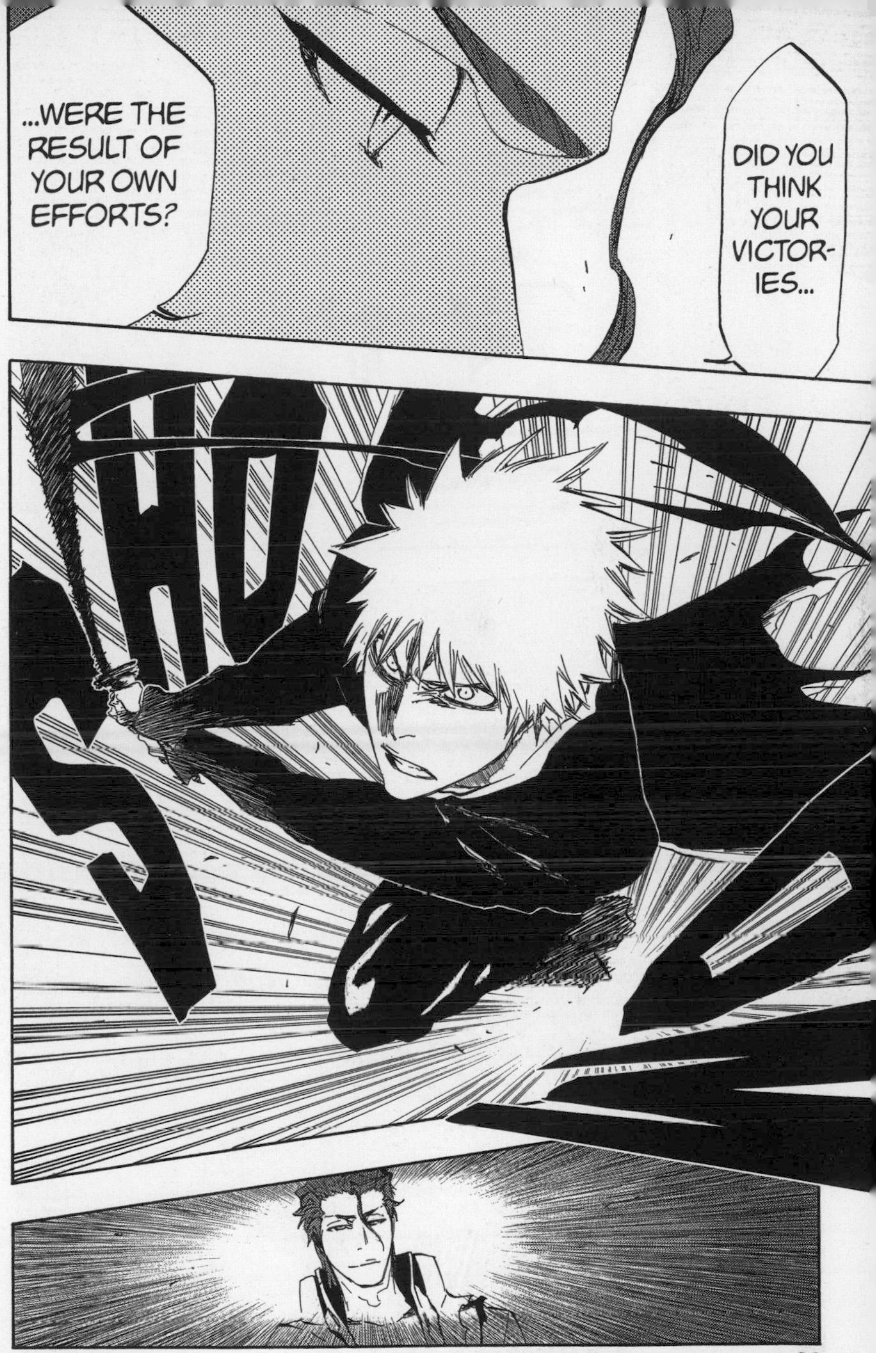
DID YOU THINK YOUR VICTOR-IES...
...WERE THE RESULT OF YOUR OWN EFFORTS?

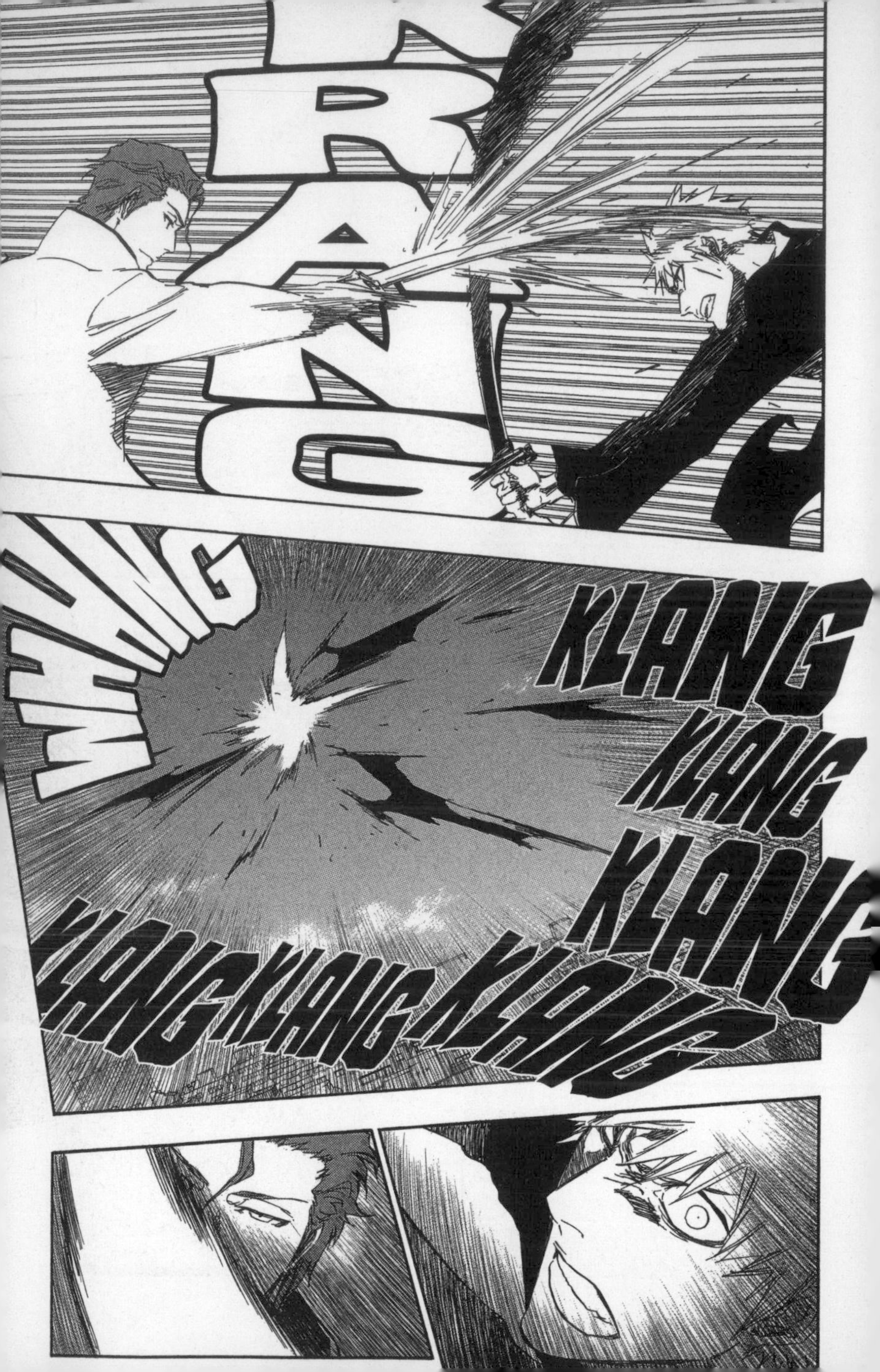
RANG
KLANG
KLANG
KLANG
KLANG KLANG KLANG
WHANG

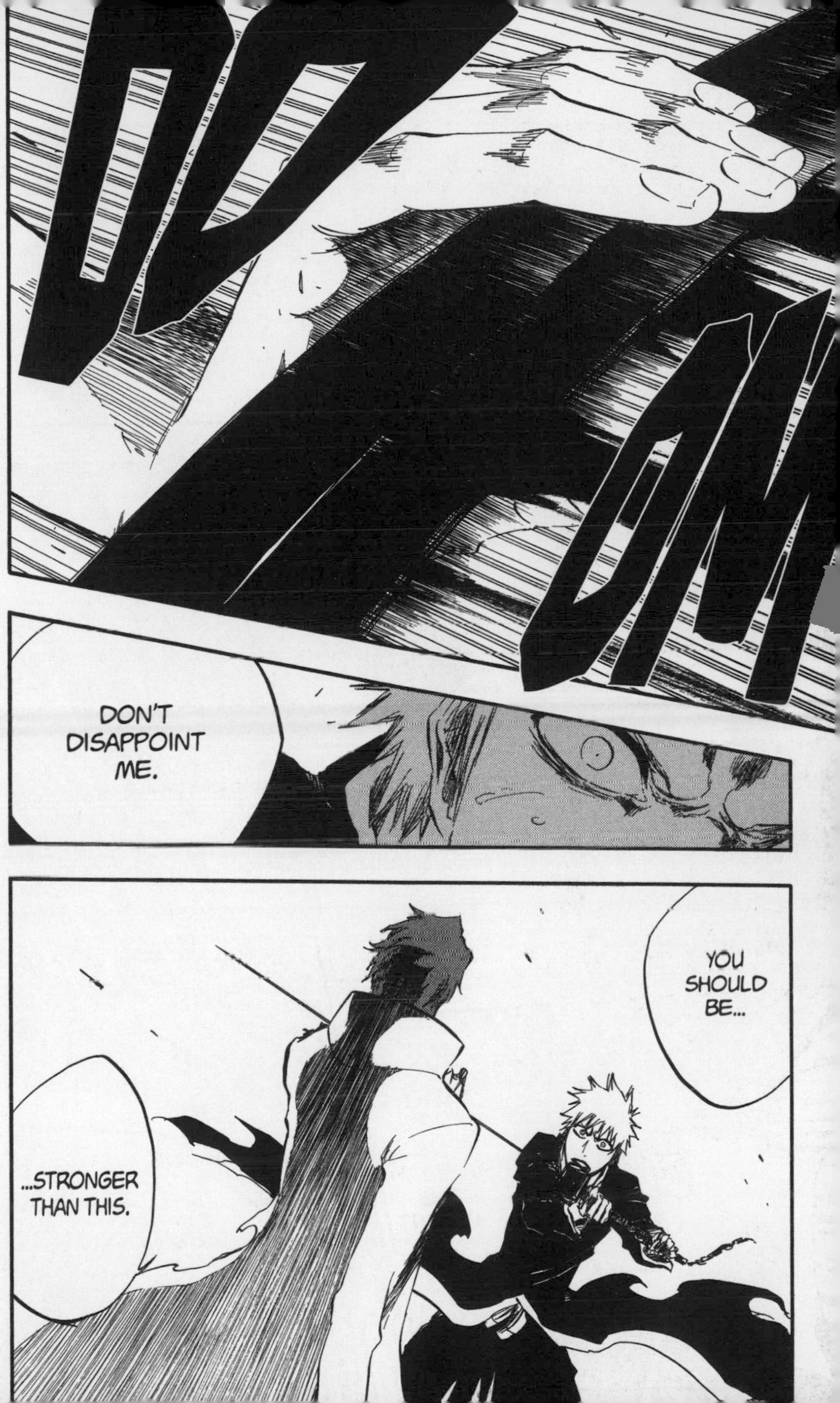
DON'T DISAPPOINT ME.
YOU SHOULD BE...
...STRONGER THAN THIS.

READ THIS WAY

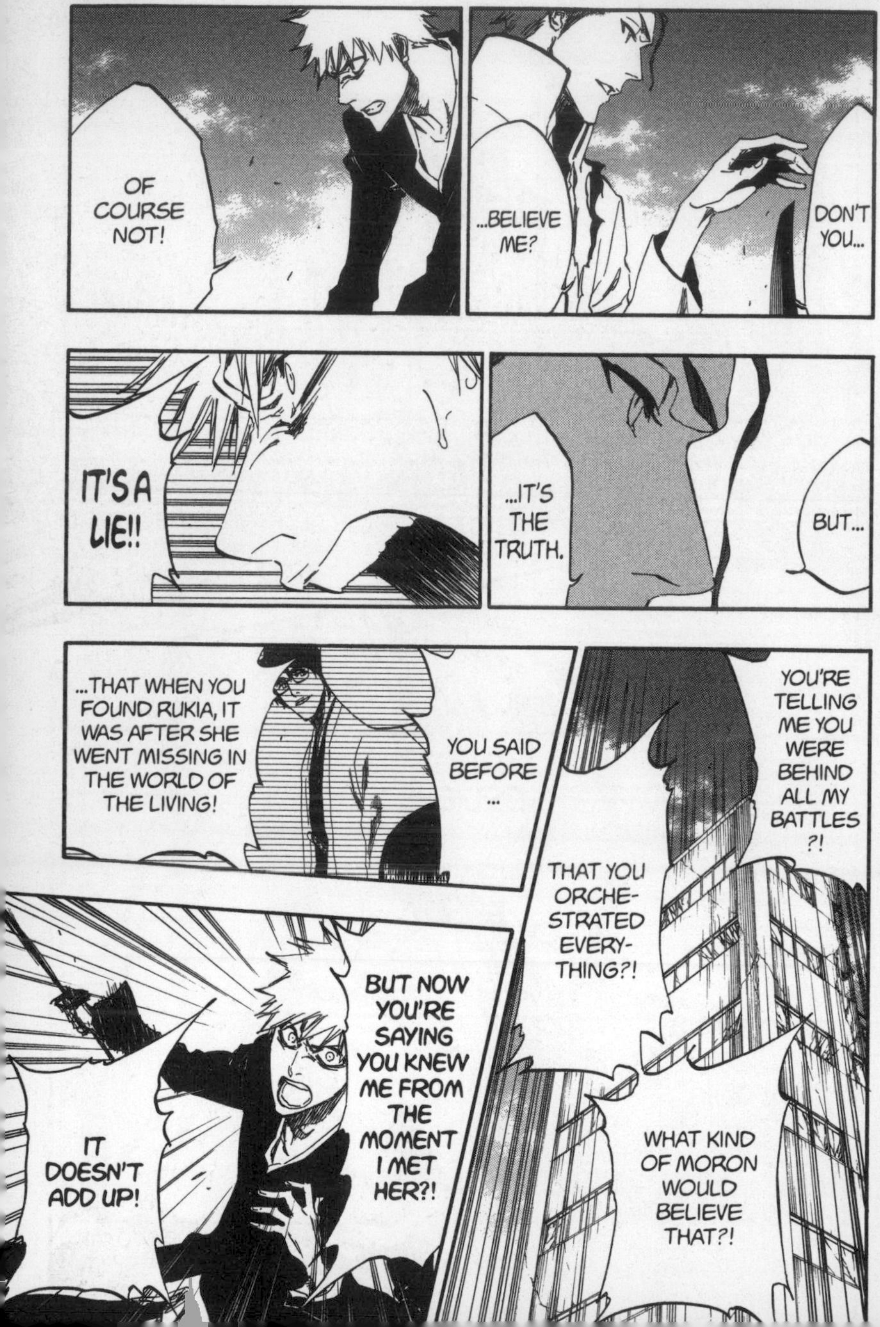

DON'T YOU...
...BELIEVE ME?
OF COURSE NOT!
BUT...
...IT'S THE TRUTH.
IT'S A LIE!!
YOU'RE TELLING ME YOU WERE BEHIND ALL MY BATTLES?!
THAT YOU ORCHESTRATED EVERYTHING?!
WHAT KIND OF MORON WOULD BELIEVE THAT?!
YOU SAID BEFORE...
...THAT WHEN YOU FOUND RUKIA, IT WAS AFTER SHE WENT MISSING IN THE WORLD OF THE LIVING!
BUT NOW YOU'RE SAYING YOU KNEW ME FROM THE MOMENT I MET HER?!
IT DOESN'T ADD UP!

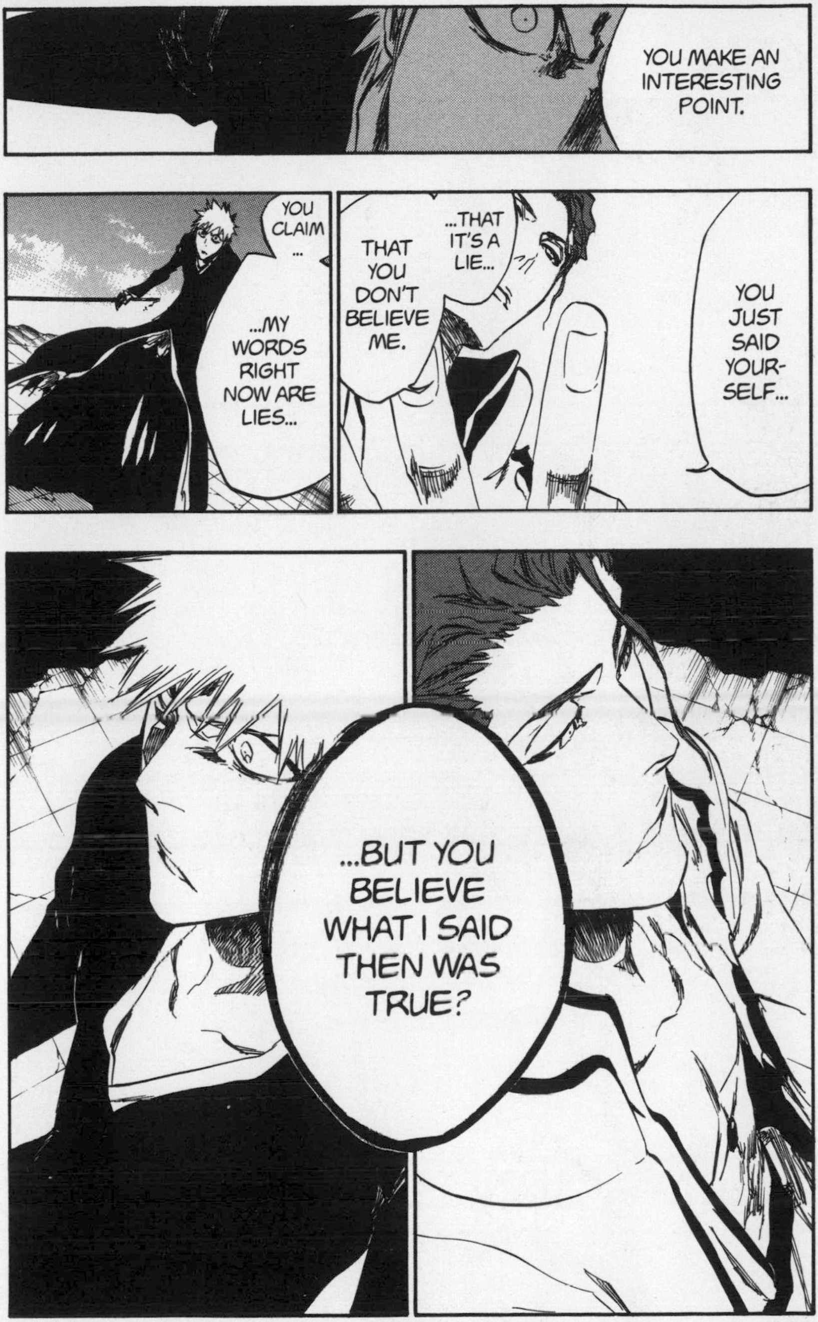
YOU MAKE AN INTERESTING POINT.
YOU JUST SAID YOURSELF...
...THAT IT'S A LIE...
THAT YOU DON'T BELIEVE ME.
YOU CLAIM ...
...MY WORDS RIGHT NOW ARE LIES...
...BUT YOU BELIEVE WHAT I SAID THEN WAS TRUE?

READ THIS WAY

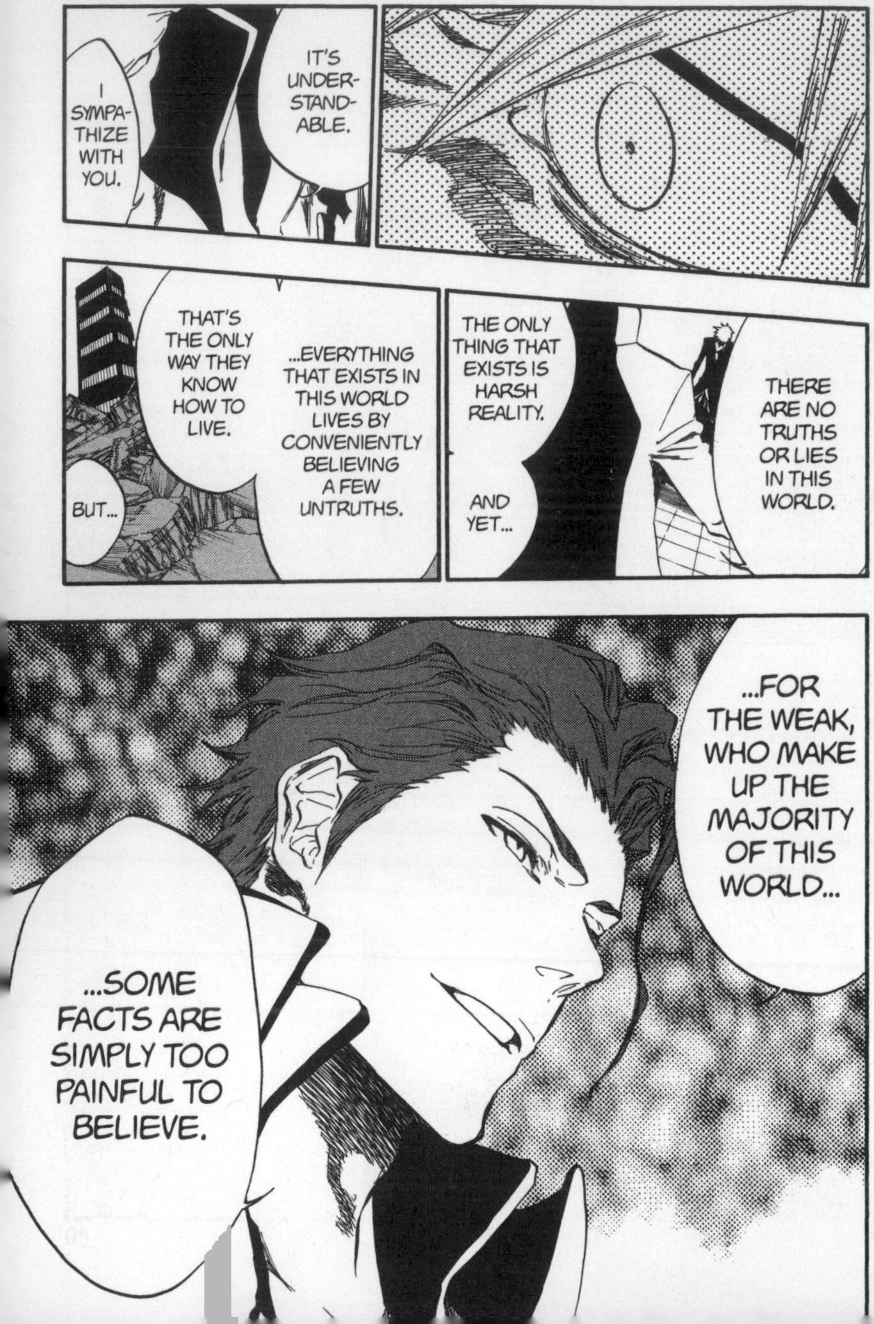
IT'S UNDERSTANDABLE.
I SYMPATHIZE WITH YOU.
THERE ARE NO TRUTHS OR LIES IN THIS WORLD.
THE ONLY THING THAT EXISTS IS HARSH REALITY.
AND YET...
...EVERYTHING THAT EXISTS IN THIS WORLD LIVES BY CONVENIENTLY BELIEVING A FEW UNTRUTHS.
THAT'S THE ONLY WAY THEY KNOW HOW TO LIVE.
BUT...
...FOR THE WEAK, WHO MAKE UP THE MAJORITY OF THIS WORLD...
...SOME FACTS ARE SIMPLY TOO PAINFUL TO BELIEVE.

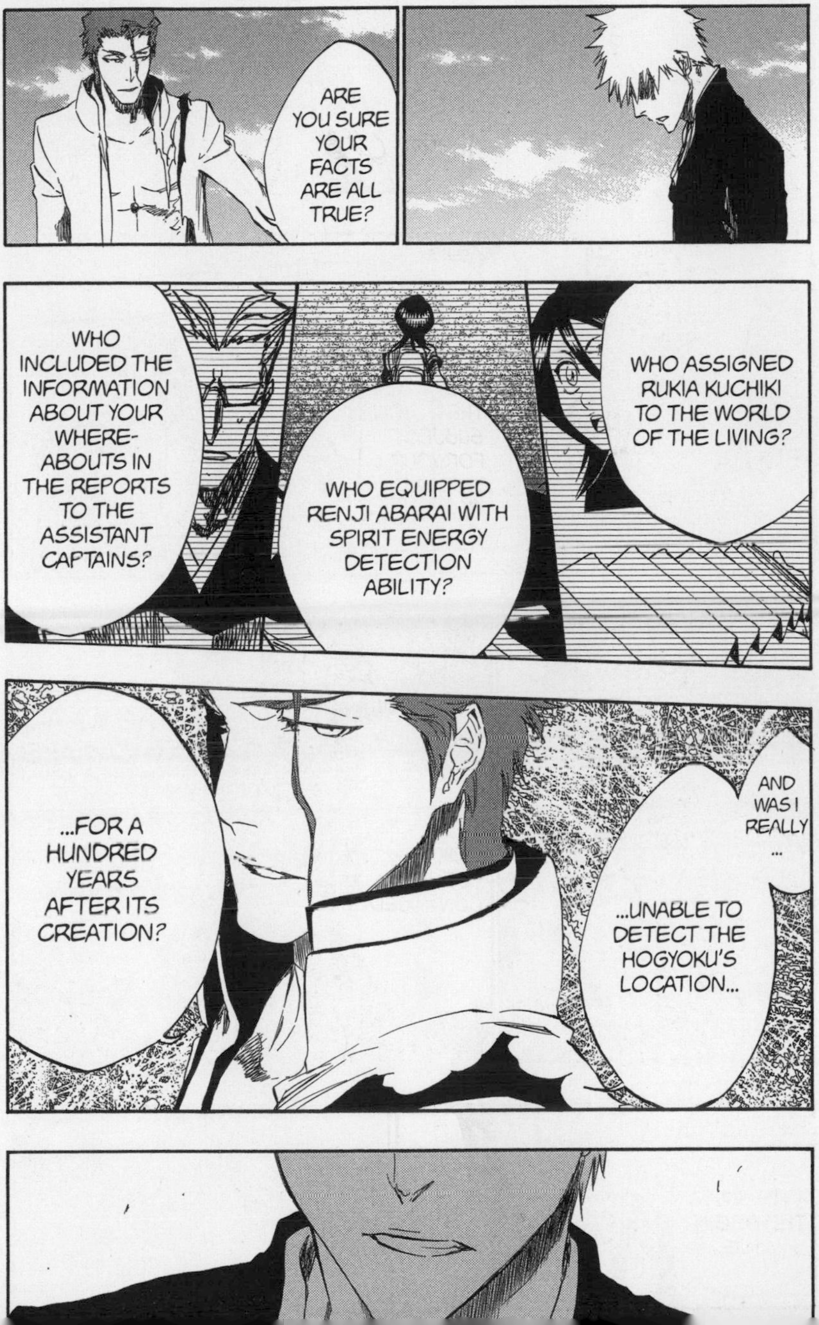
ARE YOU SURE YOUR FACTS ARE ALL TRUE?
WHO ASSIGNED RUKIA KUCHIKI TO THE WORLD OF THE LIVING?
WHO EQUIPPED RENJI ABARAI WITH SPIRIT ENERGY DETECTION ABILITY?
WHO INCLUDED THE INFORMATION ABOUT YOUR WHERE-ABOUTS IN THE REPORTS TO THE ASSISTANT CAPTAINS?
AND WAS I REALLY ...
...UNABLE TO DETECT THE HOGYOKU'S LOCATION...
...FOR A HUNDRED YEARS AFTER ITS CREATION?

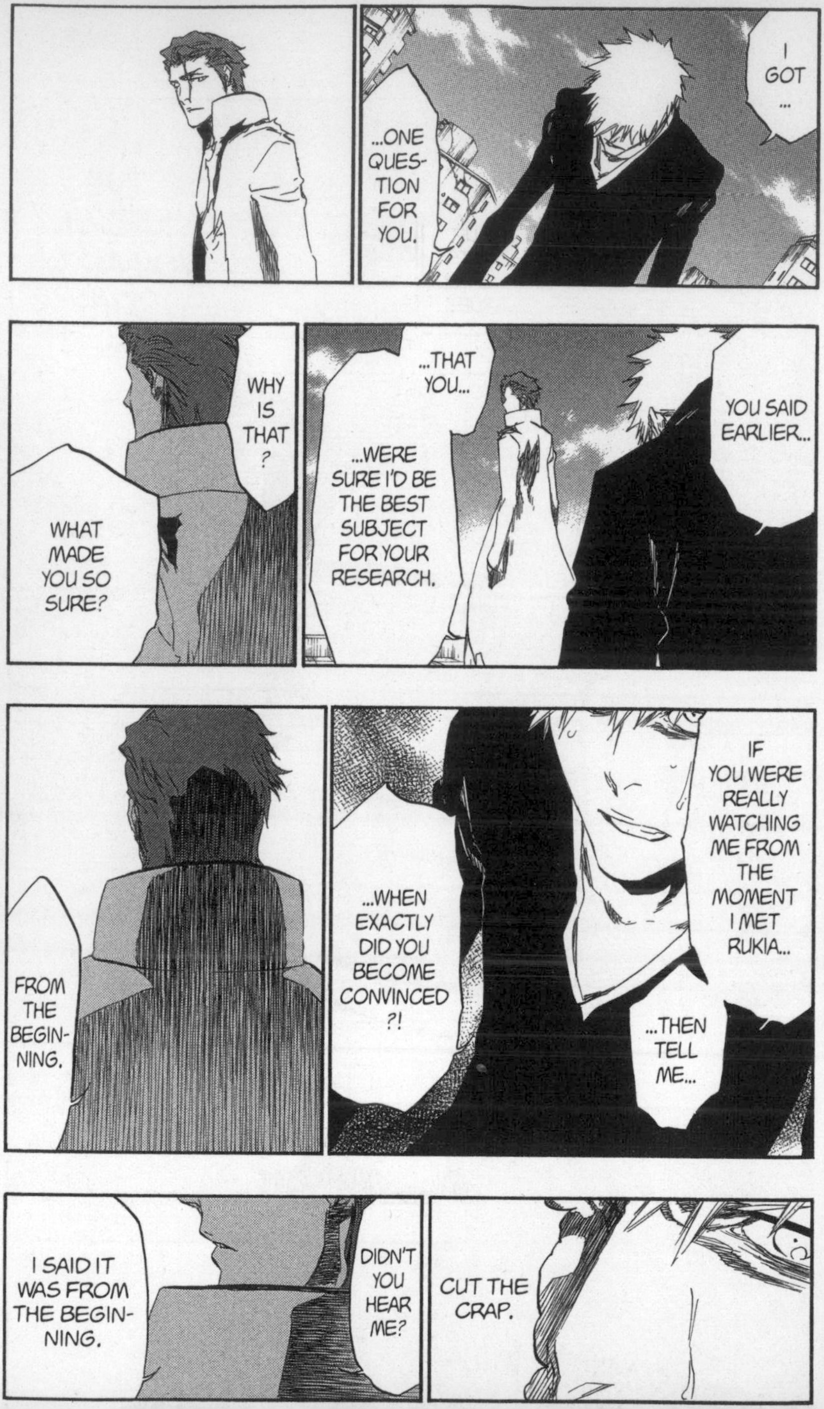
I GOT ...
...ONE QUESTION FOR YOU.
YOU SAID EARLIER...
...THAT YOU...
...WERE SURE I'D BE THE BEST SUBJECT FOR YOUR RESEARCH.
WHY IS THAT?
WHAT MADE YOU SO SURE?
IF YOU WERE REALLY WATCHING ME FROM THE MOMENT I MET RUKIA...
...THEN TELL ME...
...WHEN EXACTLY DID YOU BECOME CONVINCED?!
FROM THE BEGINNING.
CUT THE CRAP.
DIDN'T YOU HEAR ME?
I SAID IT WAS FROM THE BEGINNING.

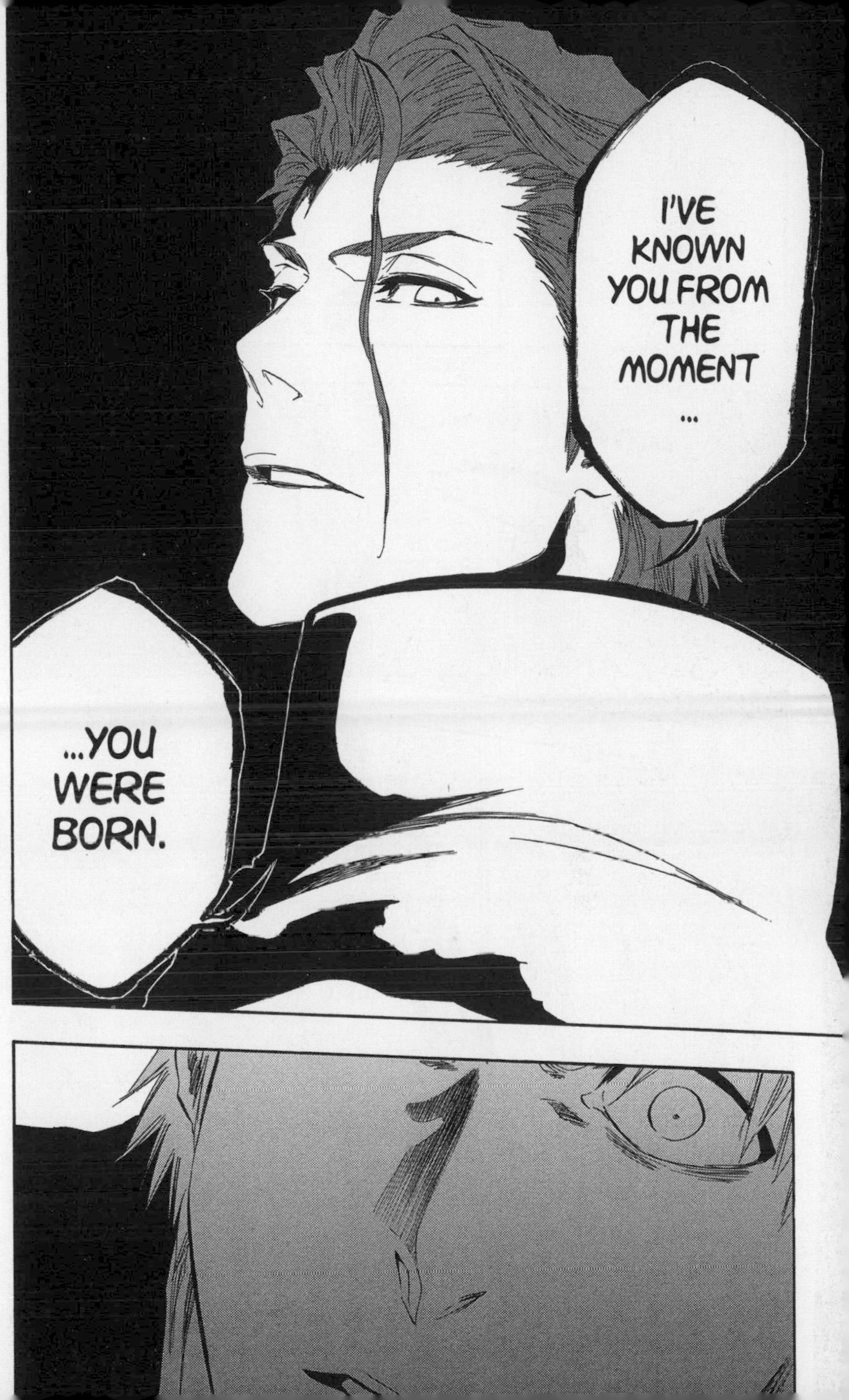
I'VE KNOWN YOU FROM THE MOMENT ...
...YOU WERE BORN.

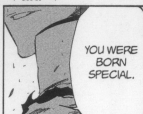

YOU WERE BORN SPECIAL.

WHAT ?!

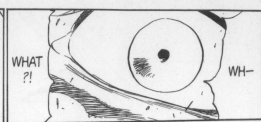

WH—

BECAUSE YOU ARE HUMAN AND...

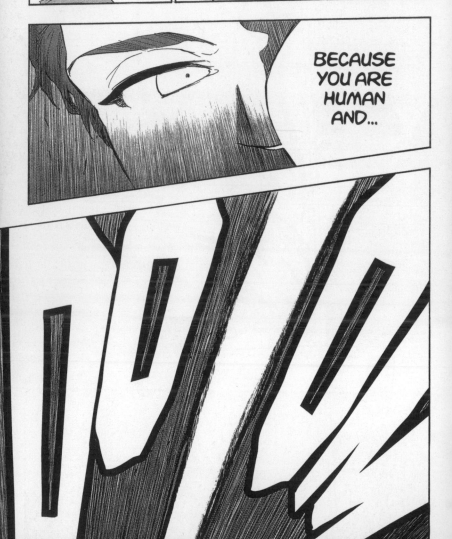

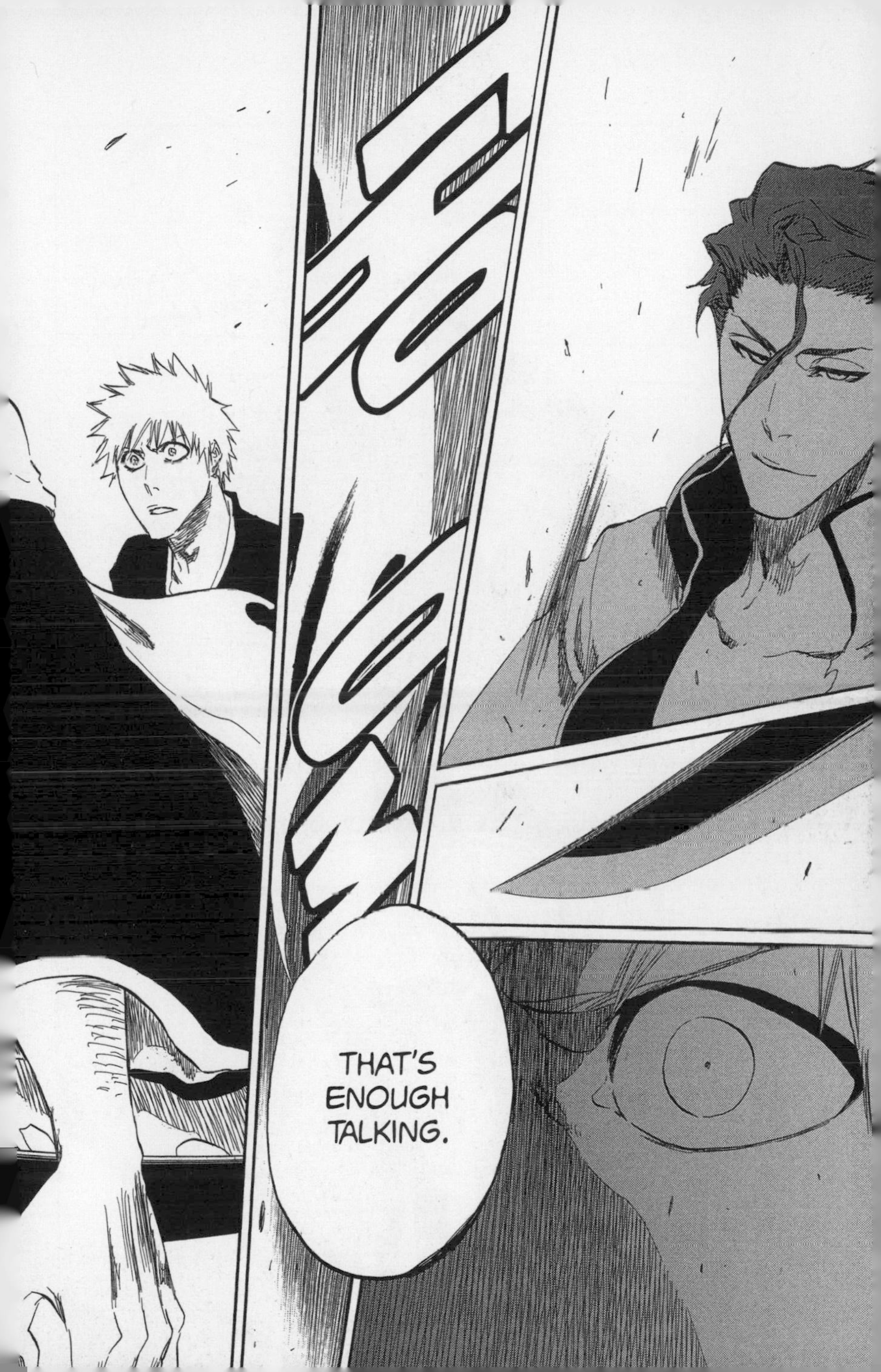
THAT'S ENOUGH TALKING.

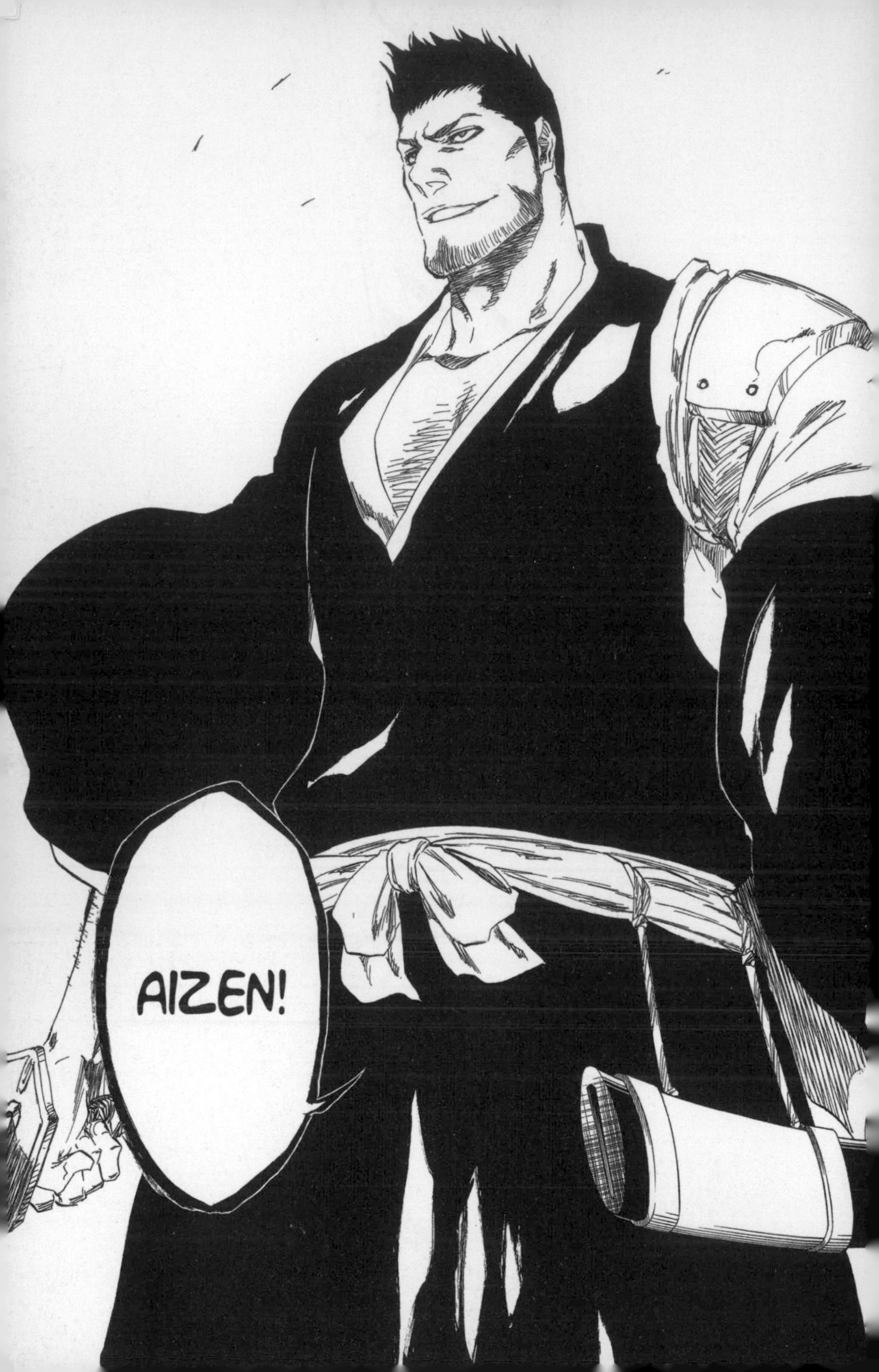
AIZEN!

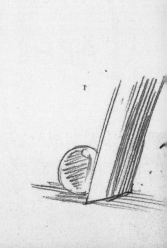

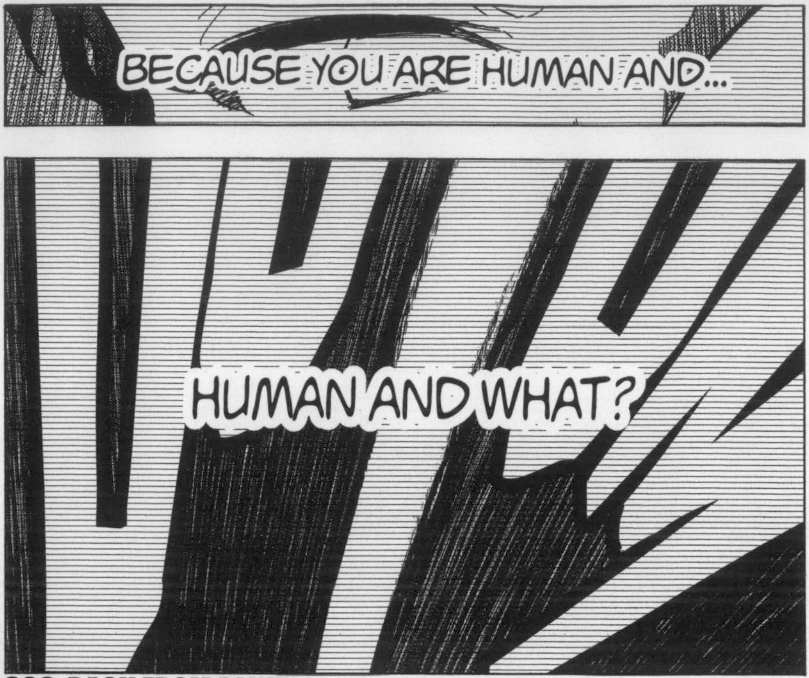
BECAUSE YOU ARE HUMAN AND...
HUMAN AND WHAT?

398. BACK FROM BLIND

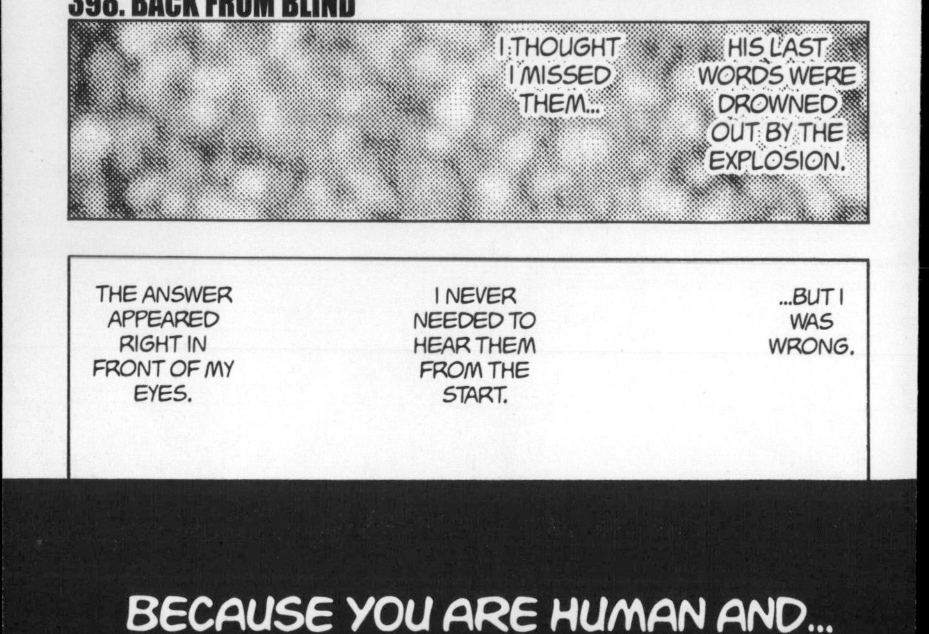
HIS LAST WORDS WERE DROWNED OUT BY THE EXPLOSION.
I THOUGHT I MISSED THEM...
...BUT I WAS WRONG.
I NEVER NEEDED TO HEAR THEM FROM THE START.
THE ANSWER APPEARED RIGHT IN FRONT OF MY EYES.
BECAUSE YOU ARE HUMAN AND...

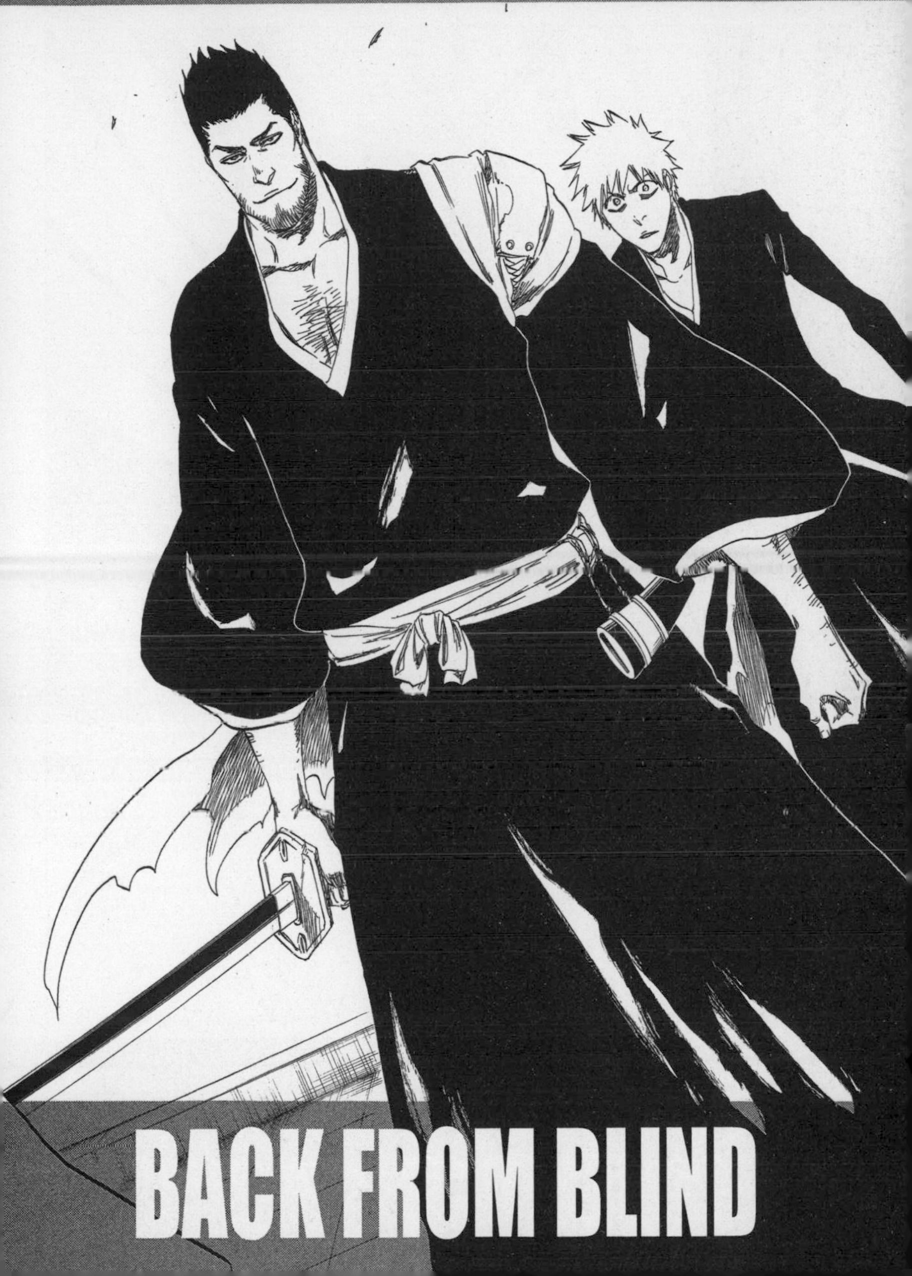
BACK FROM BLIND

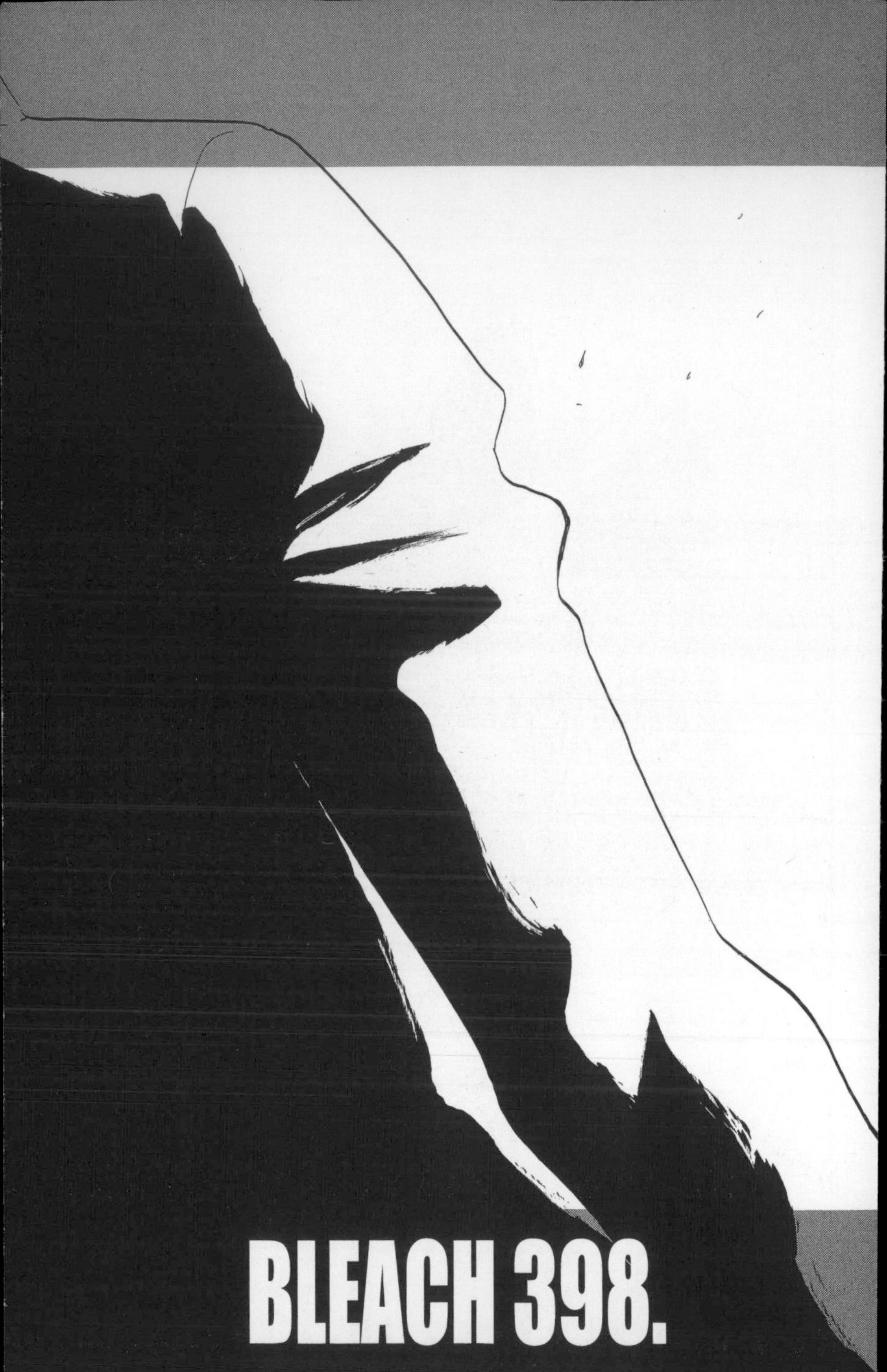

BLEACH 398.

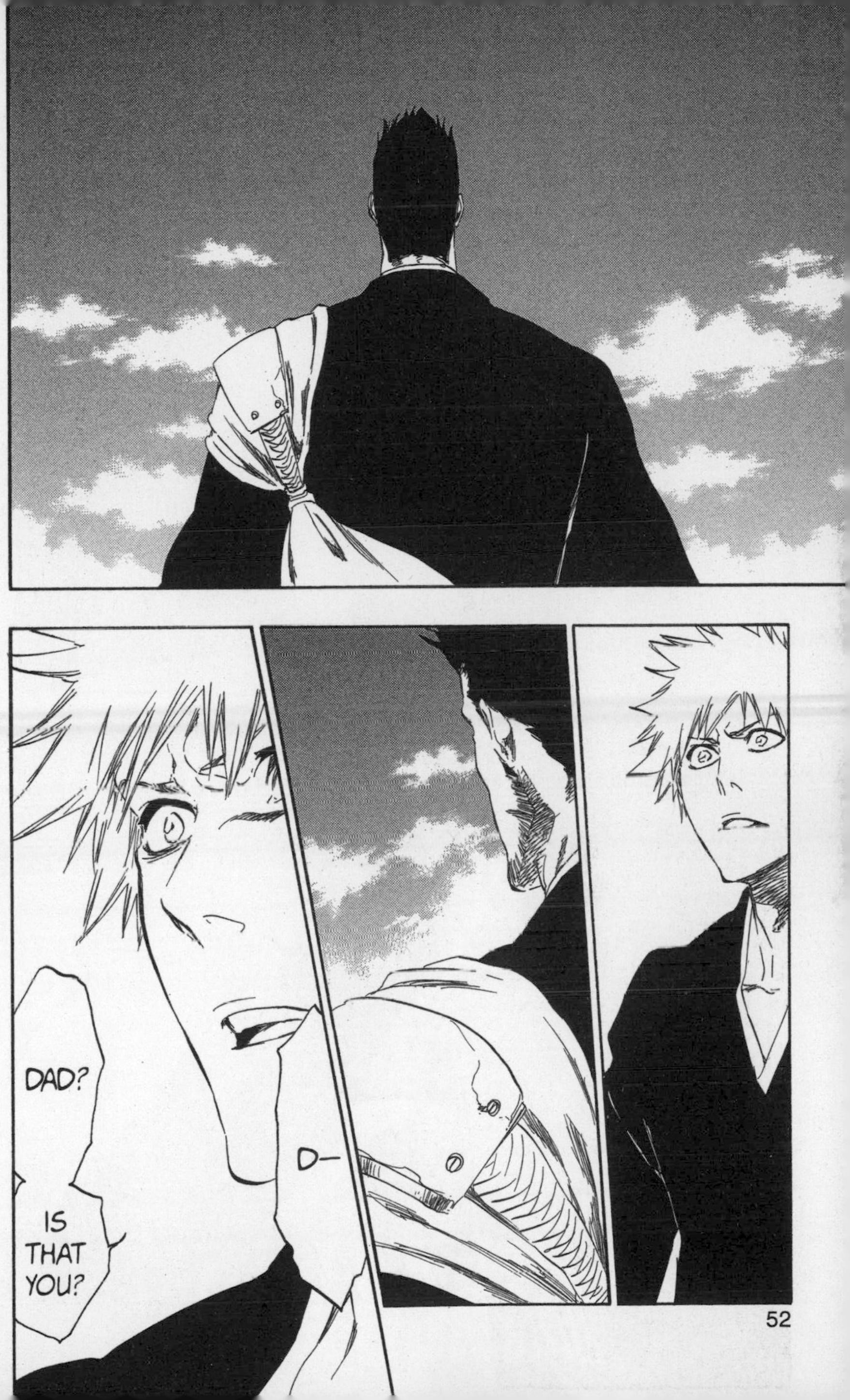
DAD?
D-
IS THAT YOU?

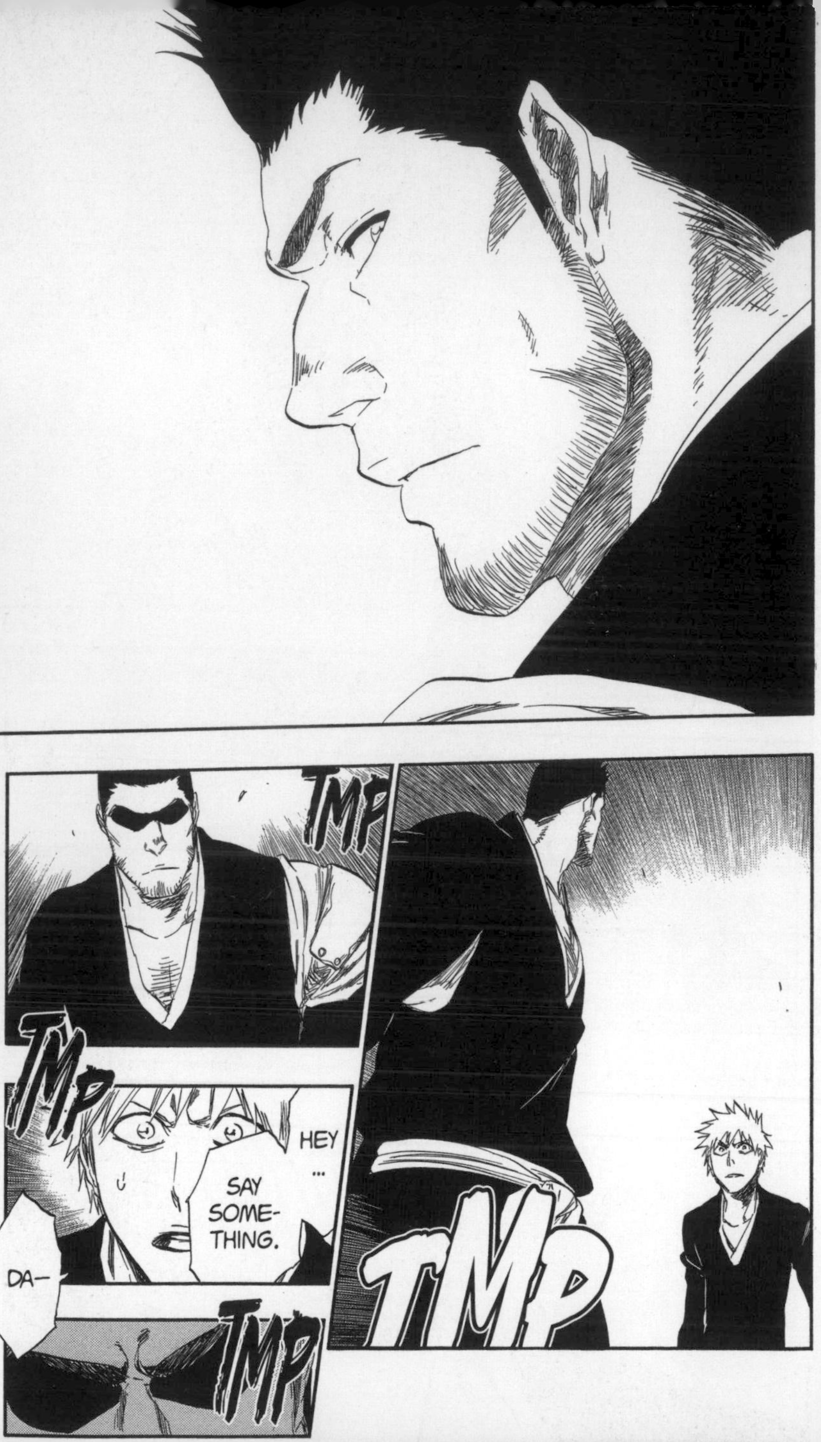
TMP
TMP
TMP
HEY
...
SAY SOMETHING.
DA—
TMP

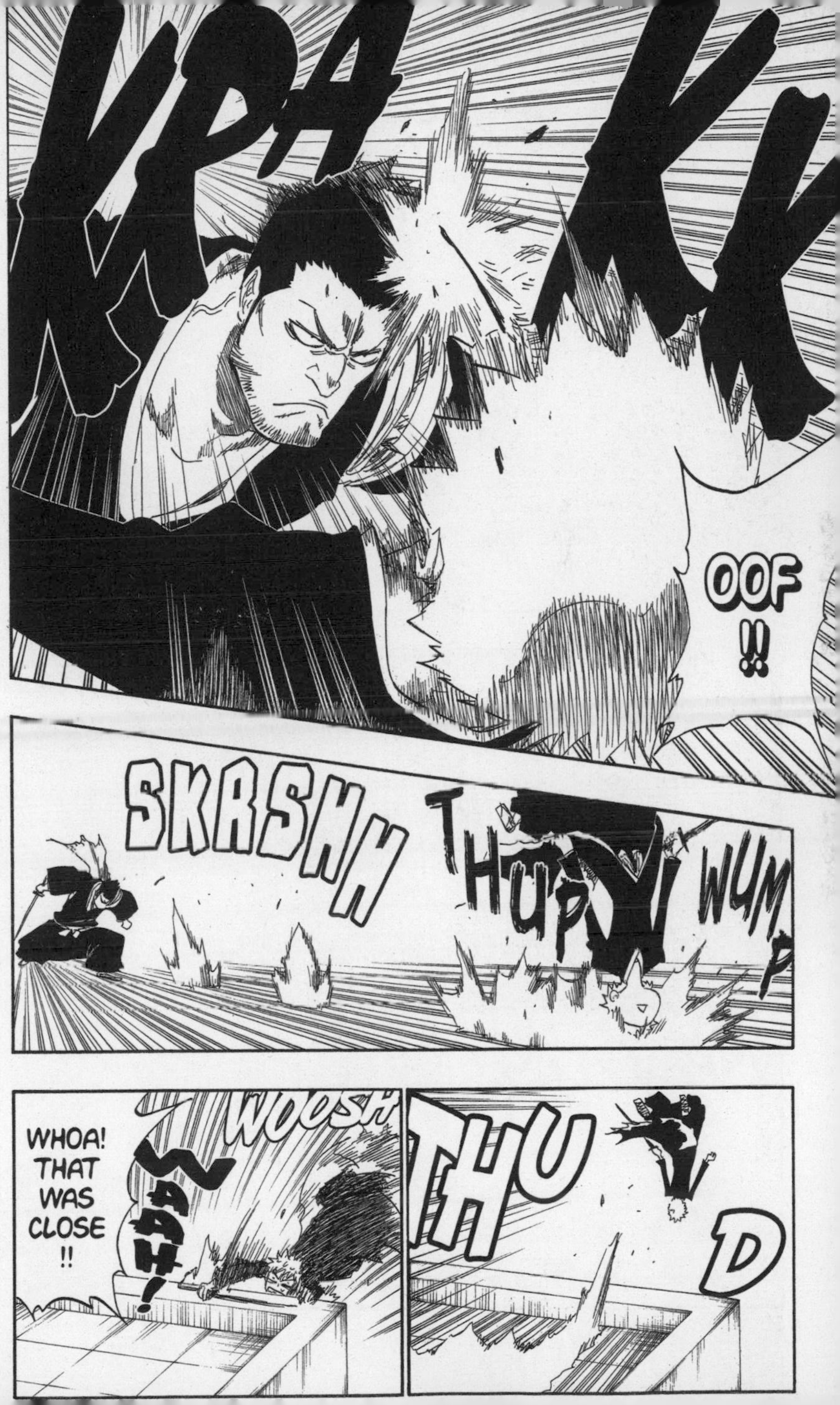
KRAKK
OOF !!
WUMP
THUP
SKRASHH
THUD
WOOSH
WAAAH!
WHOA! THAT WAS CLOSE !!

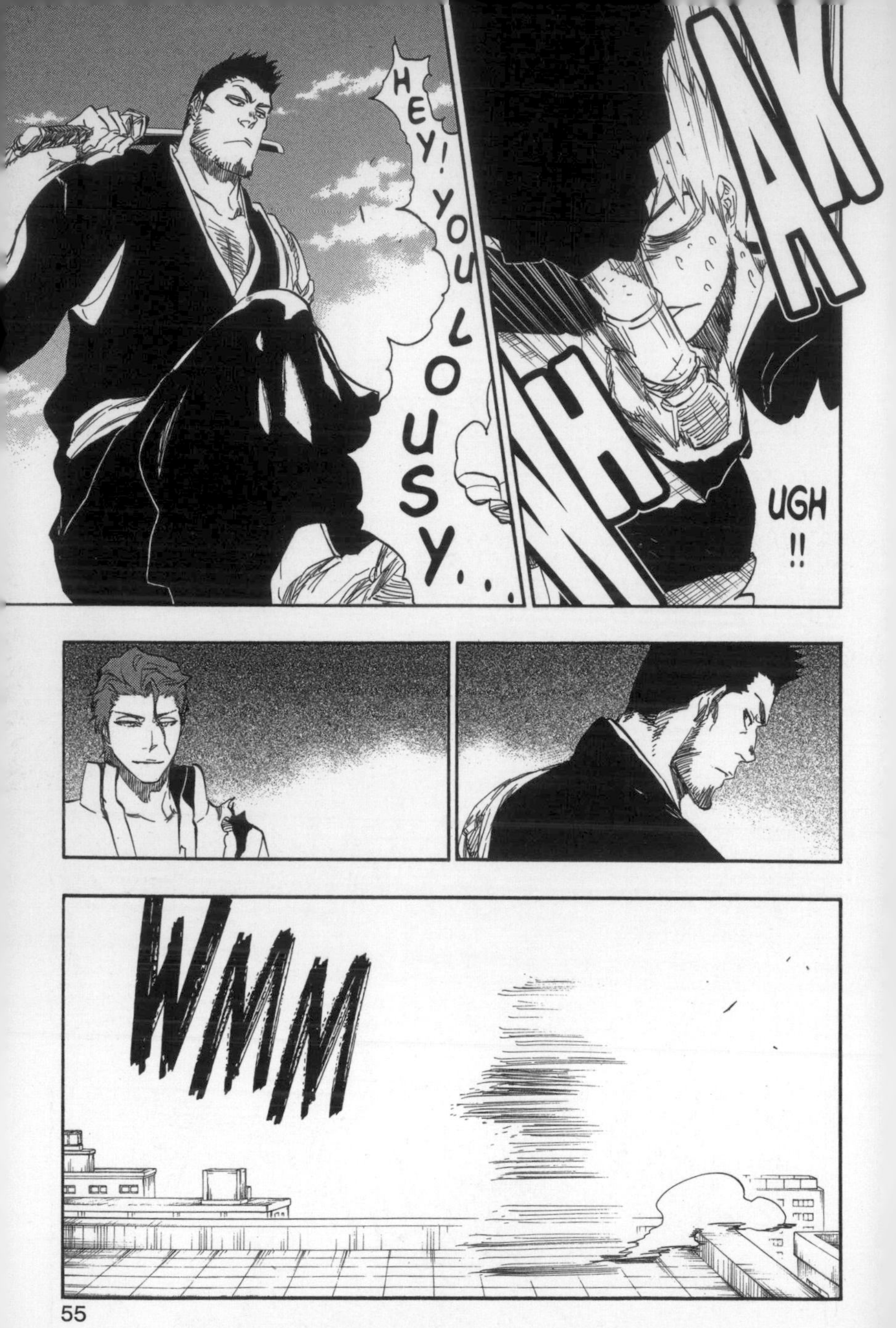
WHAK
UGH !!
HEY! YOU LOUSY...
WMM

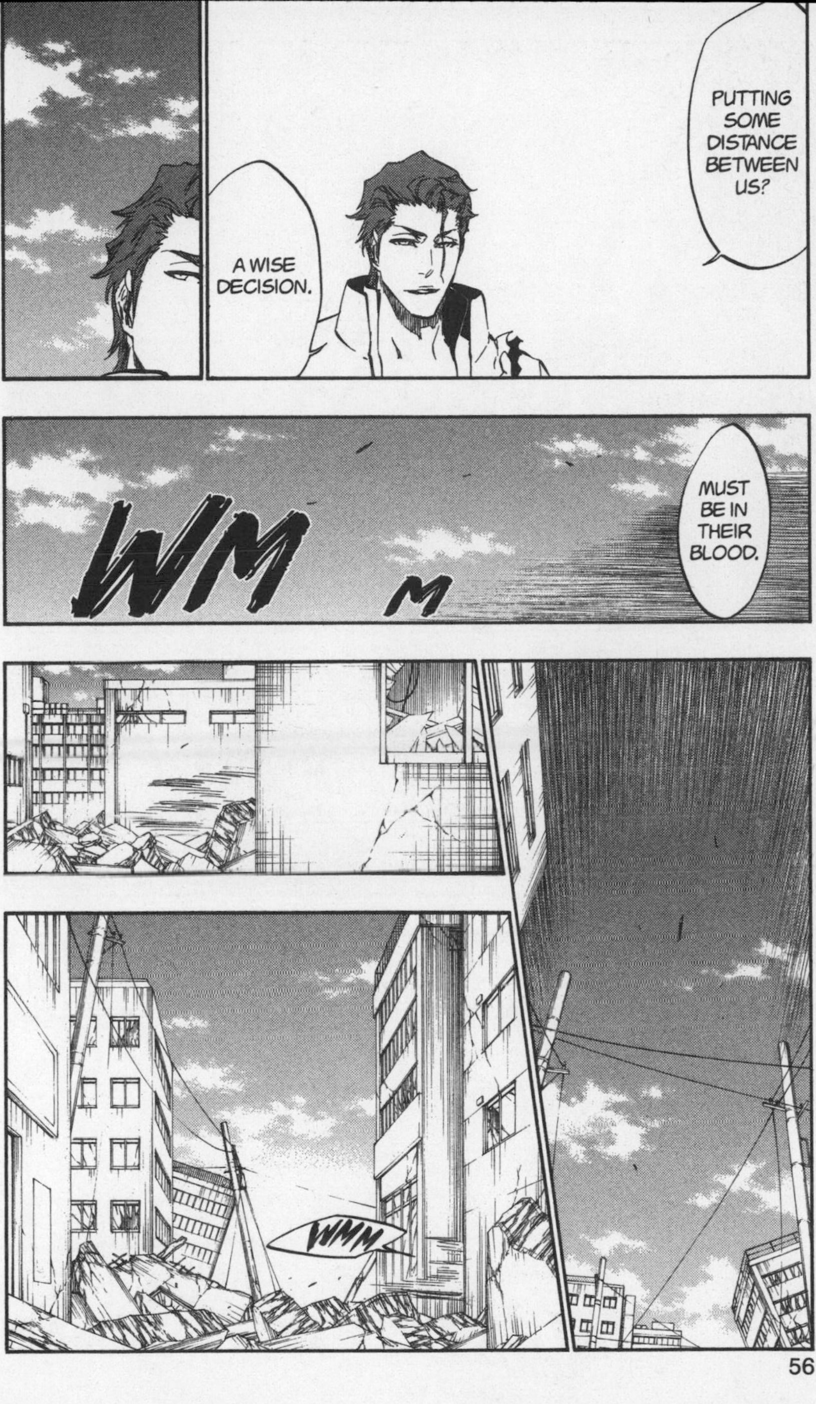
PUTTING SOME DISTANCE BETWEEN US?
A WISE DECISION.
MUST BE IN THEIR BLOOD.
WM M
WMM

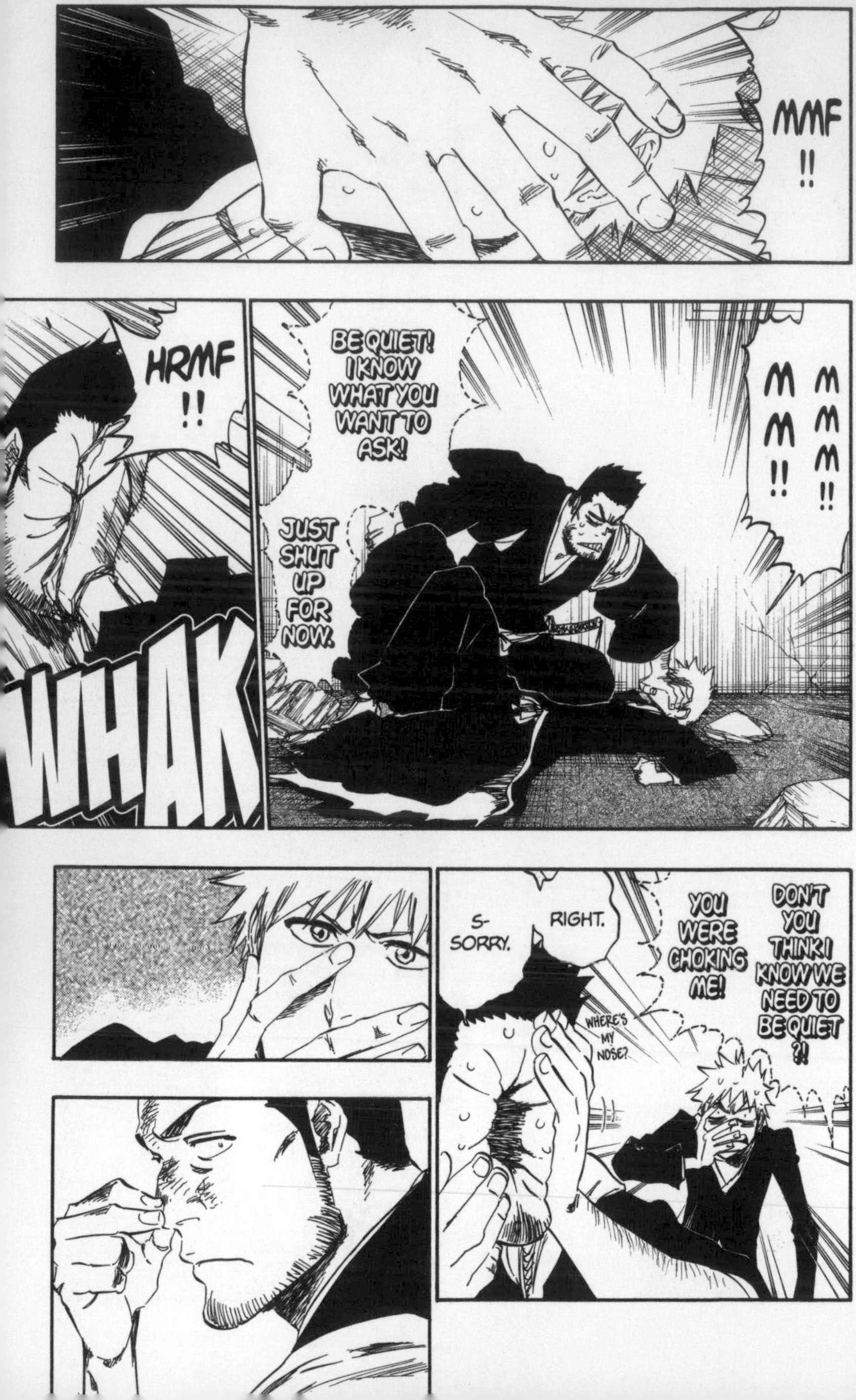
MMF !!
MMM !!
MM !!
BE QUIET! I KNOW WHAT YOU WANT TO ASK!
JUST SHUT UP FOR NOW.
HRMF !!
WHAK
DON'T YOU THINK I KNOW WE NEED TO BE QUIET ?!
YOU WERE CHOKING ME!
RIGHT.
S- SORRY.
WHERE'S MY NOSE?

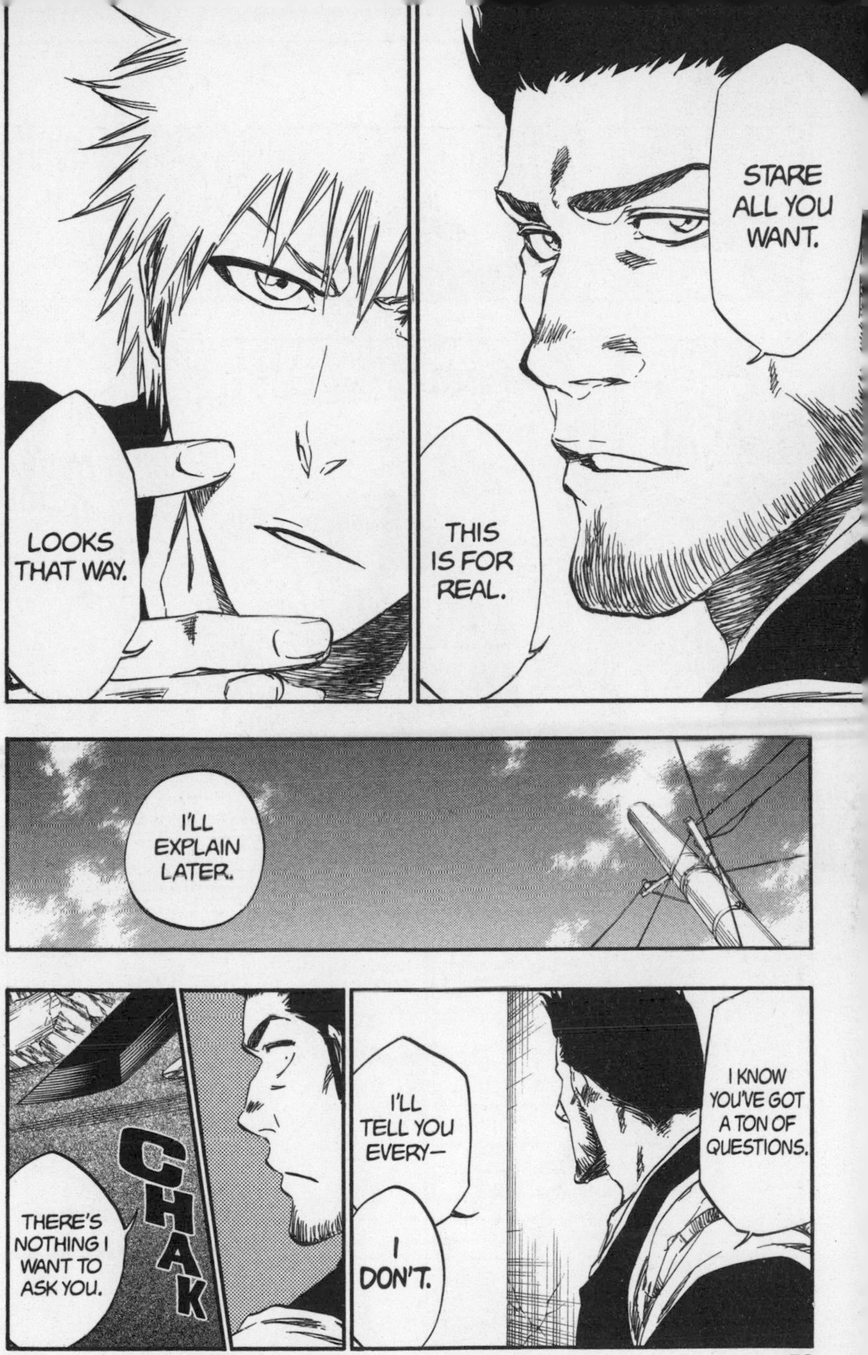
STARE ALL YOU WANT.
THIS IS FOR REAL.
LOOKS THAT WAY.
I'LL EXPLAIN LATER.
I KNOW YOU'VE GOT A TON OF QUESTIONS.
I'LL TELL YOU EVERY—
I DON'T.
CHAK
THERE'S NOTHING I WANT TO ASK YOU.

READ THIS WAY

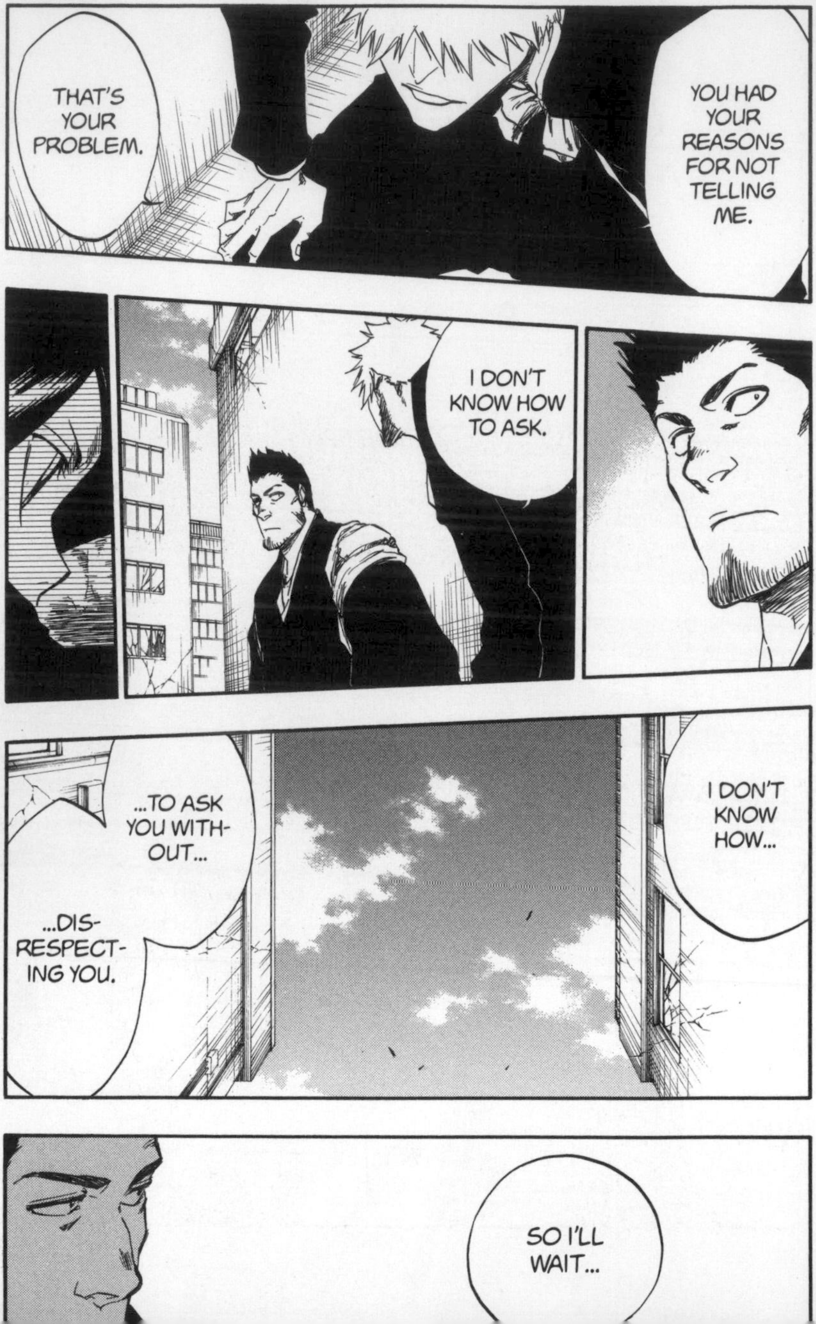
YOU HAD YOUR REASONS FOR NOT TELLING ME.
THAT'S YOUR PROBLEM.
I DON'T KNOW HOW TO ASK.
I DON'T KNOW HOW...
...TO ASK YOU WITH-OUT...
...DIS-RESPECT-ING YOU.
SO I'LL WAIT...

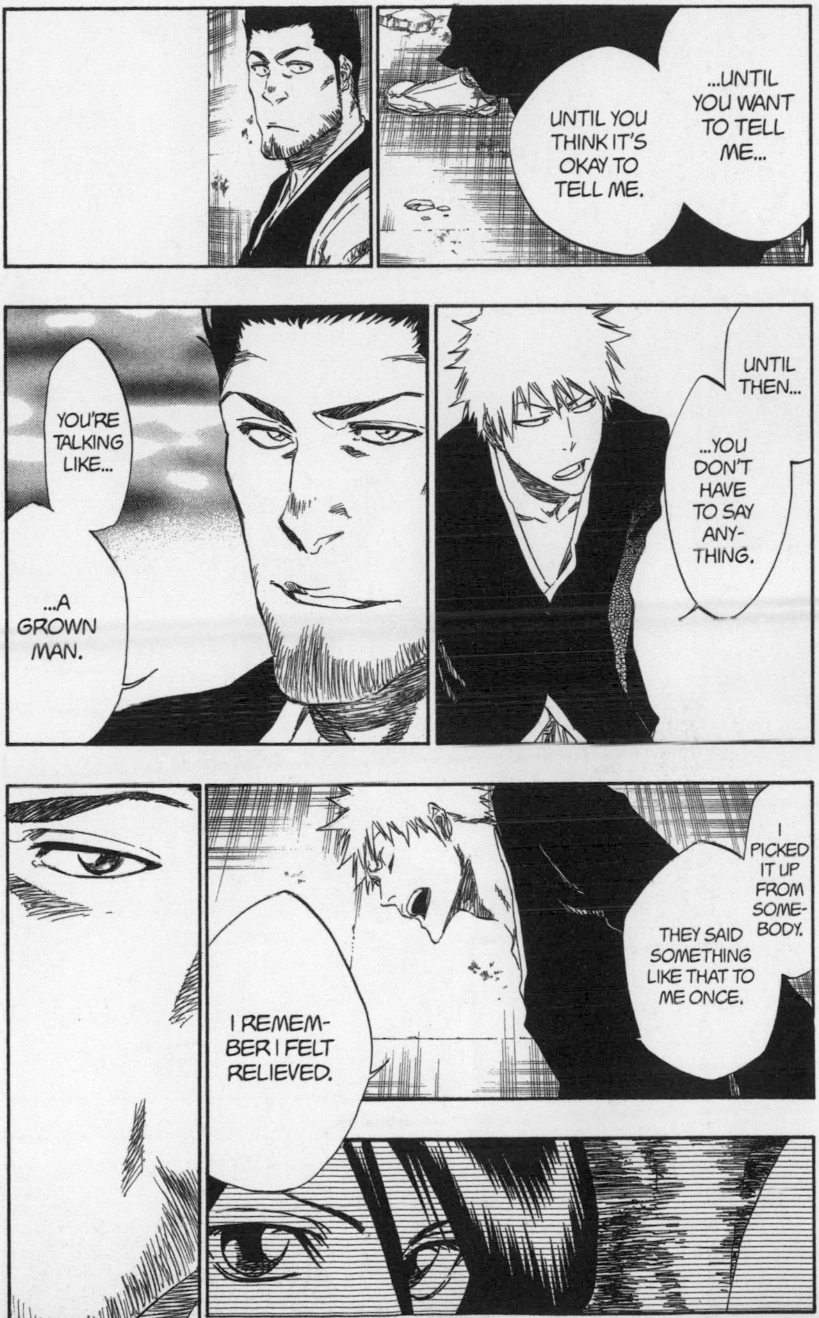
...UNTIL YOU WANT TO TELL ME...
UNTIL YOU THINK IT'S OKAY TO TELL ME.
UNTIL THEN...
...YOU DON'T HAVE TO SAY ANY-THING.
YOU'RE TALKING LIKE...
...A GROWN MAN.
I PICKED IT UP FROM SOME-BODY.
THEY SAID SOMETHING LIKE THAT TO ME ONCE.
I REMEM-BER I FELT RELIEVED.

READ THIS WAY

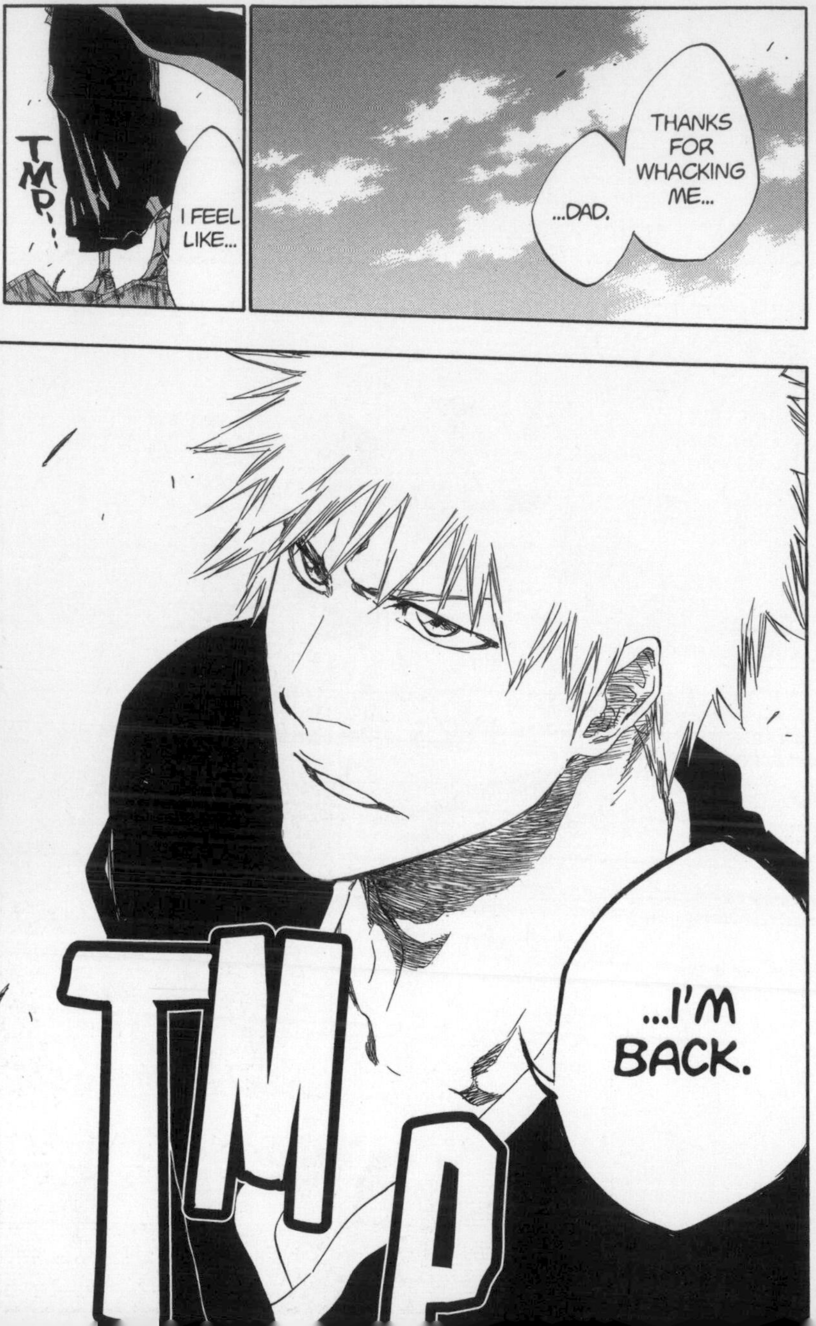
THANKS FOR WHACKING ME...
...DAD.
I FEEL LIKE...
TMP...
...I'M BACK.
TMP

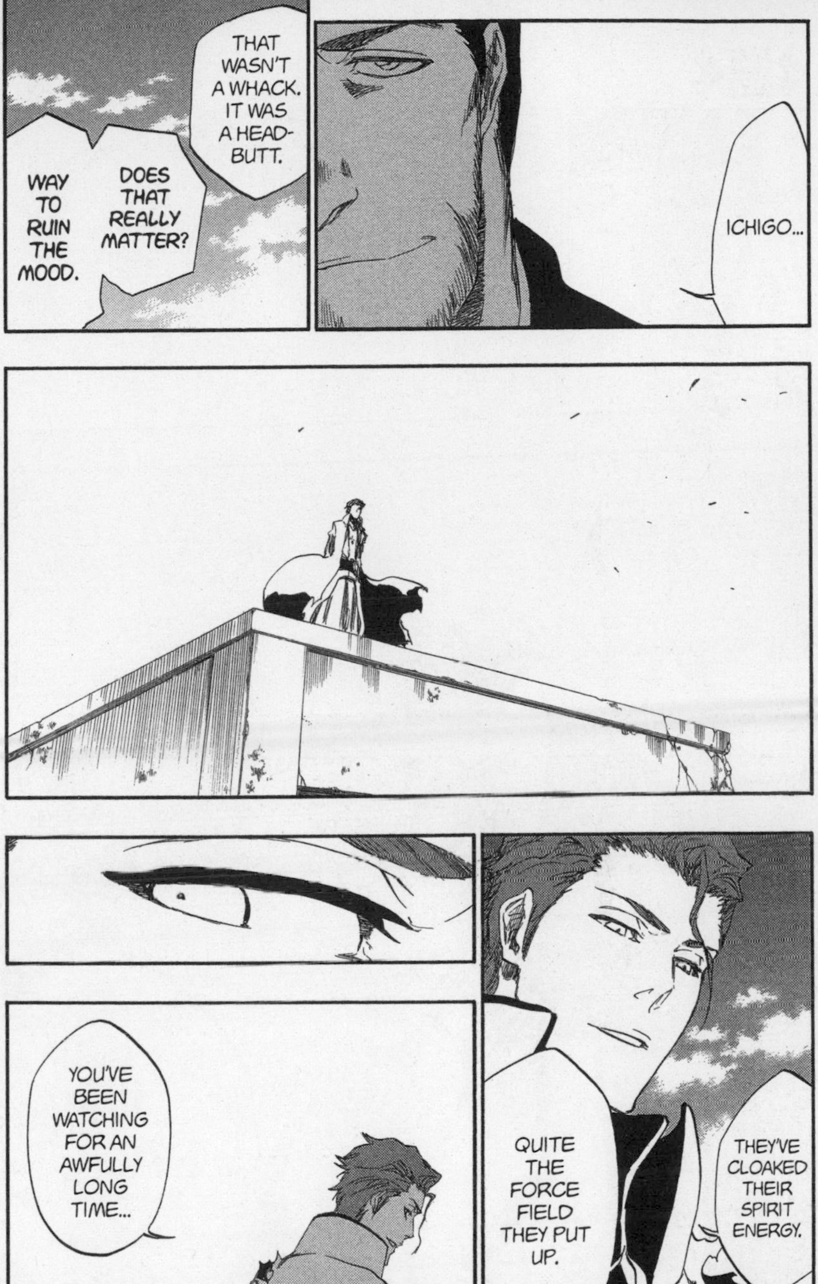
ICHIGO...
THAT WASN'T A WHACK. IT WAS A HEAD-BUTT.
DOES THAT REALLY MATTER?
WAY TO RUIN THE MOOD.
THEY'VE CLOAKED THEIR SPIRIT ENERGY.
QUITE THE FORCE FIELD THEY PUT UP.
YOU'VE BEEN WATCHING FOR AN AWFULLY LONG TIME...

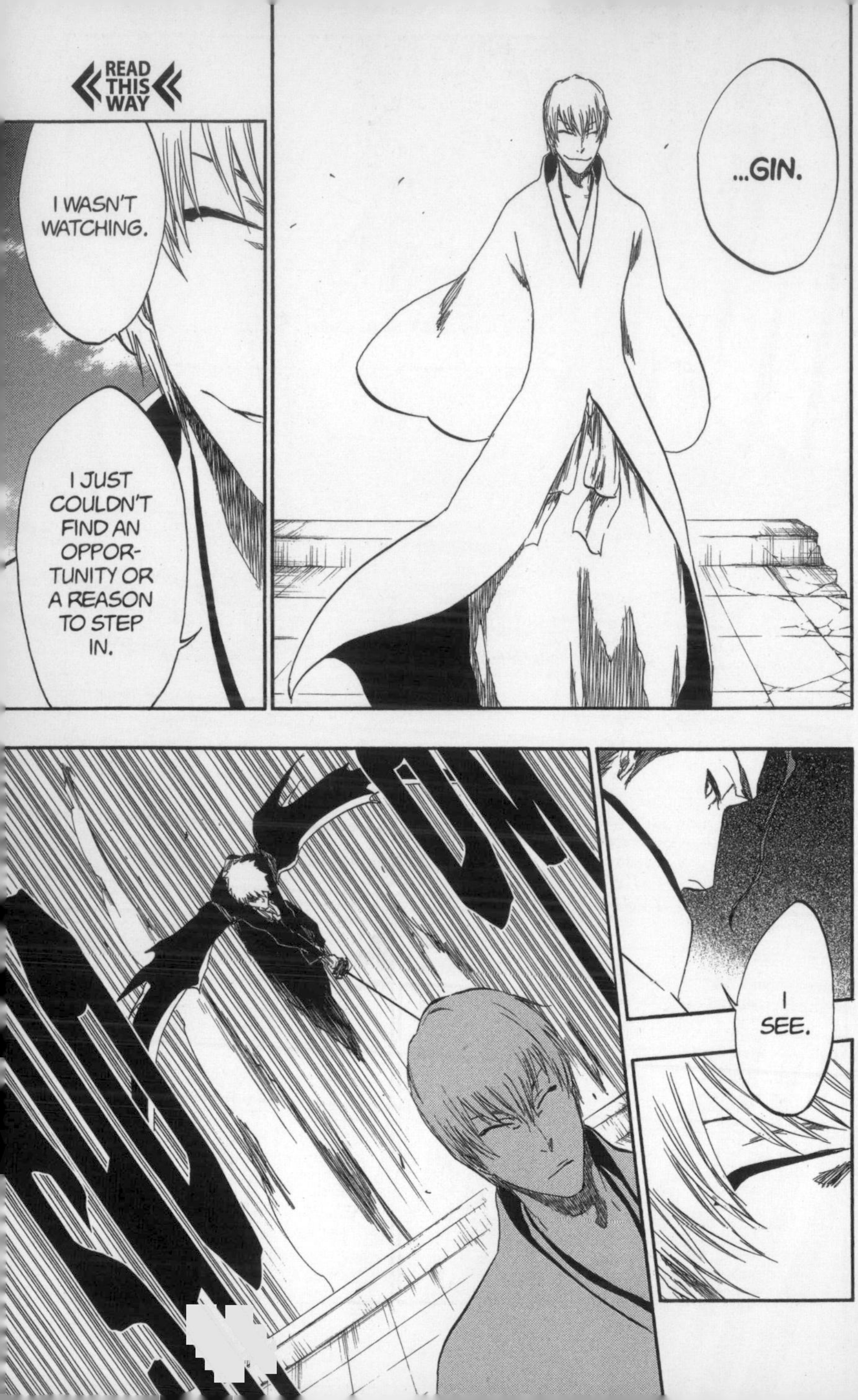
READ THIS WAY
...GIN.
I WASN'T WATCHING.
I JUST COULDN'T FIND AN OPPOR-TUNITY OR A REASON TO STEP IN.
I SEE.

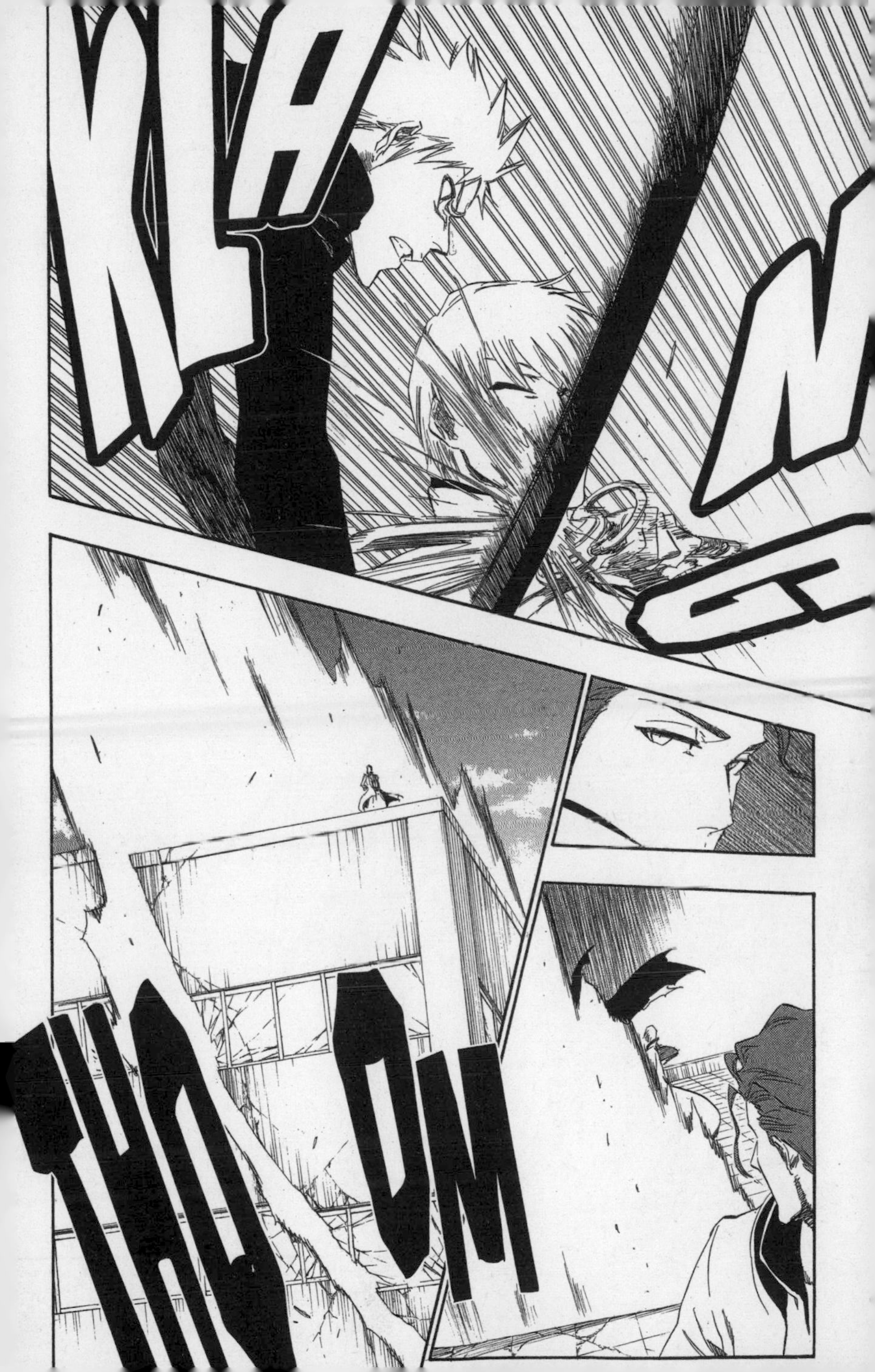
THOOM

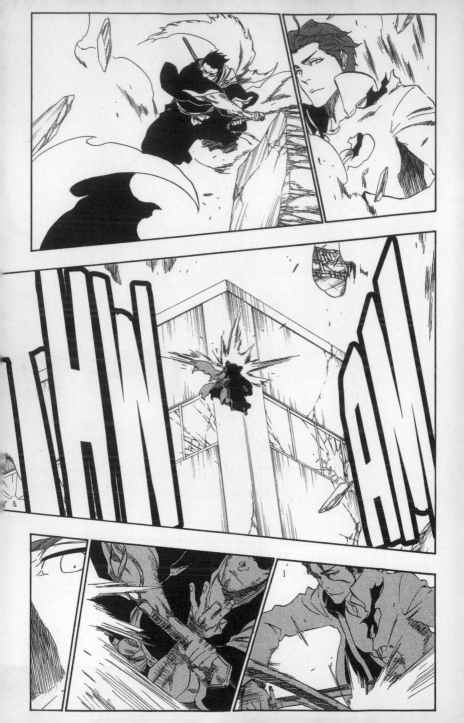

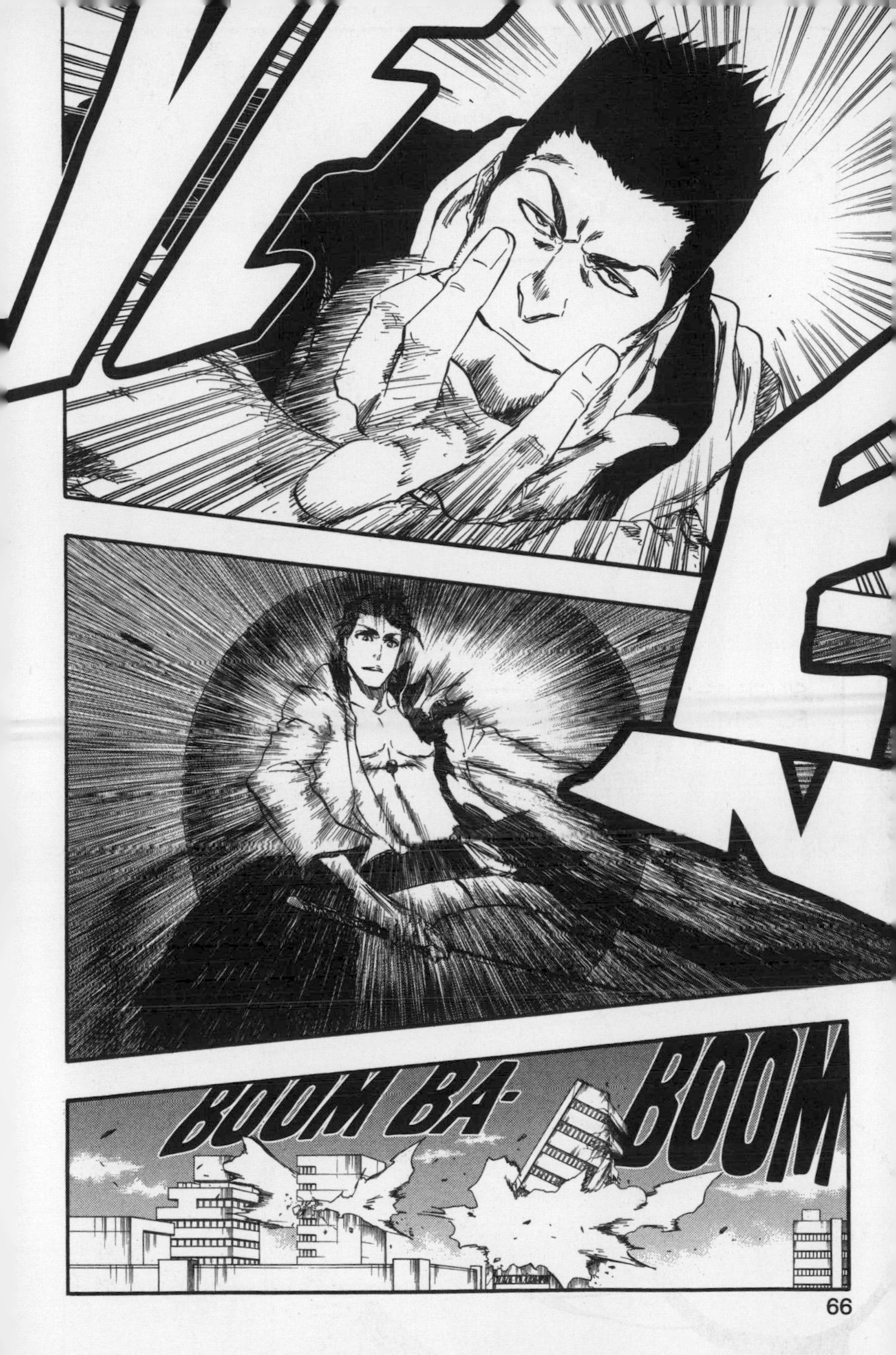
BOOM BA-BOOM

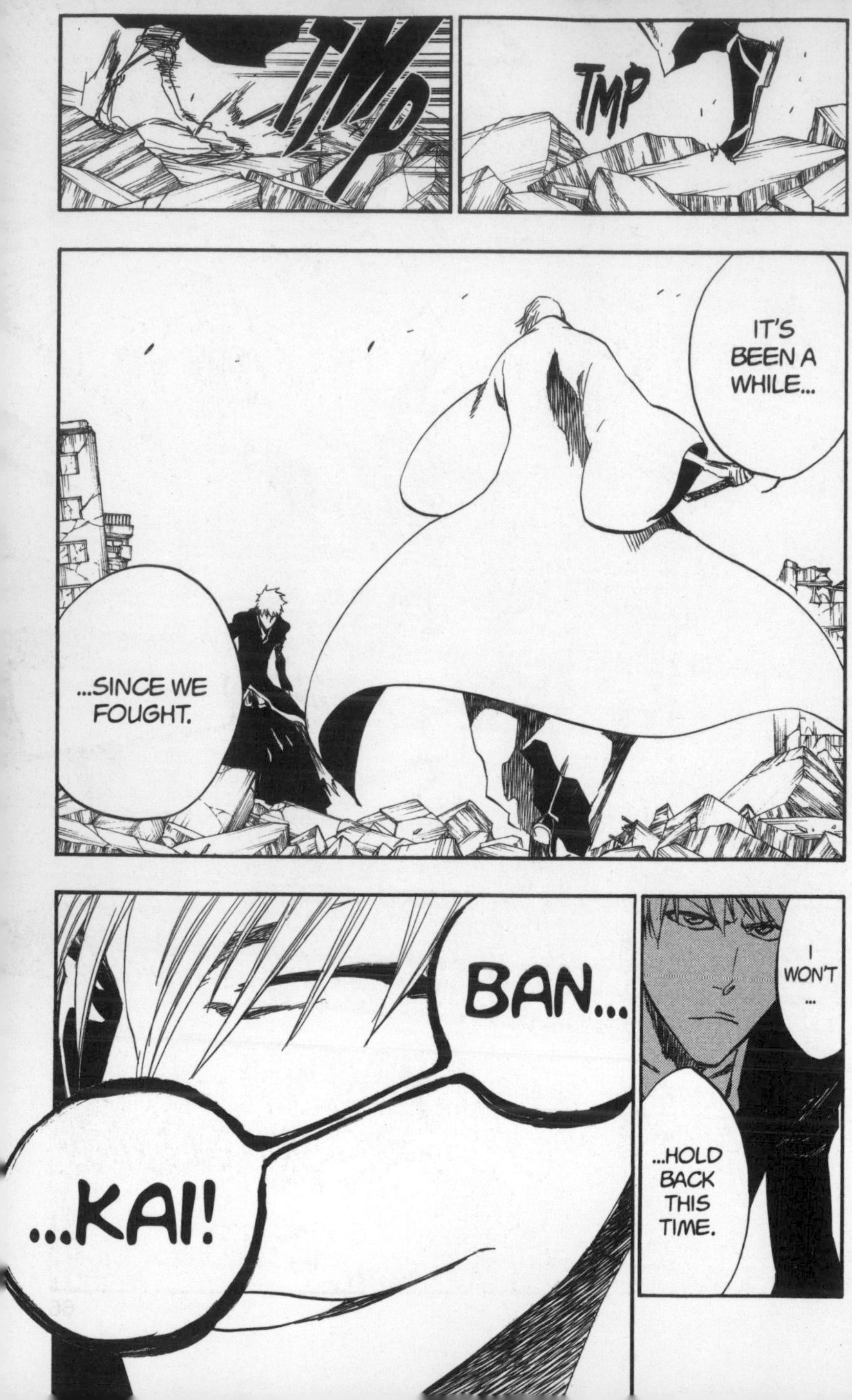
TMP
TMP
IT'S BEEN A WHILE...
...SINCE WE FOUGHT.
I WON'T ...
...HOLD BACK THIS TIME.
BAN...
...KAI!

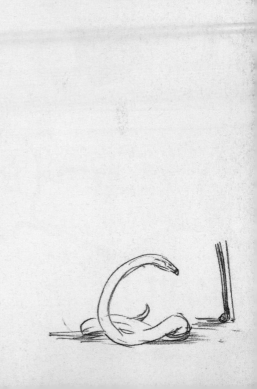

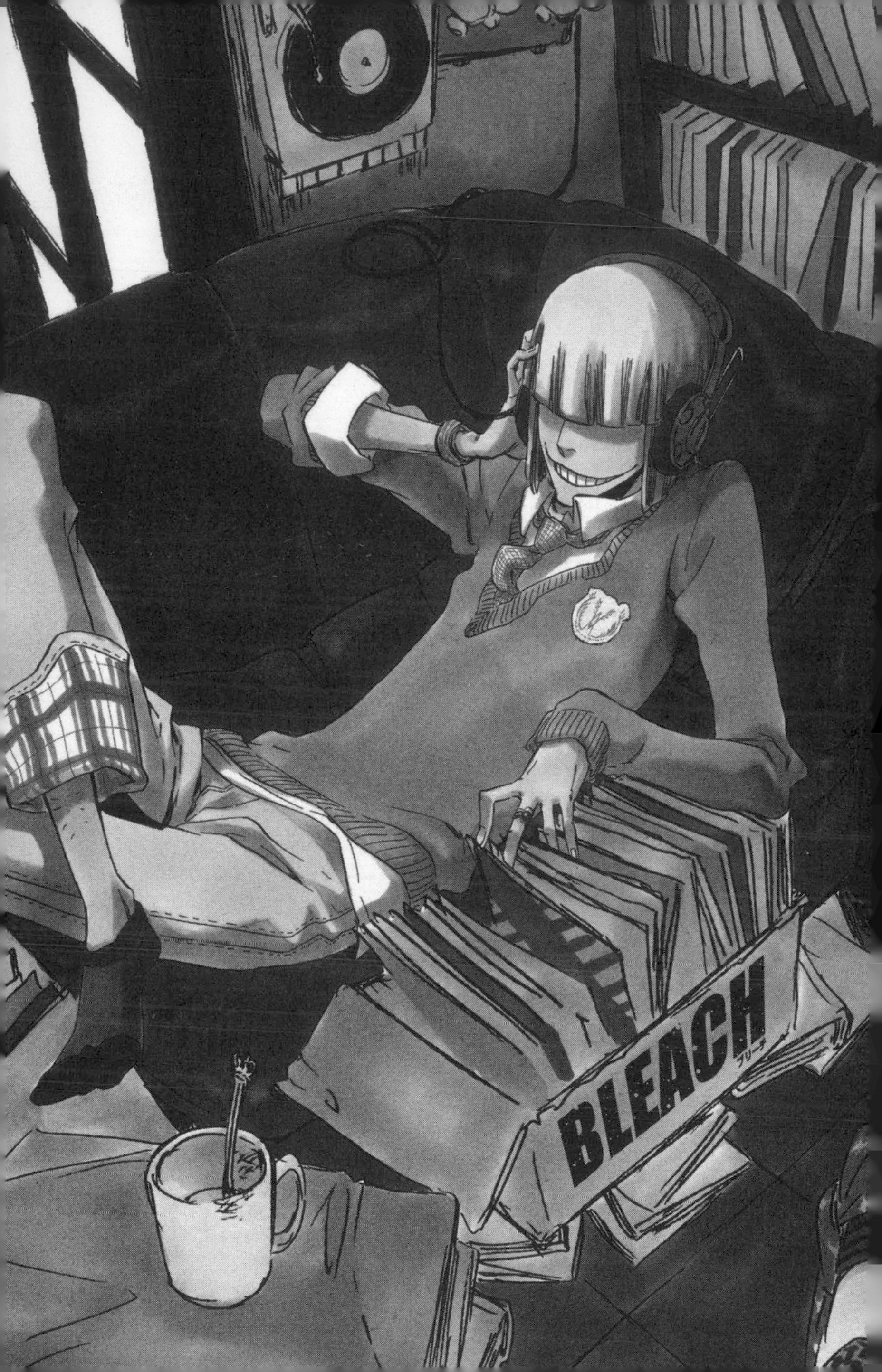
BLEACH
ブリーチ

BLEACH
ブリーチ

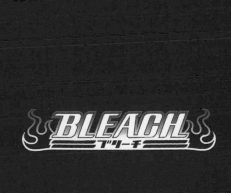

READ THIS WAY

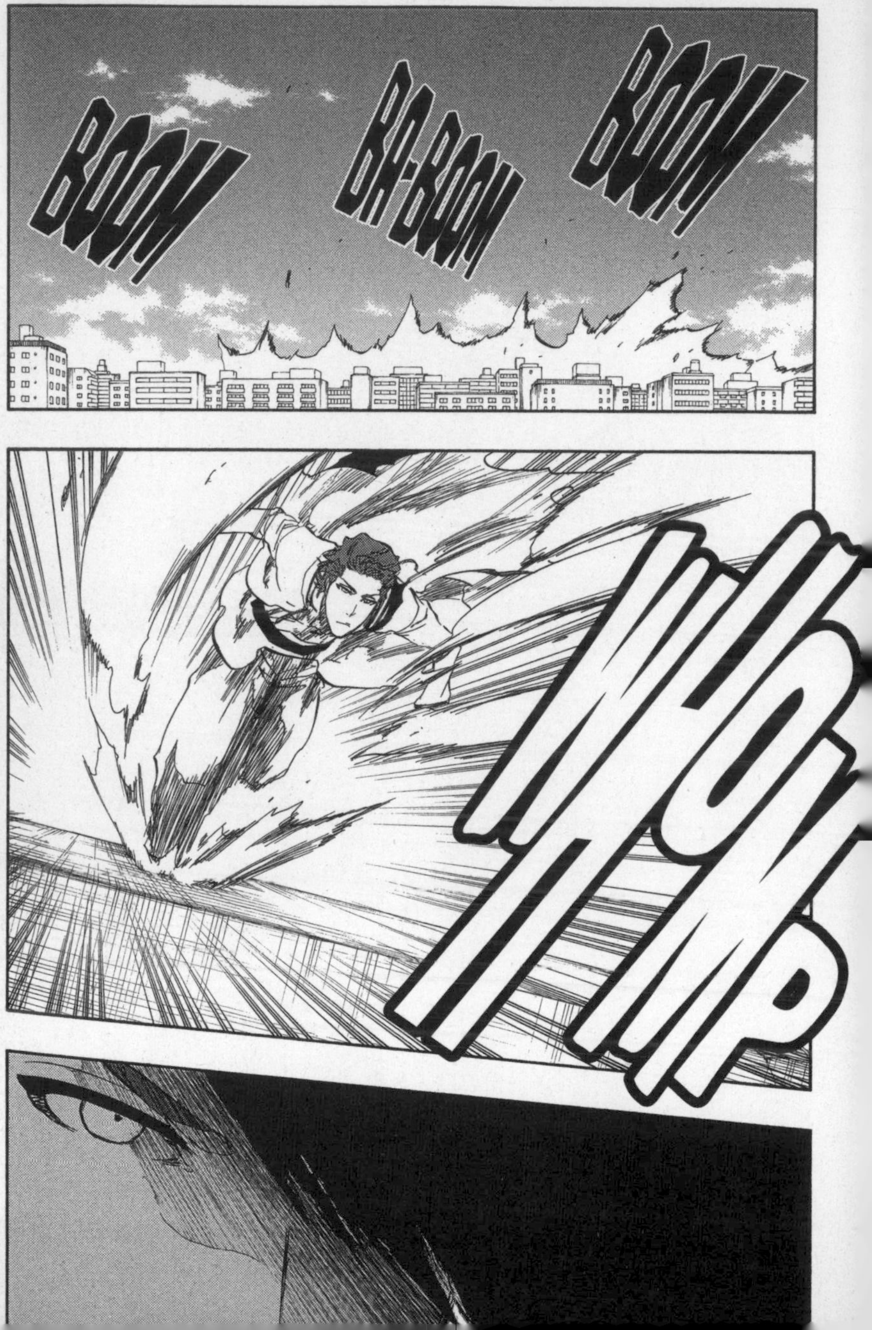
BOOM
BA-BOOM
BOOM
WHOMP

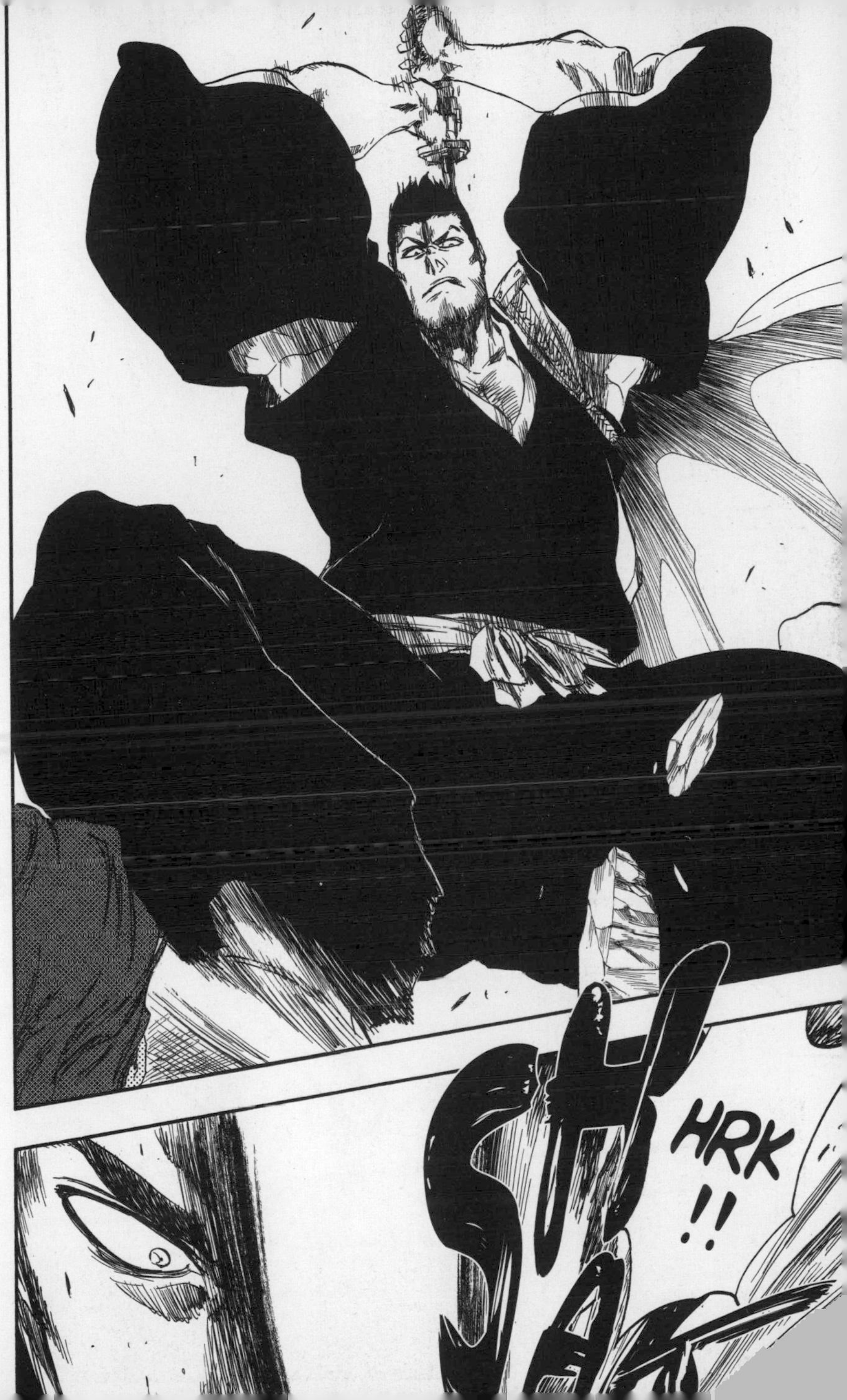
HRK
!!

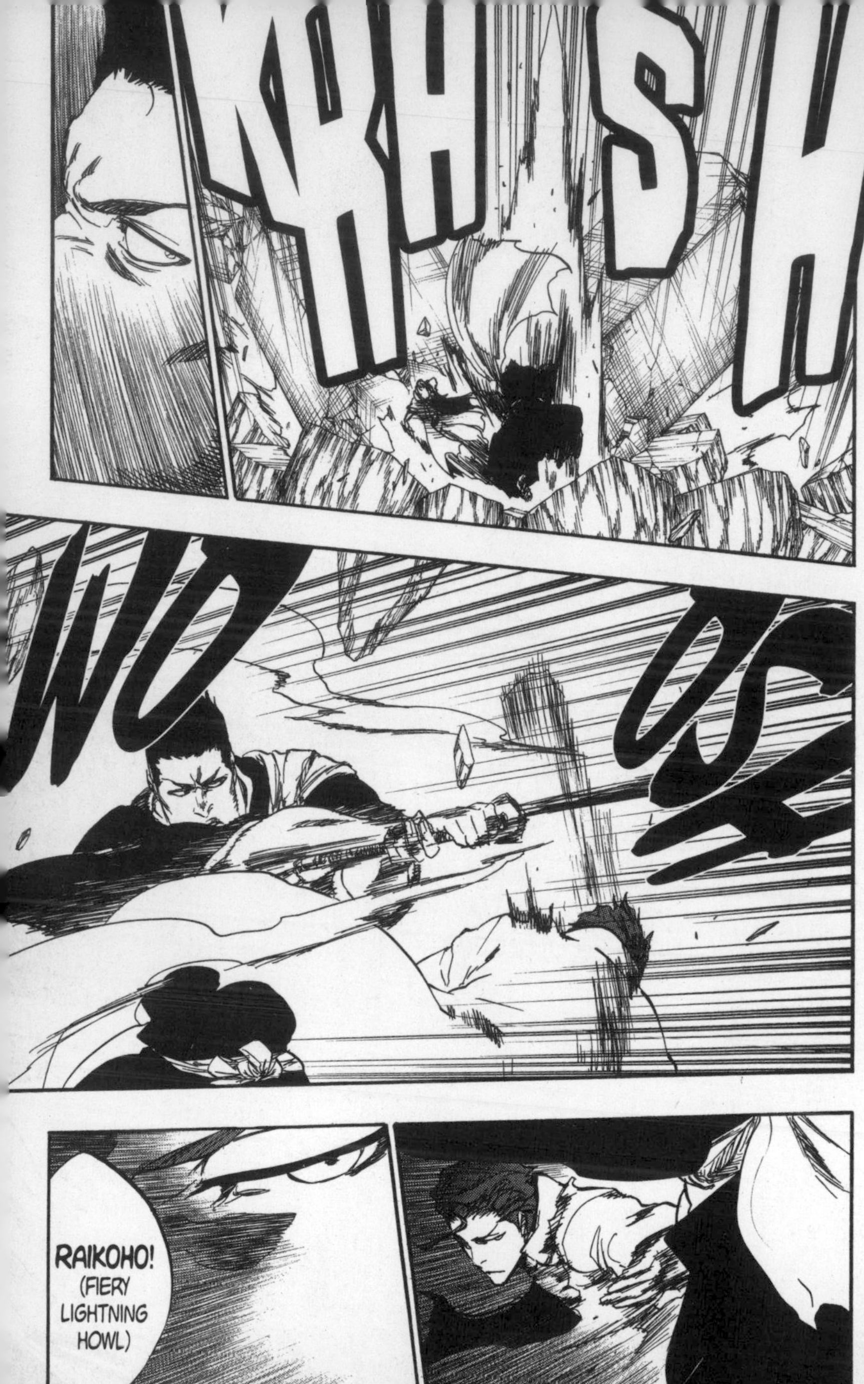
RAIKOHO!
(FIERY LIGHTNING HOWL)

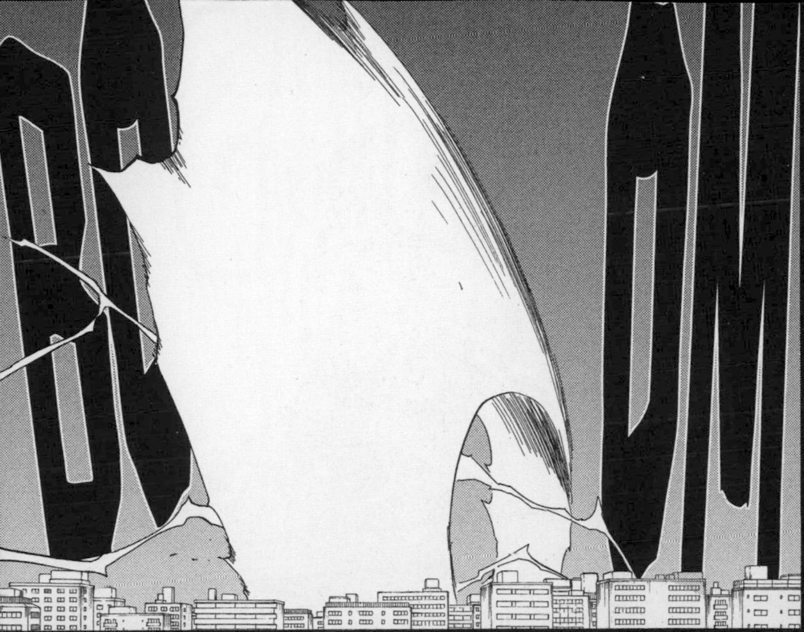

BLEACH

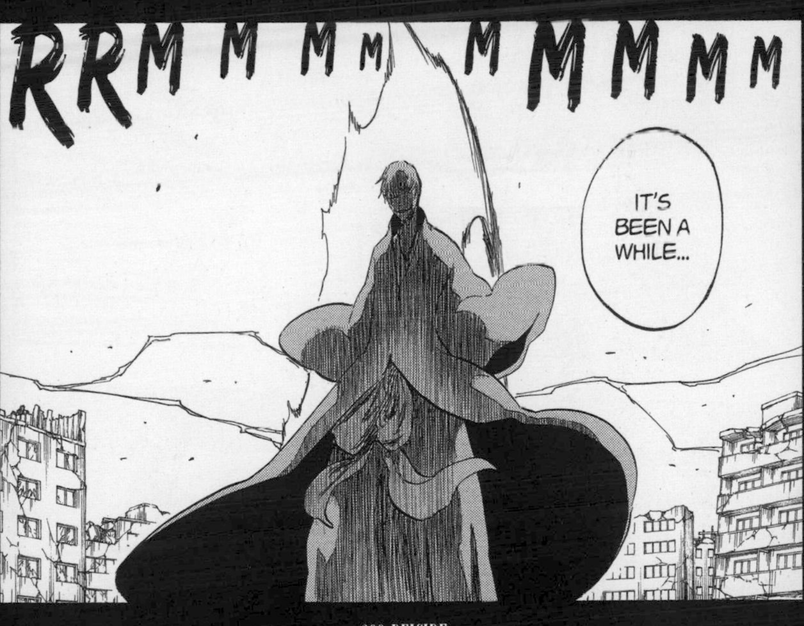
RRMMMMM MMMMM
IT'S BEEN A WHILE...

399. DEICIDE

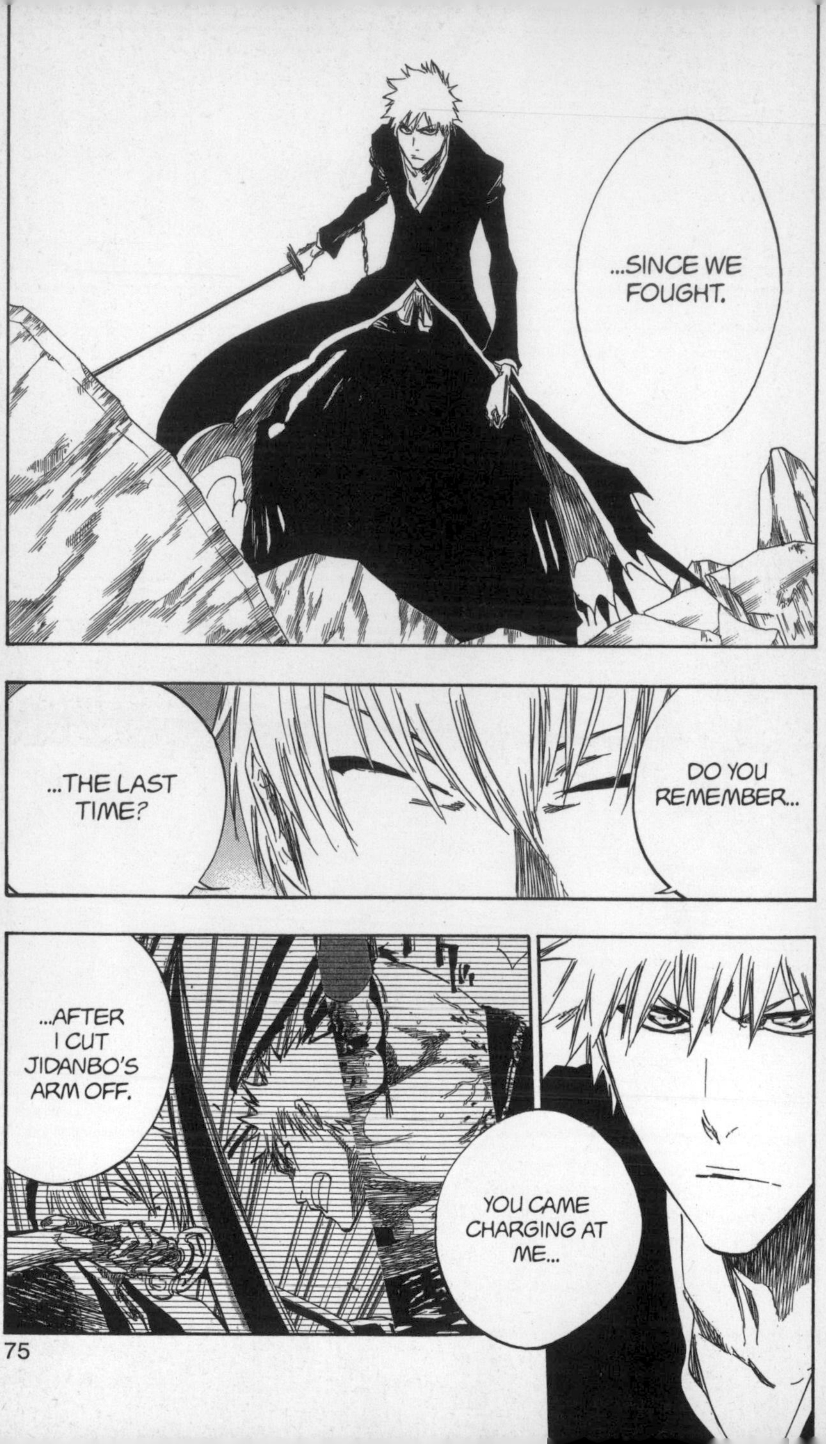
...SINCE WE FOUGHT.
DO YOU REMEMBER...
...THE LAST TIME?
YOU CAME CHARGING AT ME...
...AFTER I CUT JIDANBO'S ARM OFF.

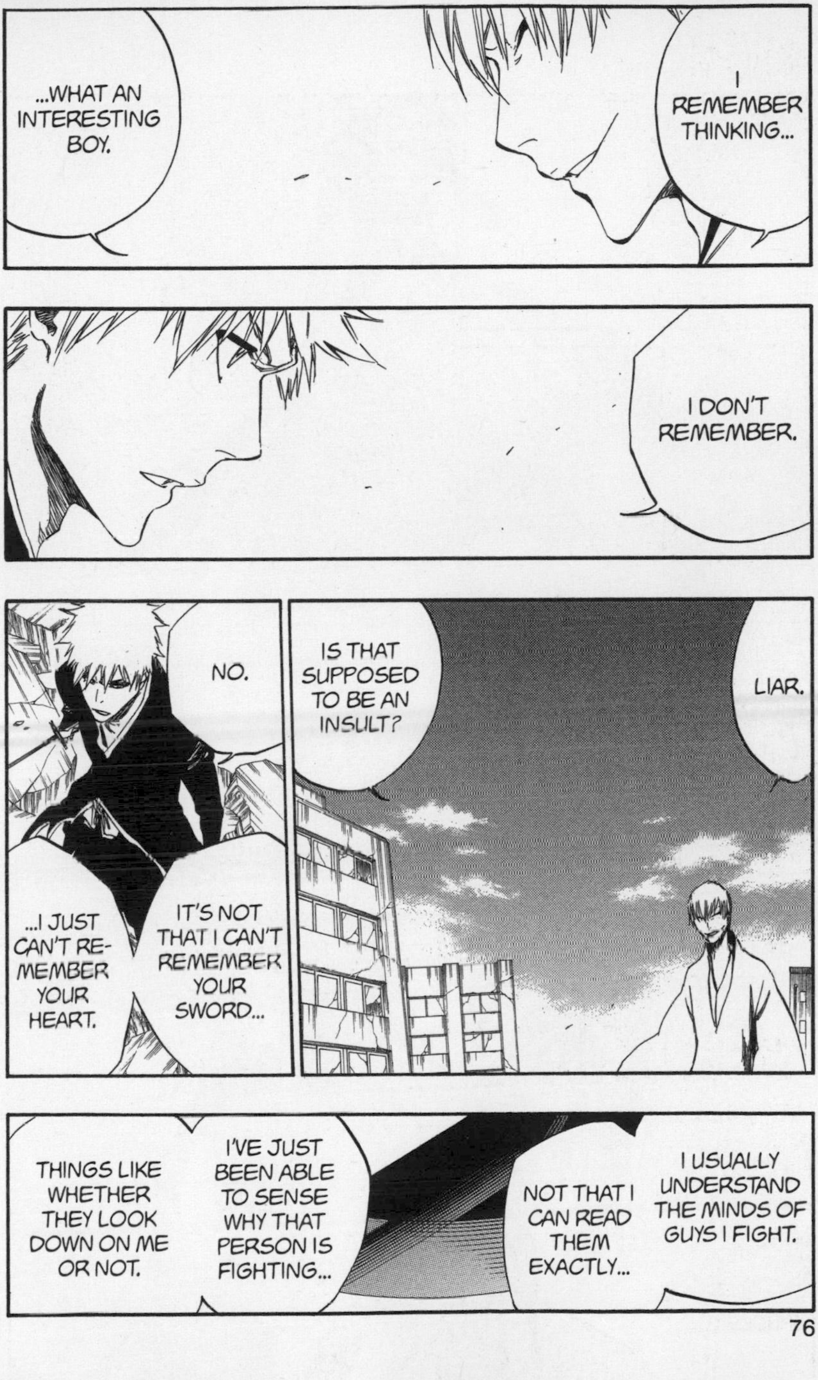
I REMEMBER THINKING...
...WHAT AN INTERESTING BOY.
I DON'T REMEMBER.
LIAR.
IS THAT SUPPOSED TO BE AN INSULT?
NO.
IT'S NOT THAT I CAN'T REMEMBER YOUR SWORD...
...I JUST CAN'T RE-MEMBER YOUR HEART.
I USUALLY UNDERSTAND THE MINDS OF GUYS I FIGHT.
NOT THAT I CAN READ THEM EXACTLY...
I'VE JUST BEEN ABLE TO SENSE WHY THAT PERSON IS FIGHTING...
THINGS LIKE WHETHER THEY LOOK DOWN ON ME OR NOT.

READ THIS WAY

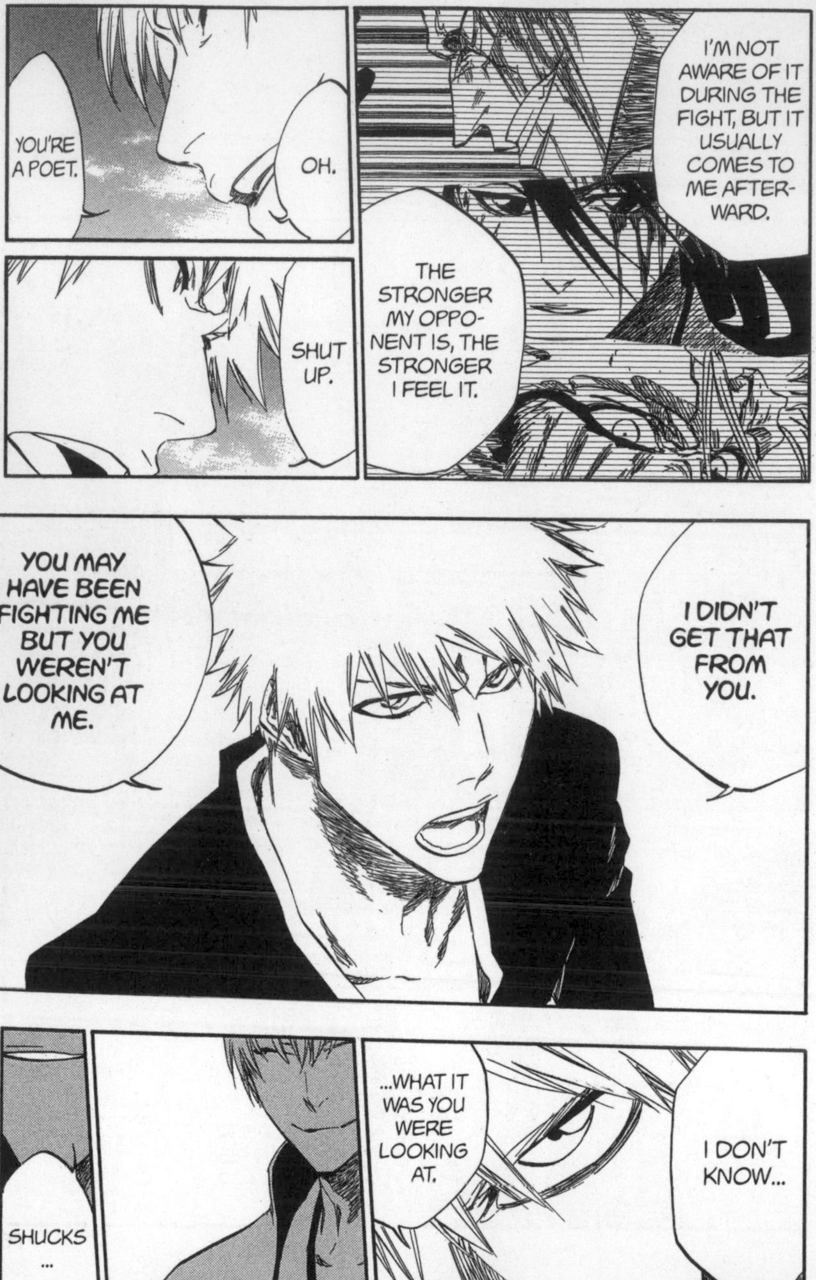

I'M NOT AWARE OF IT DURING THE FIGHT, BUT IT USUALLY COMES TO ME AFTER-WARD.
THE STRONGER MY OPPO-NENT IS, THE STRONGER I FEEL IT.
OH.
YOU'RE A POET.
SHUT UP.
I DIDN'T GET THAT FROM YOU.
YOU MAY HAVE BEEN FIGHTING ME BUT YOU WEREN'T LOOKING AT ME.
I DON'T KNOW...
...WHAT IT WAS YOU WERE LOOKING AT.
SHUCKS ...

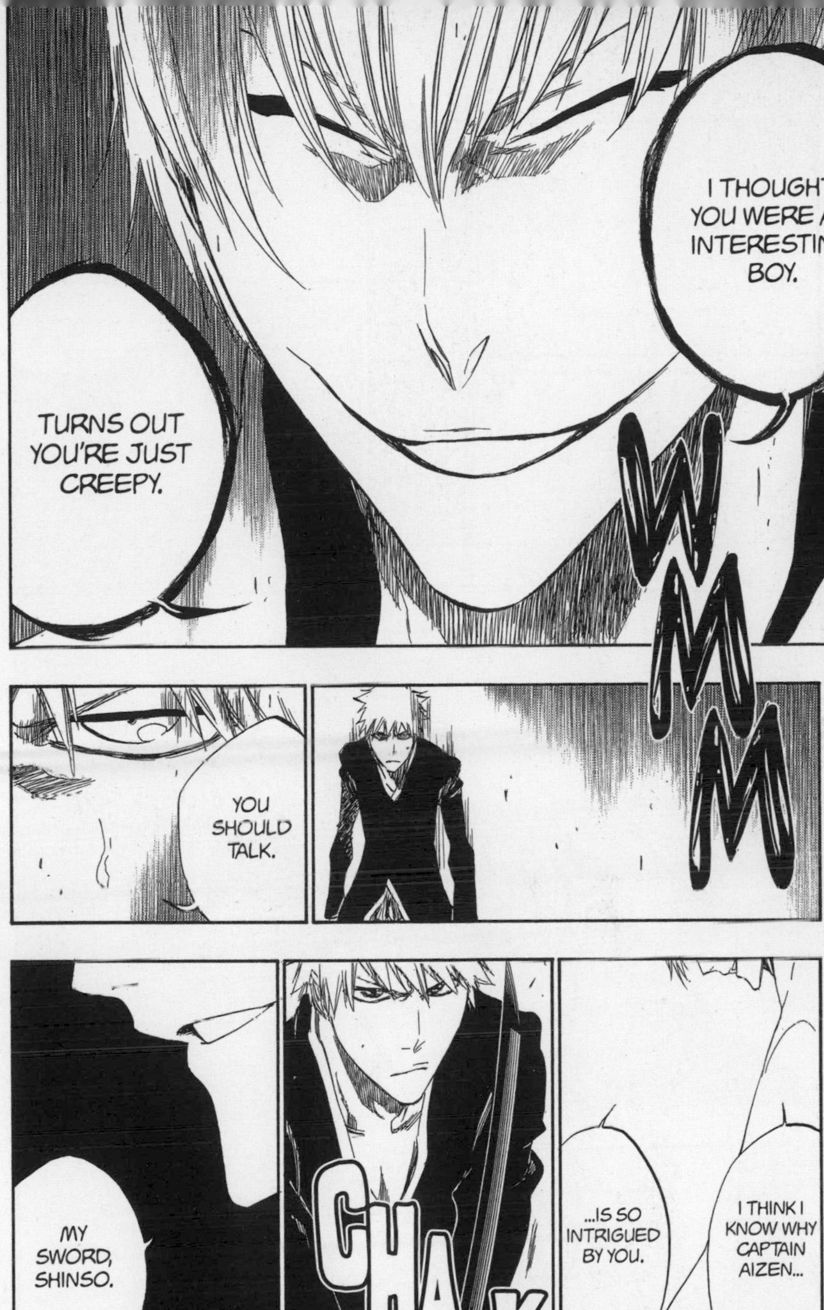
I THOUGHT YOU WERE AN INTERESTING BOY.
TURNS OUT YOU'RE JUST CREEPY.
WMM
YOU SHOULD TALK.
I THINK I KNOW WHY CAPTAIN AIZEN...
...IS SO INTRIGUED BY YOU.
CHAK
MY SWORD, SHINSO.

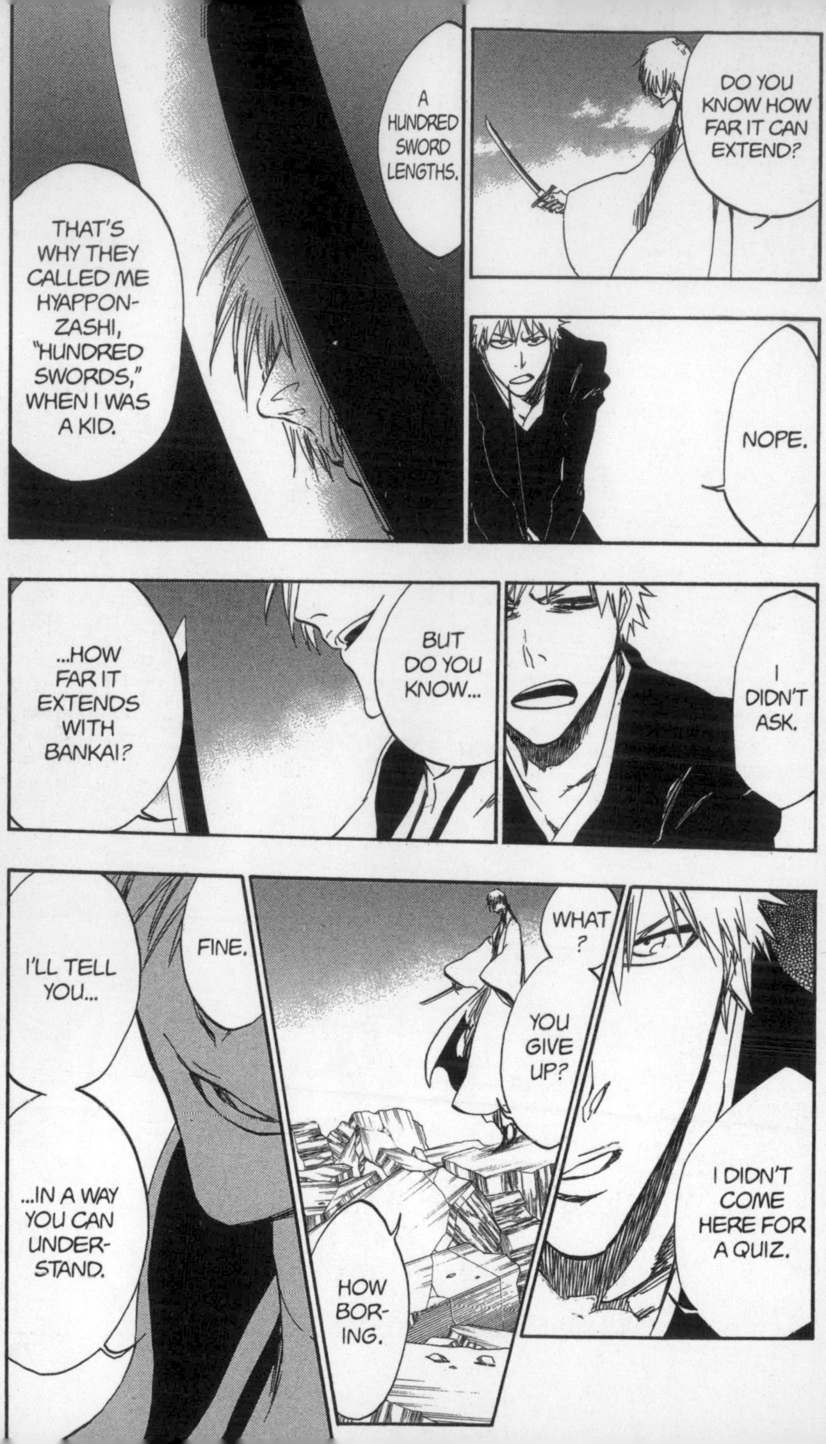
DO YOU KNOW HOW FAR IT CAN EXTEND?
NOPE.
A HUNDRED SWORD LENGTHS.
THAT'S WHY THEY CALLED ME HYAPPON-ZASHI, "HUNDRED SWORDS," WHEN I WAS A KID.
I DIDN'T ASK.
BUT DO YOU KNOW...
...HOW FAR IT EXTENDS WITH BANKAI?
WHAT?
YOU GIVE UP?
I DIDN'T COME HERE FOR A QUIZ.
HOW BOR-ING.
FINE.
I'LL TELL YOU...
...IN A WAY YOU CAN UNDER-STAND.

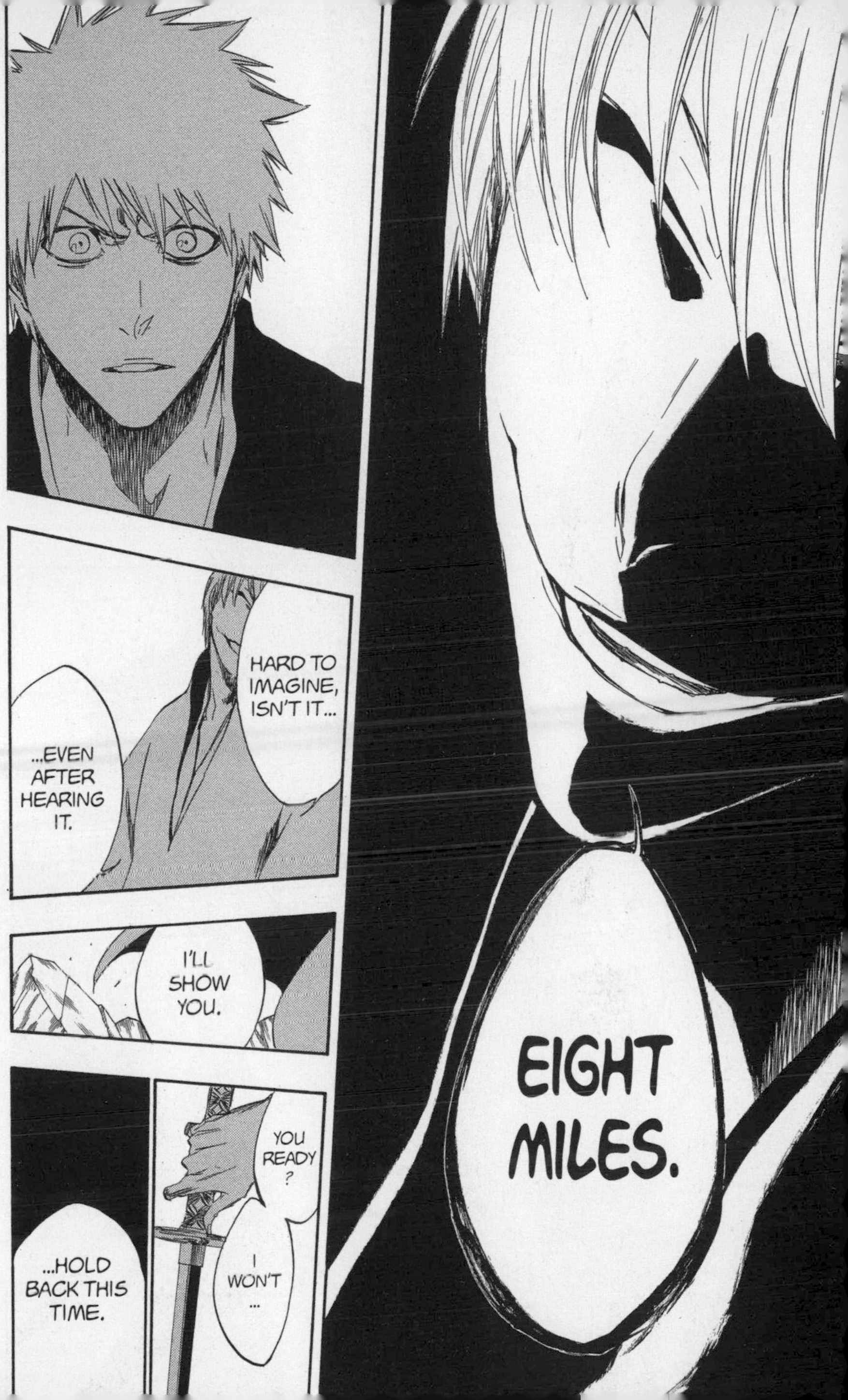
EIGHT MILES.
HARD TO IMAGINE, ISN'T IT...
...EVEN AFTER HEARING IT.
I'LL SHOW YOU.
YOU READY?
I WON'T...
...HOLD BACK THIS TIME.

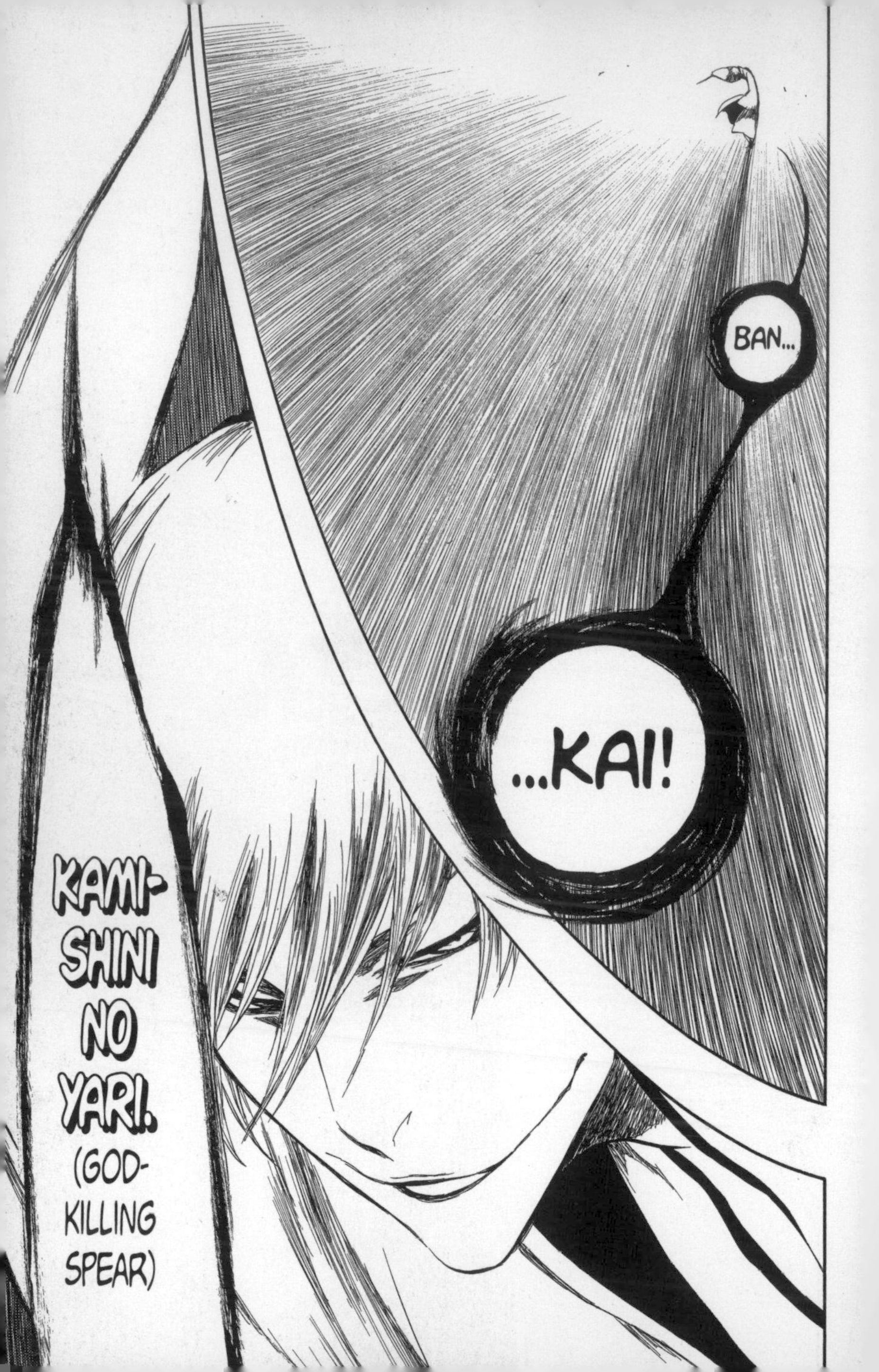
BAN...
...KAI!
KAMI-SHINI NO YARI.
(GOD-KILLING SPEAR)

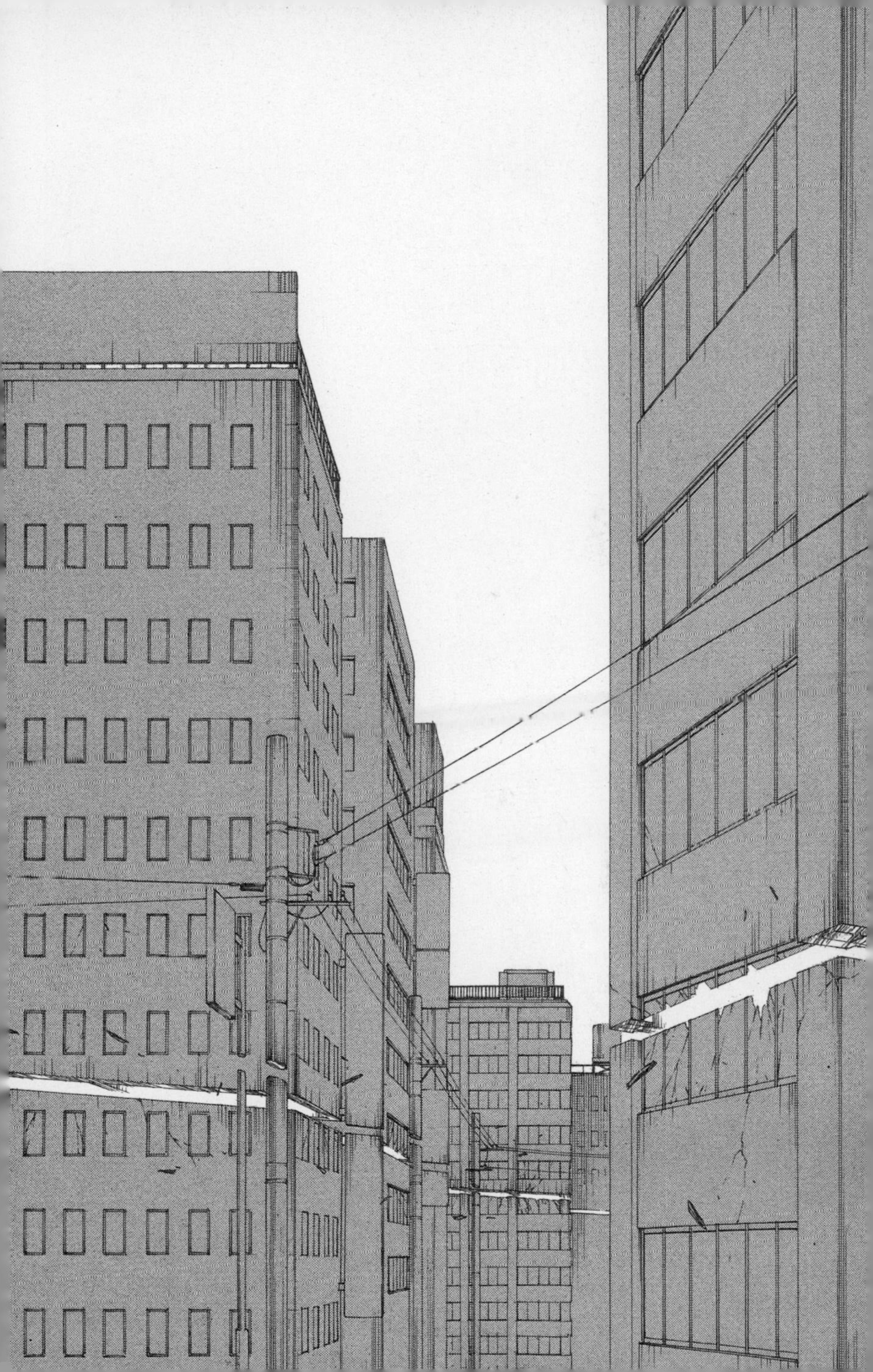

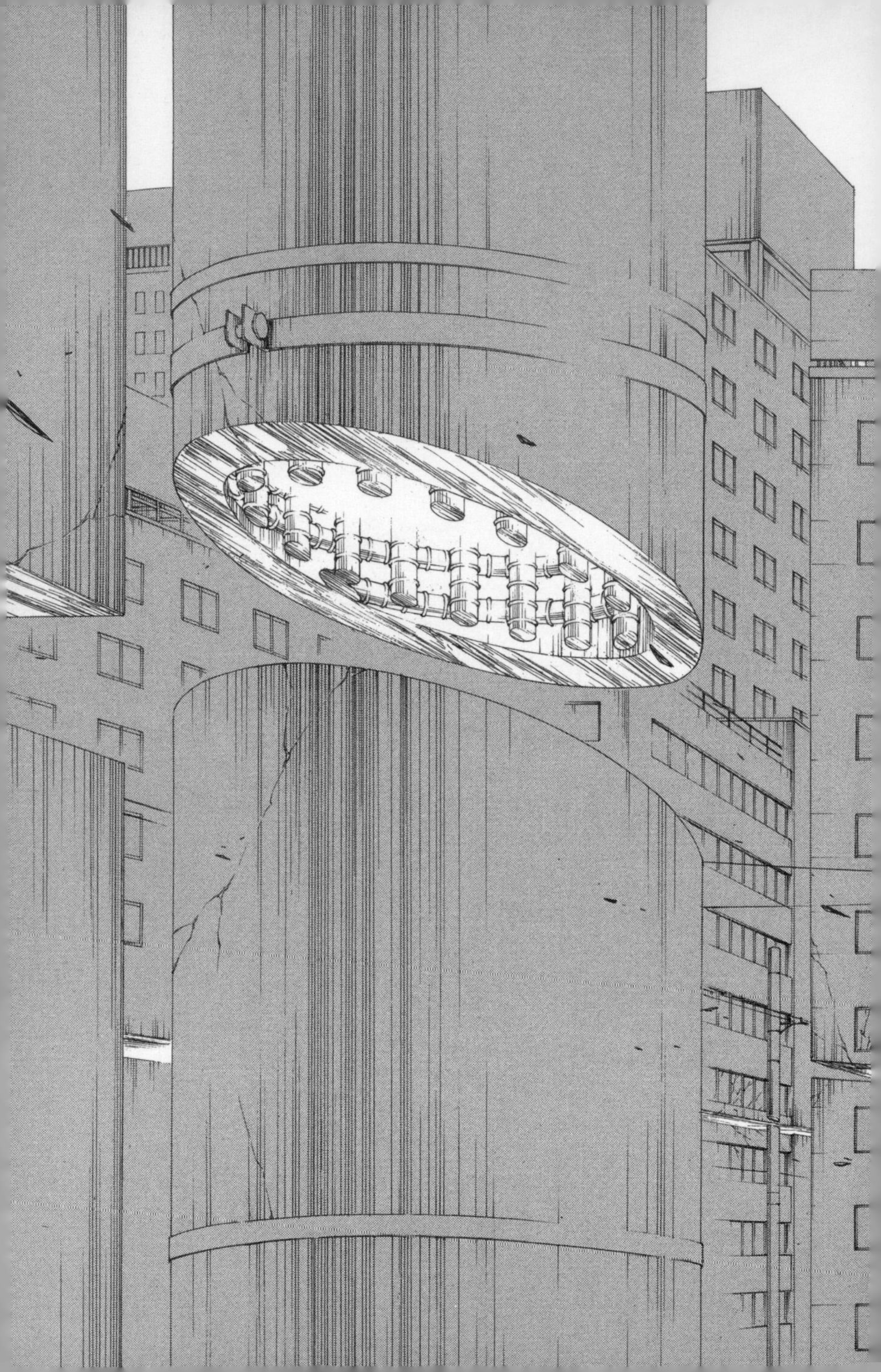

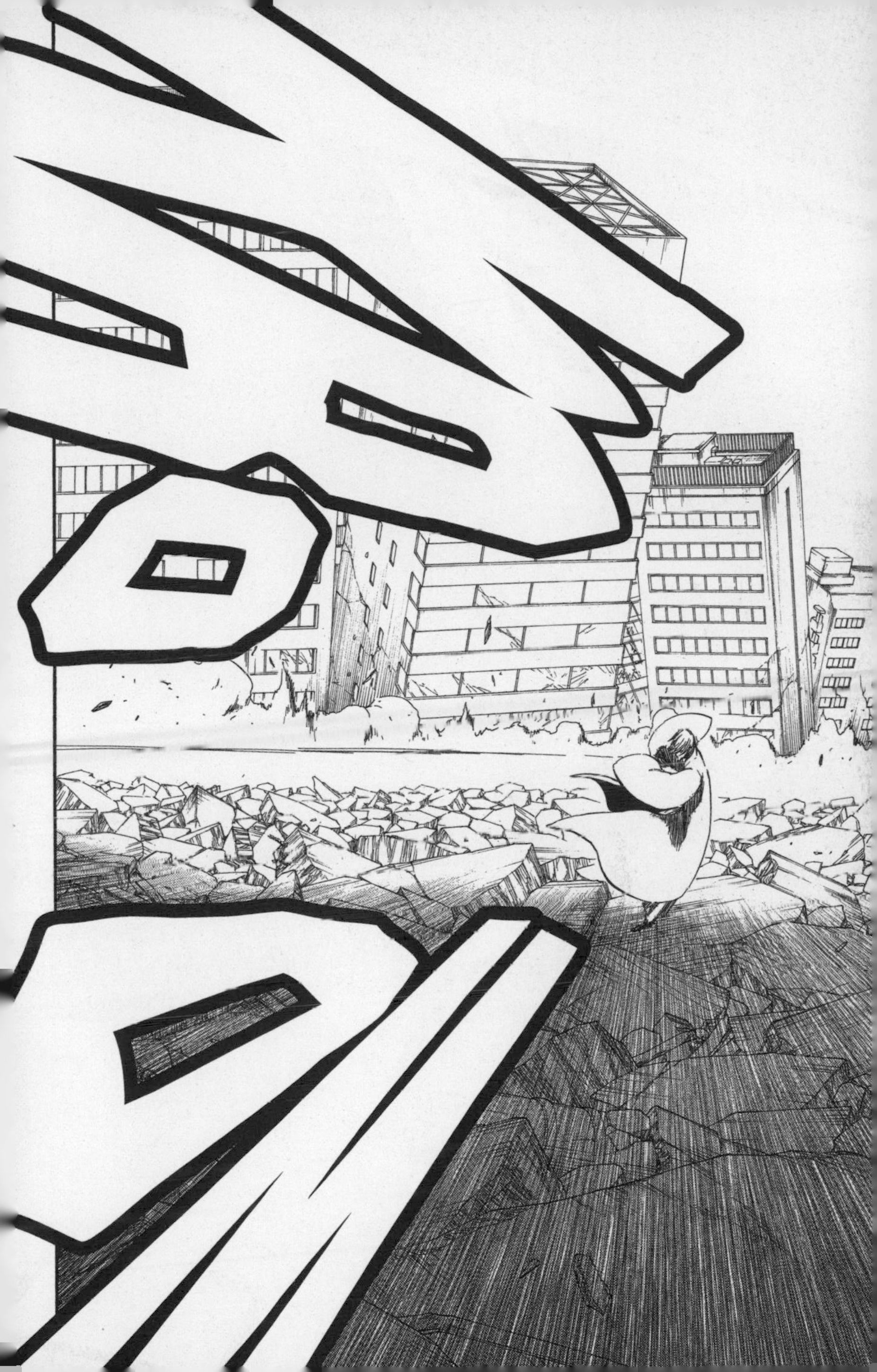

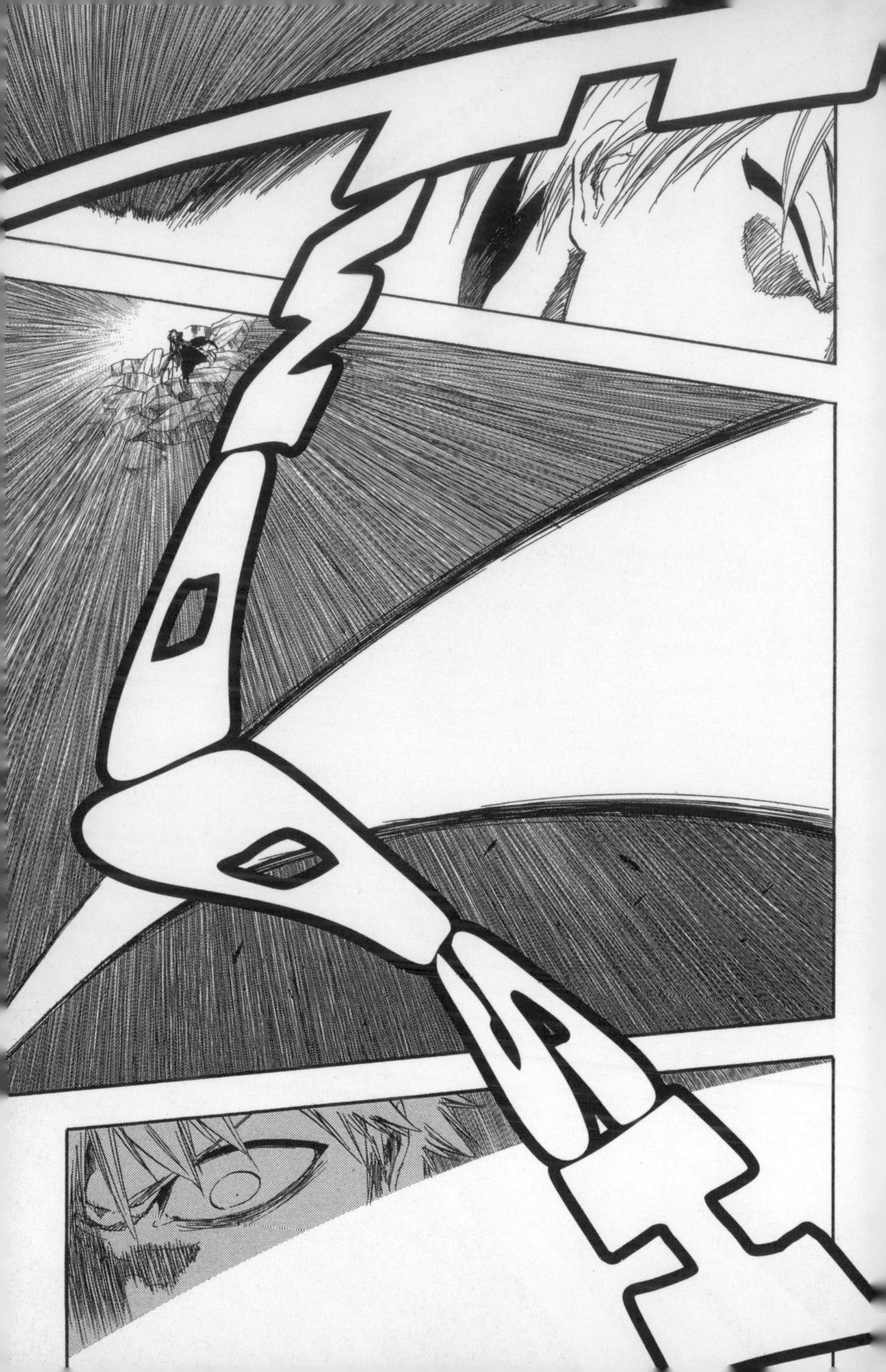

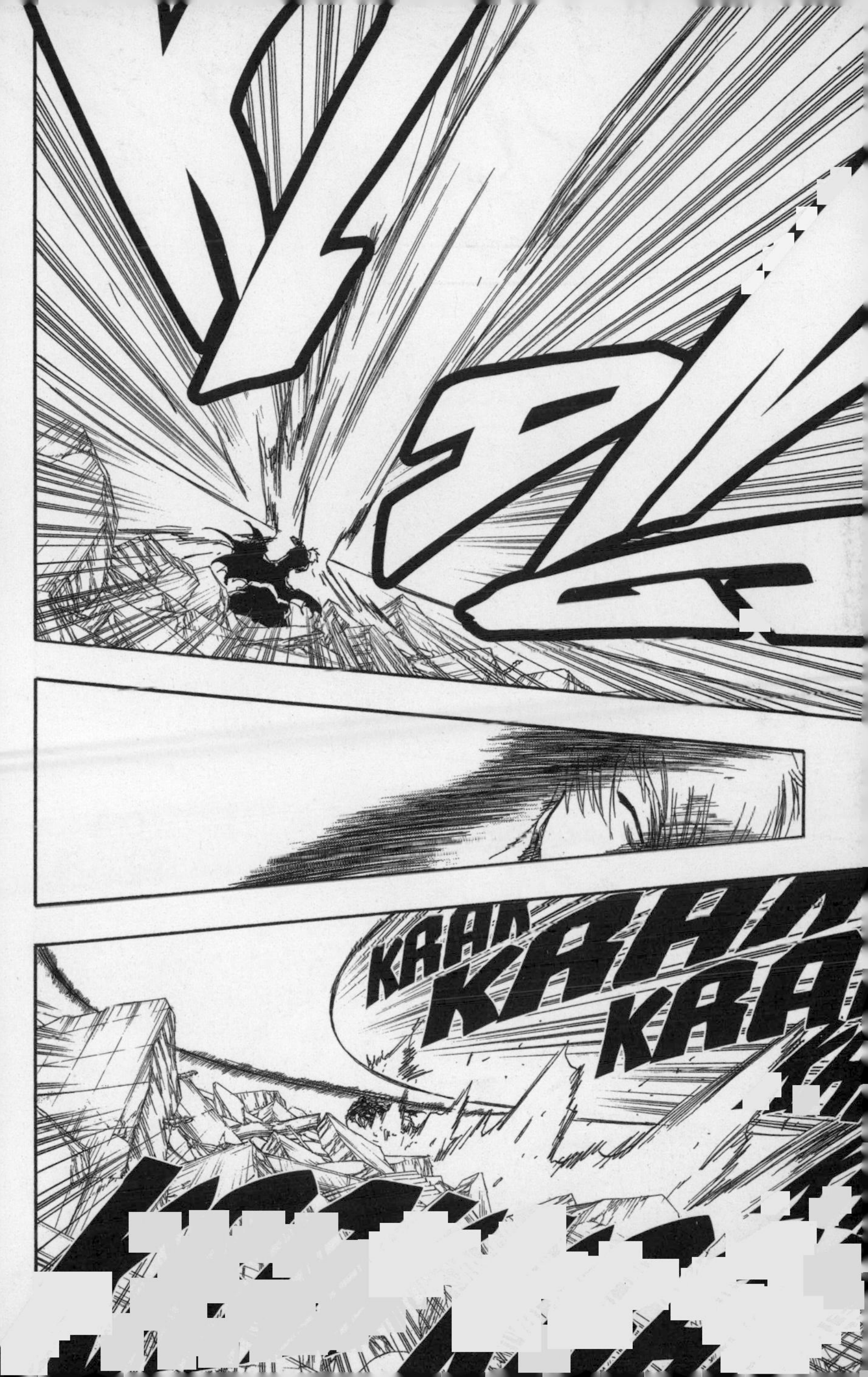

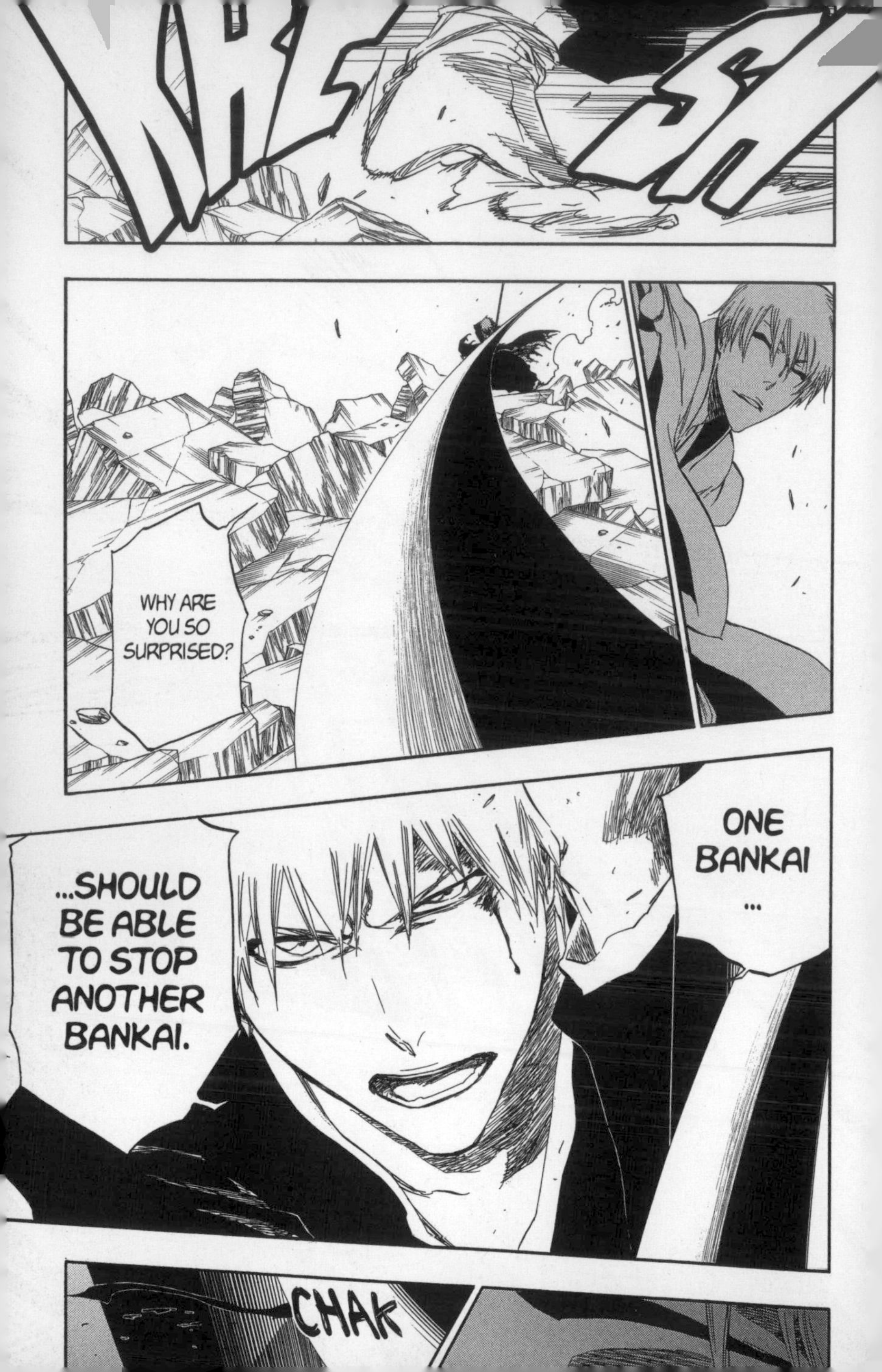
WHY ARE YOU SO SURPRISED?
ONE BANKAI ...
...SHOULD BE ABLE TO STOP ANOTHER BANKAI.
CHAK

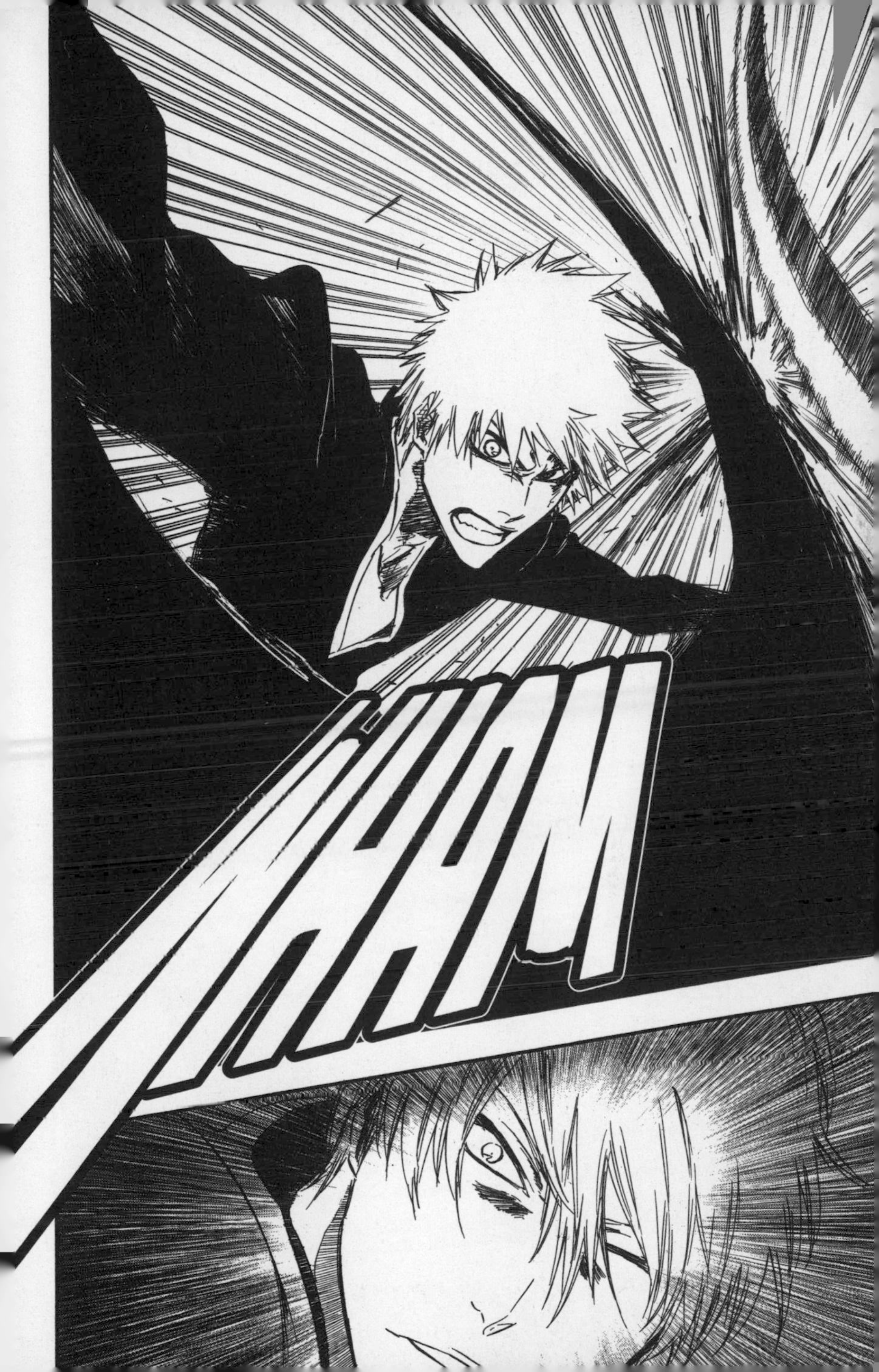
WHAM

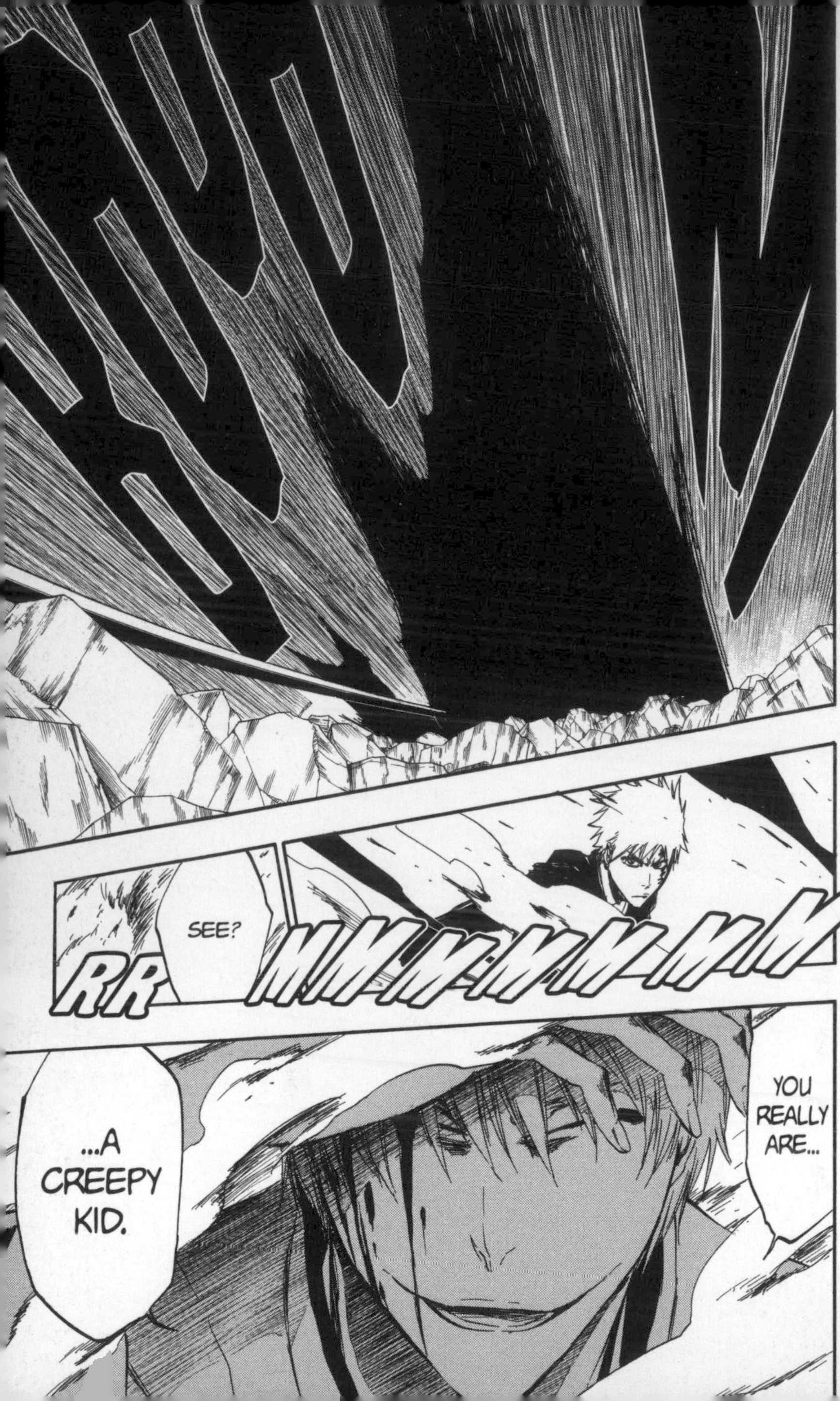
SEE?
RRMMMMMMM
YOU REALLY ARE...
...A CREEPY KID.

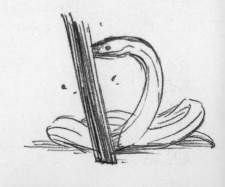

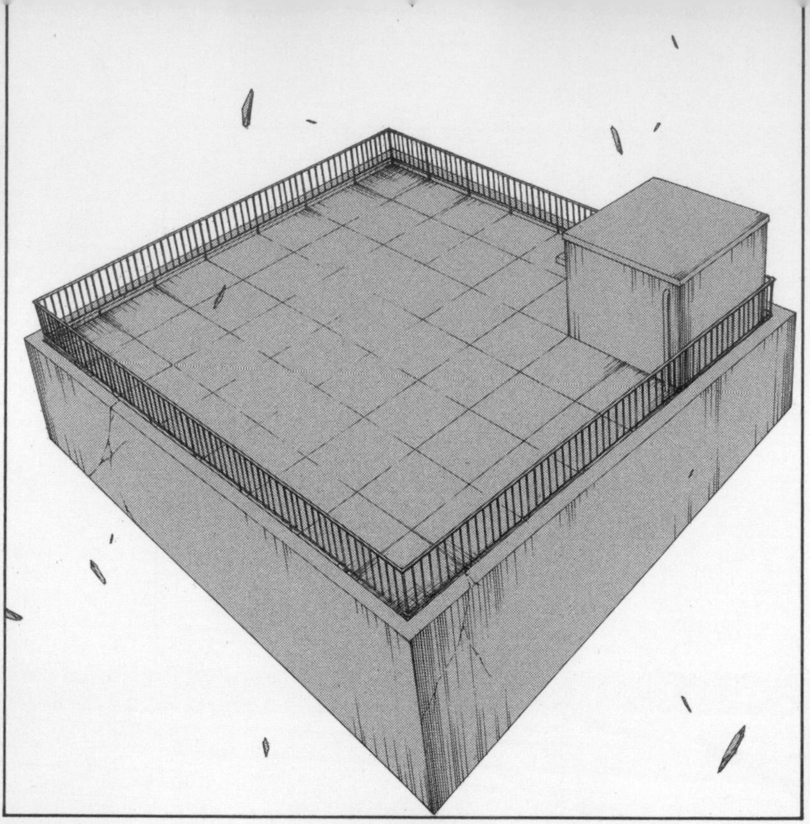

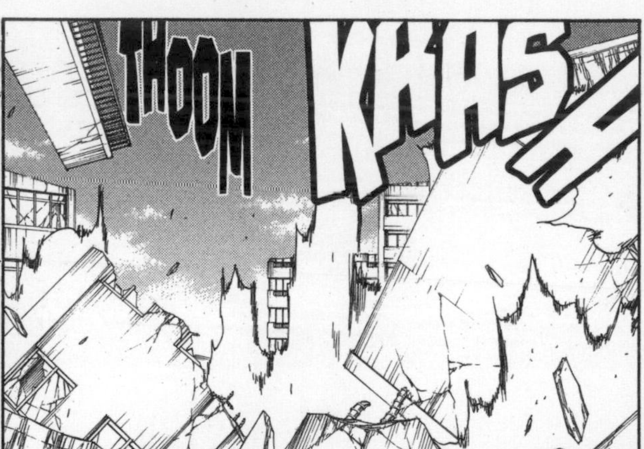
KRASH
THOOM

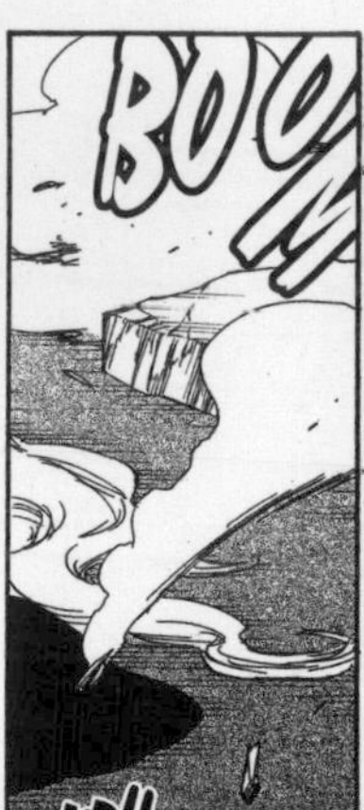
BOOM
KRUK KRUK

400. DEICIDE 2

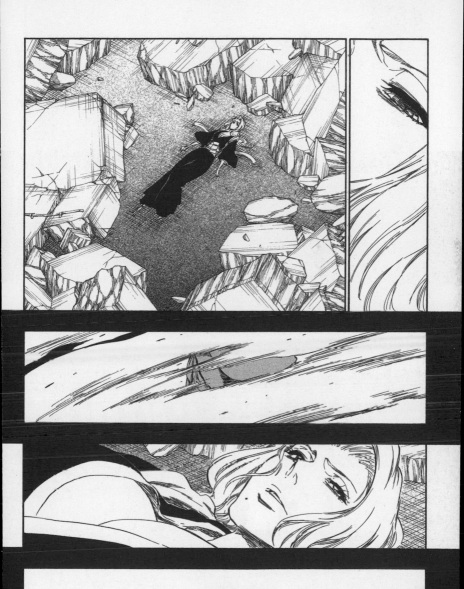

BLEACH

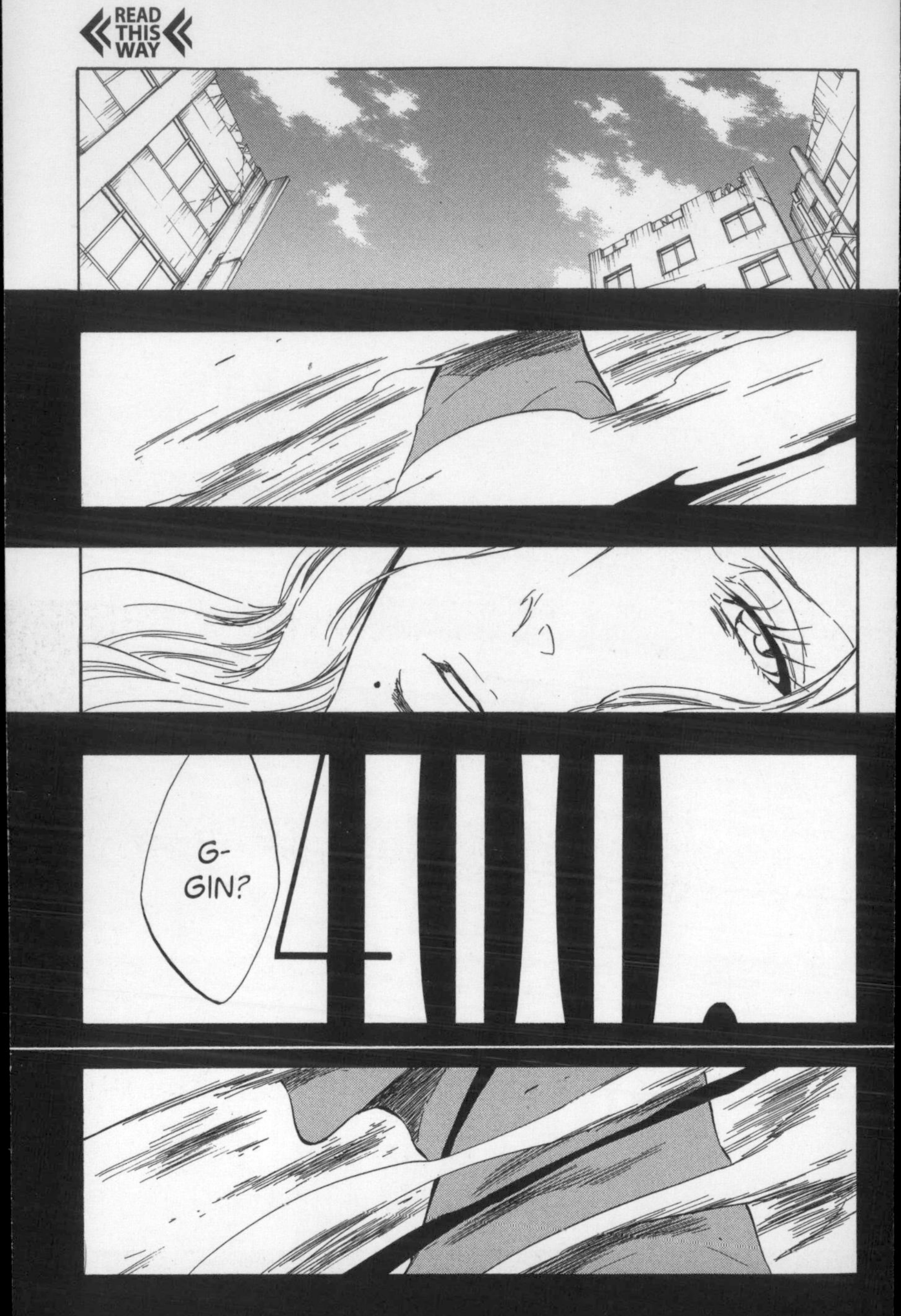
READ THIS WAY
G-GIN?

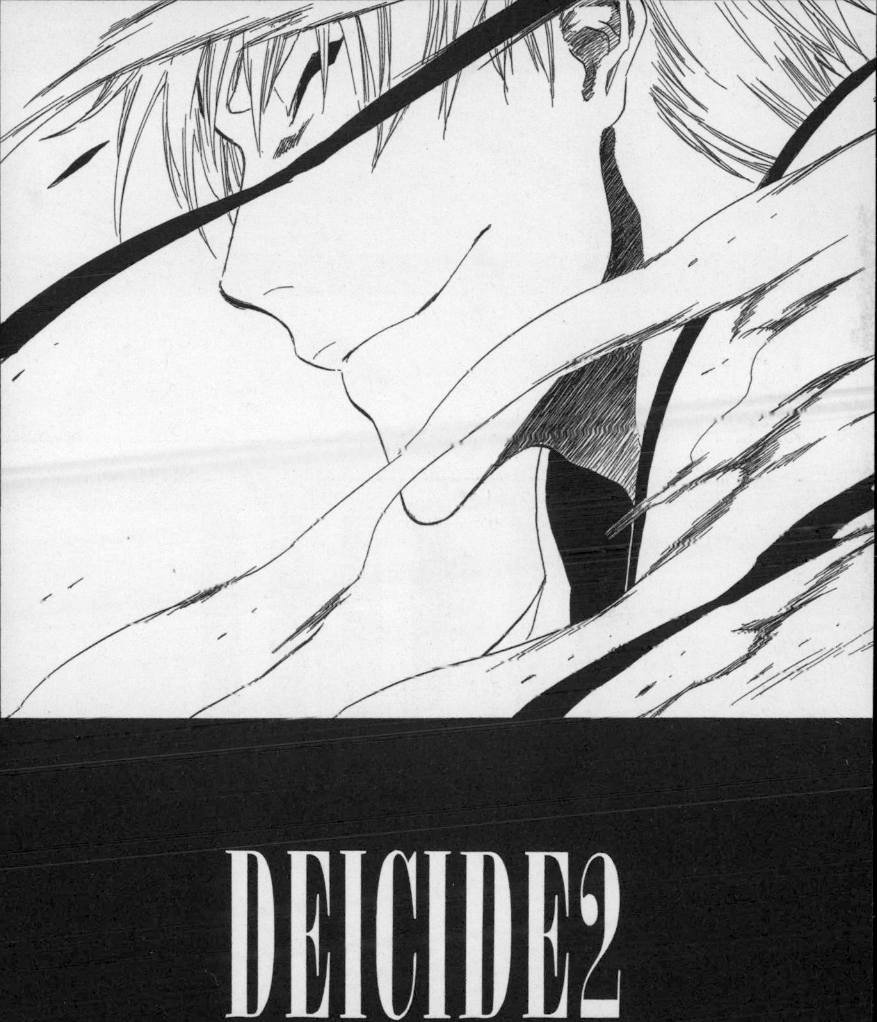

DEICIDE2

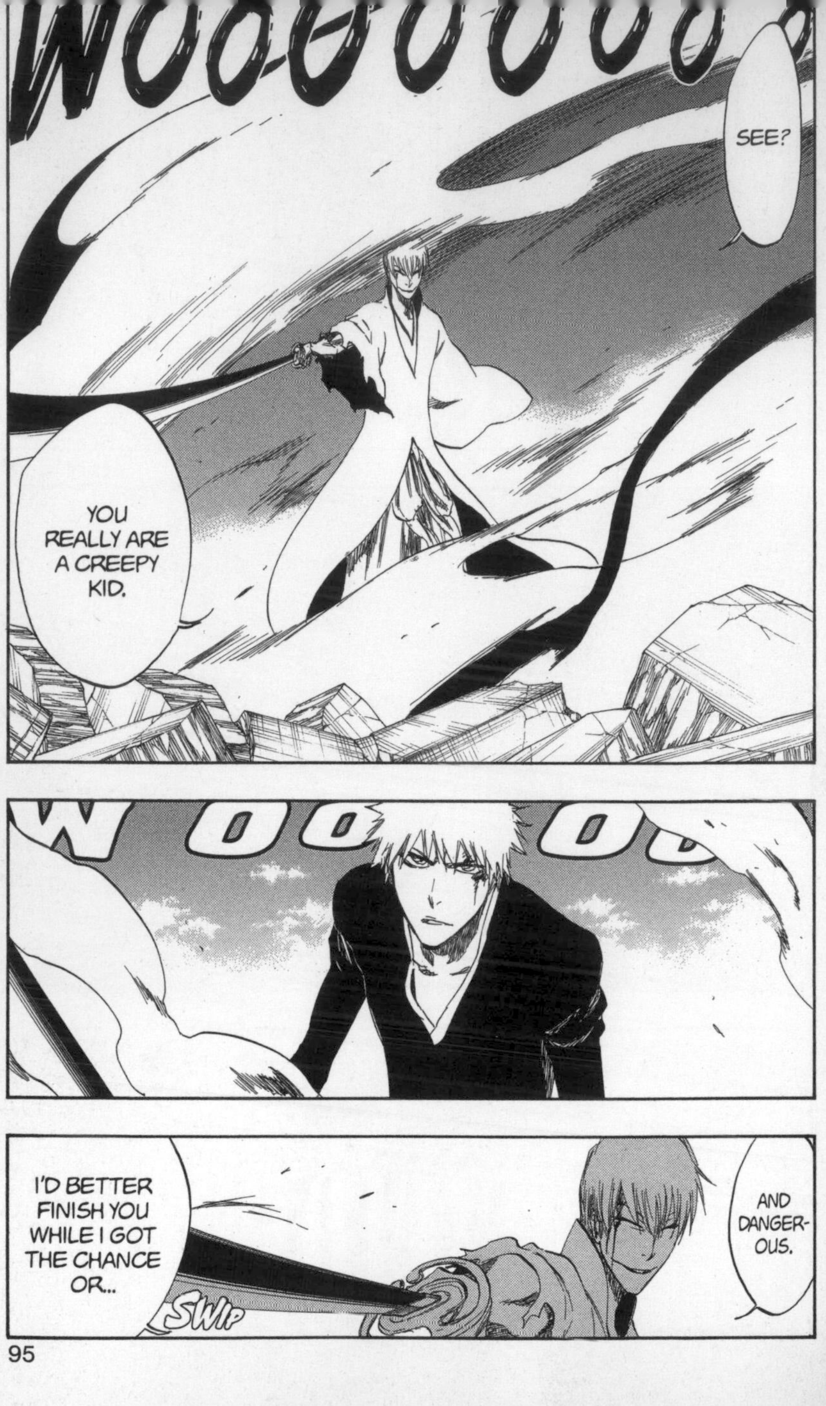
WOOOOOOOO
SEE?
YOU REALLY ARE A CREEPY KID.
WOOOOO
AND DANGER-OUS.
I'D BETTER FINISH YOU WHILE I GOT THE CHANCE OR...
SWIP

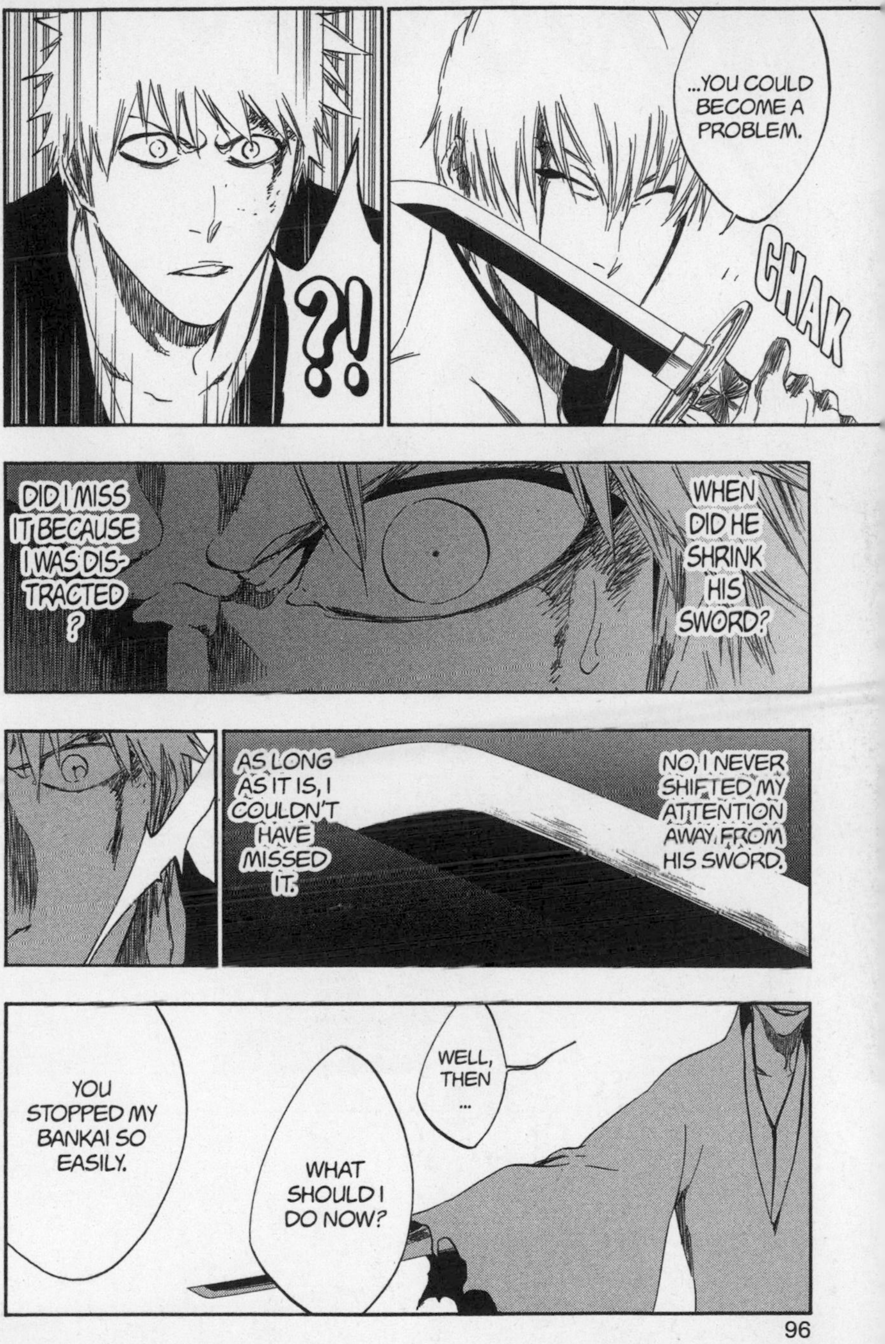
...YOU COULD BECOME A PROBLEM.
CHAK
?!
WHEN DID HE SHRINK HIS SWORD?
DID I MISS IT BECAUSE I WAS DISTRACTED?
NO, I NEVER SHIFTED MY ATTENTION AWAY FROM HIS SWORD.
AS LONG AS IT IS, I COULDN'T HAVE MISSED IT.
WELL, THEN ...
WHAT SHOULD I DO NOW?
YOU STOPPED MY BANKAI SO EASILY.

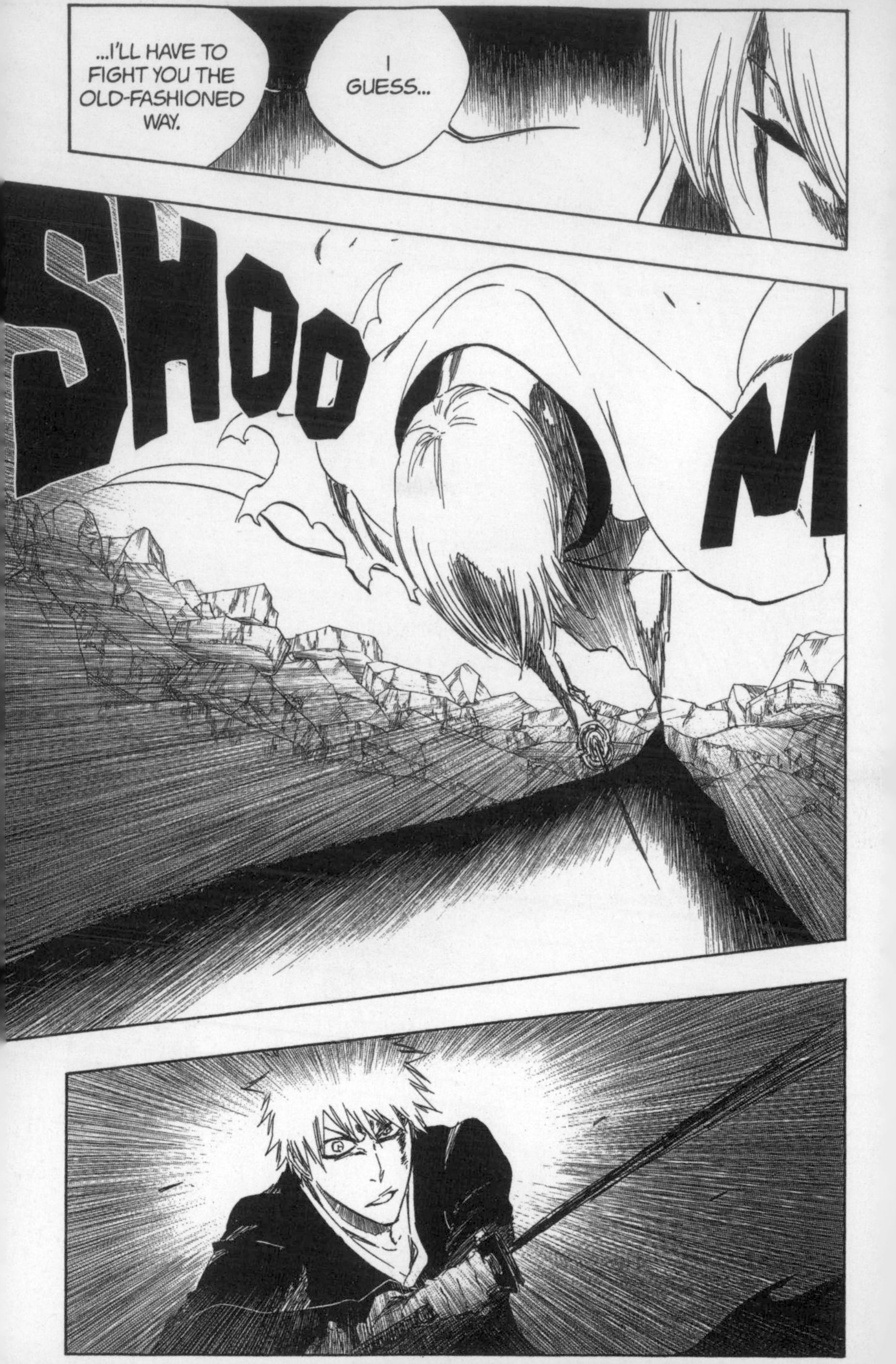
I GUESS...
...I'LL HAVE TO FIGHT YOU THE OLD-FASHIONED WAY.
SHOOM

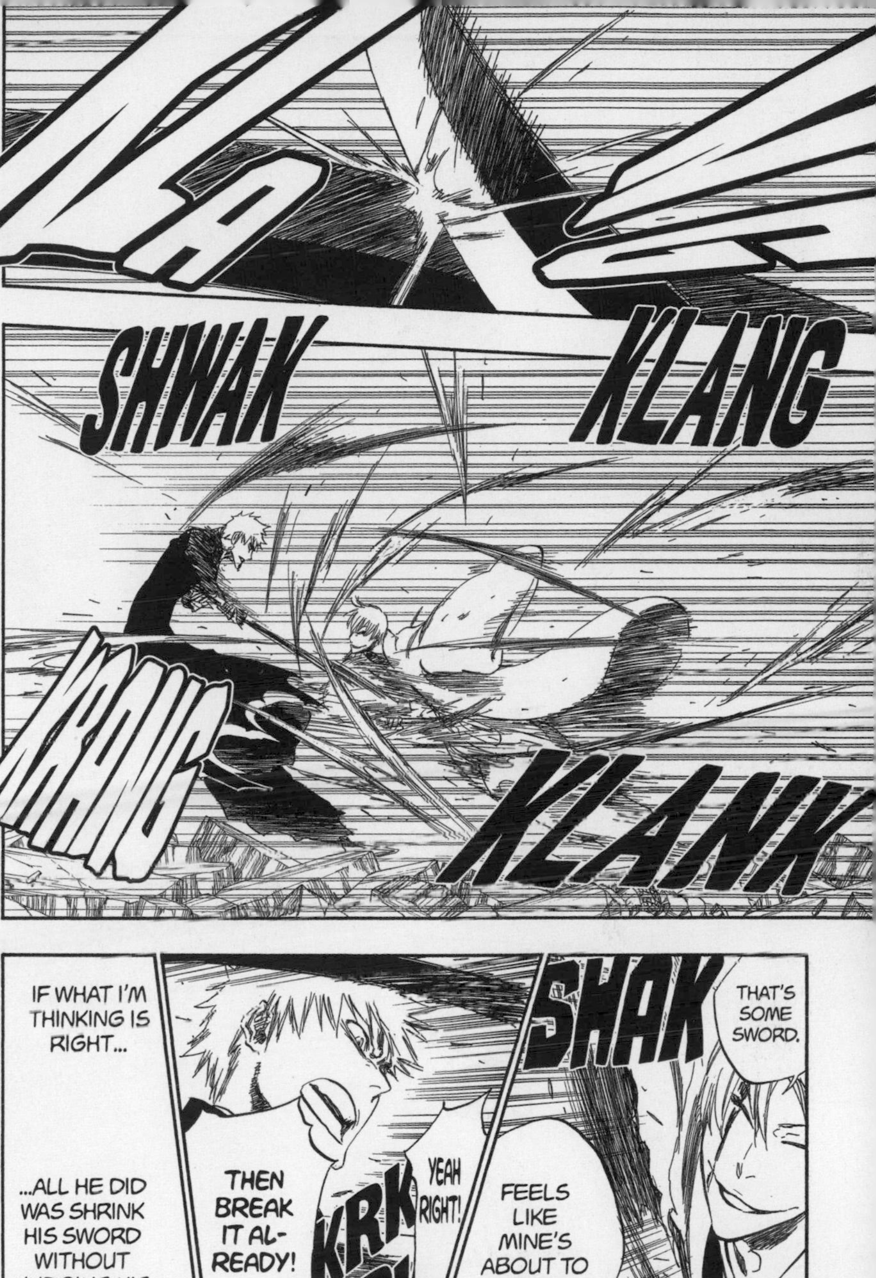
KLANG
SHWAK
KLANK
KRANG
SHAK
THAT'S SOME SWORD.
FEELS LIKE MINE'S ABOUT TO BREAK.
YEAH RIGHT!
KRK KRK
THEN BREAK IT AL-READY!
IF WHAT I'M THINKING IS RIGHT...
...ALL HE DID WAS SHRINK HIS SWORD WITHOUT UNDOING HIS BANKAI.

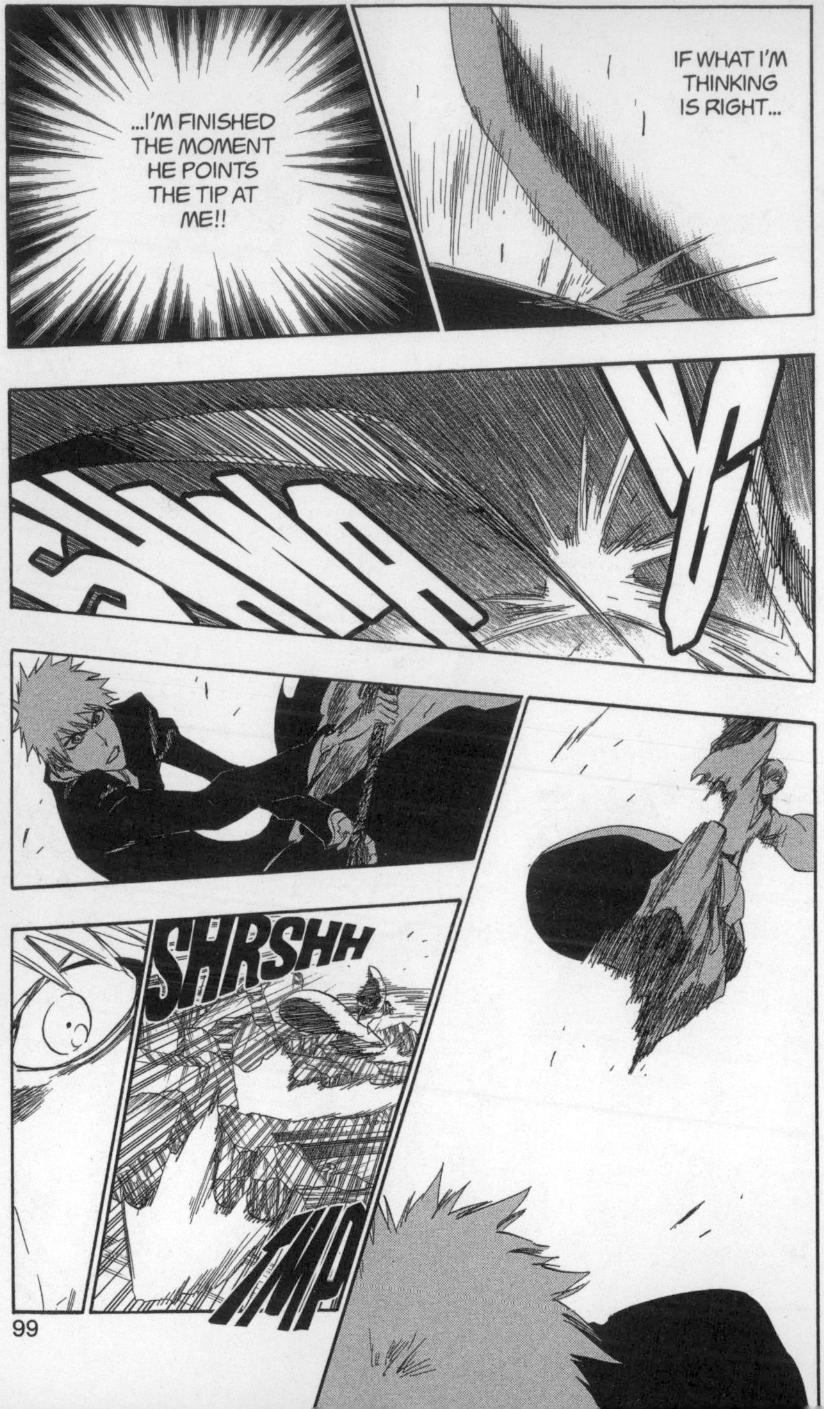
IF WHAT I'M THINKING IS RIGHT...
...I'M FINISHED THE MOMENT HE POINTS THE TIP AT ME!!
SHRSHH
TMP

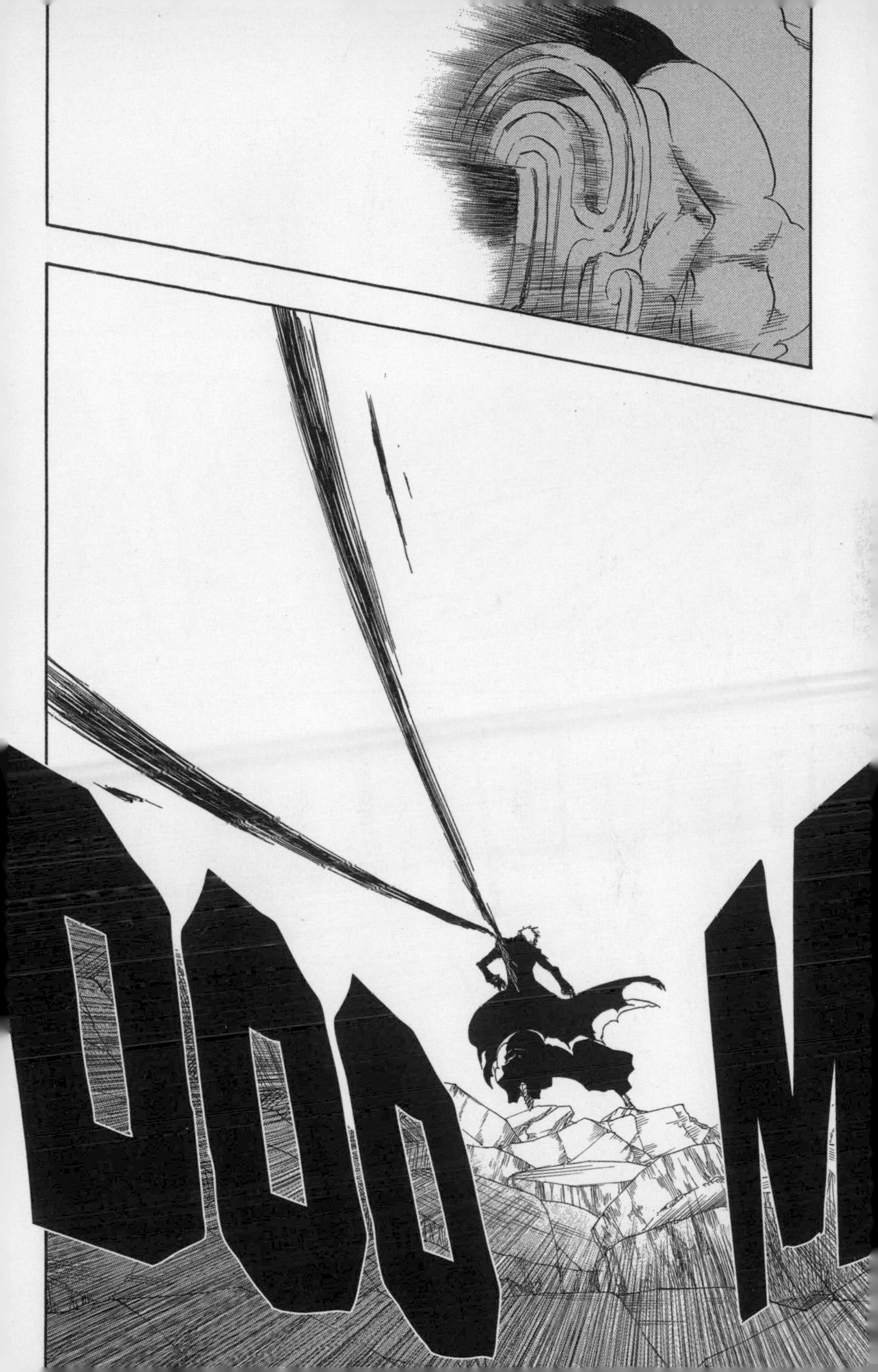
DOOM

READ THIS WAY

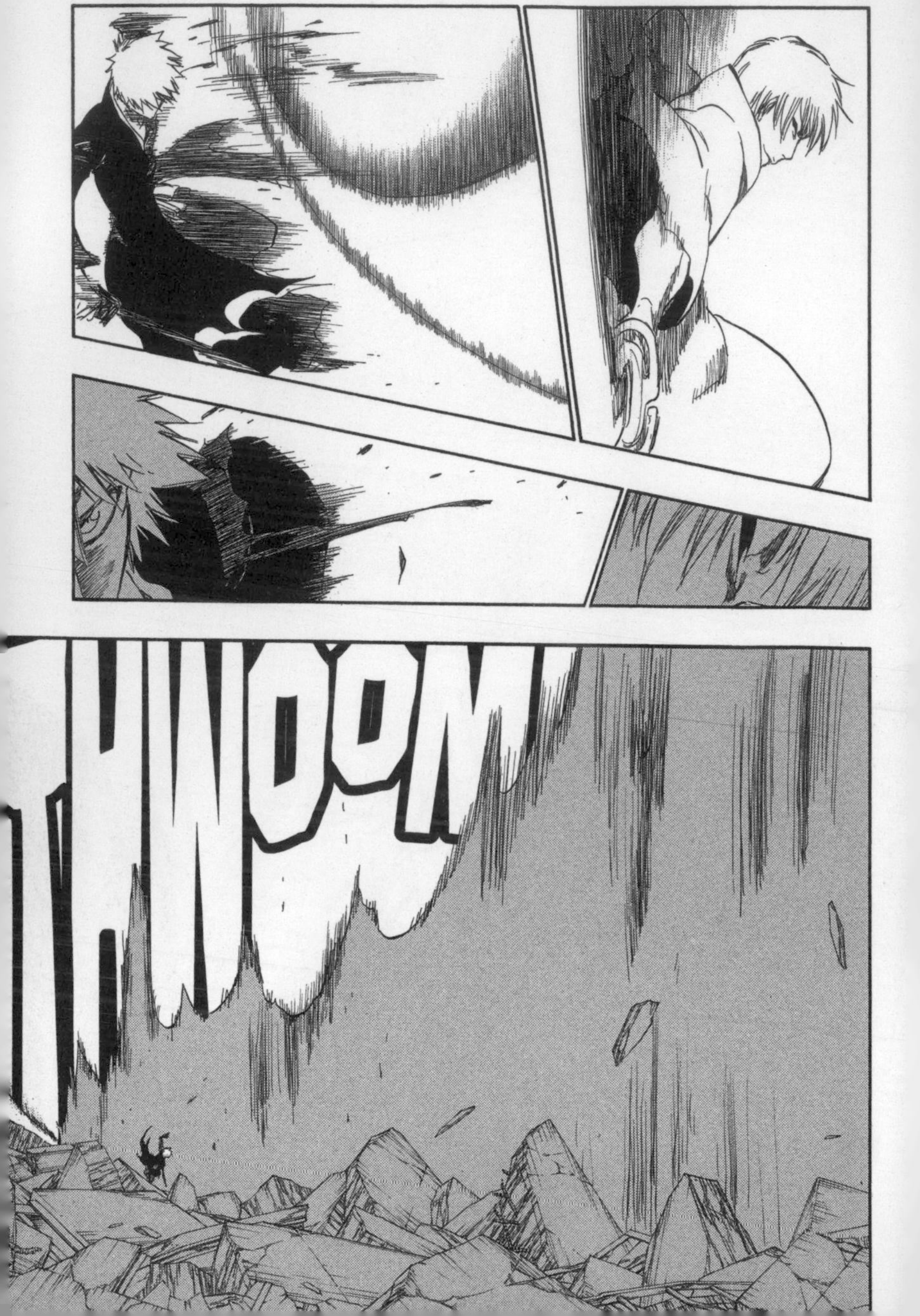
THWOOM

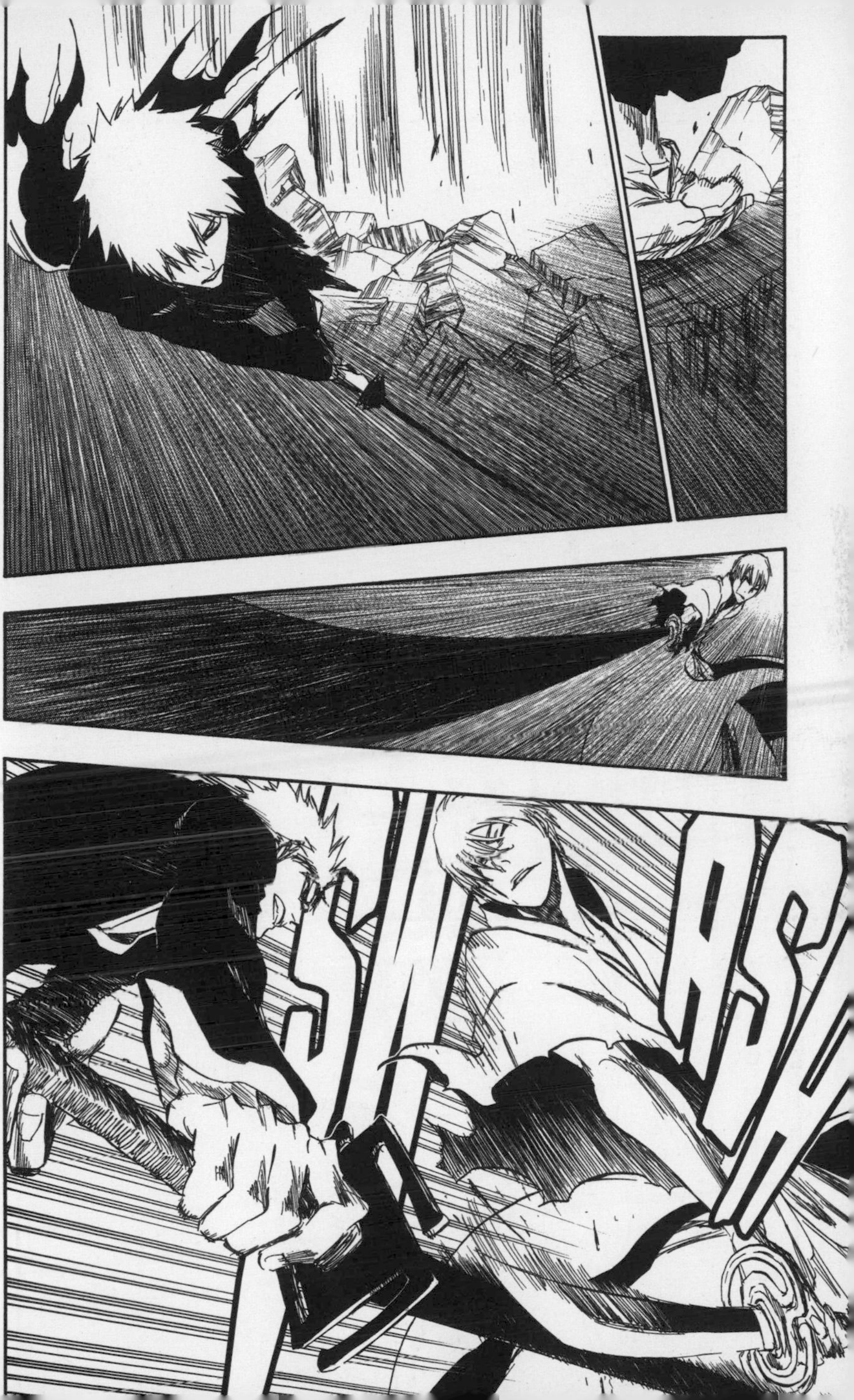
SWAS

READ THIS WAY

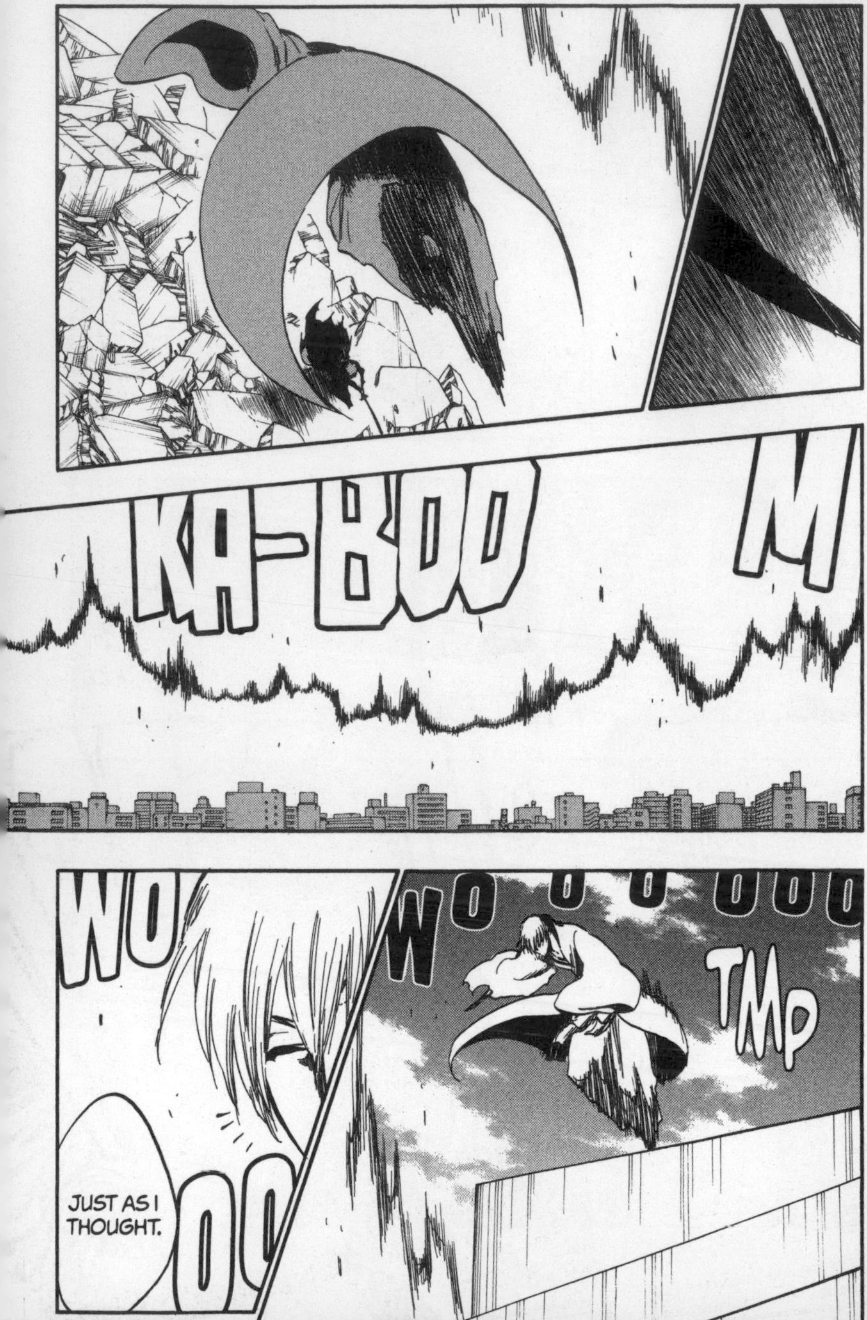
KA-BOOM
WOOOOOO
TMP
WOOO
JUST AS I THOUGHT.

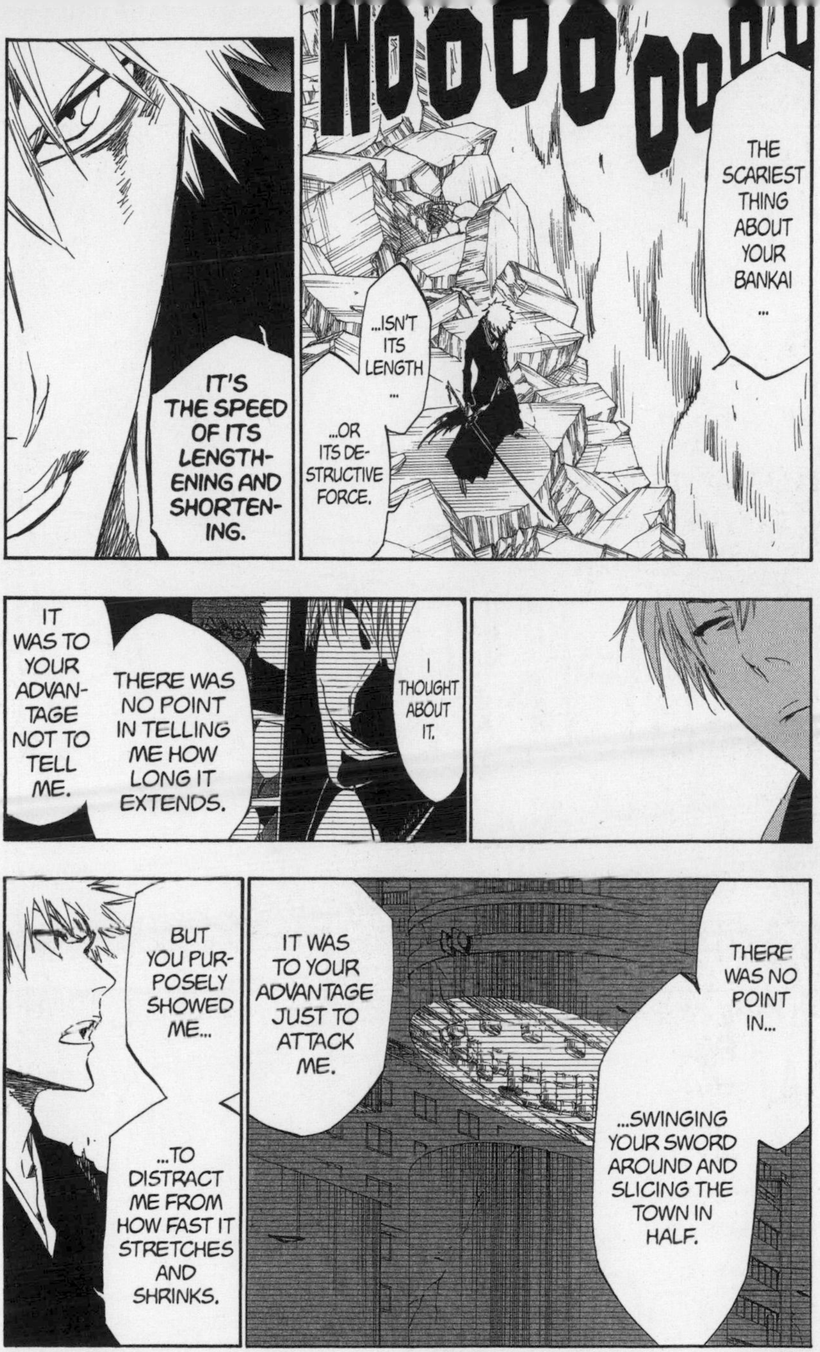
WOOOOOOOOO
THE SCARIEST THING ABOUT YOUR BANKAI ...
...ISN'T ITS LENGTH ...
...OR ITS DESTRUCTIVE FORCE.
IT'S THE SPEED OF ITS LENGTHENING AND SHORTENING.
I THOUGHT ABOUT IT.
THERE WAS NO POINT IN TELLING ME HOW LONG IT EXTENDS.
IT WAS TO YOUR ADVANTAGE NOT TO TELL ME.
THERE WAS NO POINT IN...
...SWINGING YOUR SWORD AROUND AND SLICING THE TOWN IN HALF.
IT WAS TO YOUR ADVANTAGE JUST TO ATTACK ME.
BUT YOU PURPOSELY SHOWED ME...
...TO DISTRACT ME FROM HOW FAST IT STRETCHES AND SHRINKS.

READ THIS WAY

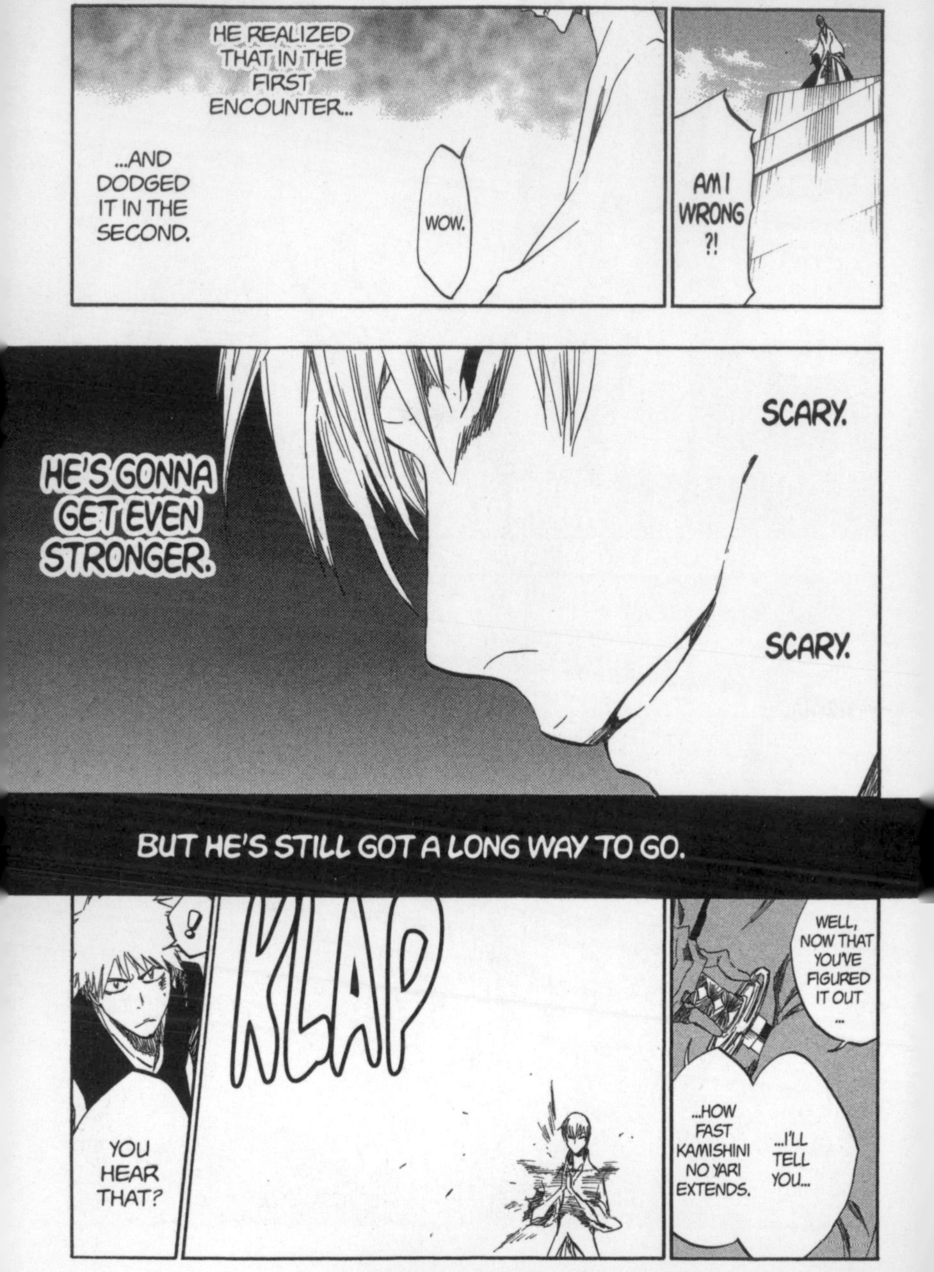
AM I WRONG ?!
WOW.
HE REALIZED THAT IN THE FIRST ENCOUNTER...
...AND DODGED IT IN THE SECOND.
SCARY.
SCARY.
HE'S GONNA GET EVEN STRONGER.
BUT HE'S STILL GOT A LONG WAY TO GO.
WELL, NOW THAT YOU'VE FIGURED IT OUT...
...I'LL TELL YOU...
...HOW FAST KAMISHINI NO YARI EXTENDS.
KLAP
!
YOU HEAR THAT?

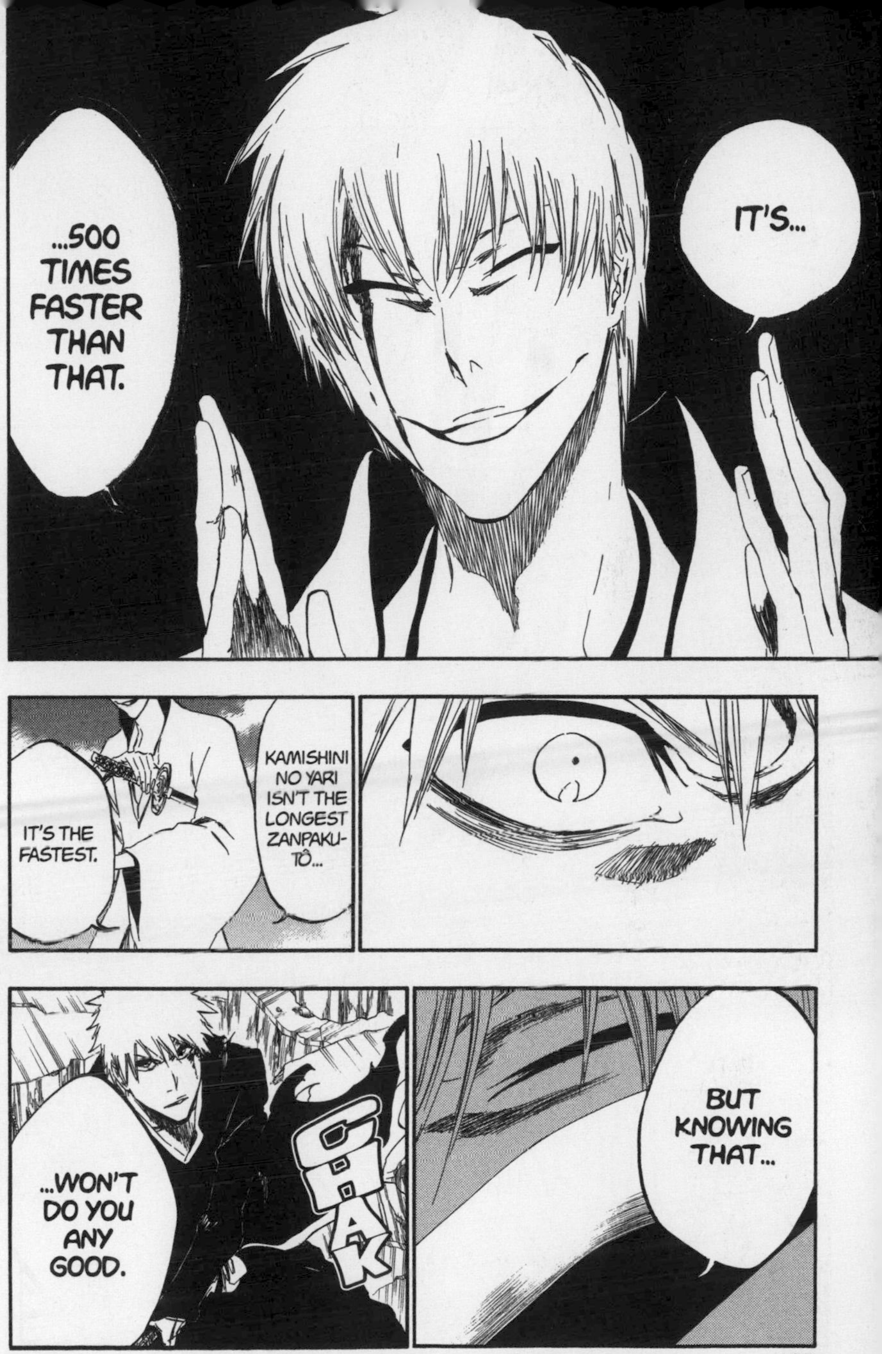
IT'S...
...500 TIMES FASTER THAN THAT.
KAMISHINI NO YARI ISN'T THE LONGEST ZANPAKU-TÔ...
IT'S THE FASTEST.
BUT KNOWING THAT...
CHAK
...WON'T DO YOU ANY GOOD.

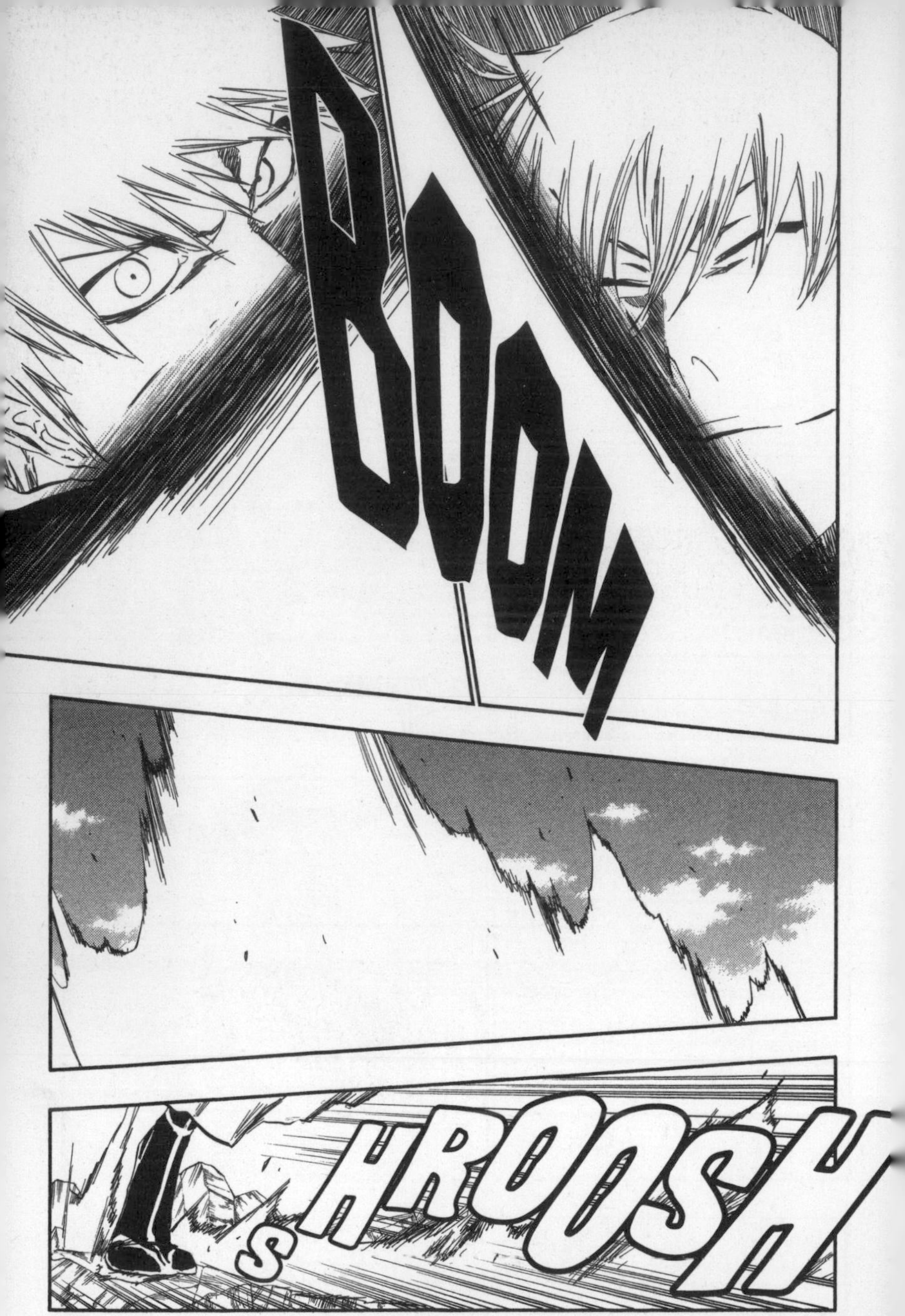
BOOM
SHROOSH

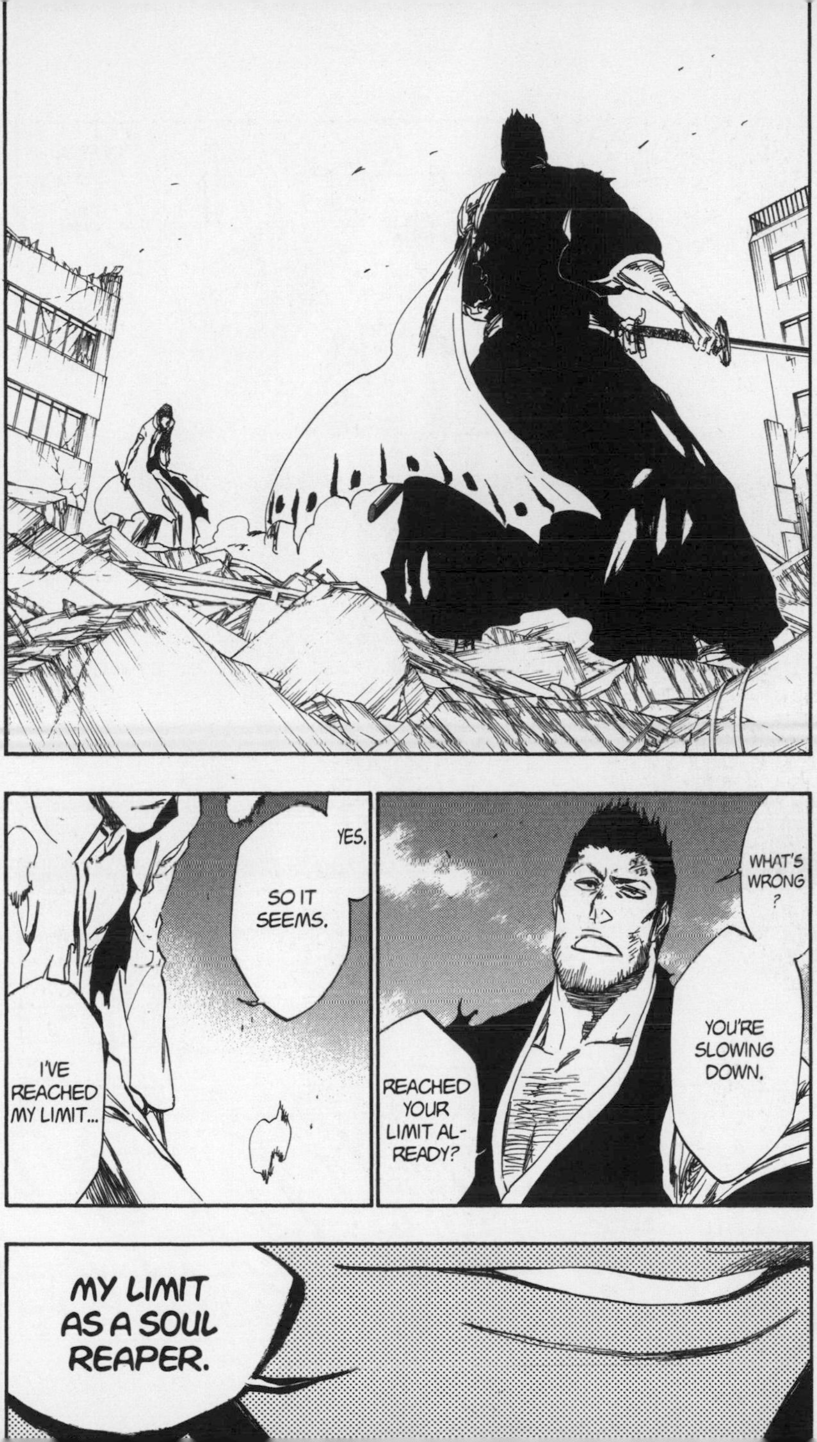
WHAT'S WRONG?
YOU'RE SLOWING DOWN.
REACHED YOUR LIMIT ALREADY?
YES.
SO IT SEEMS.
I'VE REACHED MY LIMIT...
MY LIMIT AS A SOUL REAPER.

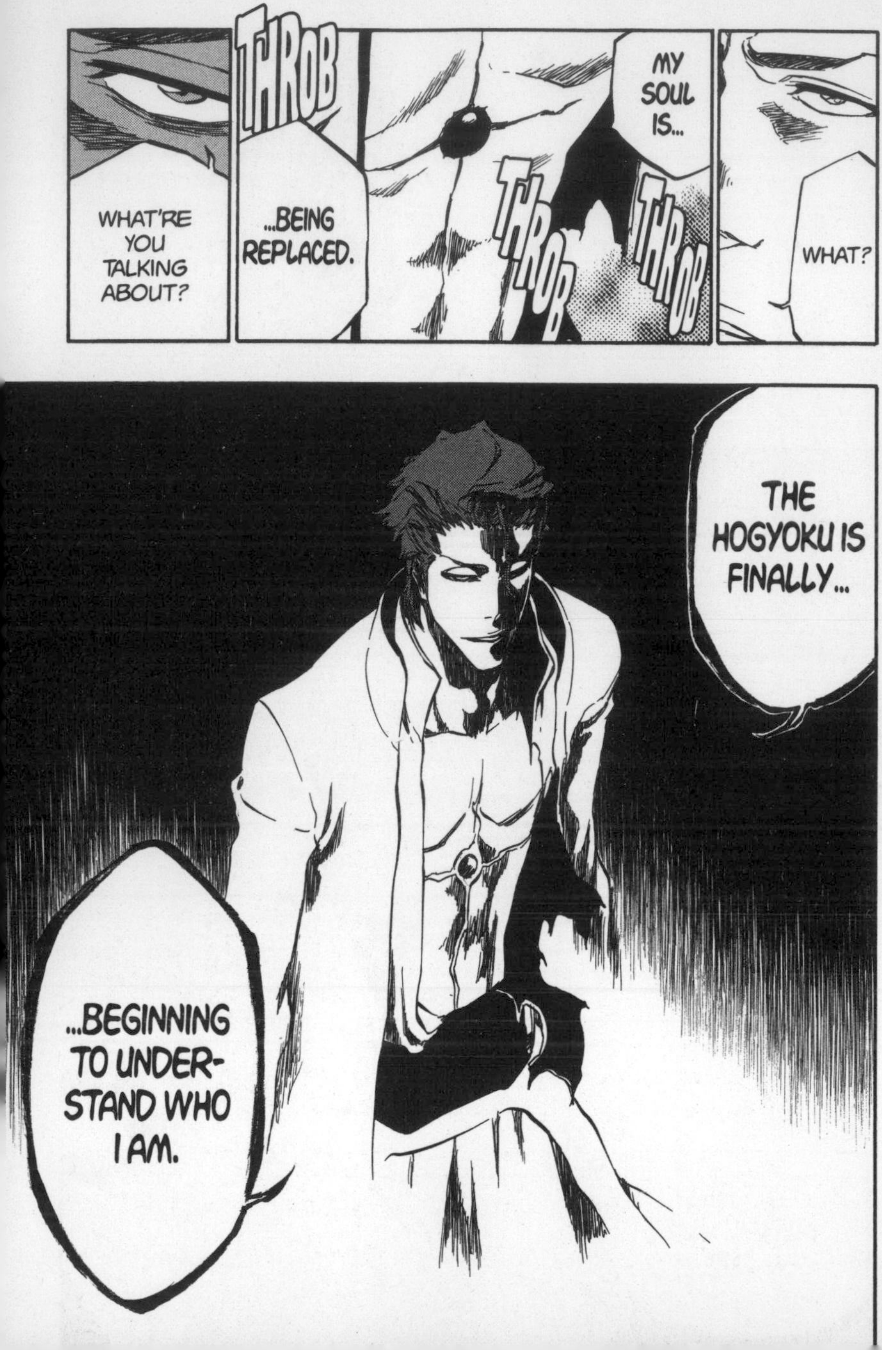
WHAT?
MY SOUL IS...
THROB
THROB
THROB
...BEING REPLACED.
WHAT'RE YOU TALKING ABOUT?
THE HOGYOKU IS FINALLY...
...BEGINNING TO UNDER-STAND WHO I AM.

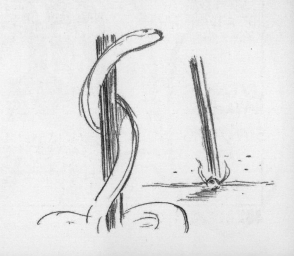

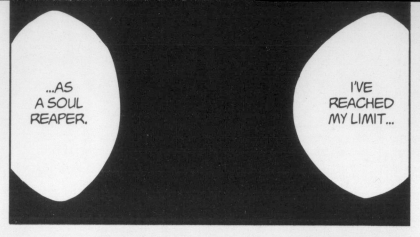

I'VE REACHED MY LIMIT...
...AS A SOUL REAPER.
WHAT'RE YOU TALKING ABOUT?
THE HOGYOKU IS FINALLY...
...BEGINNING TO UNDER-STAND WHO I AM.
YOU TALKING IN YOUR SLEEP?
DON'T YOU SEE?

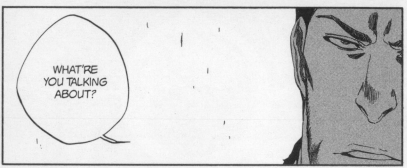

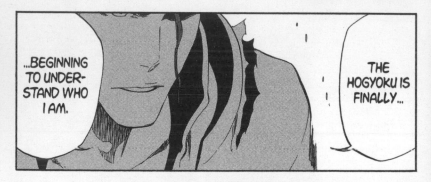

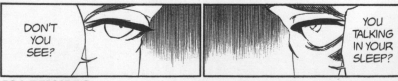

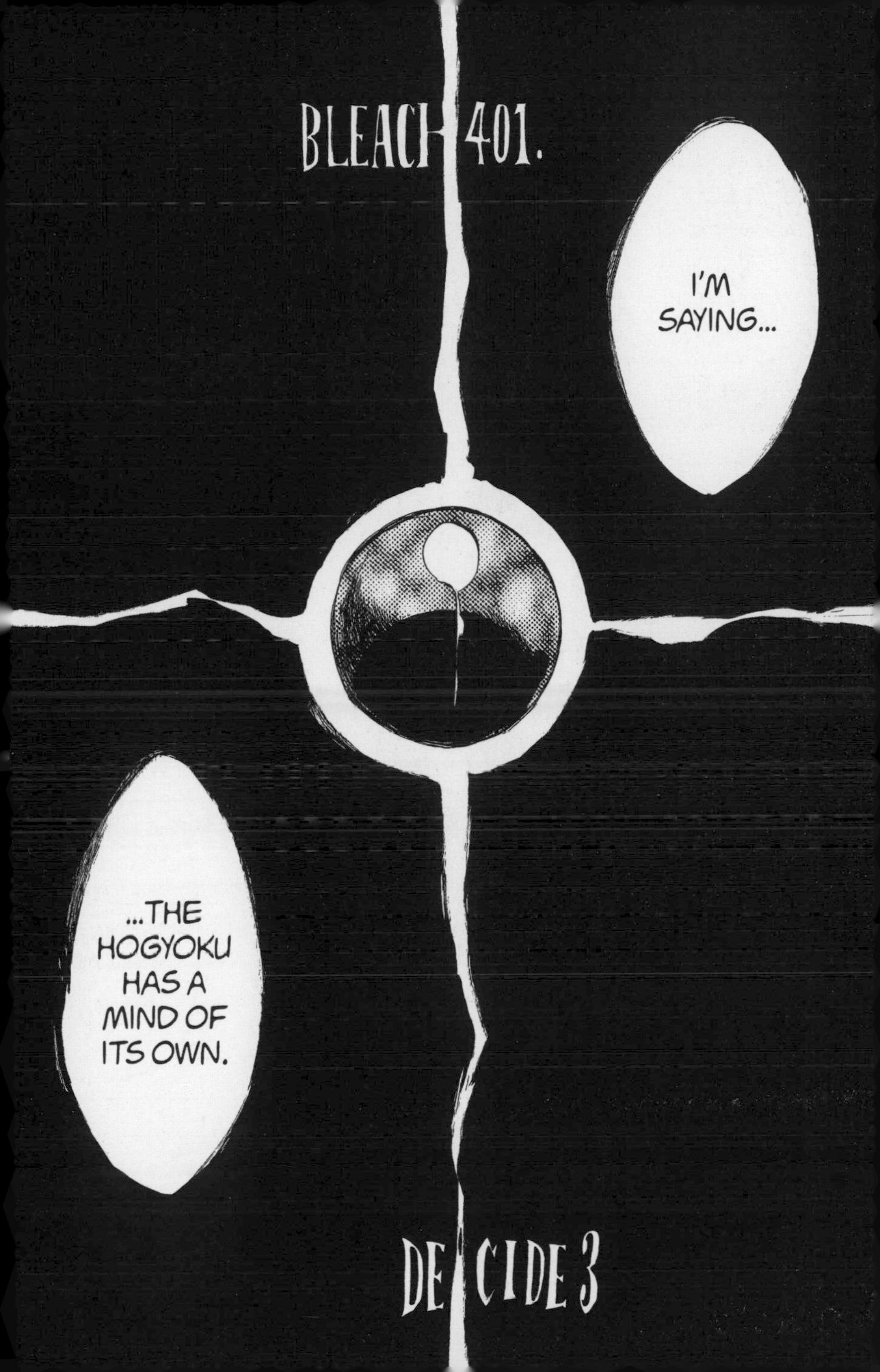
BLEACH 401.
I'M SAYING...
...THE HOGYOKU HAS A MIND OF ITS OWN.
DECIDE 3

READ THIS WAY

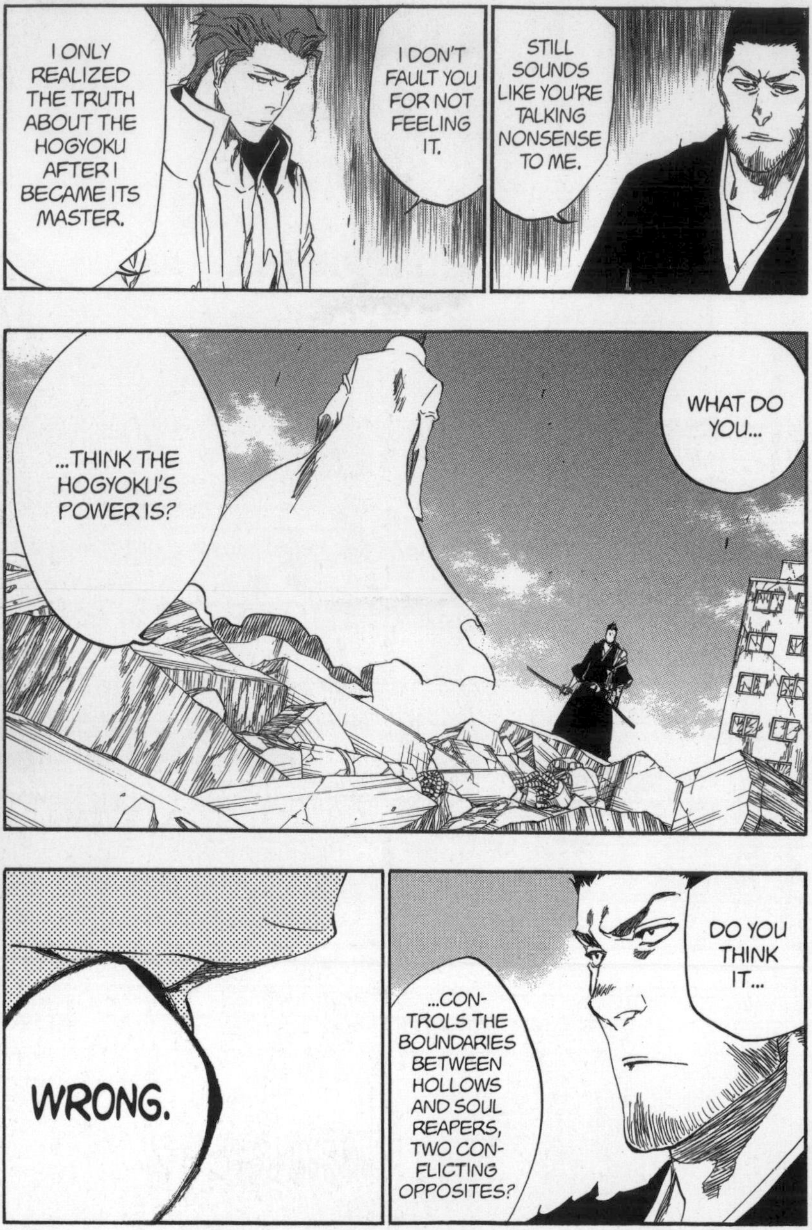
STILL SOUNDS LIKE YOU'RE TALKING NONSENSE TO ME.
I DON'T FAULT YOU FOR NOT FEELING IT.
I ONLY REALIZED THE TRUTH ABOUT THE HOGYOKU AFTER I BECAME ITS MASTER.
WHAT DO YOU...
...THINK THE HOGYOKU'S POWER IS?
DO YOU THINK IT...
...CON-TROLS THE BOUNDARIES BETWEEN HOLLOWS AND SOUL REAPERS, TWO CON-FLICTING OPPOSITES?
WRONG.

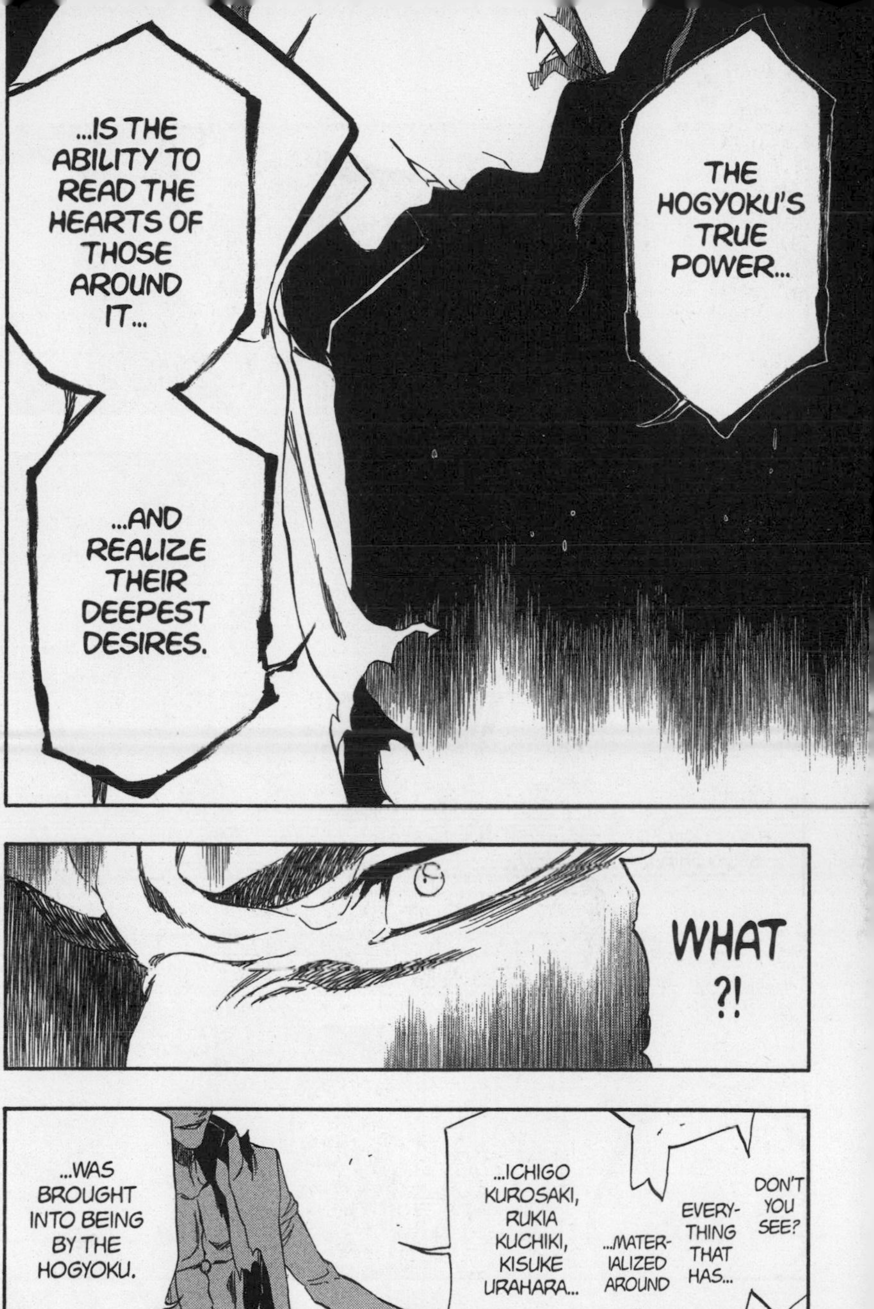
THE HOGYOKU'S TRUE POWER...
...IS THE ABILITY TO READ THE HEARTS OF THOSE AROUND IT...
...AND REALIZE THEIR DEEPEST DESIRES.
WHAT ?!
DON'T YOU SEE?
EVERYTHING THAT HAS...
...MATERIALIZED AROUND ...
...ICHIGO KUROSAKI, RUKIA KUCHIKI, KISUKE URAHARA...
...WAS BROUGHT INTO BEING BY THE HOGYOKU.

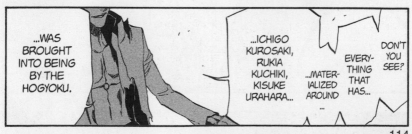

READ THIS WAY

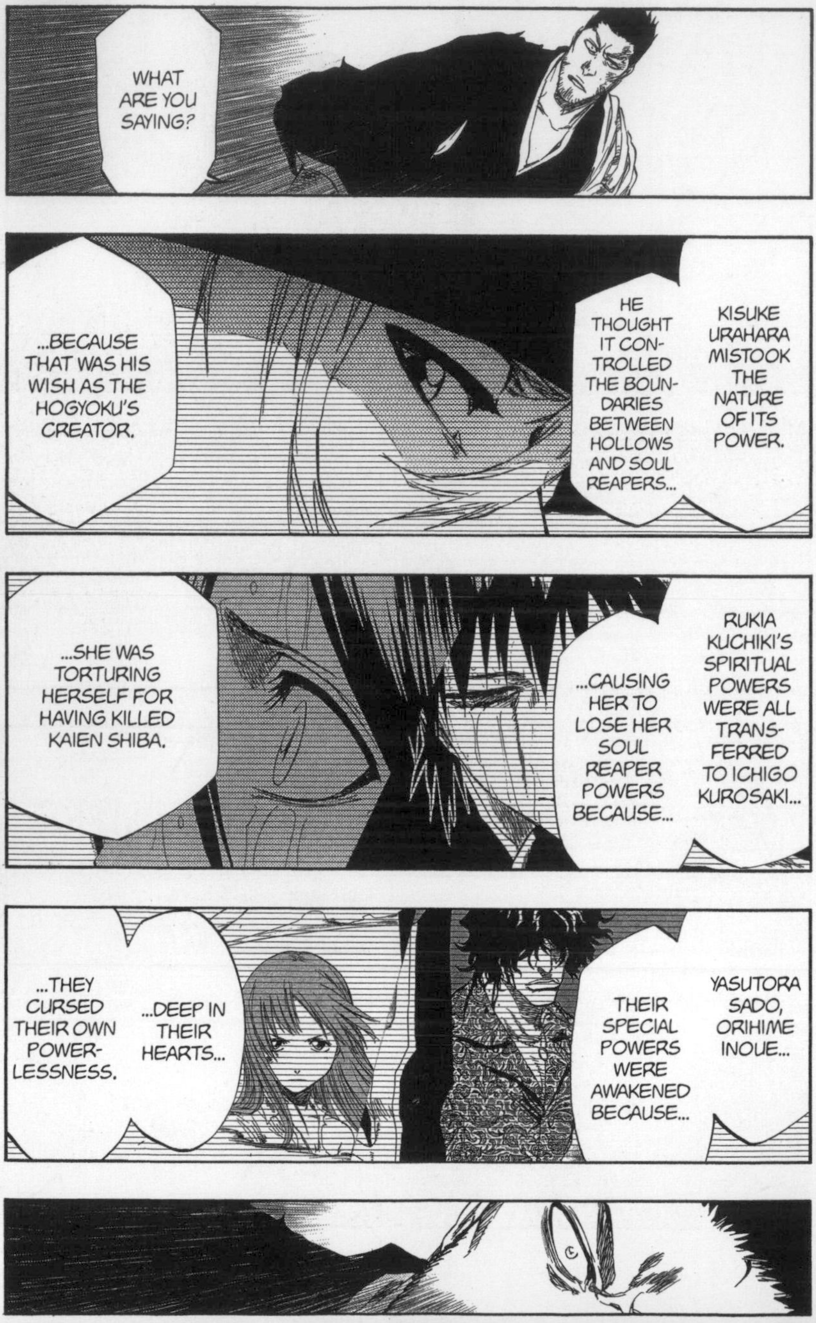
WHAT ARE YOU SAYING?
KISUKE URAHARA MISTOOK THE NATURE OF ITS POWER.
HE THOUGHT IT CONTROLLED THE BOUNDARIES BETWEEN HOLLOWS AND SOUL REAPERS...
...BECAUSE THAT WAS HIS WISH AS THE HOGYOKU'S CREATOR.
RUKIA KUCHIKI'S SPIRITUAL POWERS WERE ALL TRANSFERRED TO ICHIGO KUROSAKI...
...CAUSING HER TO LOSE HER SOUL REAPER POWERS BECAUSE...
...SHE WAS TORTURING HERSELF FOR HAVING KILLED KAIEN SHIBA.
YASUTORA SADO, ORIHIME INOUE...
THEIR SPECIAL POWERS WERE AWAKENED BECAUSE...
...DEEP IN THEIR HEARTS...
...THEY CURSED THEIR OWN POWERLESSNESS.

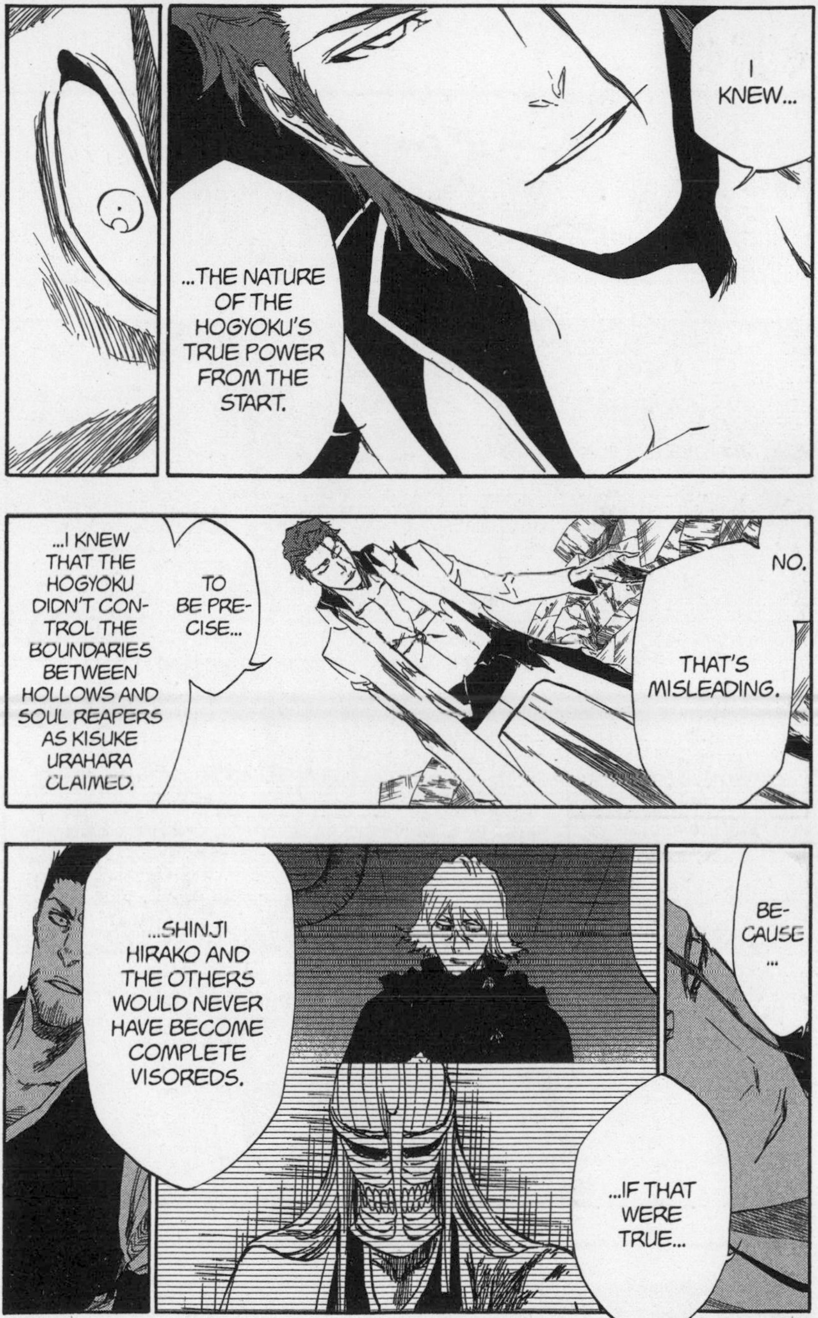
I KNEW...
...THE NATURE OF THE HOGYOKU'S TRUE POWER FROM THE START.
NO.
THAT'S MISLEADING.
TO BE PRECISE...
...I KNEW THAT THE HOGYOKU DIDN'T CONTROL THE BOUNDARIES BETWEEN HOLLOWS AND SOUL REAPERS AS KISUKE URAHARA CLAIMED.
BECAUSE...
...IF THAT WERE TRUE...
...SHINJI HIRAKO AND THE OTHERS WOULD NEVER HAVE BECOME COMPLETE VISOREDS.

READ THIS WAY

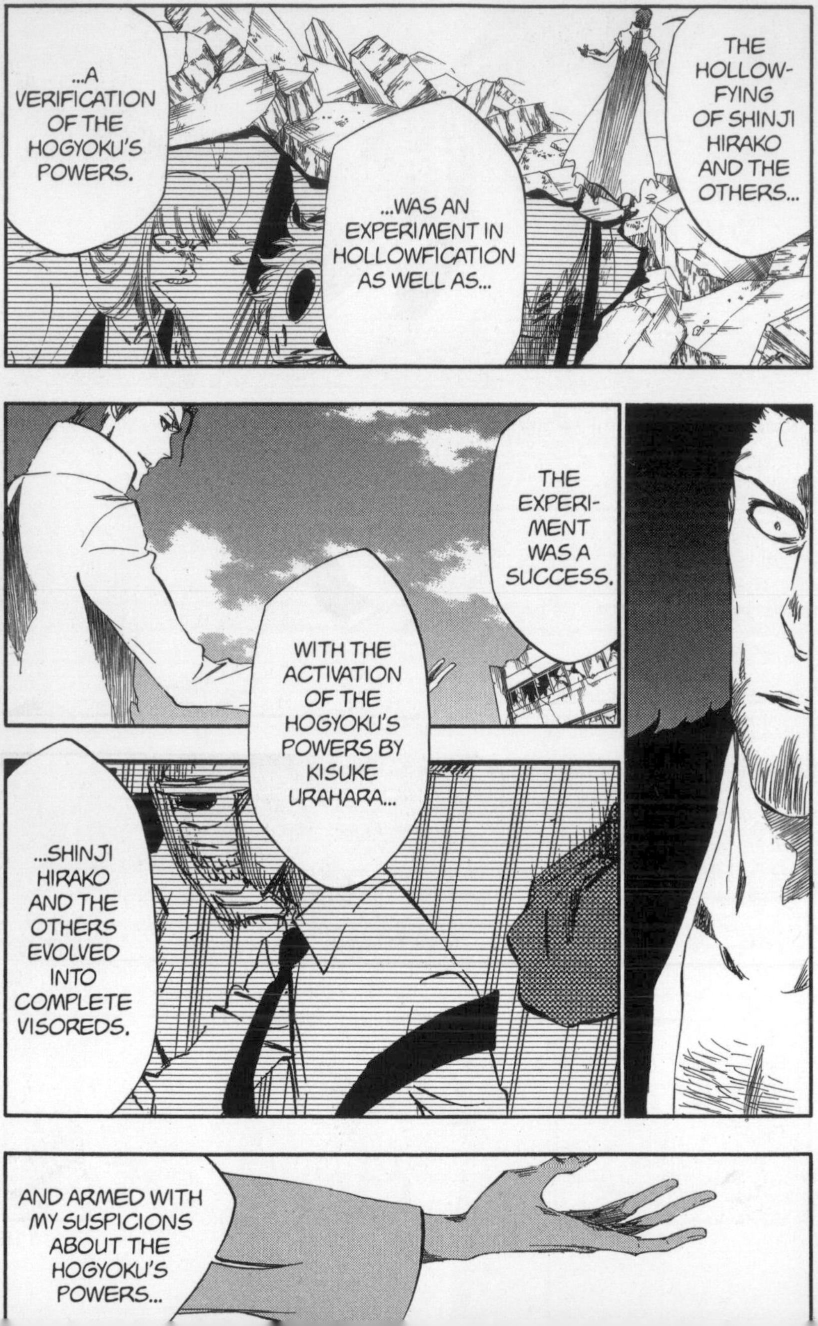
THE HOLLOW-FYING OF SHINJI HIRAKO AND THE OTHERS...
...WAS AN EXPERIMENT IN HOLLOWFICATION AS WELL AS...
...A VERIFICATION OF THE HOGYOKU'S POWERS.
THE EXPERI-MENT WAS A SUCCESS.
WITH THE ACTIVATION OF THE HOGYOKU'S POWERS BY KISUKE URAHARA...
...SHINJI HIRAKO AND THE OTHERS EVOLVED INTO COMPLETE VISOREDS.
AND ARMED WITH MY SUSPICIONS ABOUT THE HOGYOKU'S POWERS...

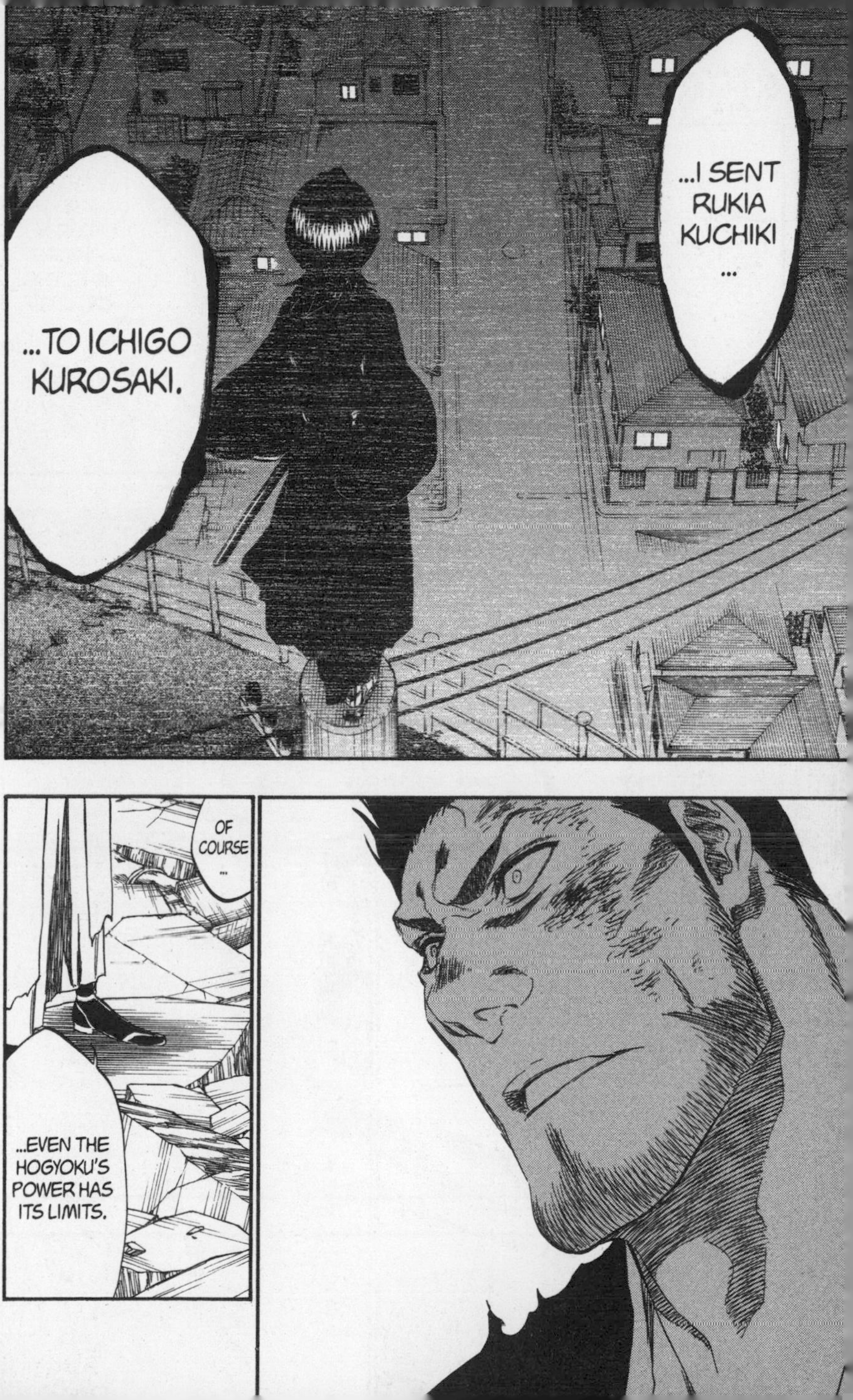
...I SENT RUKIA KUCHIKI ...
...TO ICHIGO KUROSAKI.
OF COURSE ...
...EVEN THE HOGYOKU'S POWER HAS ITS LIMITS.

READ THIS WAY

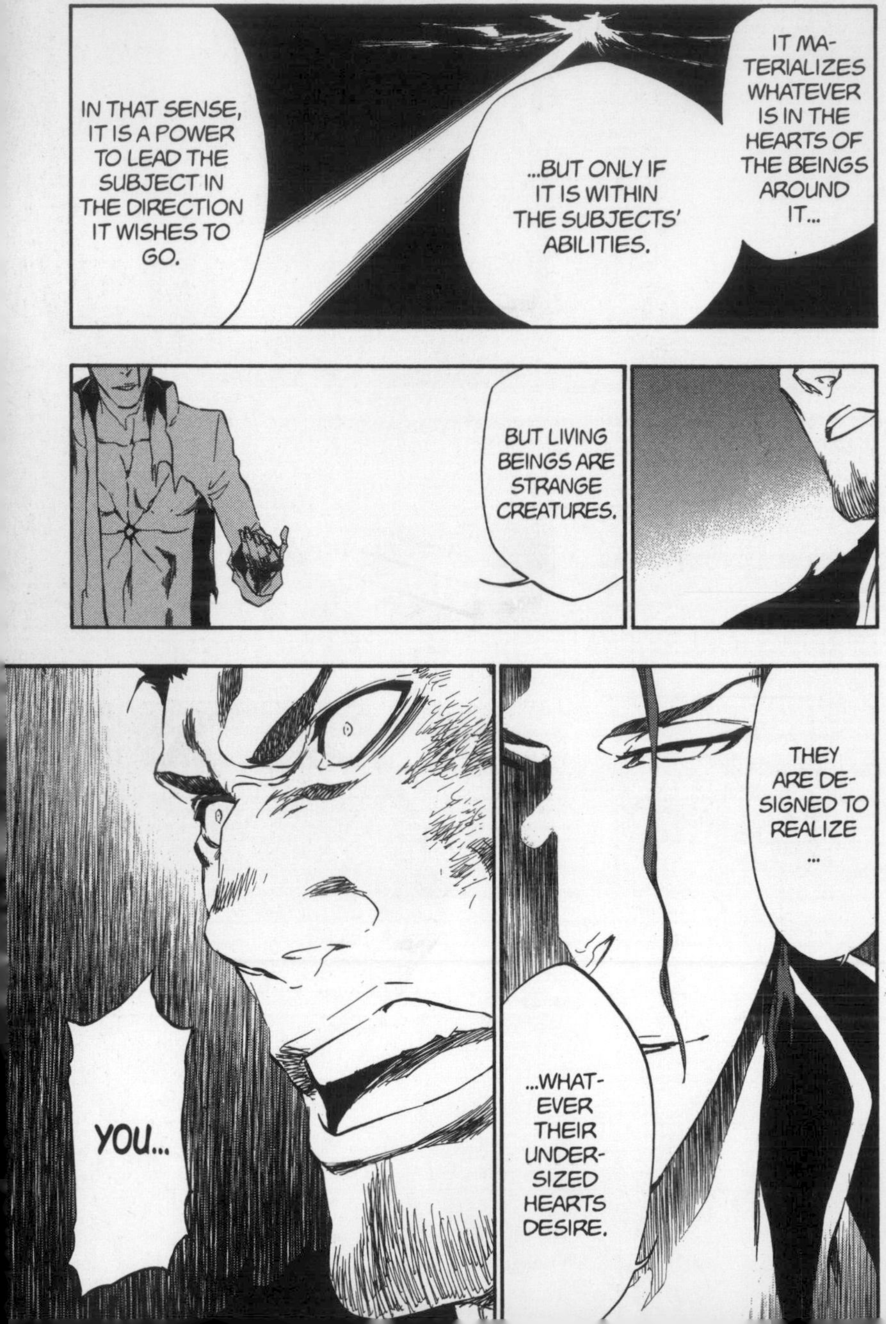
IT MA-TERIALIZES WHATEVER IS IN THE HEARTS OF THE BEINGS AROUND IT...
...BUT ONLY IF IT IS WITHIN THE SUBJECTS' ABILITIES.
IN THAT SENSE, IT IS A POWER TO LEAD THE SUBJECT IN THE DIRECTION IT WISHES TO GO.
BUT LIVING BEINGS ARE STRANGE CREATURES.
THEY ARE DE-SIGNED TO REALIZE ...
...WHAT-EVER THEIR UNDER-SIZED HEARTS DESIRE.
YOU...

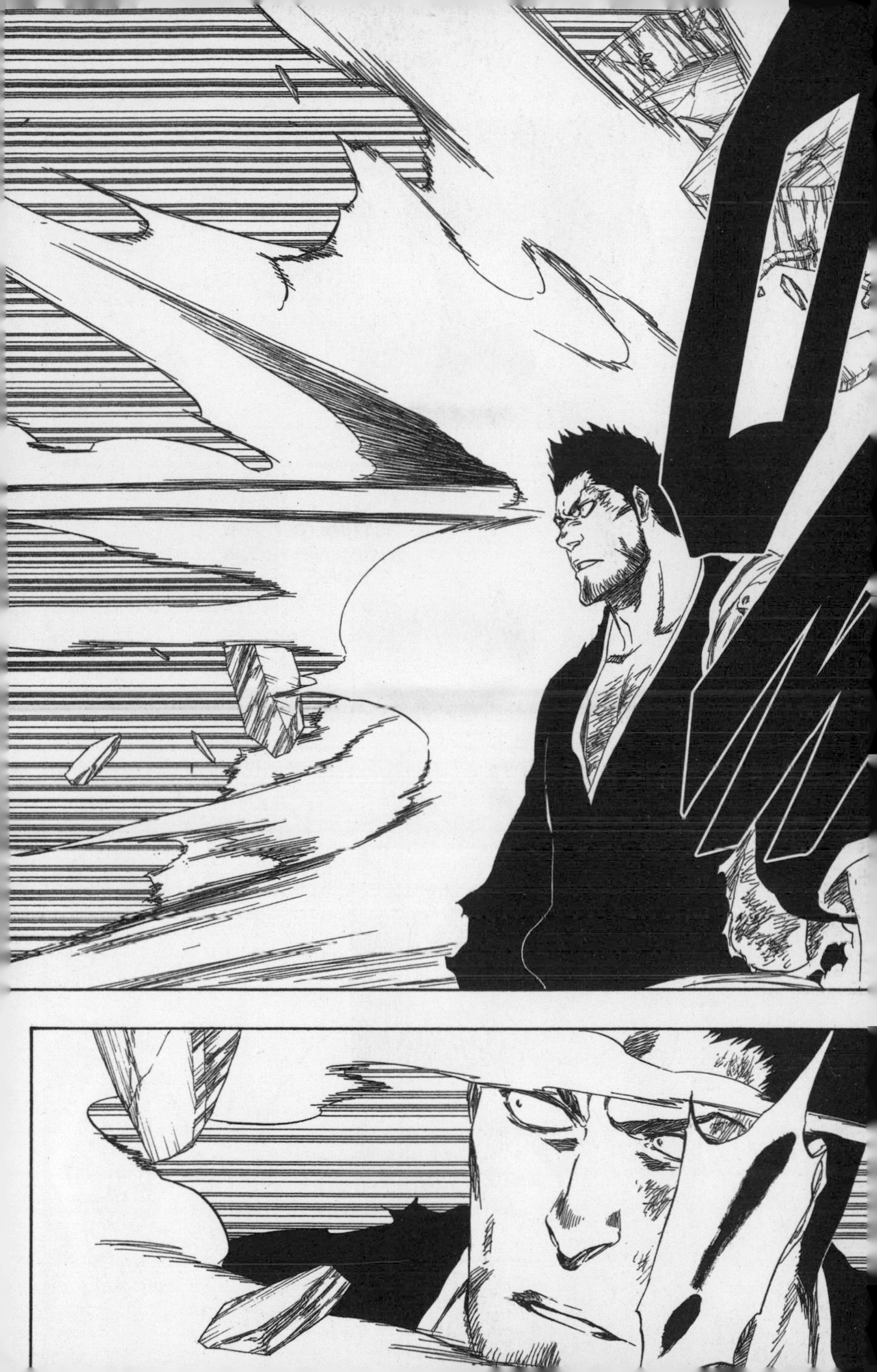

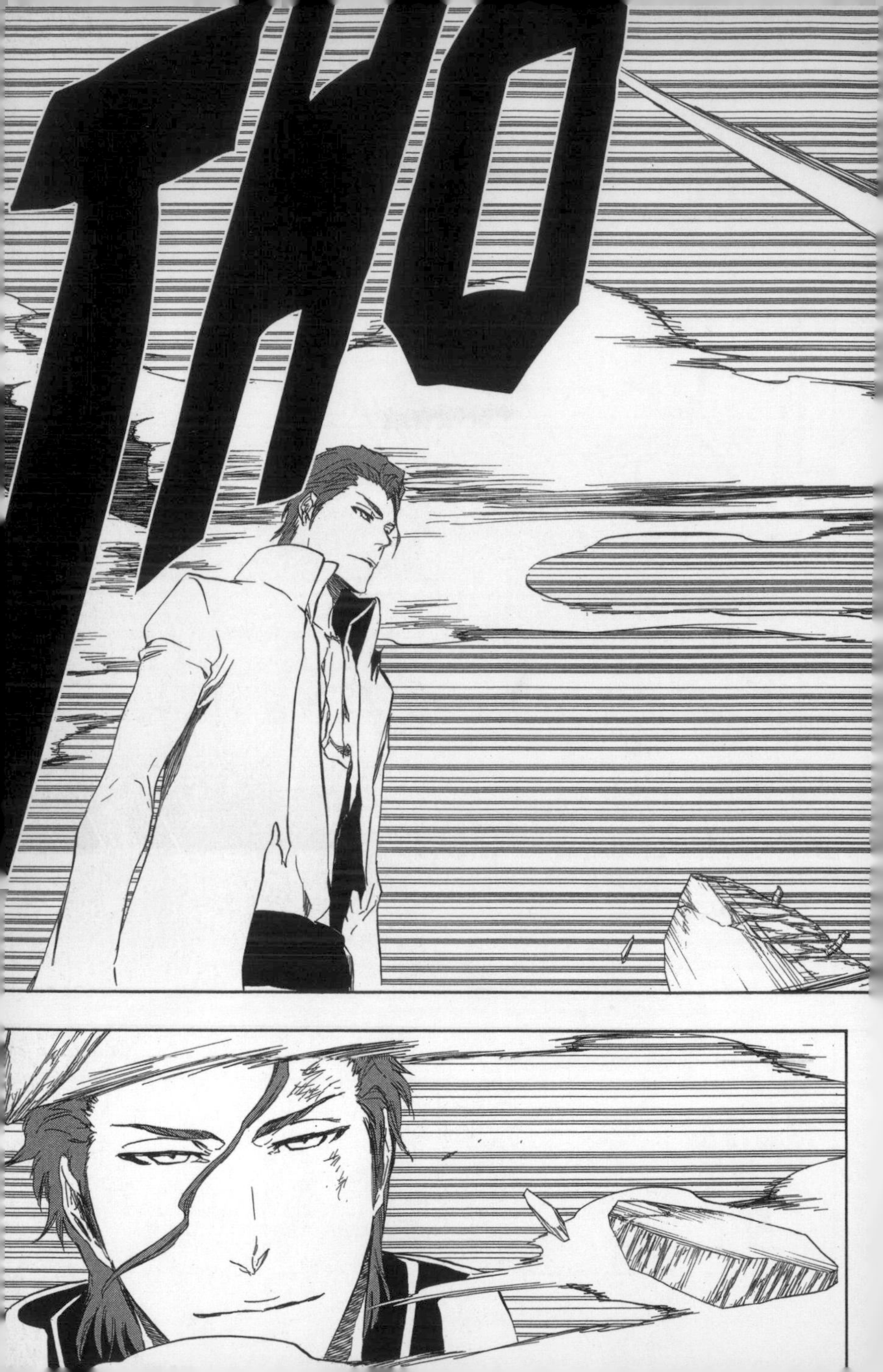

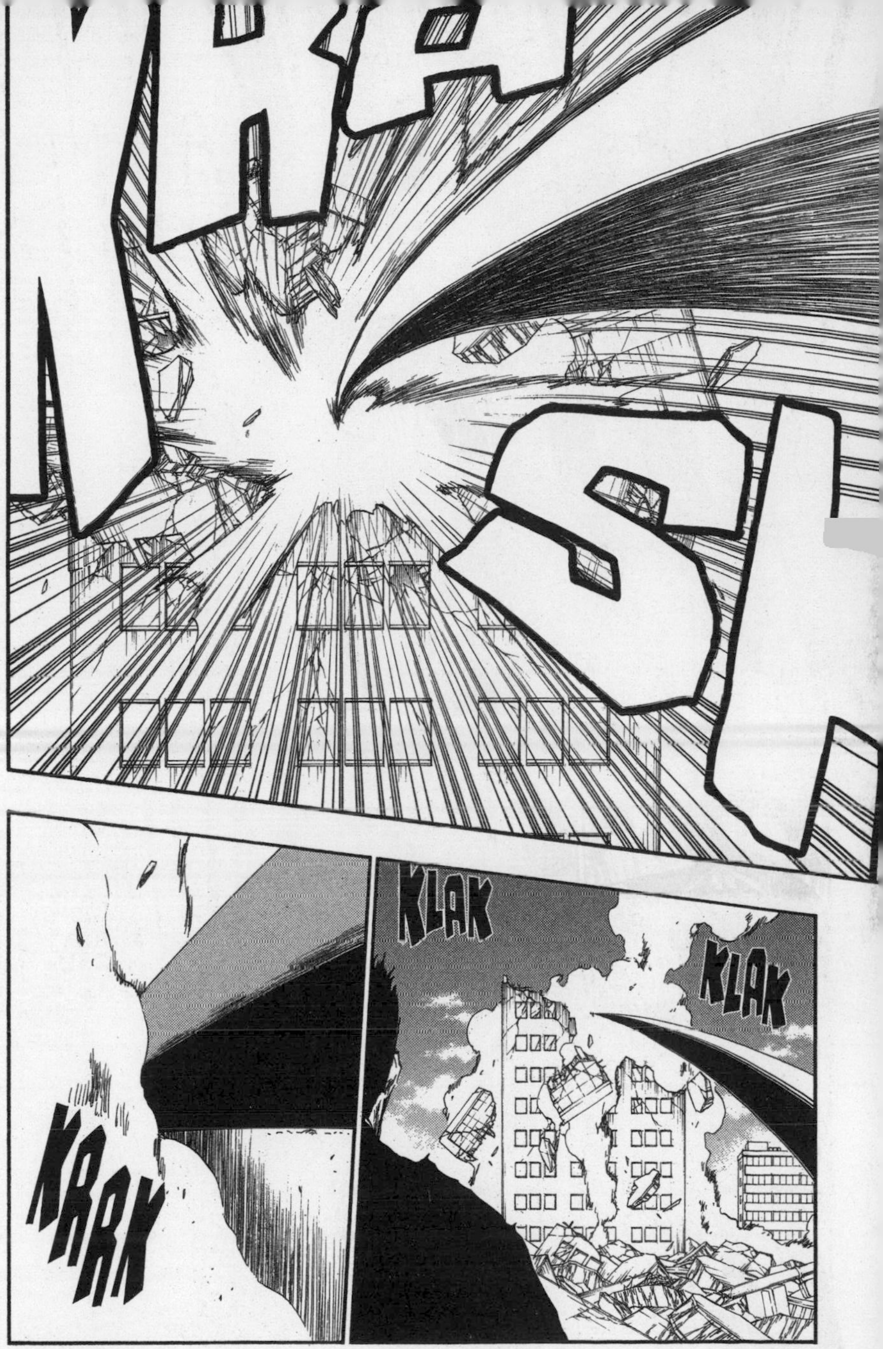
KLAK
KLAK
KRRK

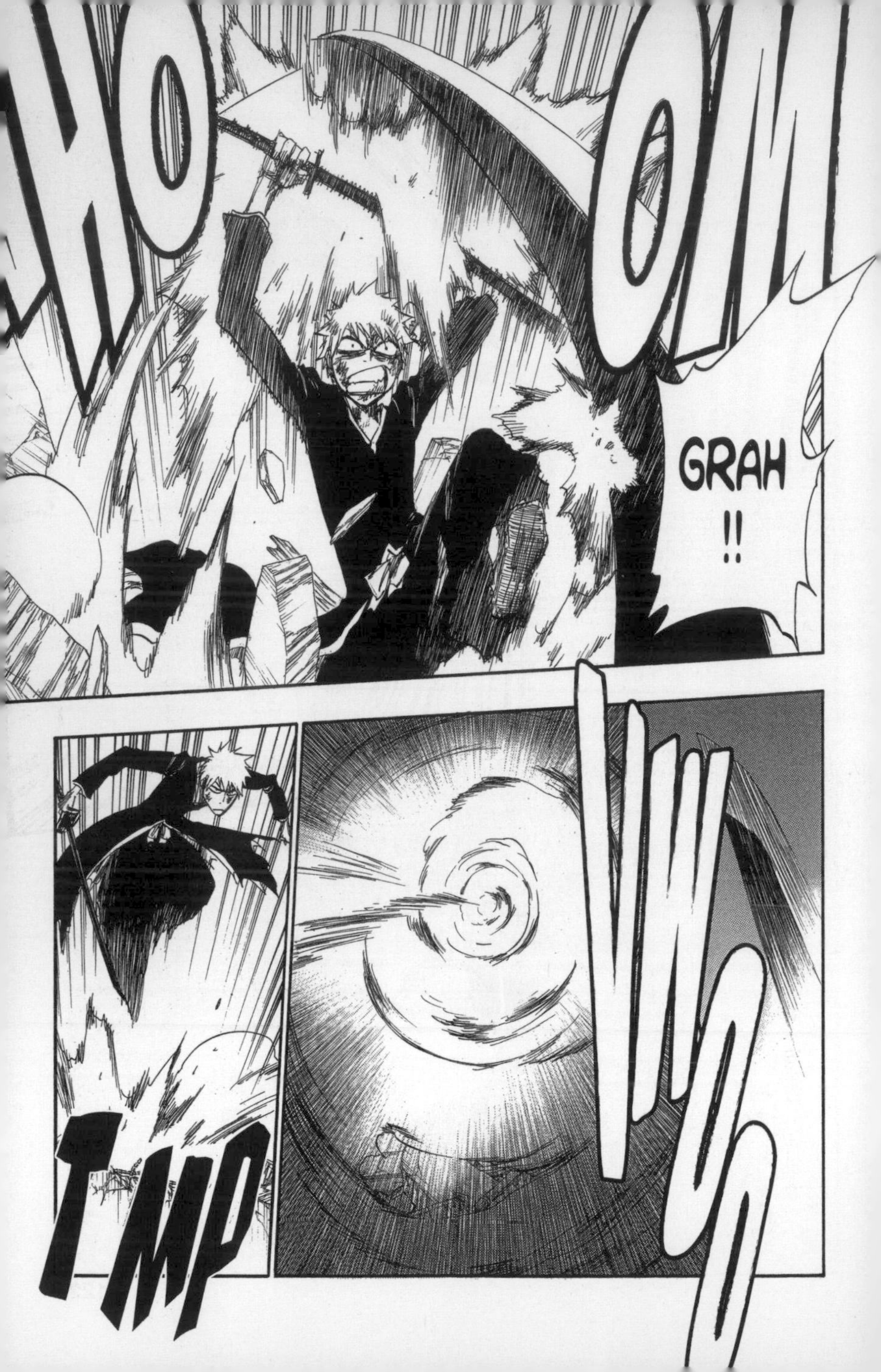
GRAH !!
TMP

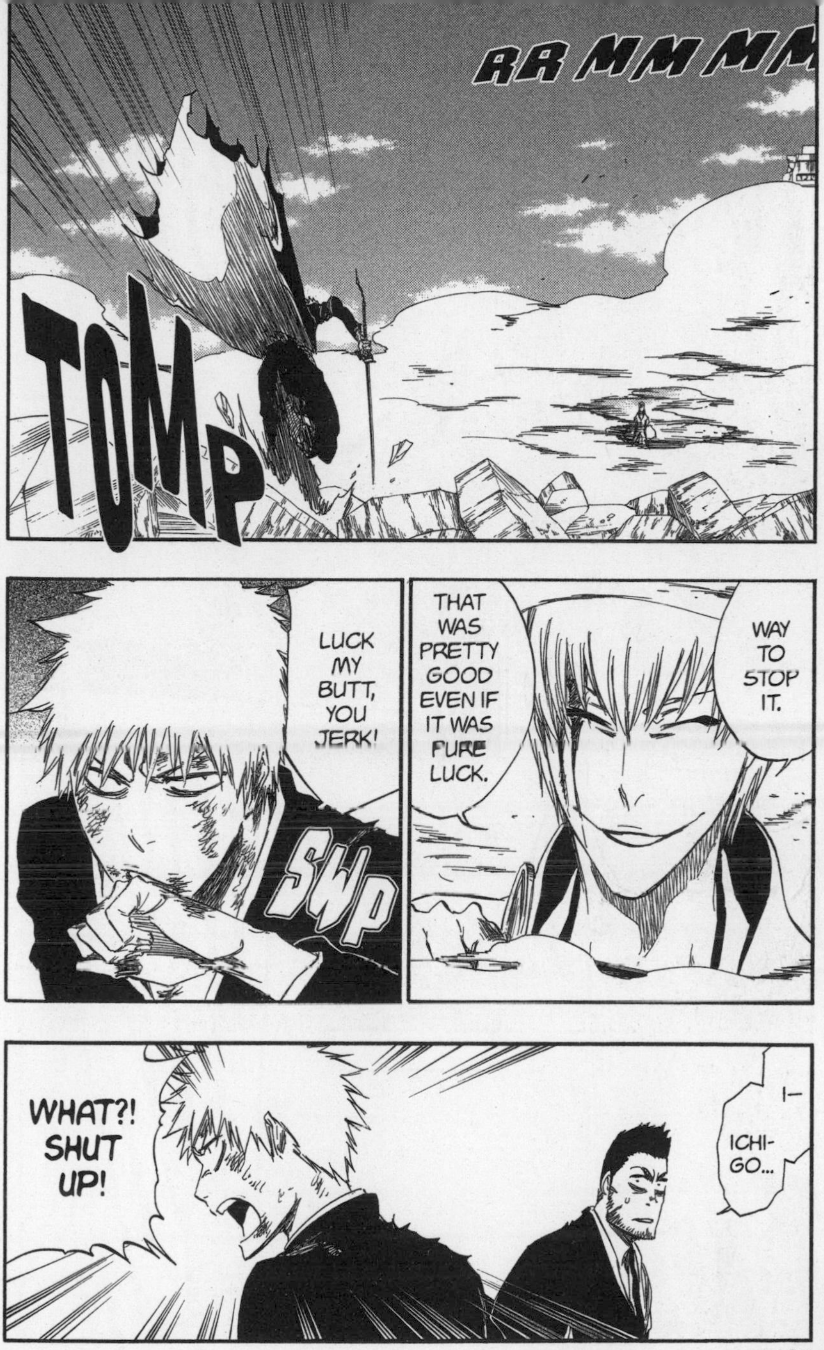
RRMMMM
TOMP
WAY TO STOP IT.
THAT WAS PRETTY GOOD EVEN IF IT WAS PURE LUCK.
LUCK MY BUTT, YOU JERK!
SWP
I— ICHIGO...
WHAT?! SHUT UP!

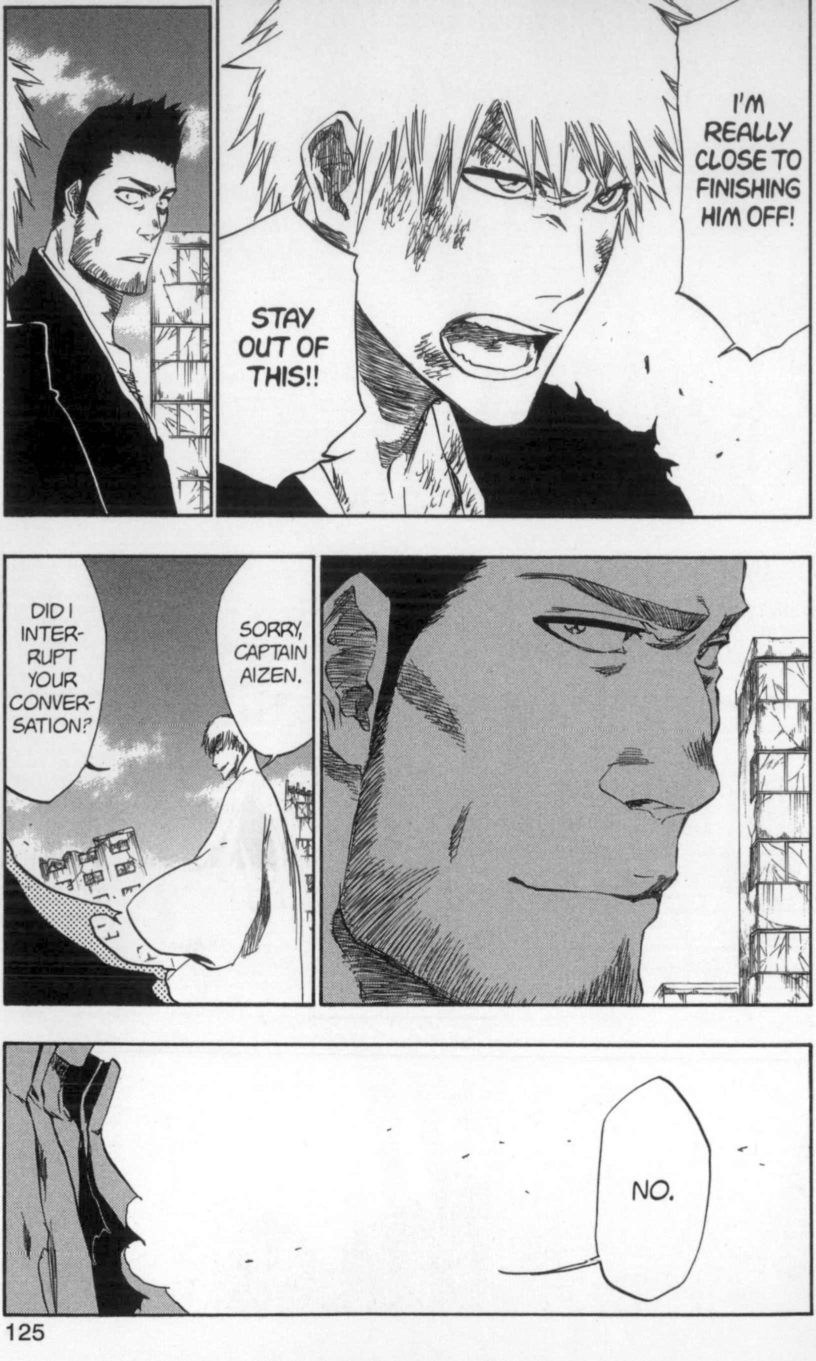
I'M REALLY CLOSE TO FINISHING HIM OFF!
STAY OUT OF THIS!!
SORRY, CAPTAIN AIZEN.
DID I INTER-RUPT YOUR CONVER-SATION?
NO.

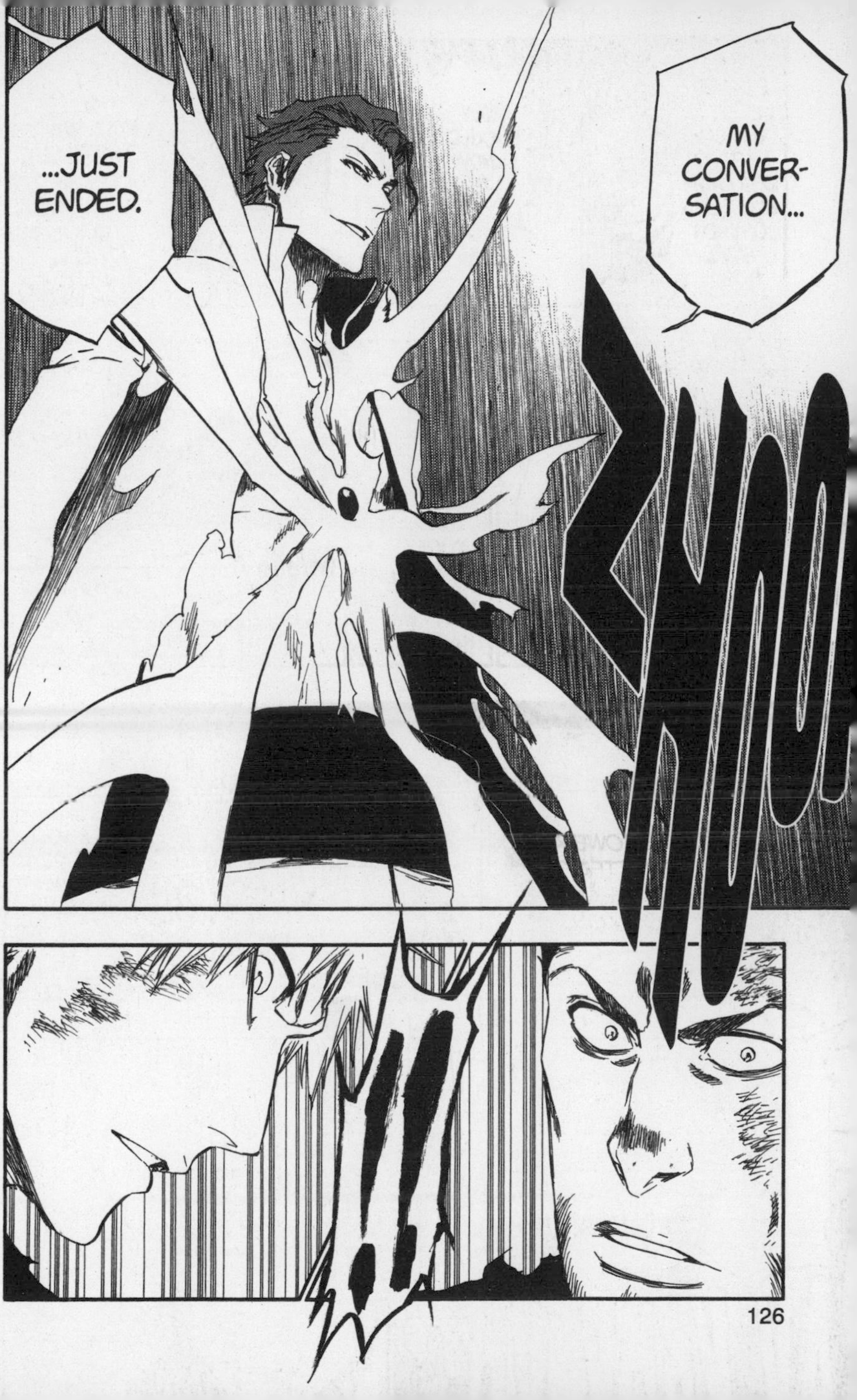
MY CONVER-
SATION...
...JUST ENDED.

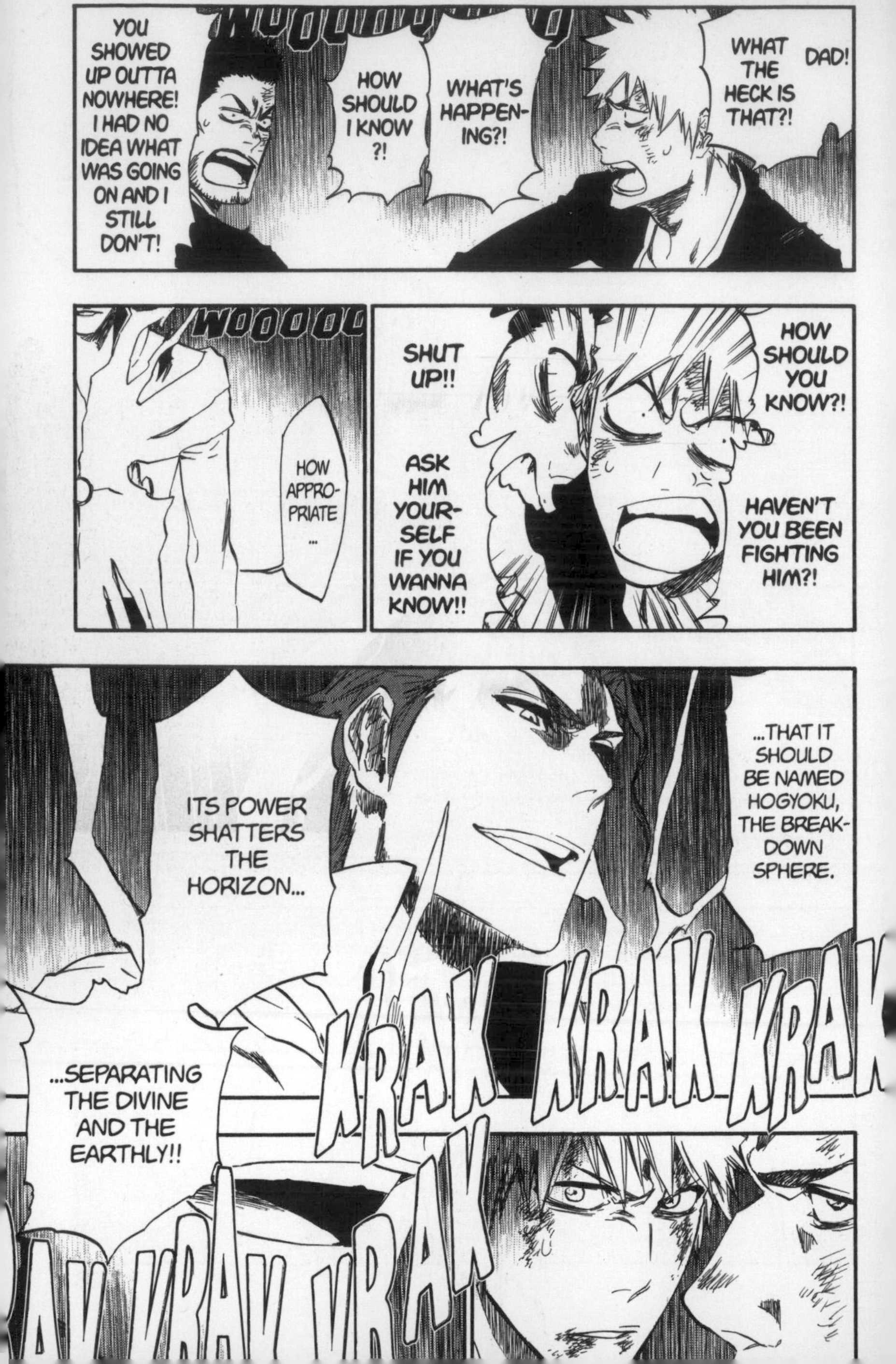
DAD!
WHAT THE HECK IS THAT?!
WHAT'S HAPPENING?!
HOW SHOULD I KNOW ?!
YOU SHOWED UP OUTTA NOWHERE! I HAD NO IDEA WHAT WAS GOING ON AND I STILL DON'T!
HOW SHOULD YOU KNOW?!
HAVEN'T YOU BEEN FIGHTING HIM?!
SHUT UP!!
ASK HIM YOURSELF IF YOU WANNA KNOW!!
HOW APPROPRIATE...
...THAT IT SHOULD BE NAMED HOGYOKU, THE BREAK-DOWN SPHERE.
ITS POWER SHATTERS THE HORIZON...
...SEPARATING THE DIVINE AND THE EARTHLY!!
KRAK KRAK KRAK
KRAK

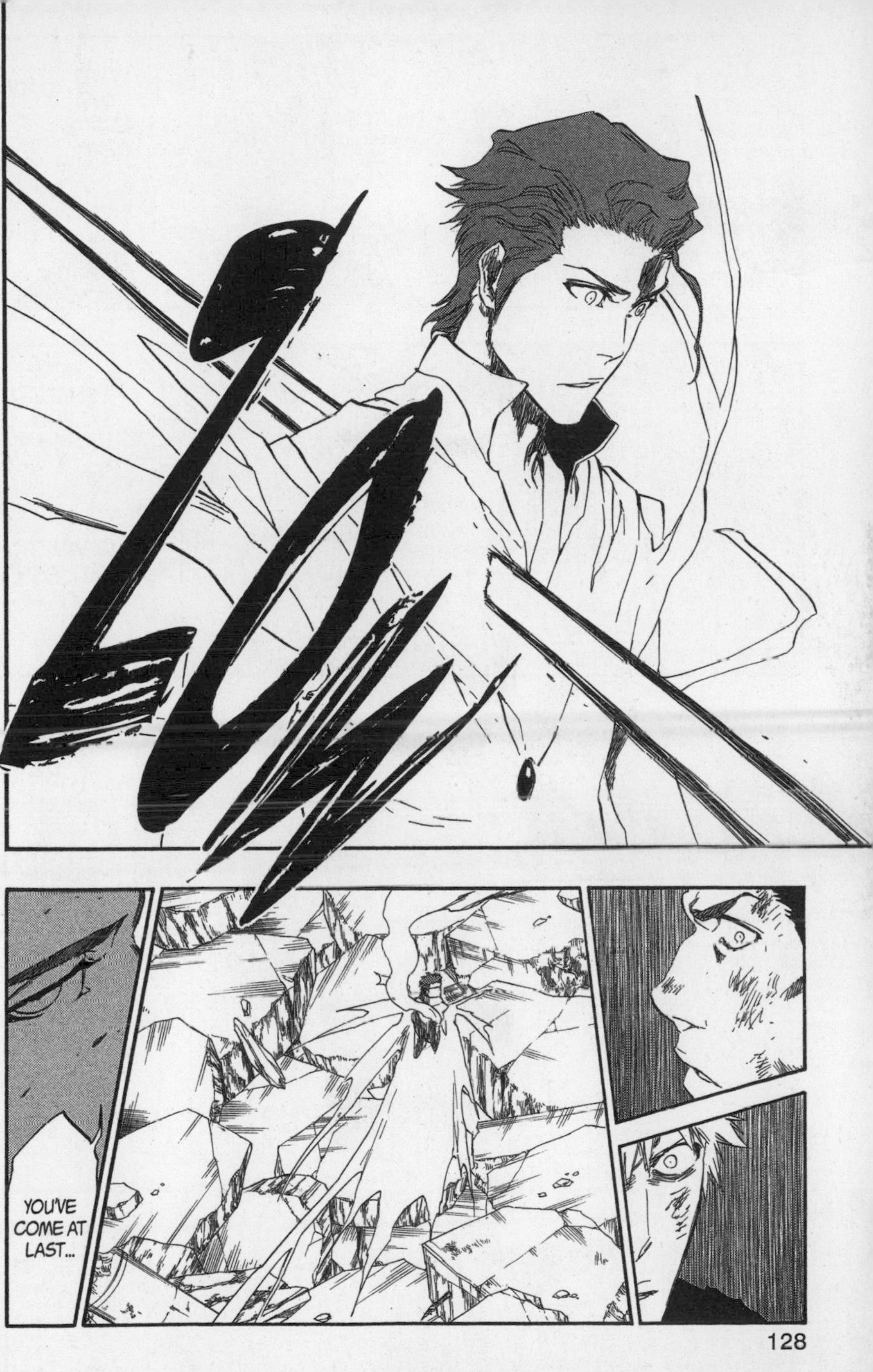
YOU'VE COME AT LAST...

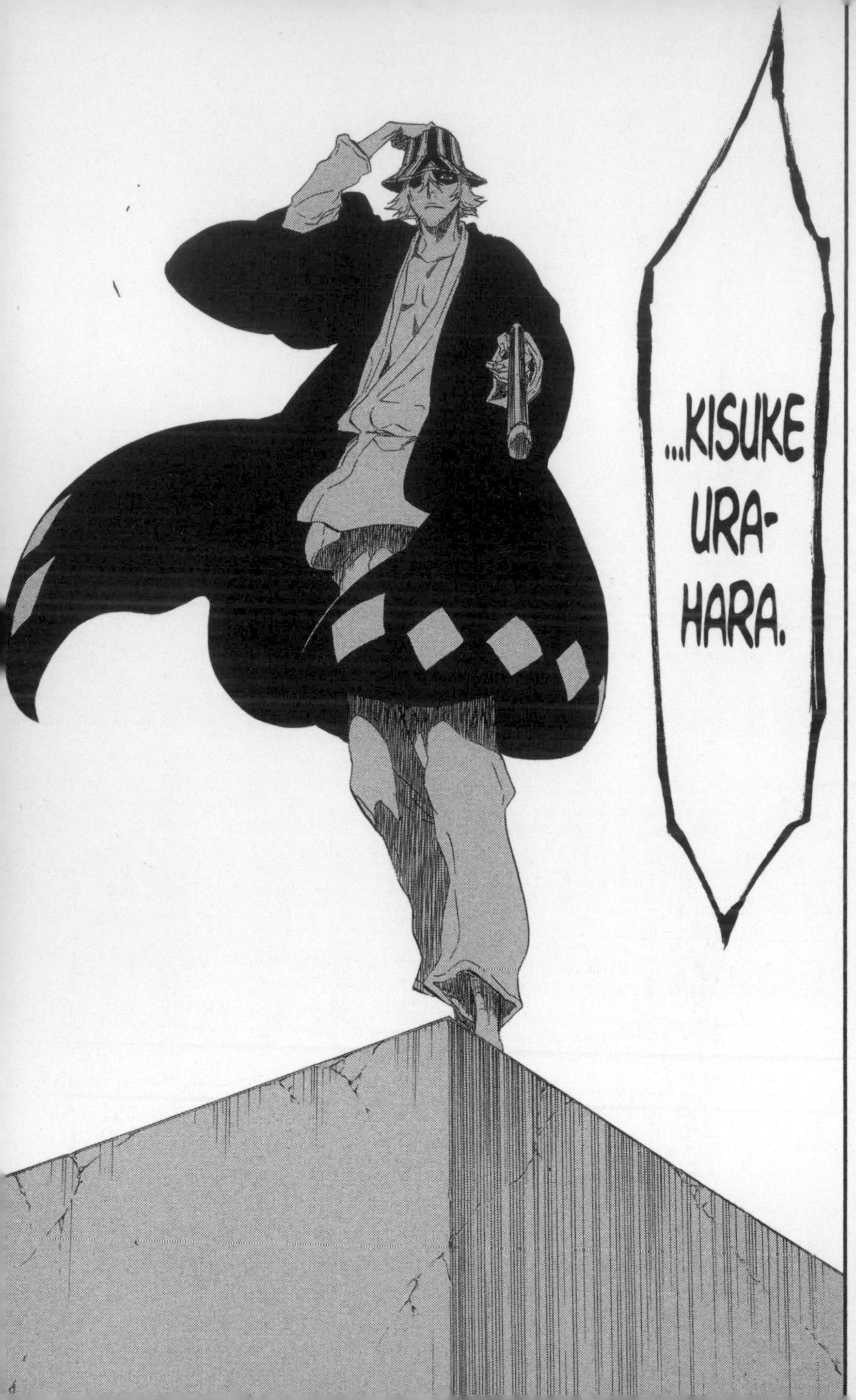
...KISUKE
URA-
HARA.

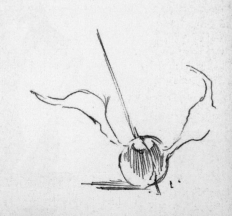

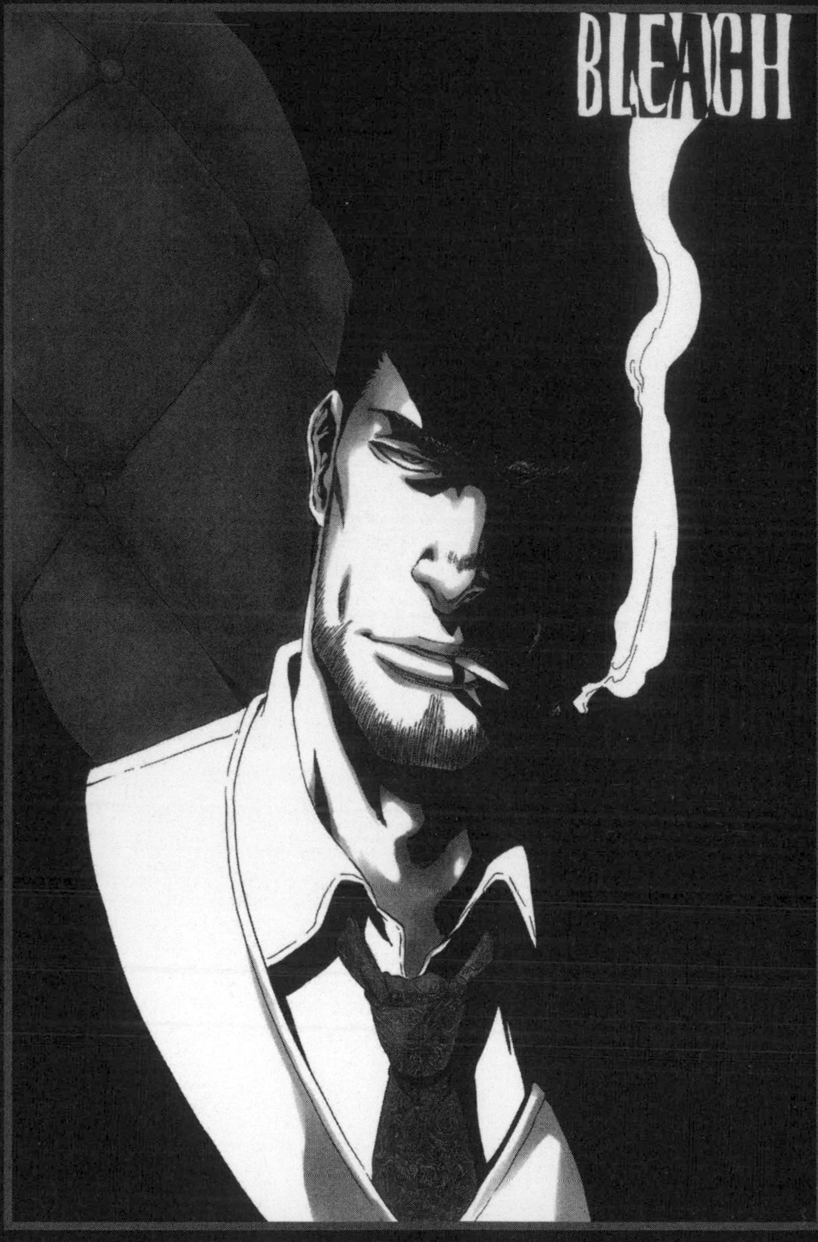
BLEACH

BLEACH
ブリーチ

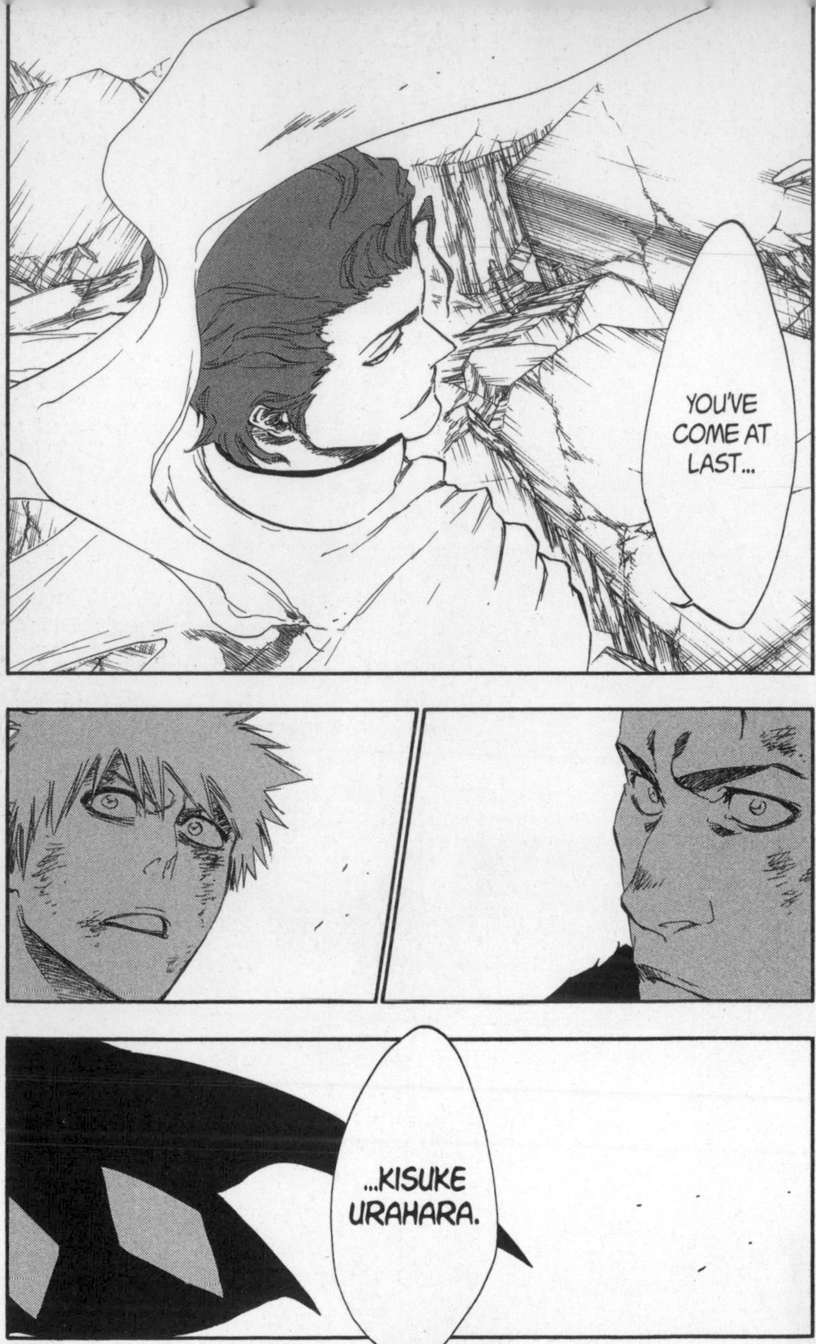
YOU'VE COME AT LAST...
...KISUKE URAHARA.

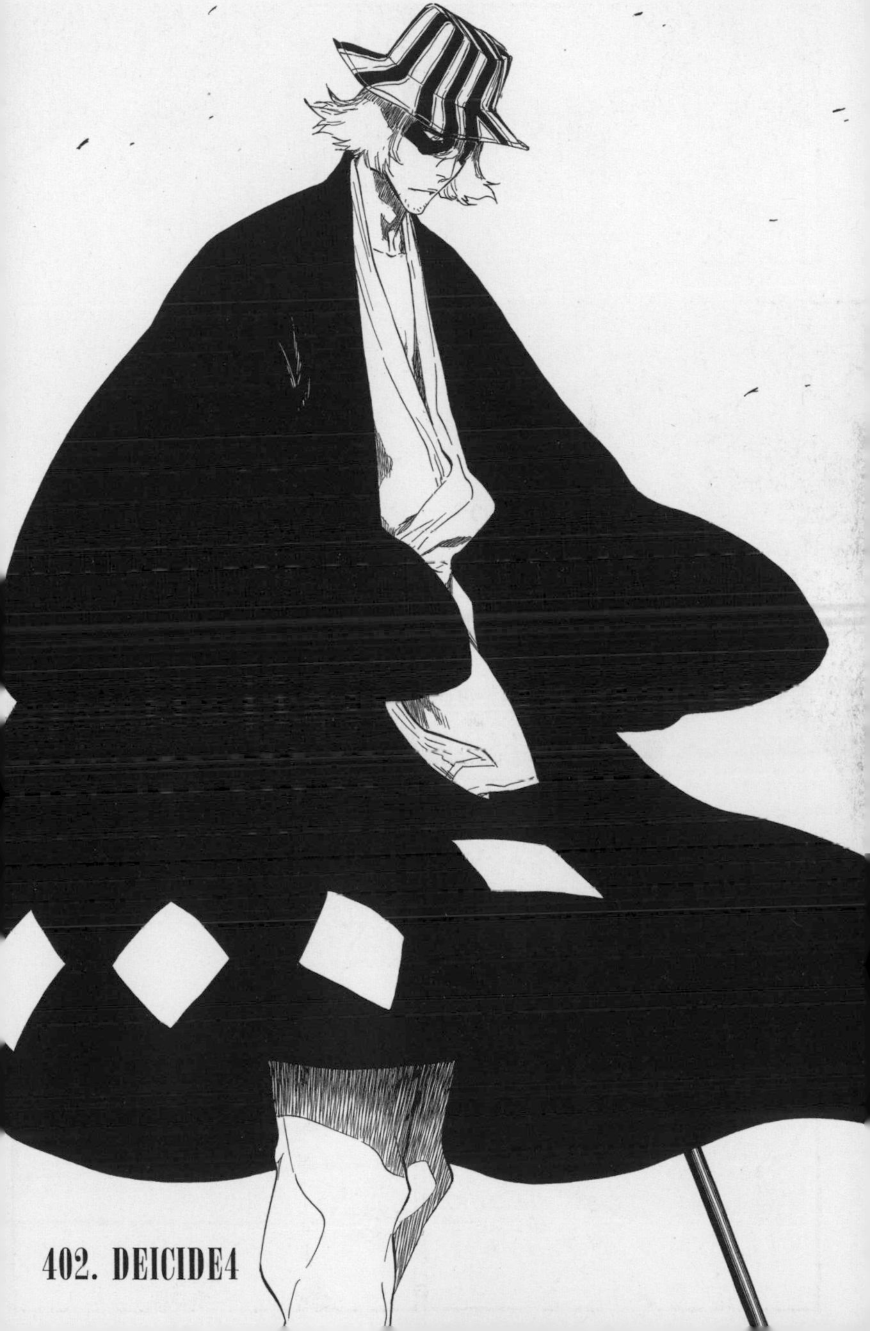

402. DEICIDE4

READ THIS WAY

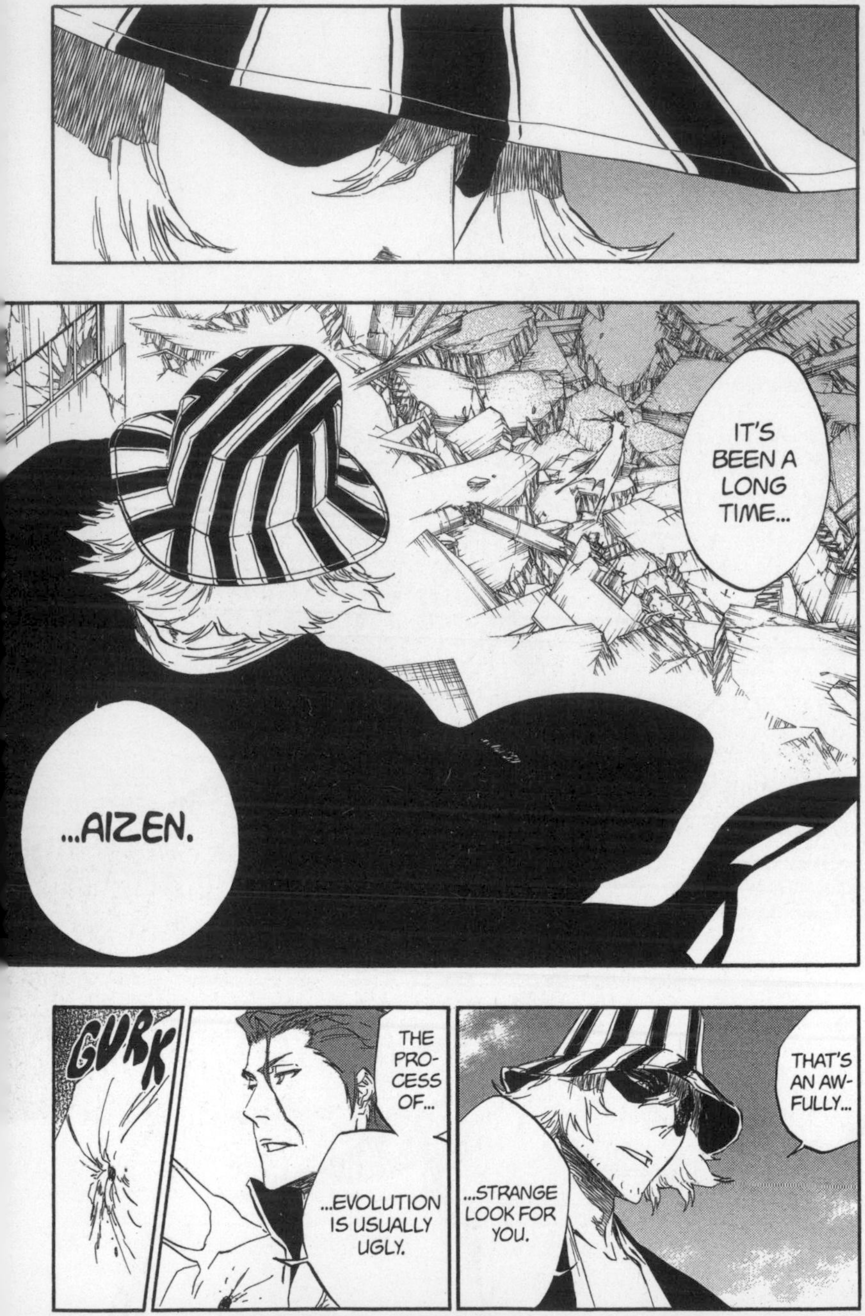
IT'S BEEN A LONG TIME...
...AIZEN.
THAT'S AN AWFULLY...
...STRANGE LOOK FOR YOU.
THE PROCESS OF...
...EVOLUTION IS USUALLY UGLY.
GURK

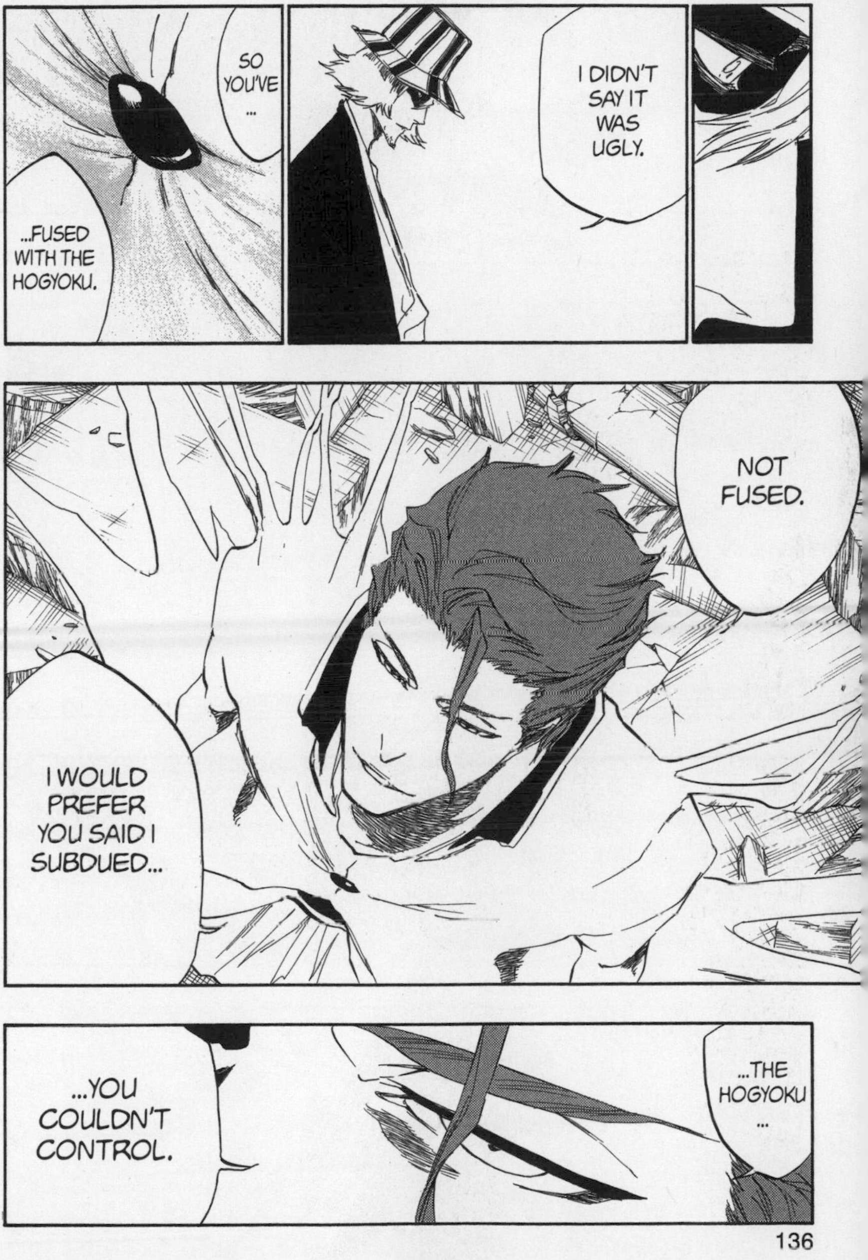
I DIDN'T SAY IT WAS UGLY.
SO YOU'VE ...
...FUSED WITH THE HOGYOKU.
NOT FUSED.
I WOULD PREFER YOU SAID I SUBDUED...
...THE HOGYOKU ...
...YOU COULDN'T CONTROL.

READ THIS WAY

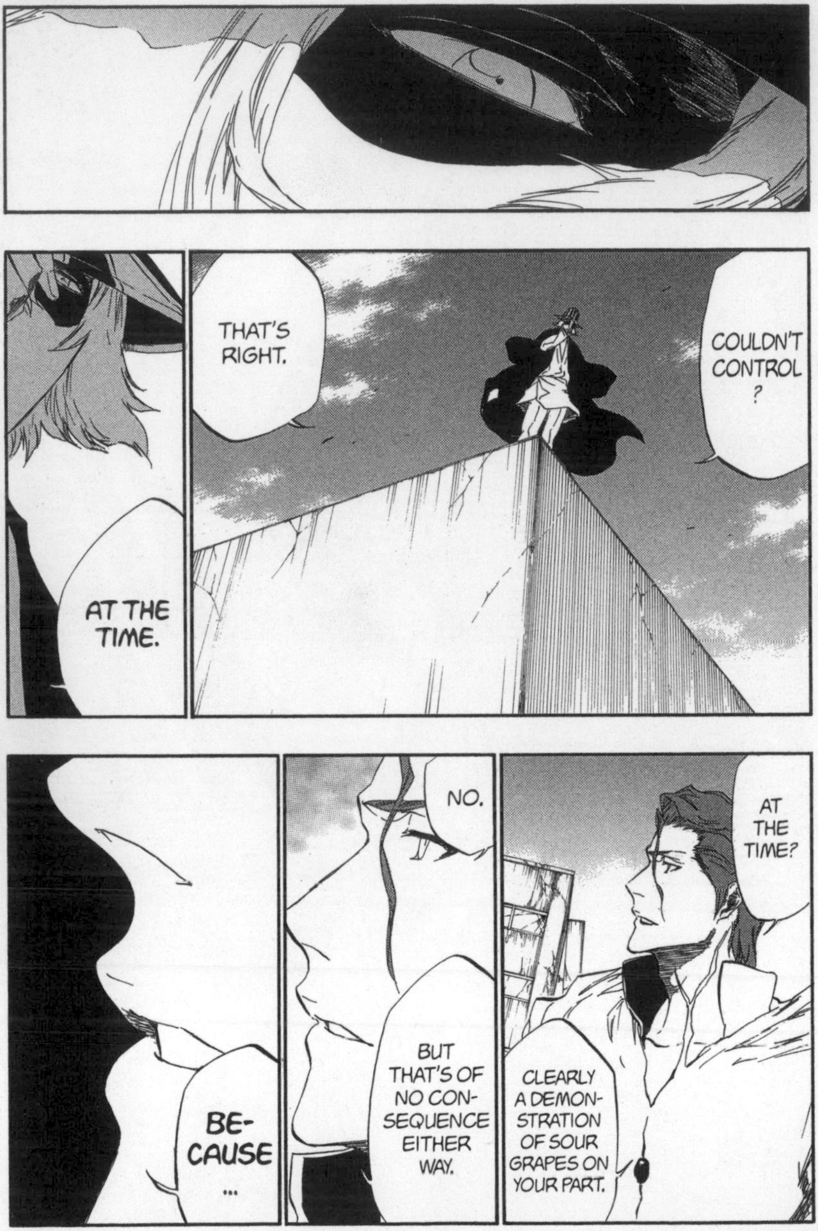
COULDN'T CONTROL?
THAT'S RIGHT.
AT THE TIME.
AT THE TIME?
CLEARLY A DEMON-STRATION OF SOUR GRAPES ON YOUR PART.
NO.
BUT THAT'S OF NO CON-SEQUENCE EITHER WAY.
BE-CAUSE ...

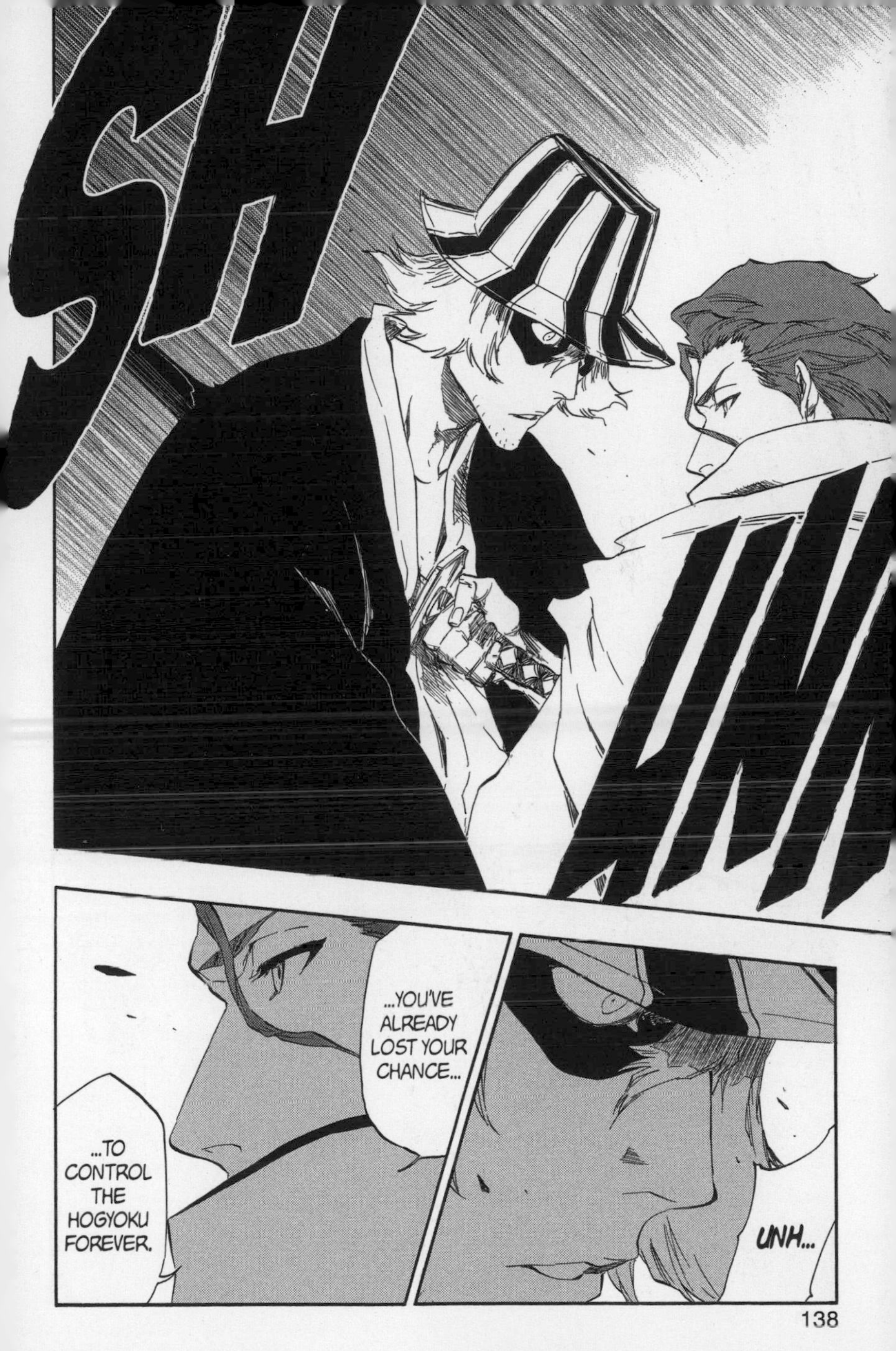
UNH...
...YOU'VE ALREADY LOST YOUR CHANCE...
...TO CONTROL THE HOGYOKU FOREVER.

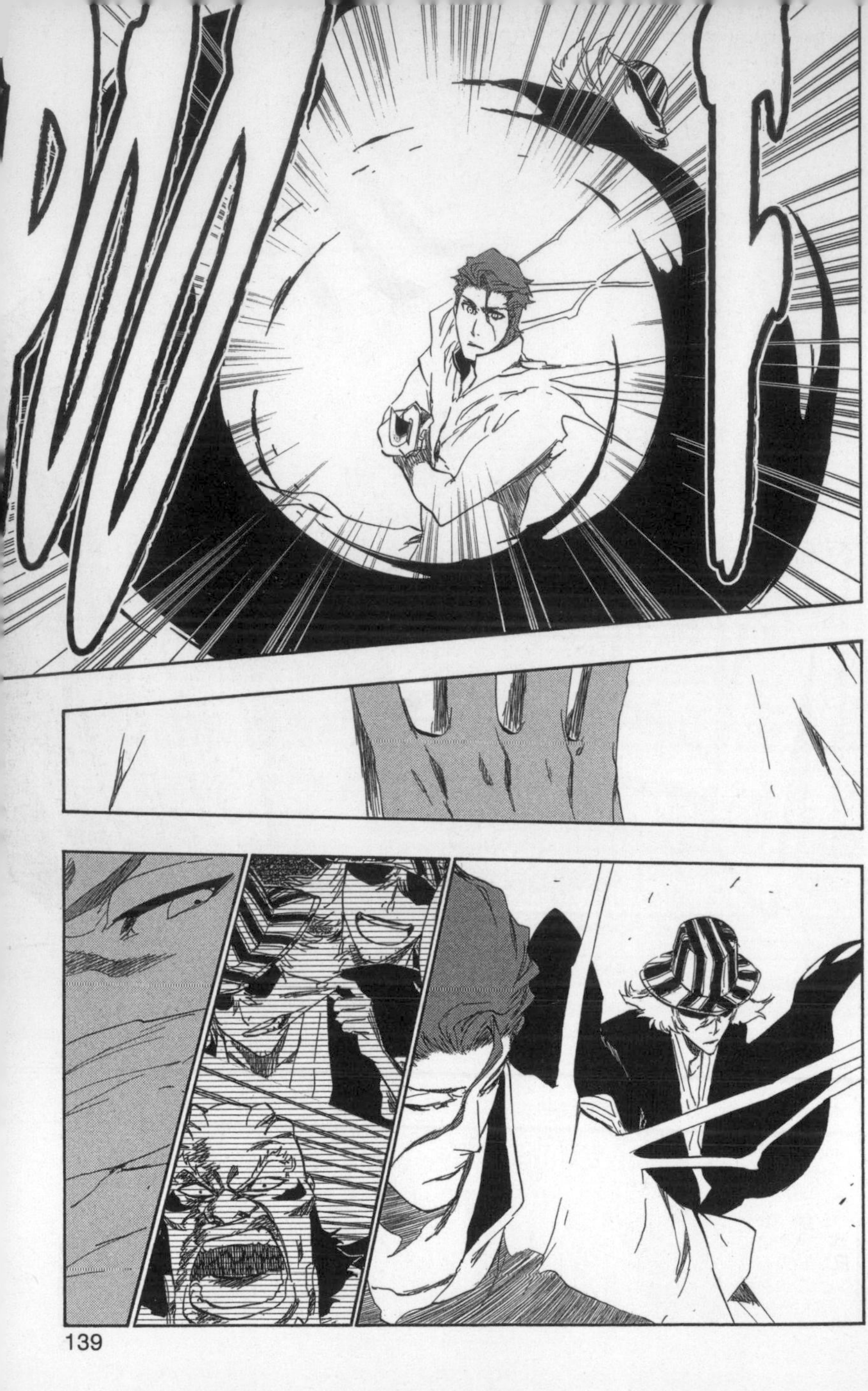

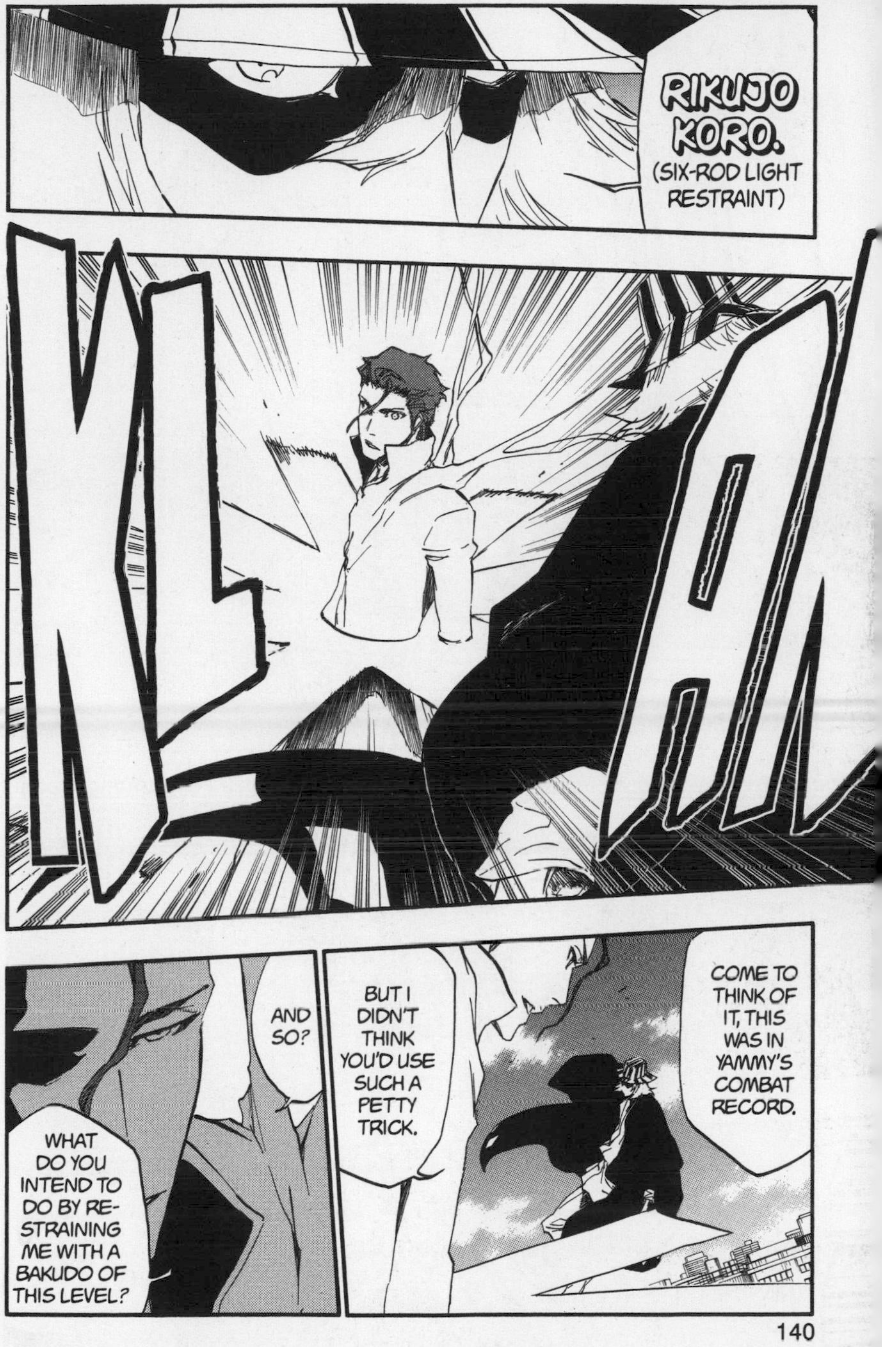
RIKUJO KORO.
(SIX-ROD LIGHT RESTRAINT)
COME TO THINK OF IT, THIS WAS IN YAMMY'S COMBAT RECORD.
BUT I DIDN'T THINK YOU'D USE SUCH A PETTY TRICK.
AND SO?
WHAT DO YOU INTEND TO DO BY RE-STRAINING ME WITH A BAKUDO OF THIS LEVEL?

READ THIS WAY

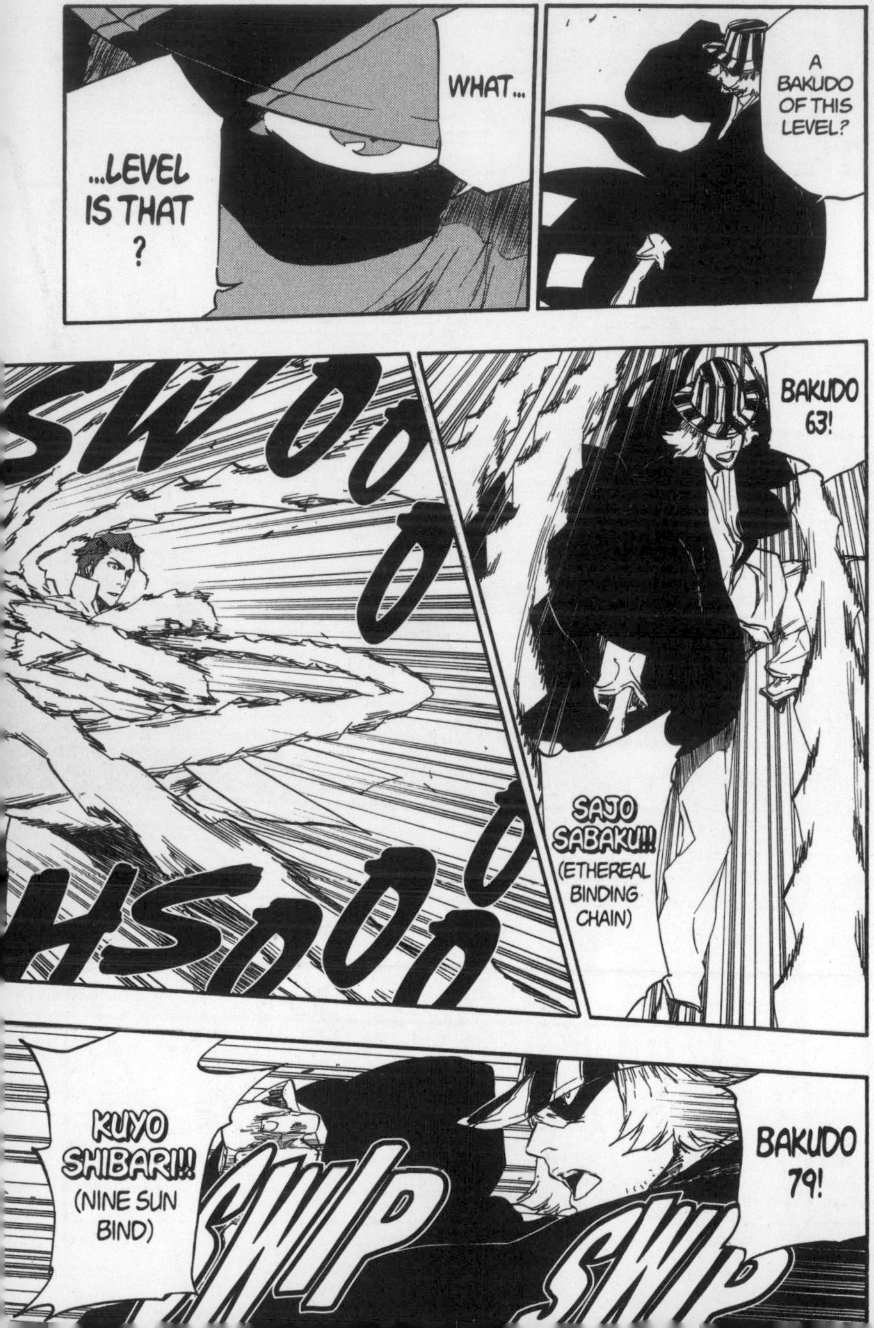
A BAKUDO OF THIS LEVEL?
WHAT...
...LEVEL IS THAT ?
BAKUDO 63!
SAJO SABAKU!!!
(ETHEREAL BINDING CHAIN)
BAKUDO 79!
KUYO SHIBARI!!!
(NINE SUN BIND)
SHIP
SHIP

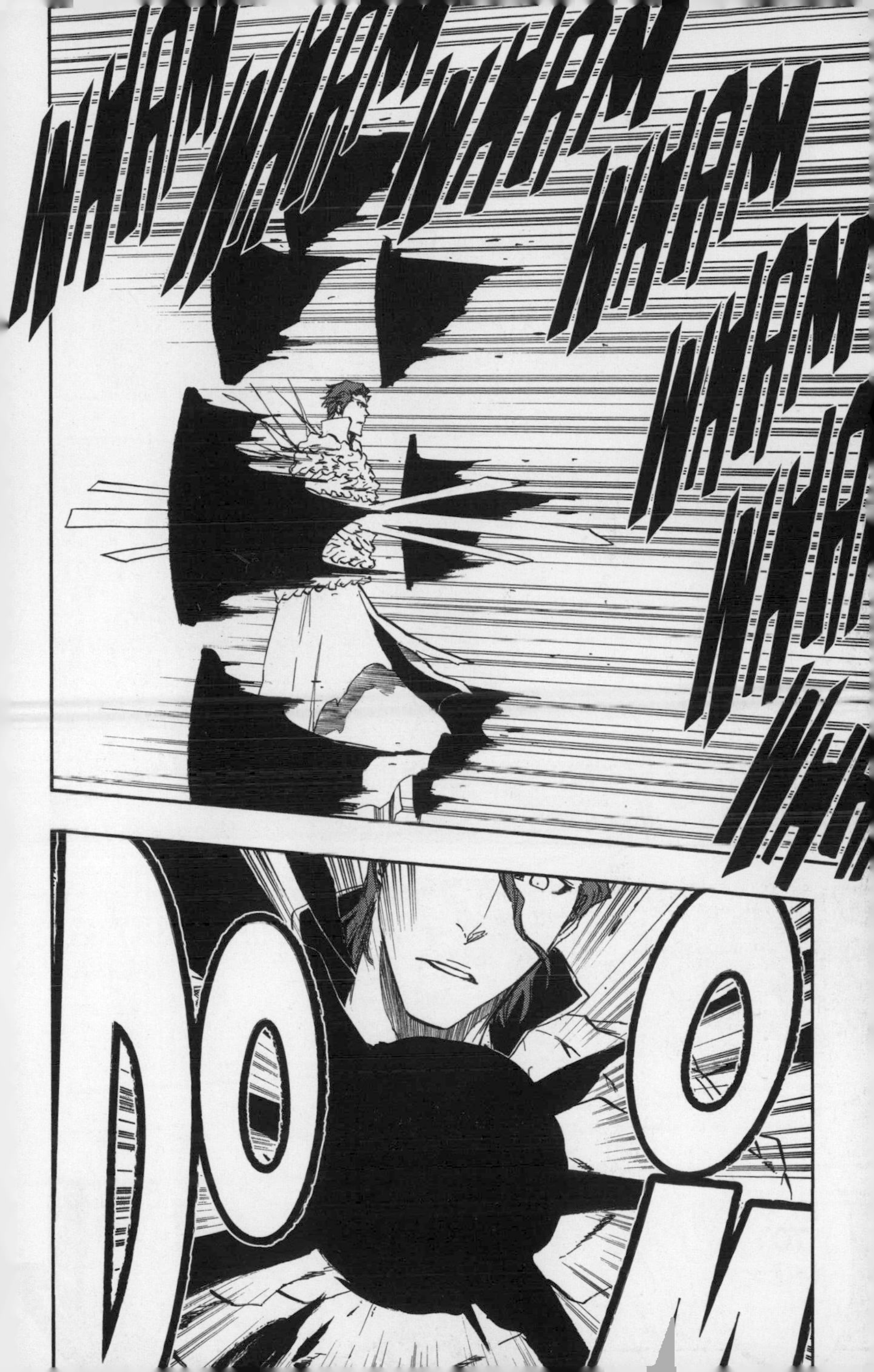
WHAM
WHAM
WHAM WHAM WHAM WHAM
DOOM

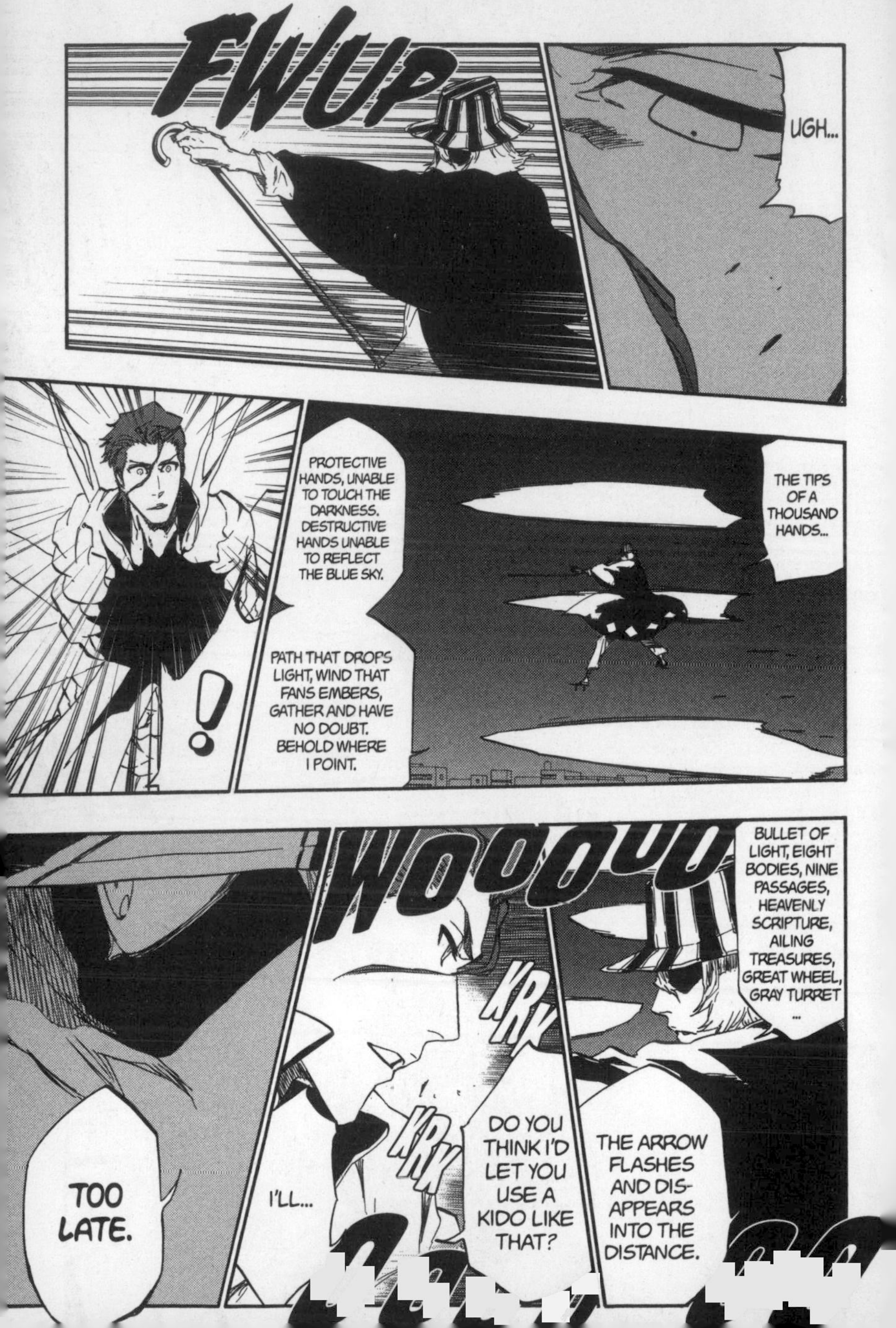
UGH...
FWUP
THE TIPS OF A THOUSAND HANDS...
PROTECTIVE HANDS, UNABLE TO TOUCH THE DARKNESS. DESTRUCTIVE HANDS UNABLE TO REFLECT THE BLUE SKY.
PATH THAT DROPS LIGHT, WIND THAT FANS EMBERS, GATHER AND HAVE NO DOUBT. BEHOLD WHERE I POINT.
!
BULLET OF LIGHT, EIGHT BODIES, NINE PASSAGES, HEAVENLY SCRIPTURE, AILING TREASURES, GREAT WHEEL, GRAY TURRET ...
THE ARROW FLASHES AND DIS-APPEARS INTO THE DISTANCE.
WOOOOO
KRK
DO YOU THINK I'D LET YOU USE A KIDO LIKE THAT?
KRK
I'LL...
TOO LATE.

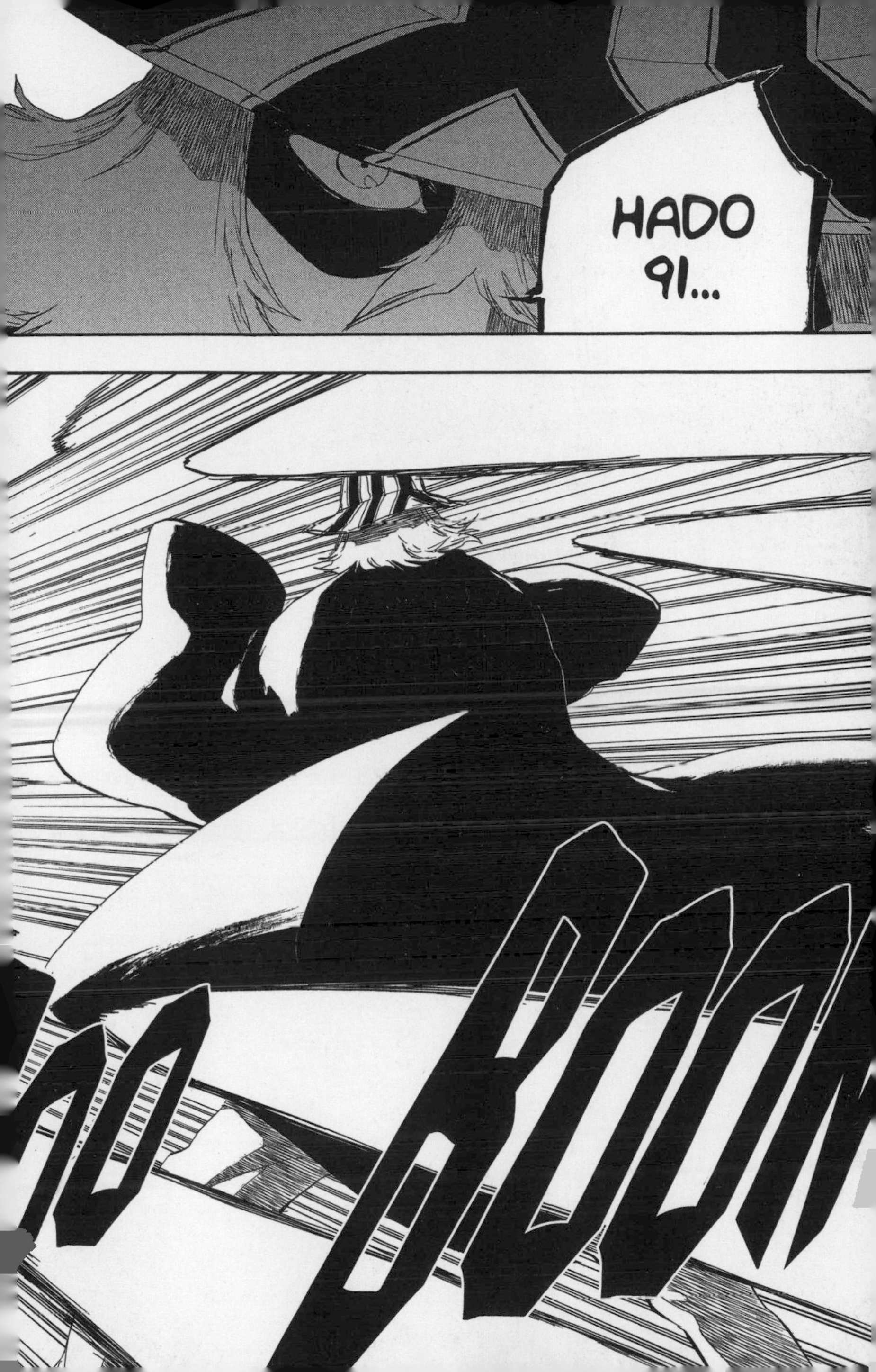
HADO 91...

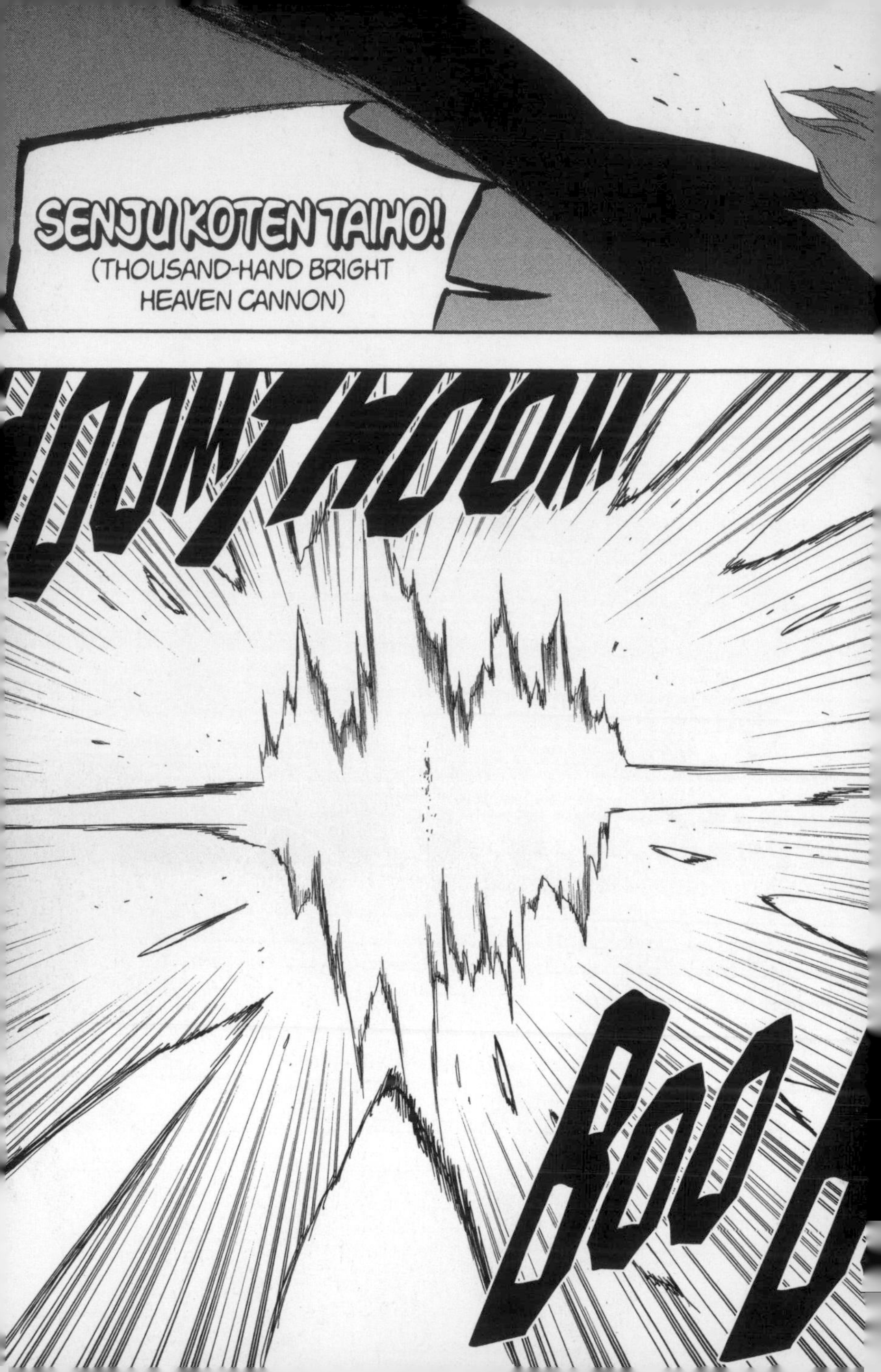
SENJU KOTEN TAIHO!
(THOUSAND-HAND BRIGHT HEAVEN CANNON)

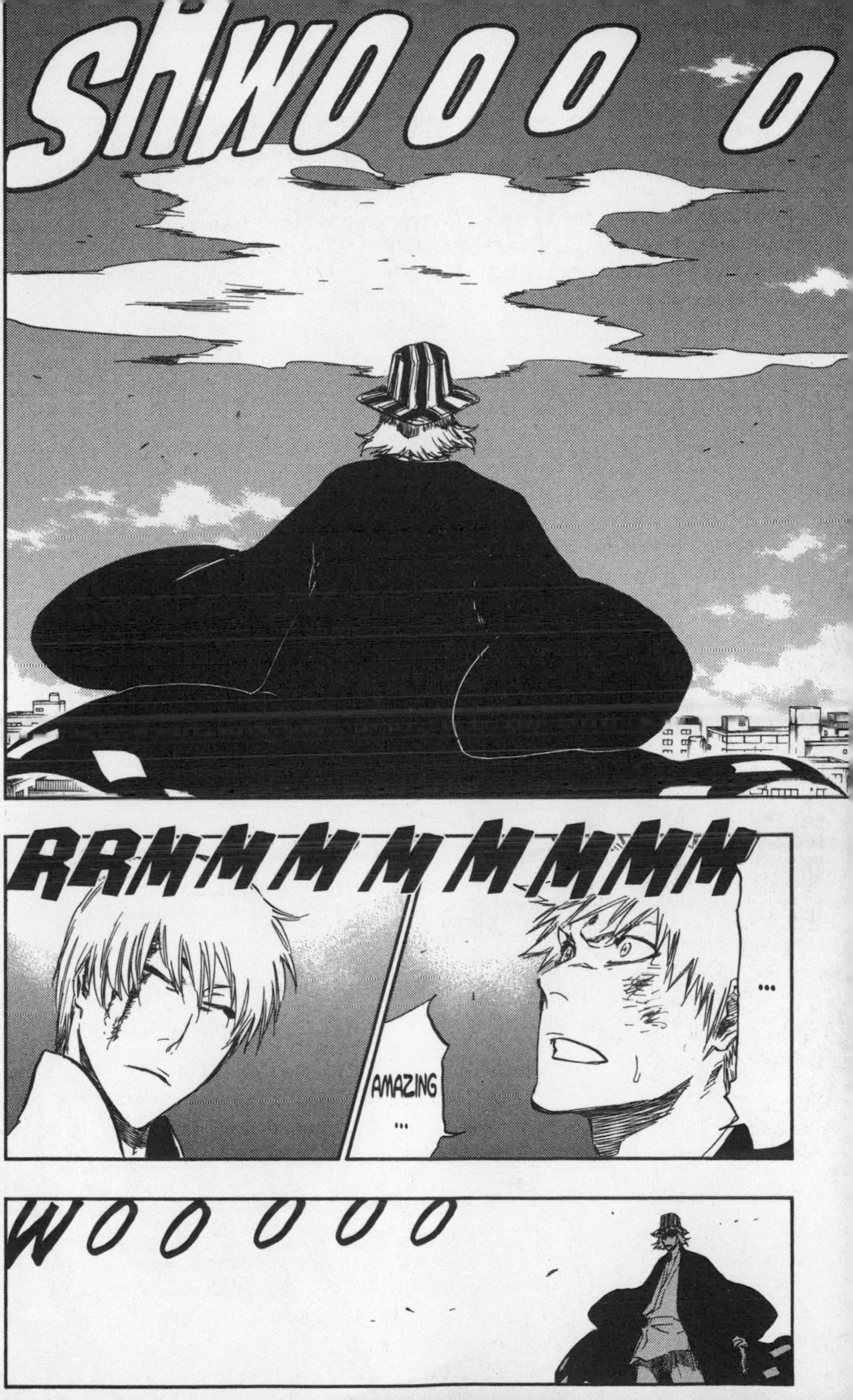
SHWOOOOO
RRMMMMMMMM
...
AMAZING
...
WOOOOO

READ THIS WAY

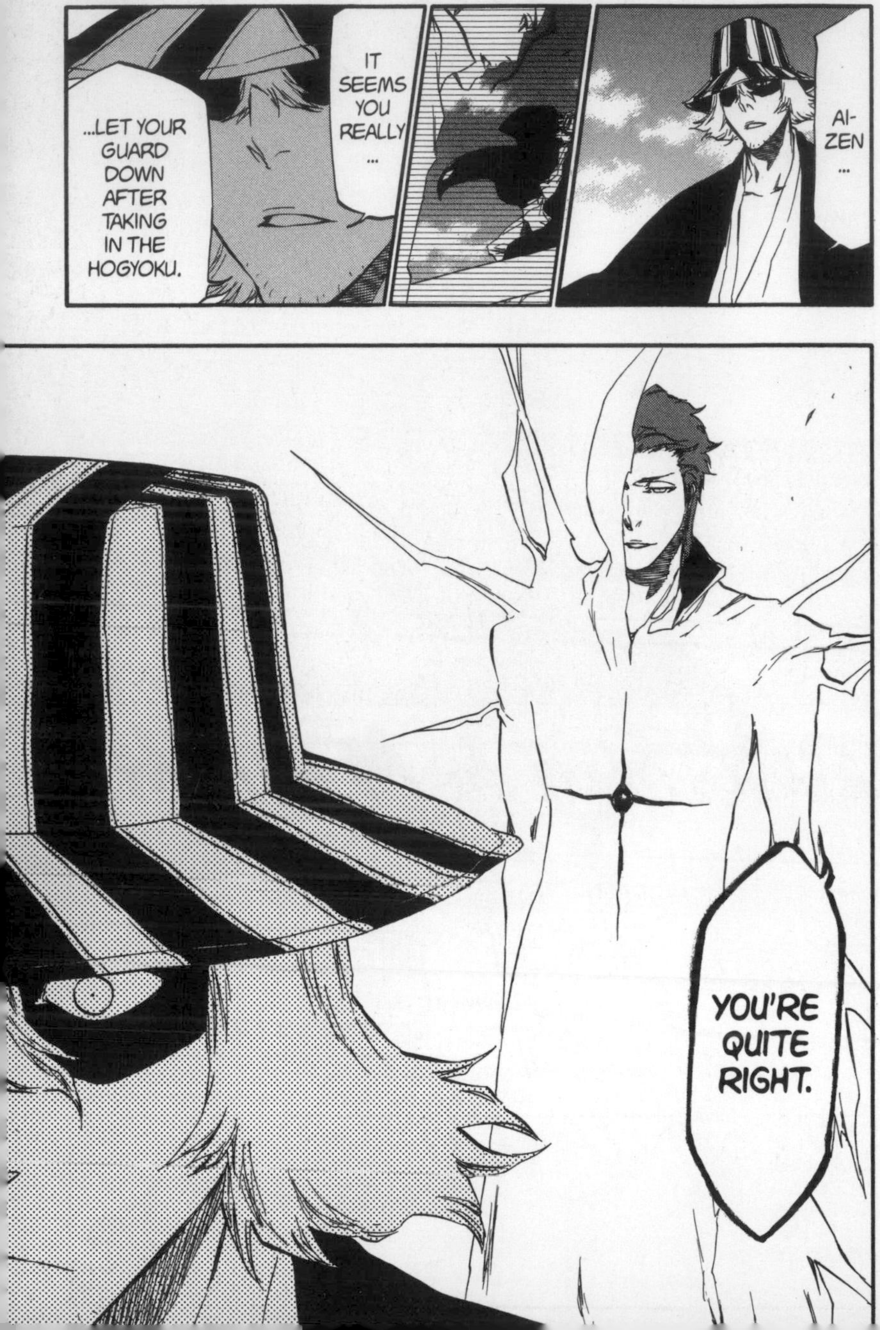
AI-ZEN ...
IT SEEMS YOU REALLY ...
...LET YOUR GUARD DOWN AFTER TAKING IN THE HOGYOKU.
YOU'RE QUITE RIGHT.

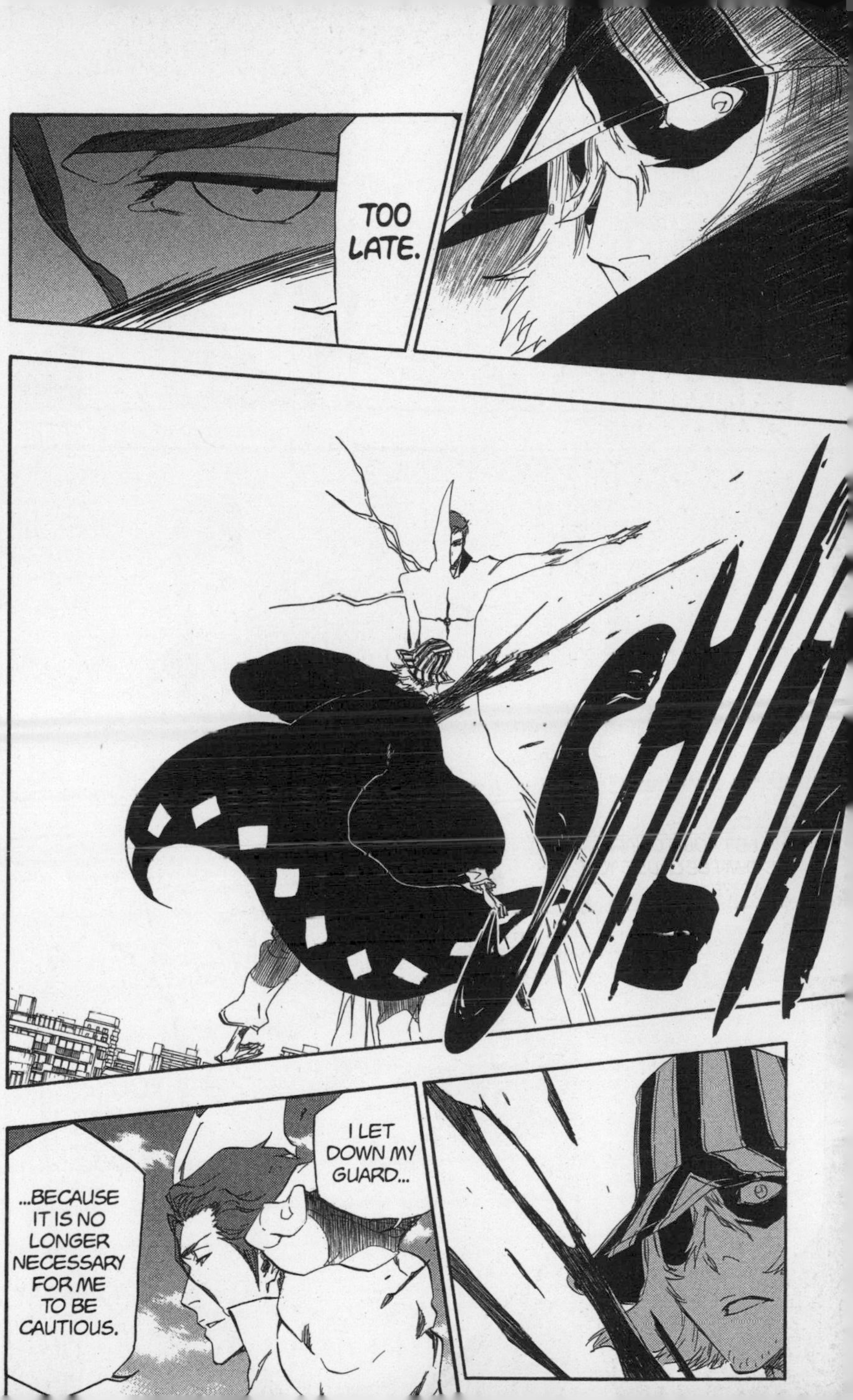
TOO LATE.
I LET DOWN MY GUARD...
...BECAUSE IT IS NO LONGER NECESSARY FOR ME TO BE CAUTIOUS.

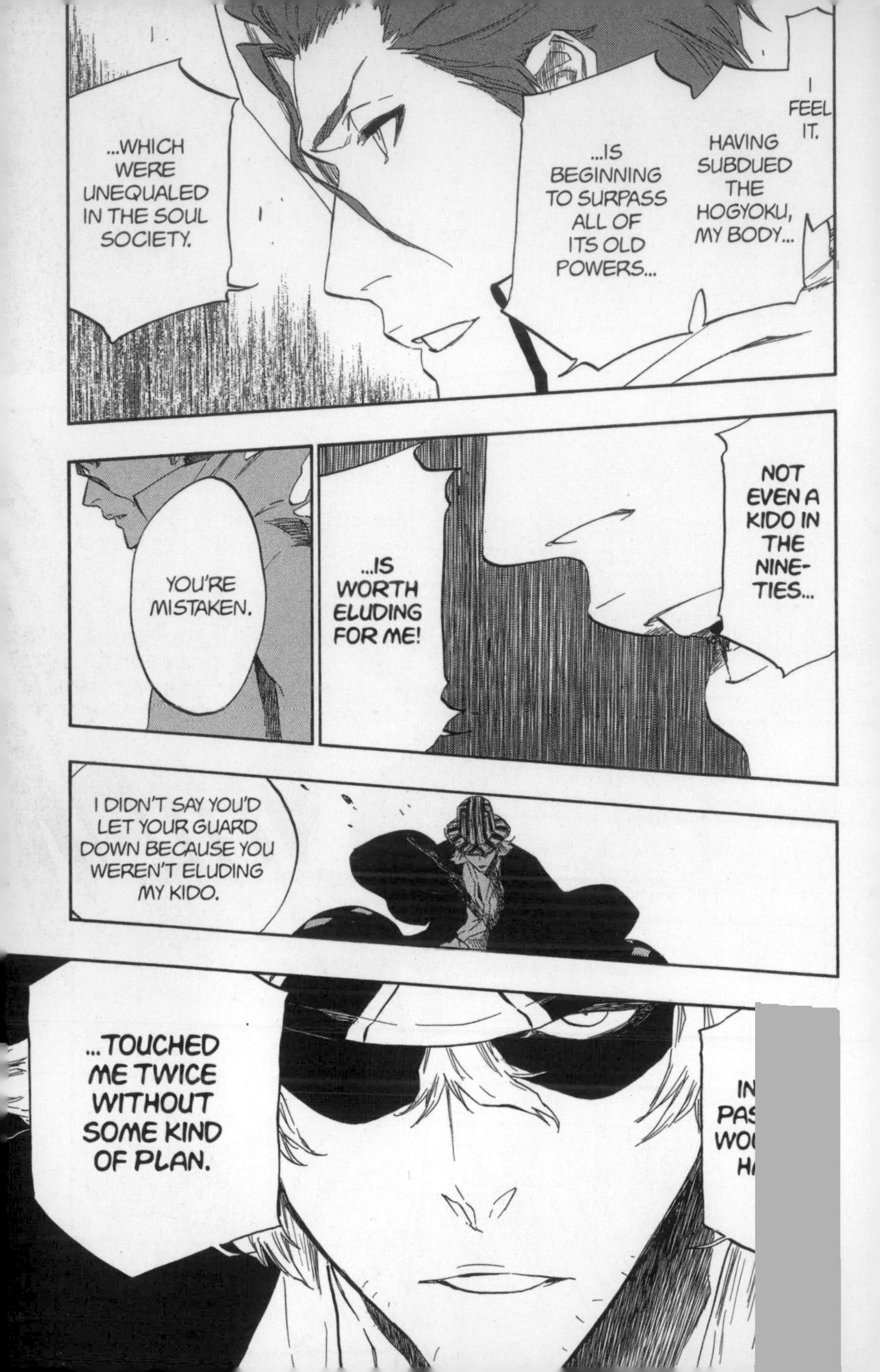
I FEEL IT.
HAVING SUBDUED THE HOGYOKU, MY BODY...
...IS BEGINNING TO SURPASS ALL OF ITS OLD POWERS...
...WHICH WERE UNEQUALED IN THE SOUL SOCIETY.
NOT EVEN A KIDO IN THE NINETIES...
...IS WORTH ELUDING FOR ME!
YOU'RE MISTAKEN.
I DIDN'T SAY YOU'D LET YOUR GUARD DOWN BECAUSE YOU WEREN'T ELUDING MY KIDO.
...TOUCHED ME TWICE WITHOUT SOME KIND OF PLAN.

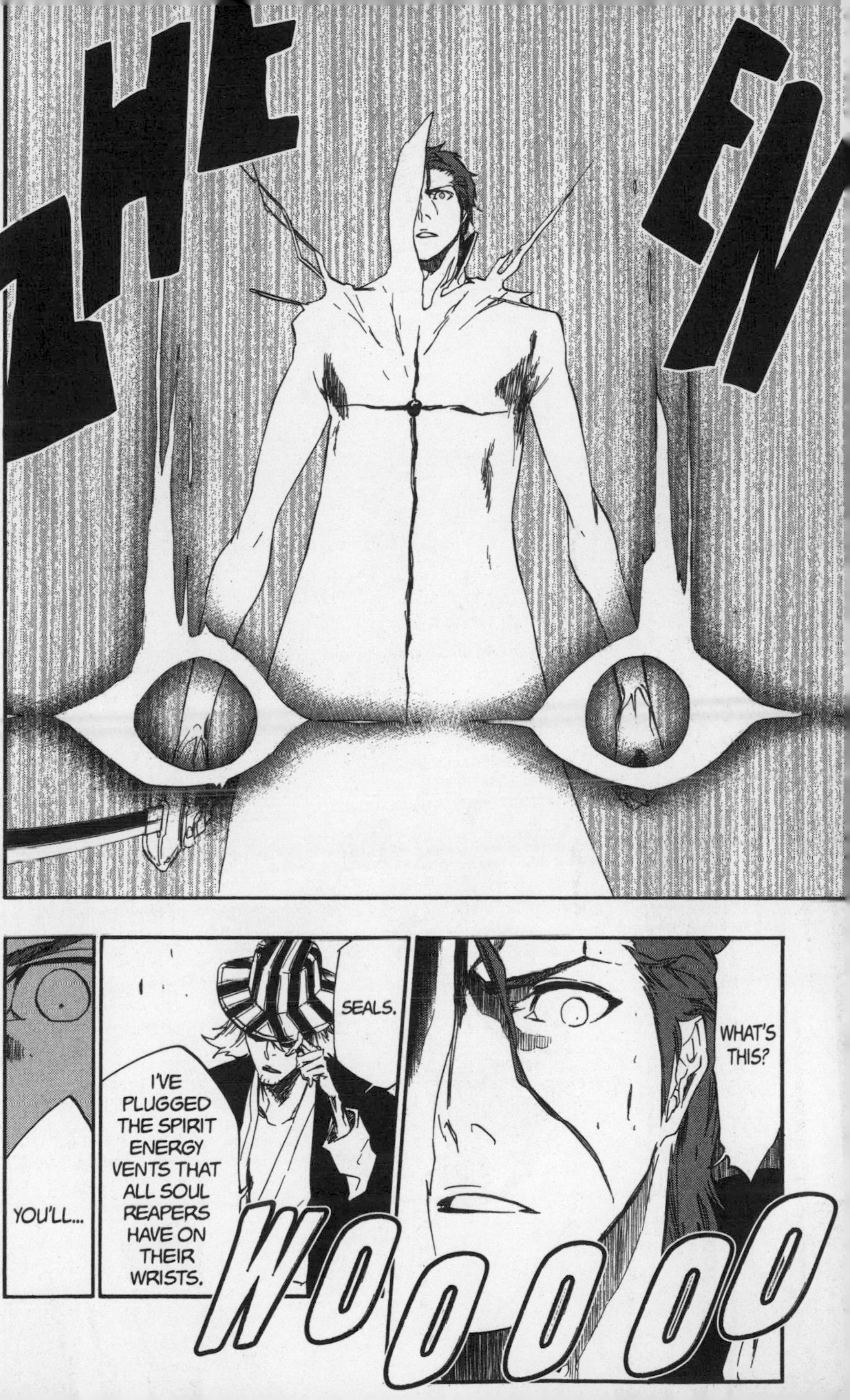
ZHE
EN
WHAT'S THIS?
SEALS.
I'VE PLUGGED THE SPIRIT ENERGY VENTS THAT ALL SOUL REAPERS HAVE ON THEIR WRISTS.
WOOOOOO
YOU'LL...

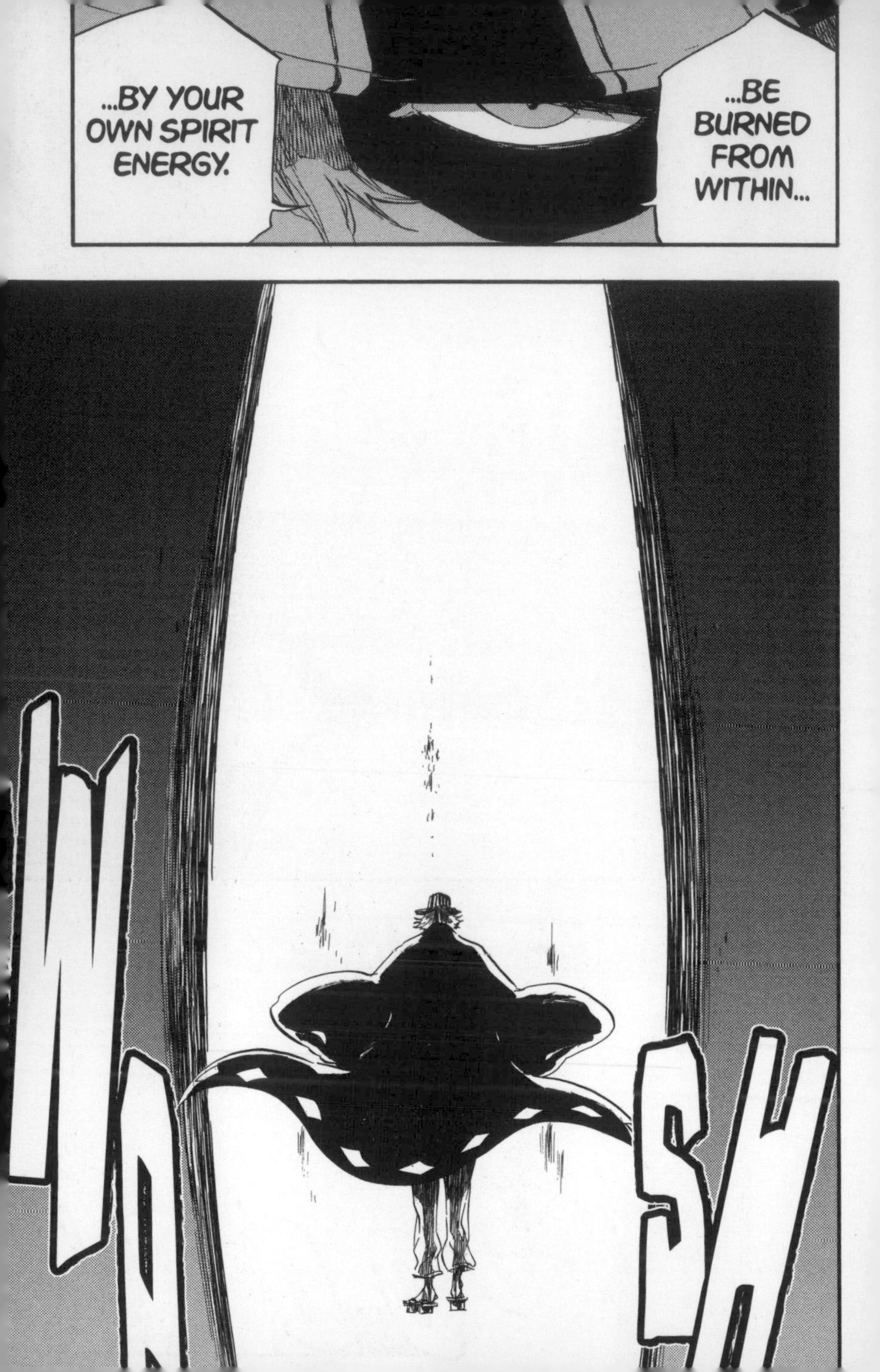
...BE BURNED FROM WITHIN...
...BY YOUR OWN SPIRIT ENERGY.

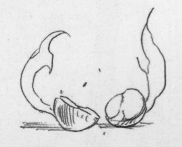

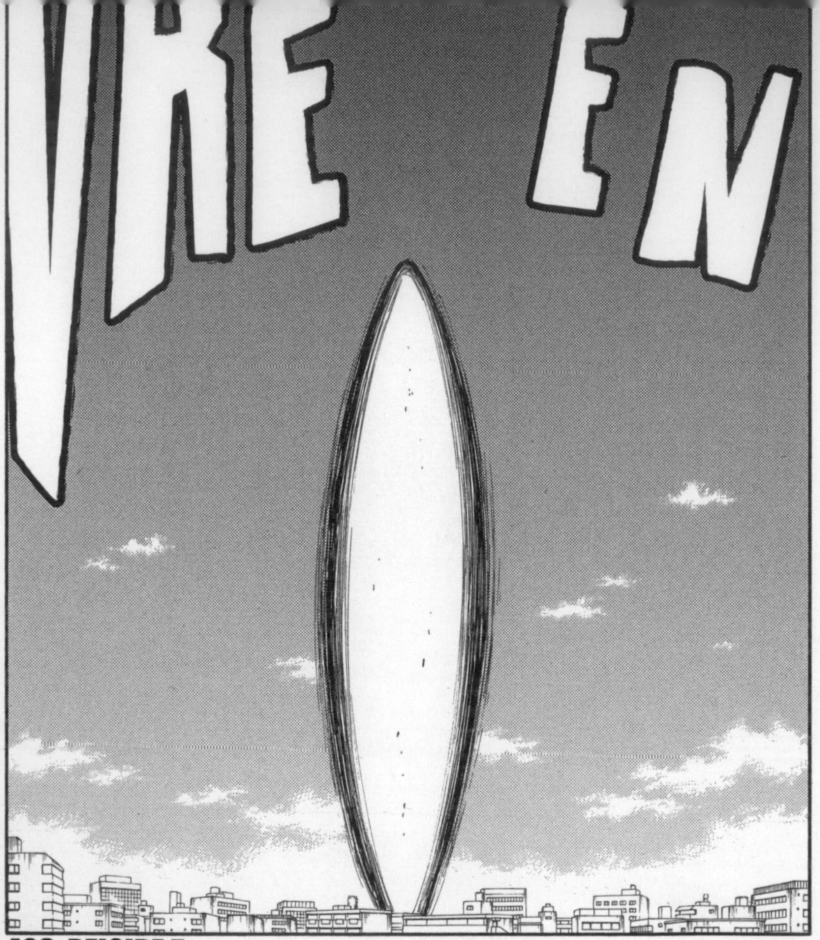
VRE EN

403. DEICIDE 5

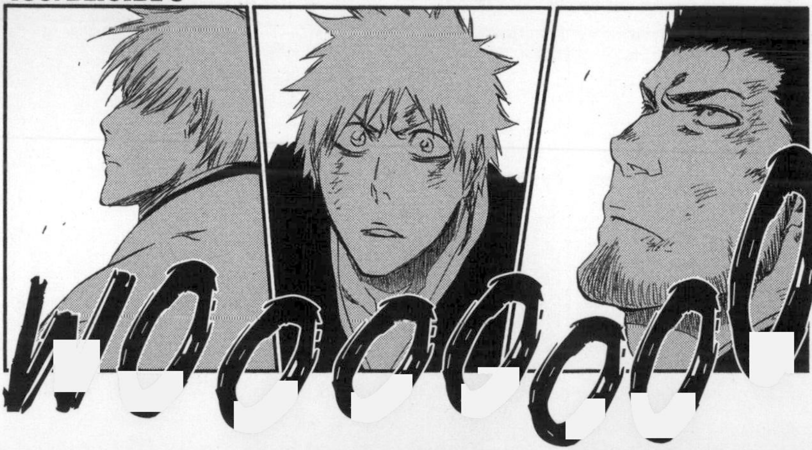
VOOOOOOO

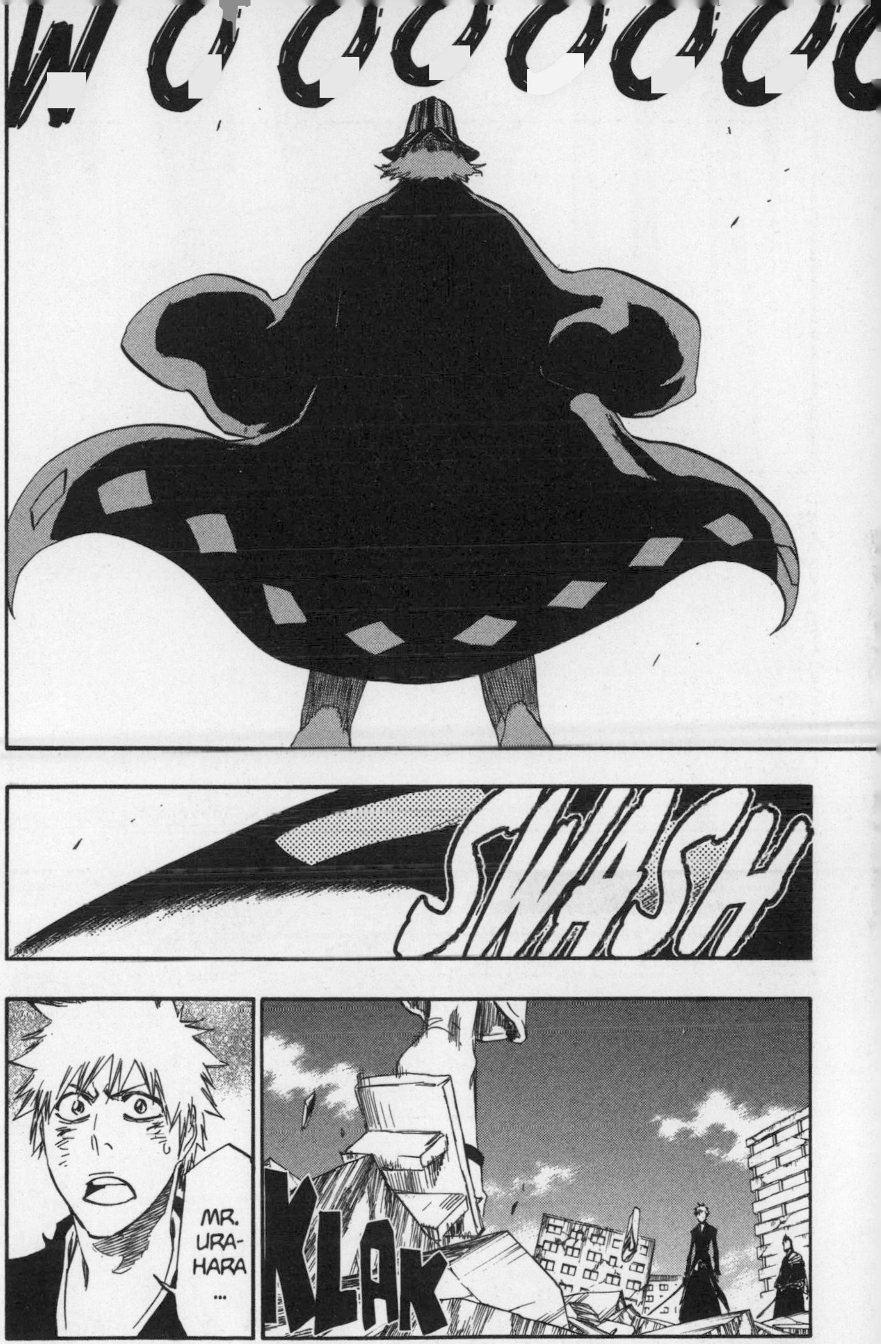
WOOOOOOO
SWASH
KLAK
MR. URA-HARA...

READ THIS WAY

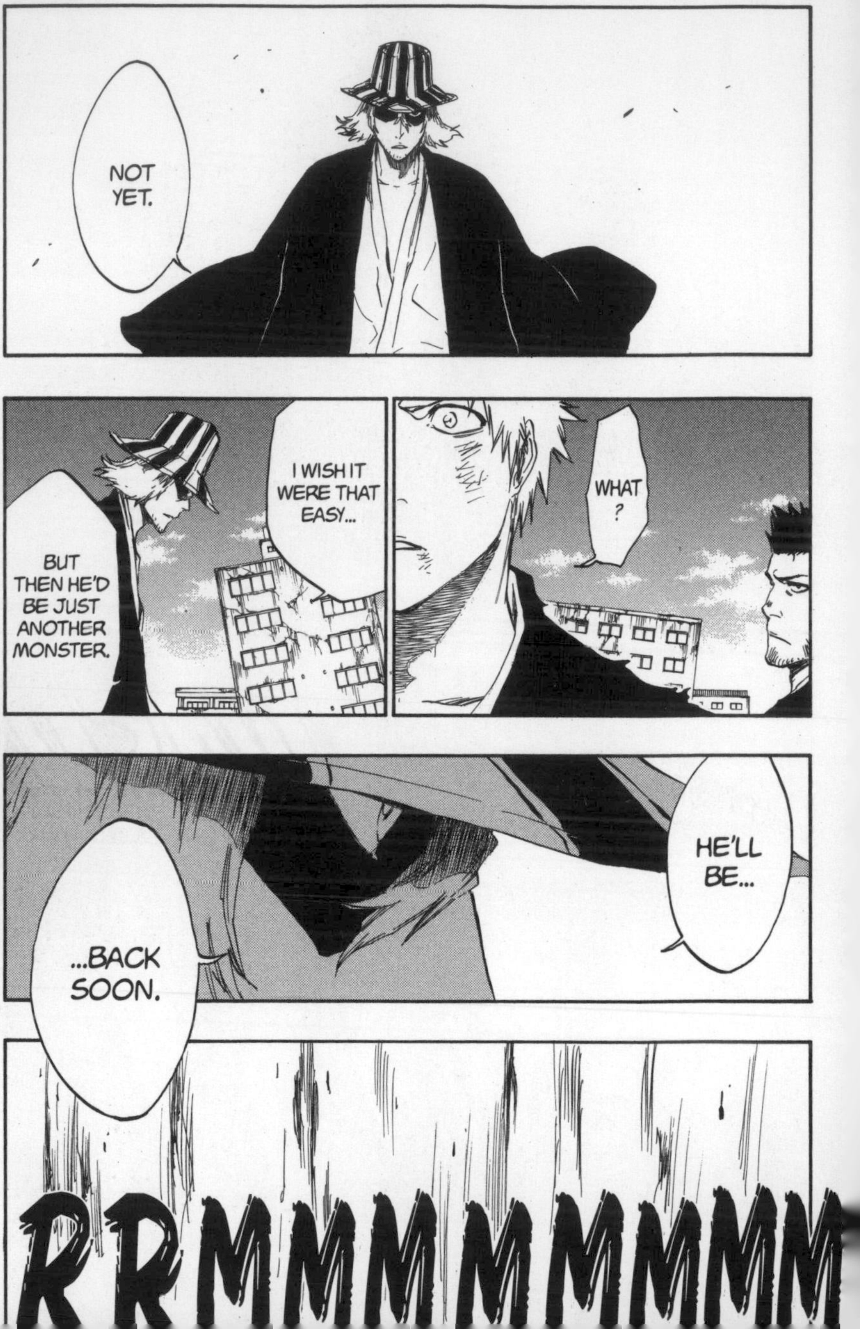
NOT YET.
WHAT?
I WISH IT WERE THAT EASY...
BUT THEN HE'D BE JUST ANOTHER MONSTER.
HE'LL BE...
...BACK SOON.
RRMMMMMMMM

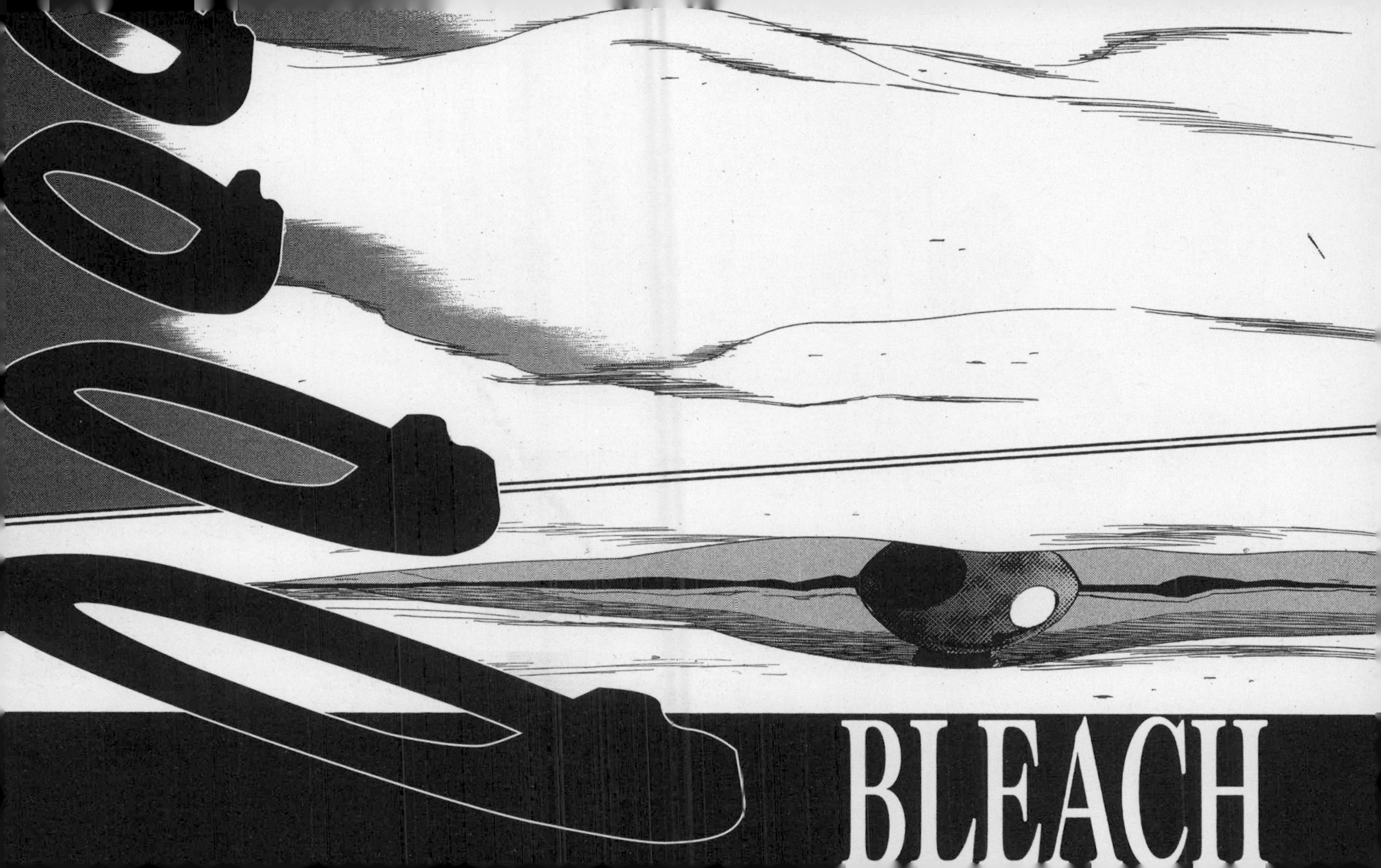
BLEACH

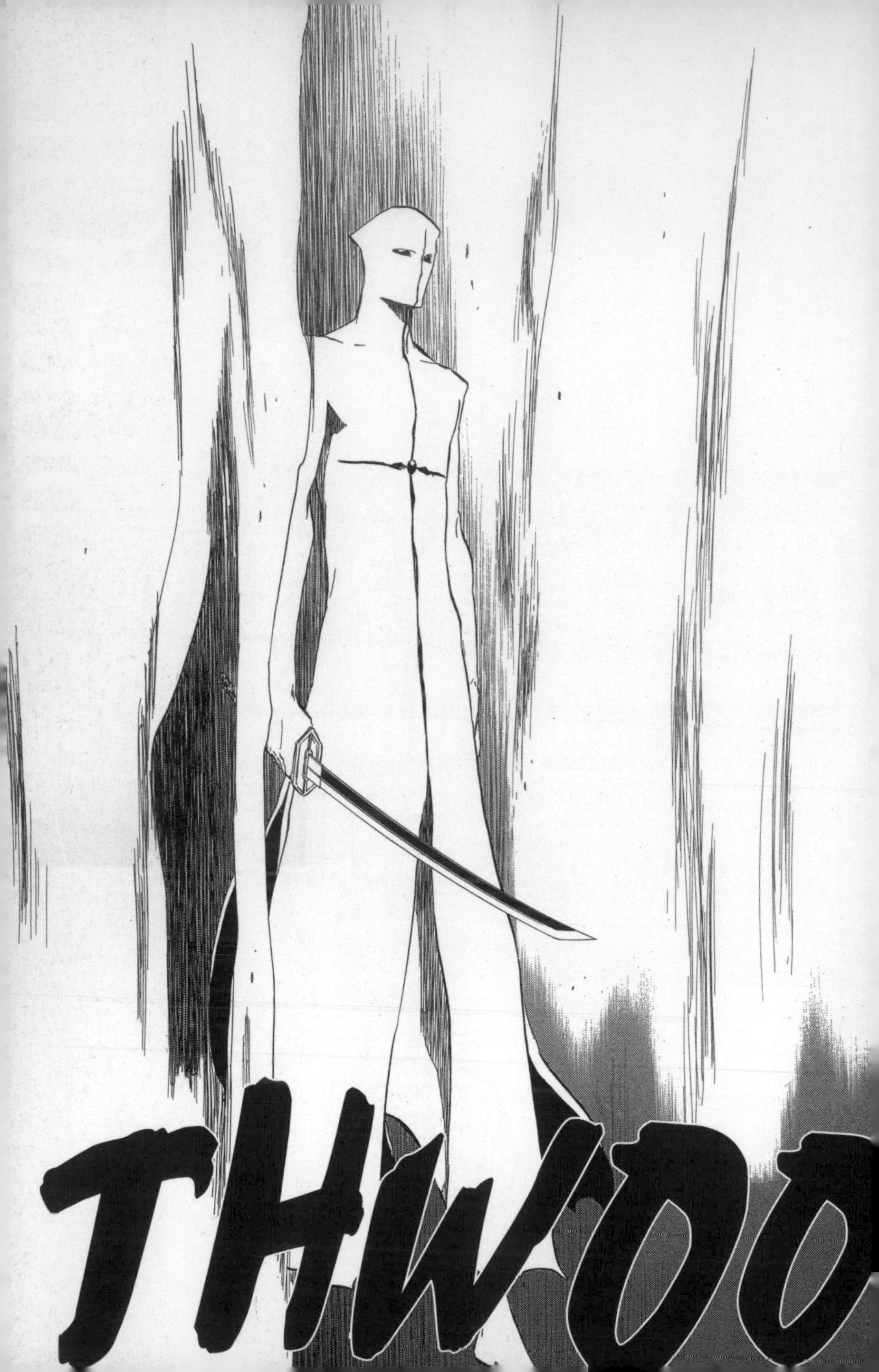
THWOOO

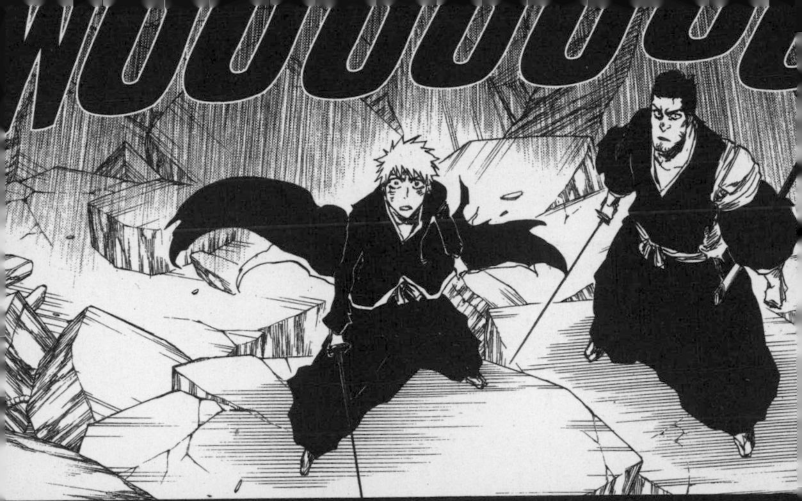

403.

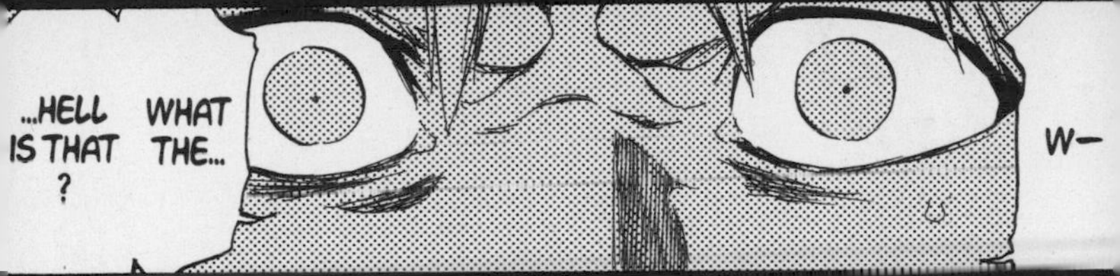
W—
WHAT THE...
...HELL IS THAT?

DEICIDE 5

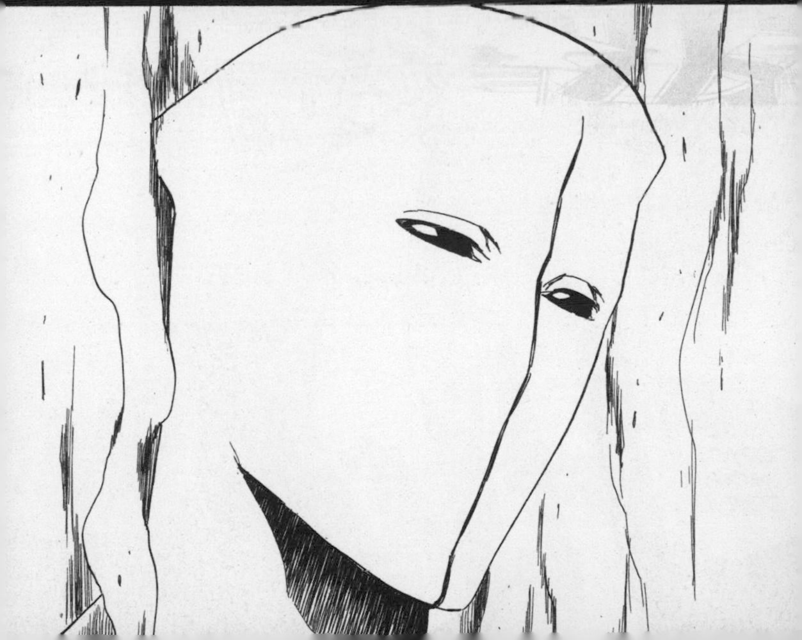

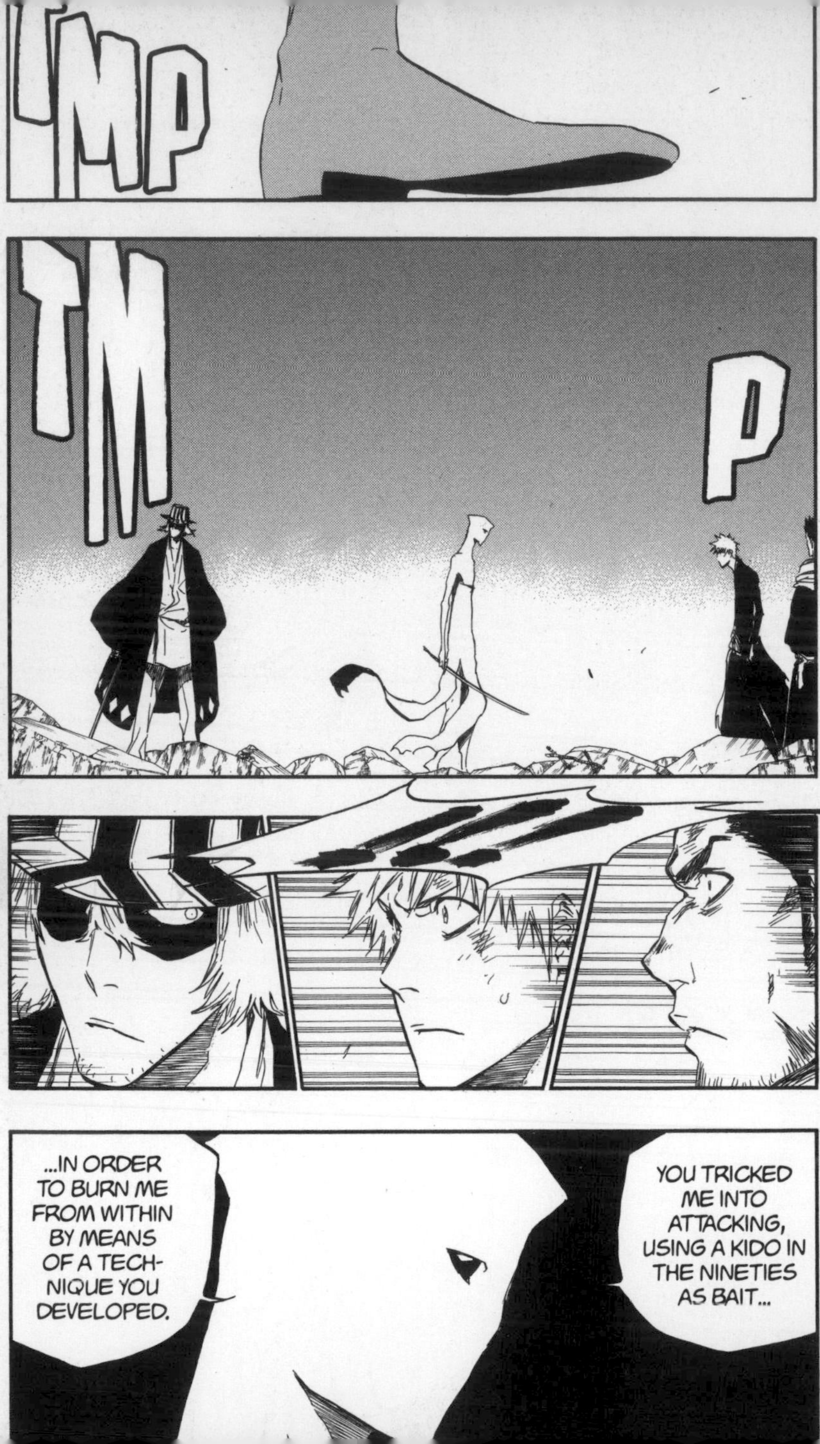
TMP
YOU TRICKED ME INTO ATTACKING, USING A KIDO IN THE NINETIES AS BAIT...
...IN ORDER TO BURN ME FROM WITHIN BY MEANS OF A TECH-NIQUE YOU DEVELOPED.

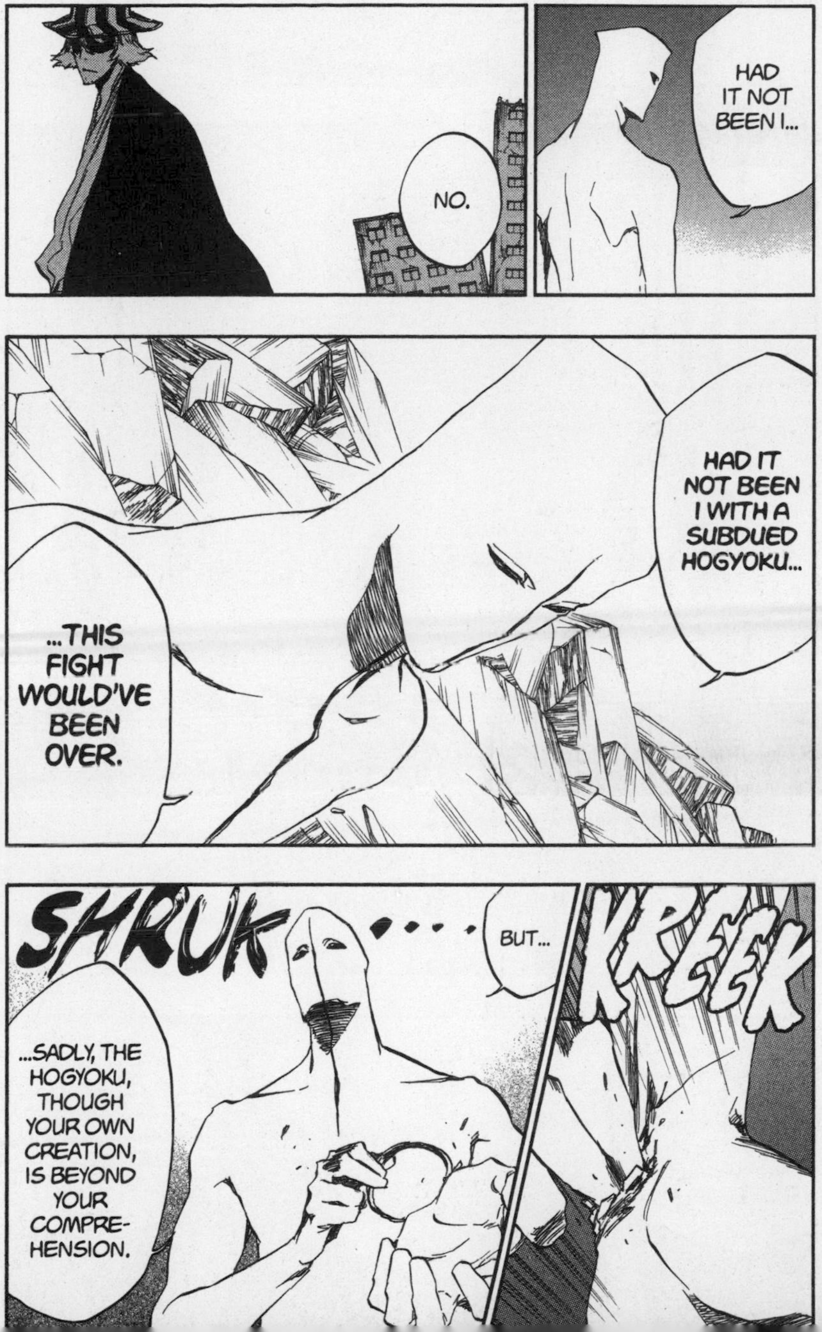
HAD IT NOT BEEN I...
NO.
HAD IT NOT BEEN I WITH A SUBDUED HOGYOKU...
...THIS FIGHT WOULD'VE BEEN OVER.
KREEK
BUT...
SHRUK
...SADLY, THE HOGYOKU, THOUGH YOUR OWN CREATION, IS BEYOND YOUR COMPRE-HENSION.

READ THIS WAY

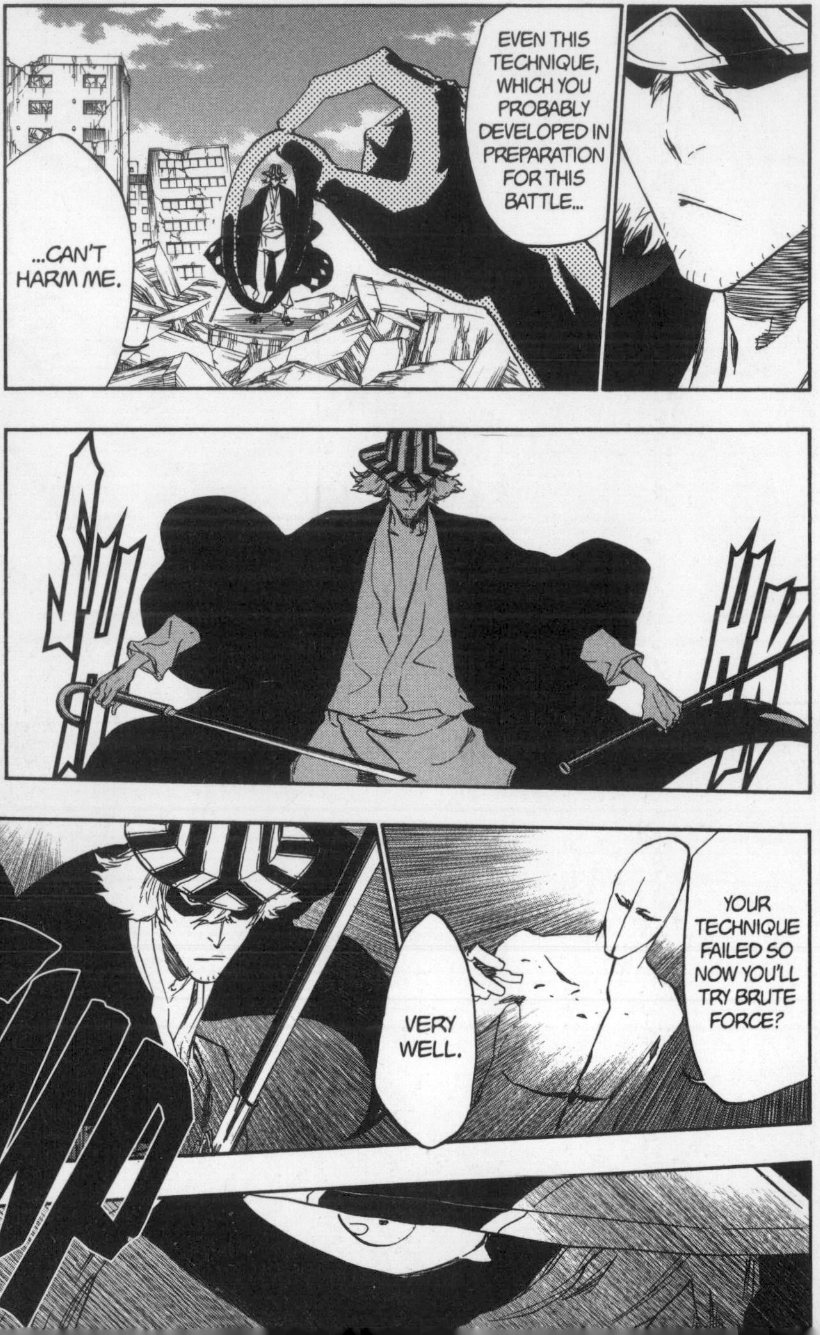
EVEN THIS TECHNIQUE, WHICH YOU PROBABLY DEVELOPED IN PREPARATION FOR THIS BATTLE...
...CAN'T HARM ME.
YOUR TECHNIQUE FAILED SO NOW YOU'LL TRY BRUTE FORCE?
VERY WELL.

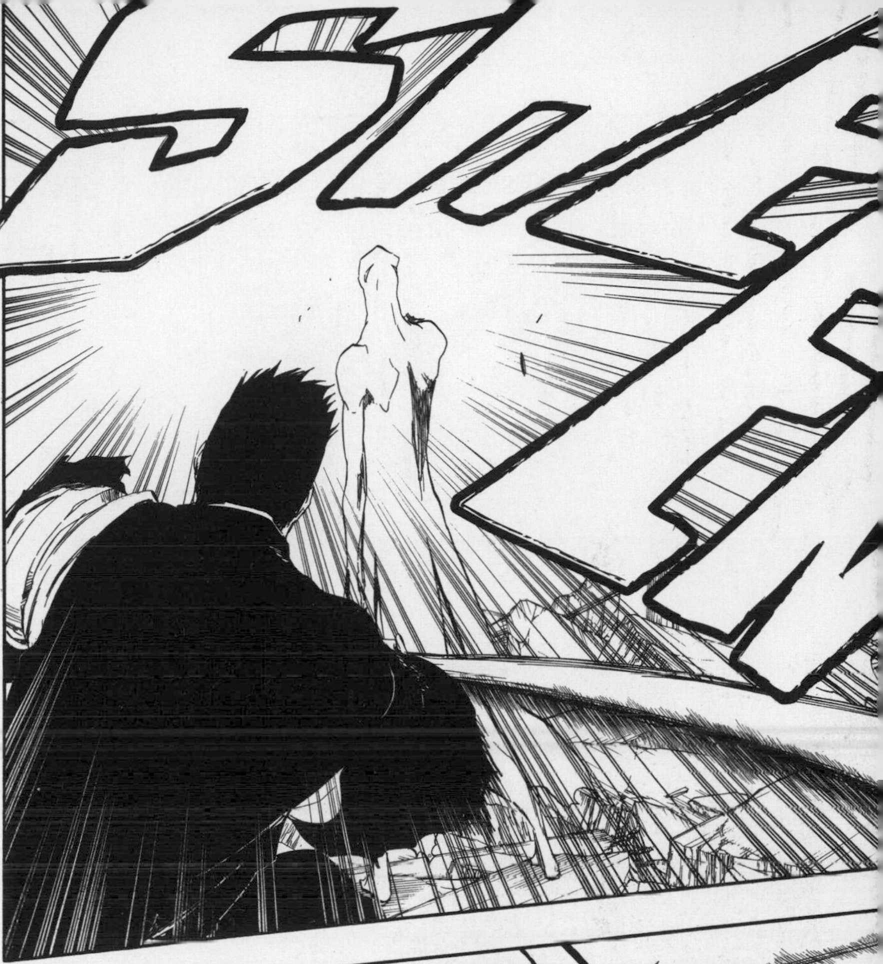
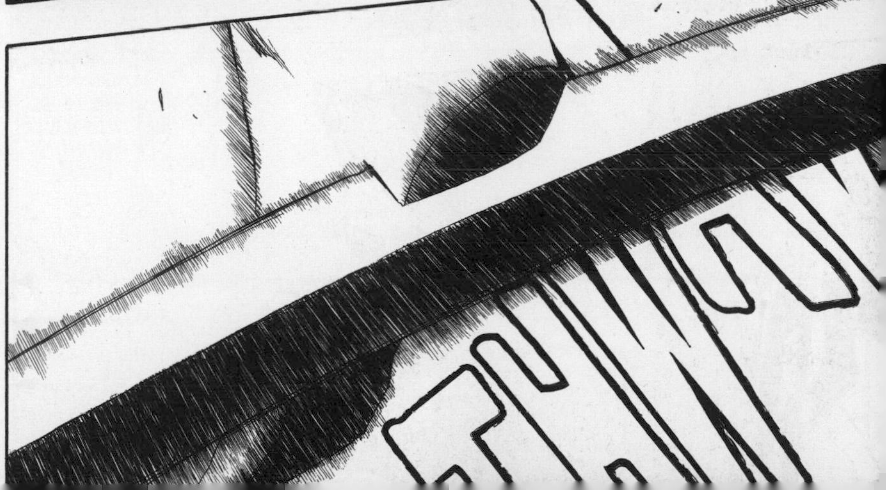

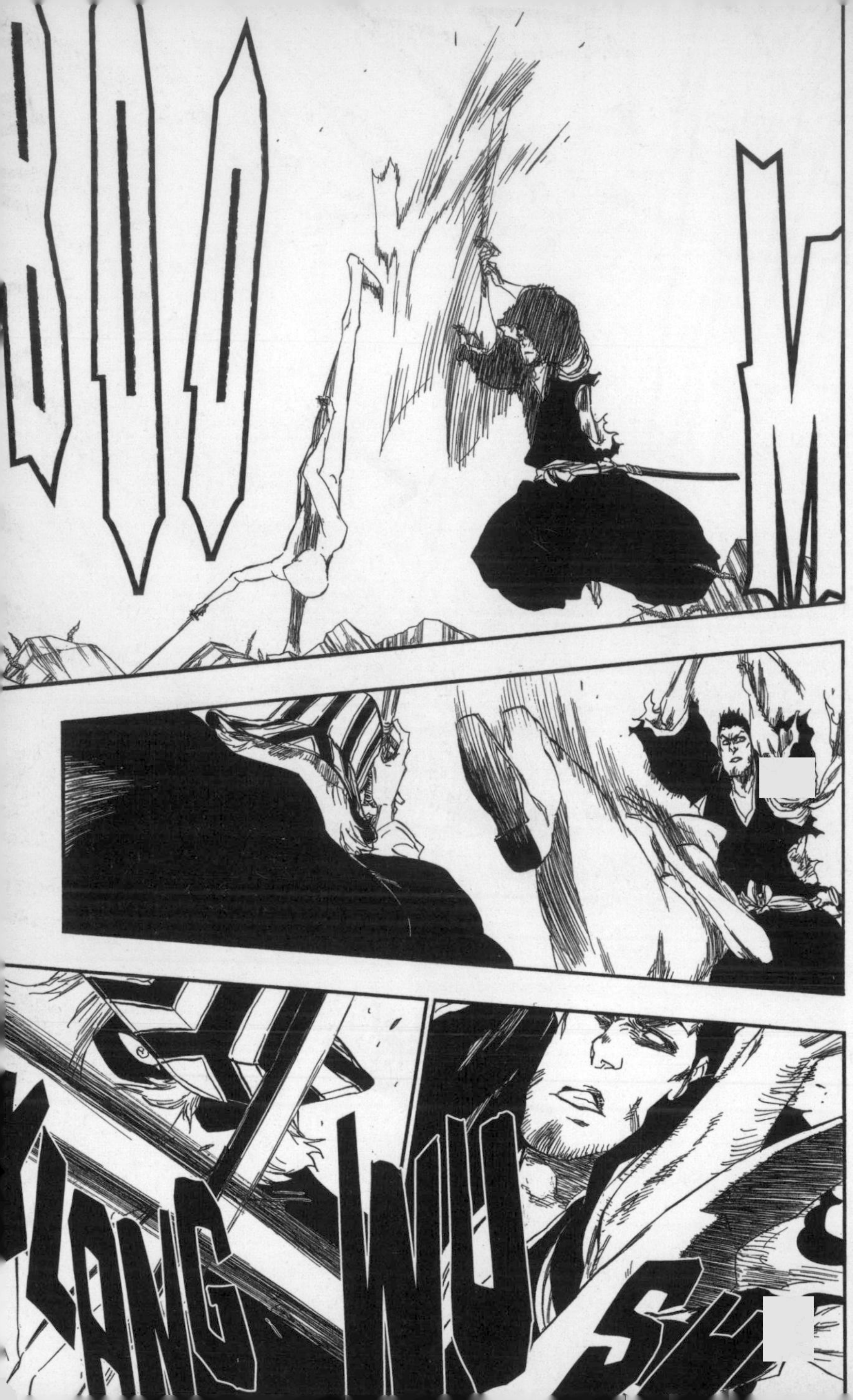
BOOM
KLANG

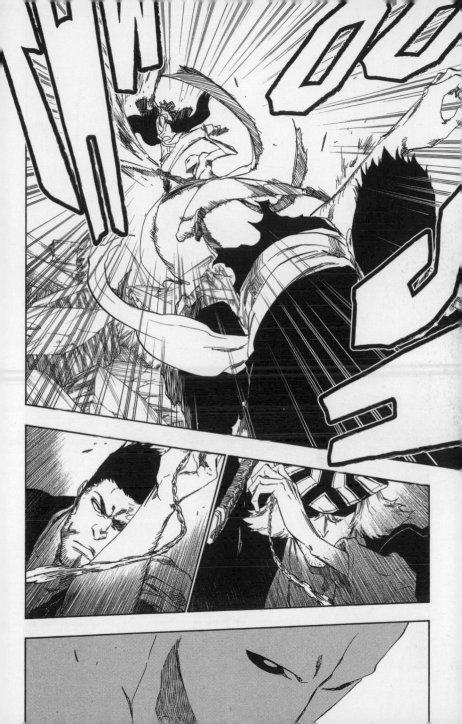

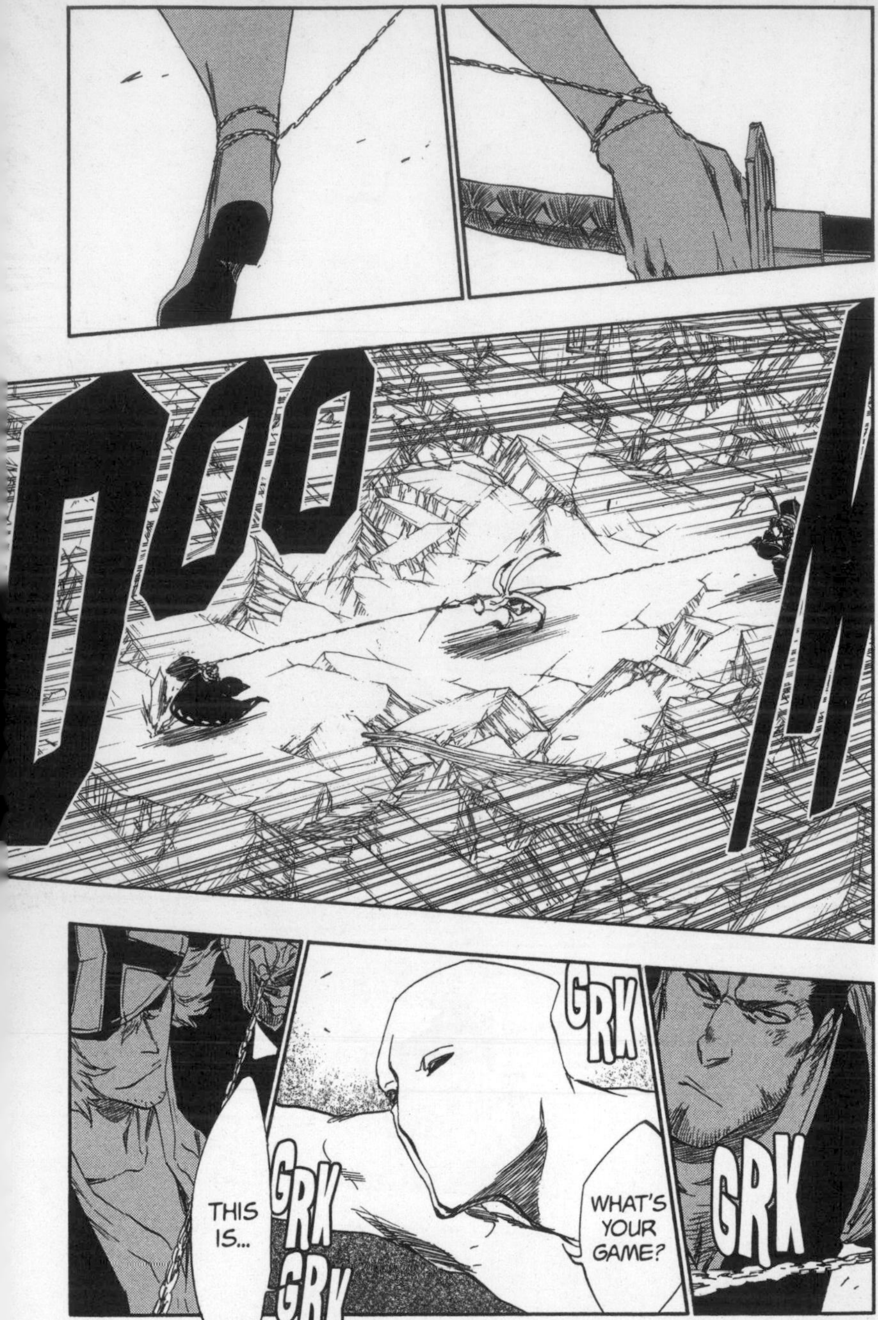
DOOM
GRK
GRK
WHAT'S YOUR GAME?
GRK GRK
THIS IS...

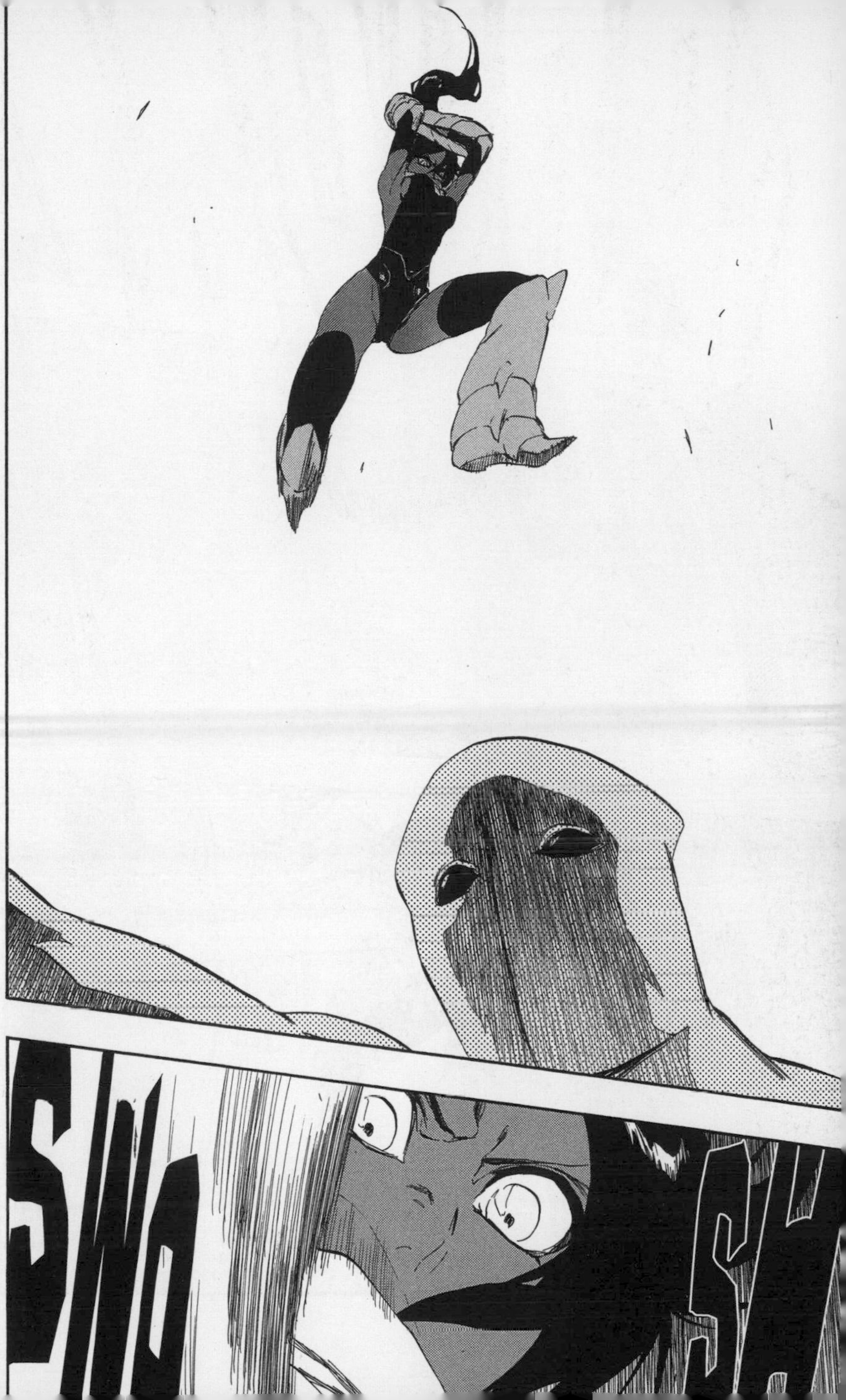
SH
SWO

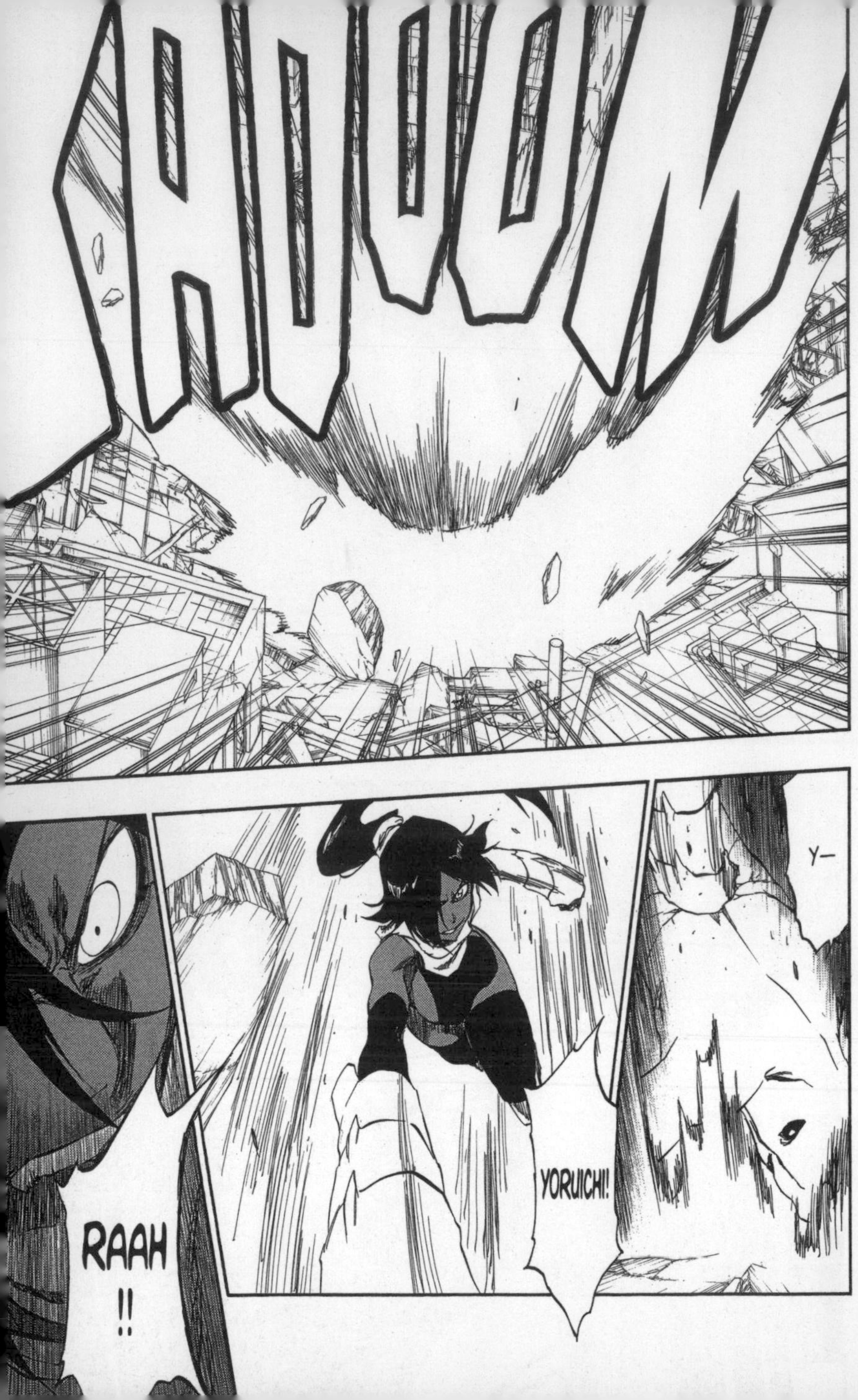
Y—
YORUICHI!
RAAH
!!

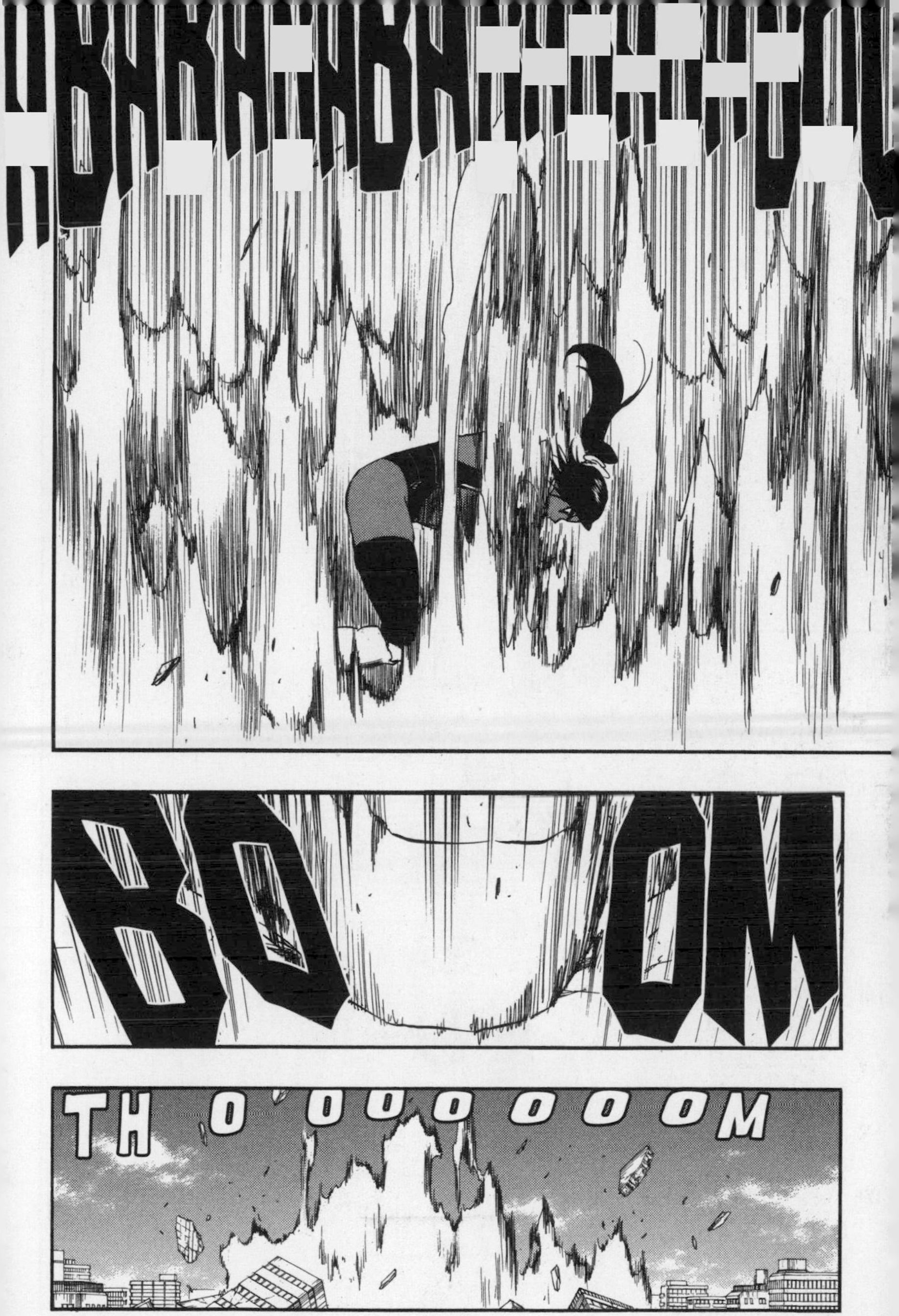
THOOOOOOOM

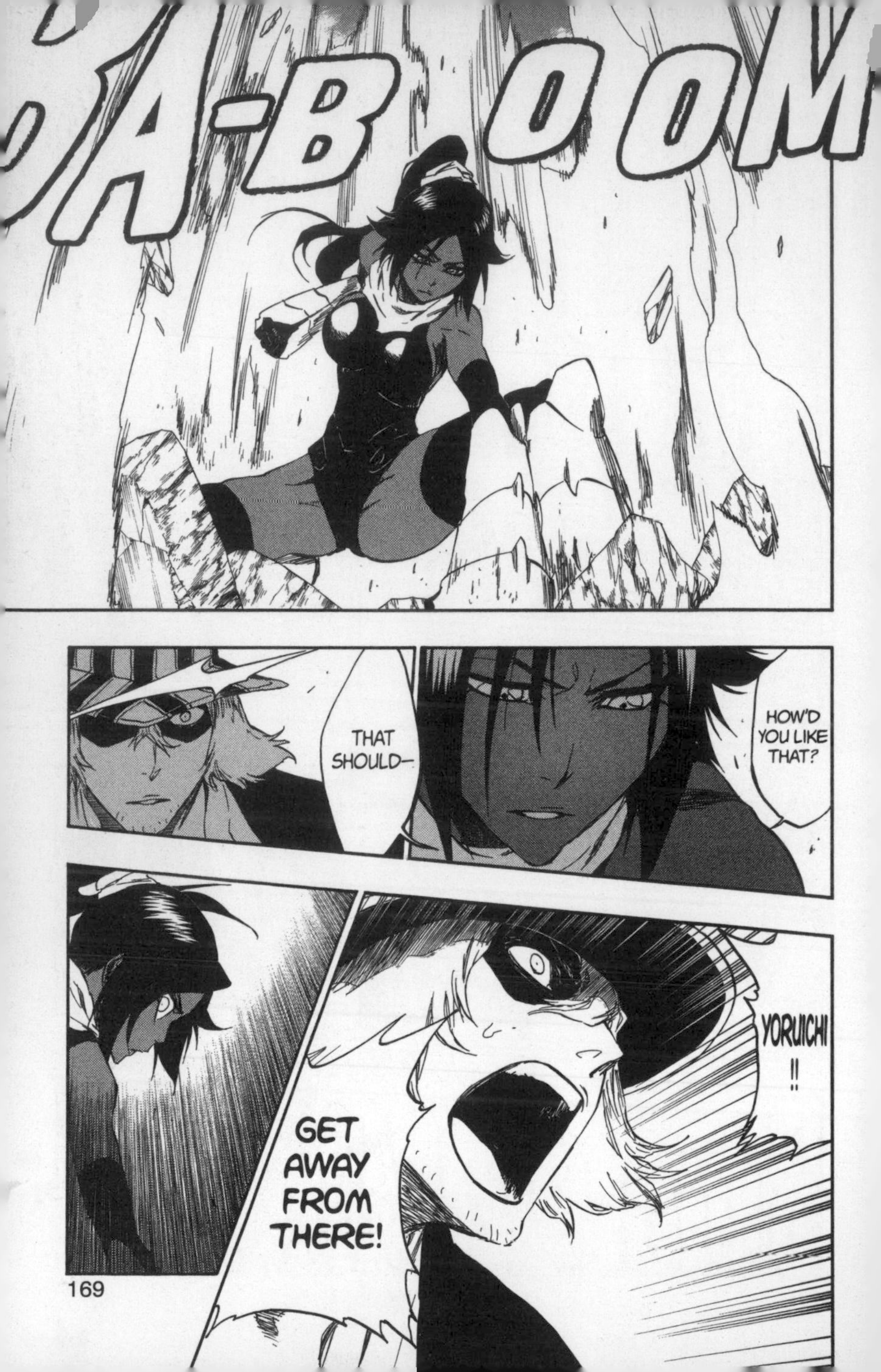
A-BOOM
HOW'D YOU LIKE THAT?
THAT SHOULD—
YORUICHI !!
GET AWAY FROM THERE!

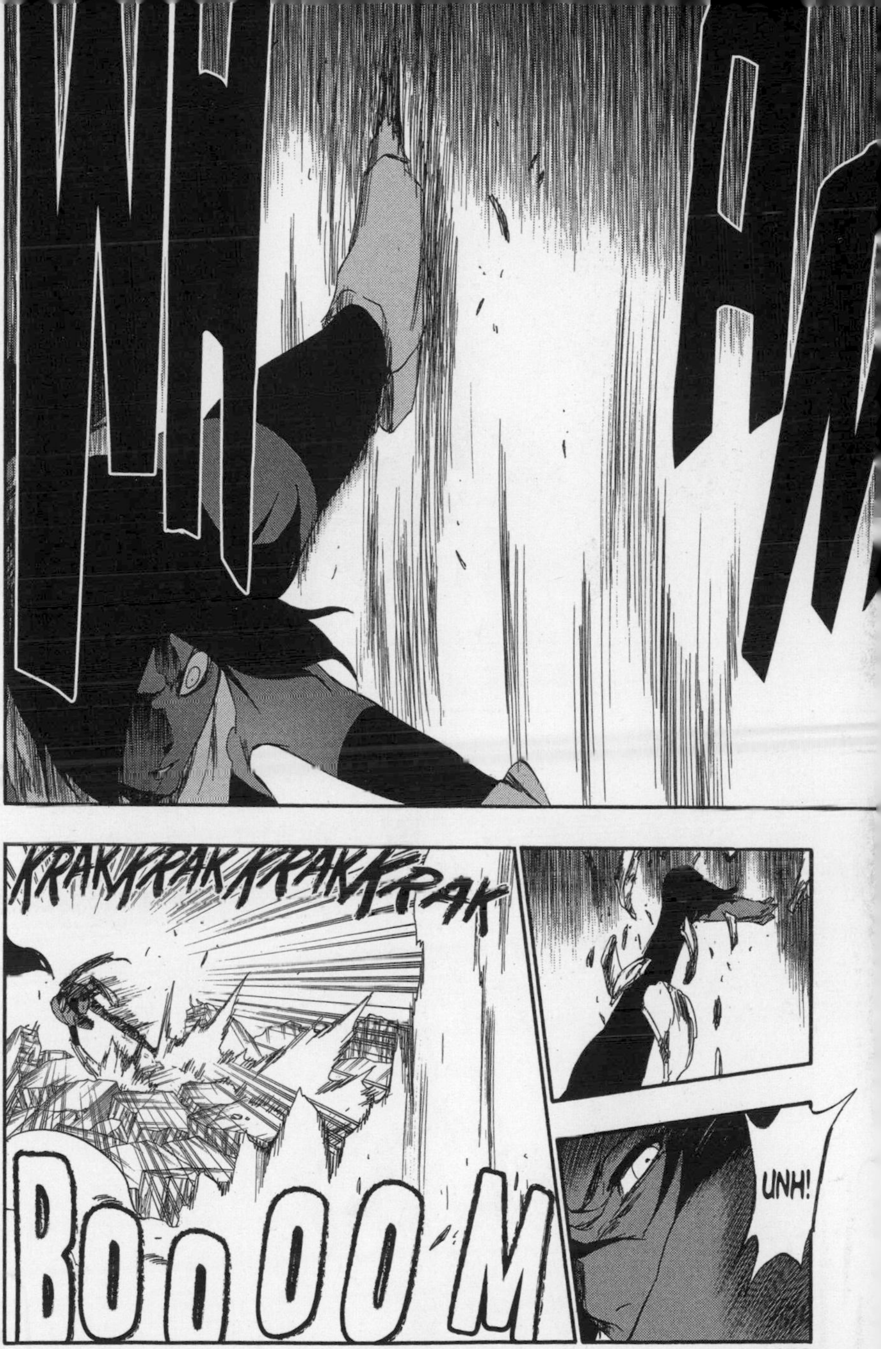
UNH!
KRAKKRAKKRAKKRAK
BOOOOM

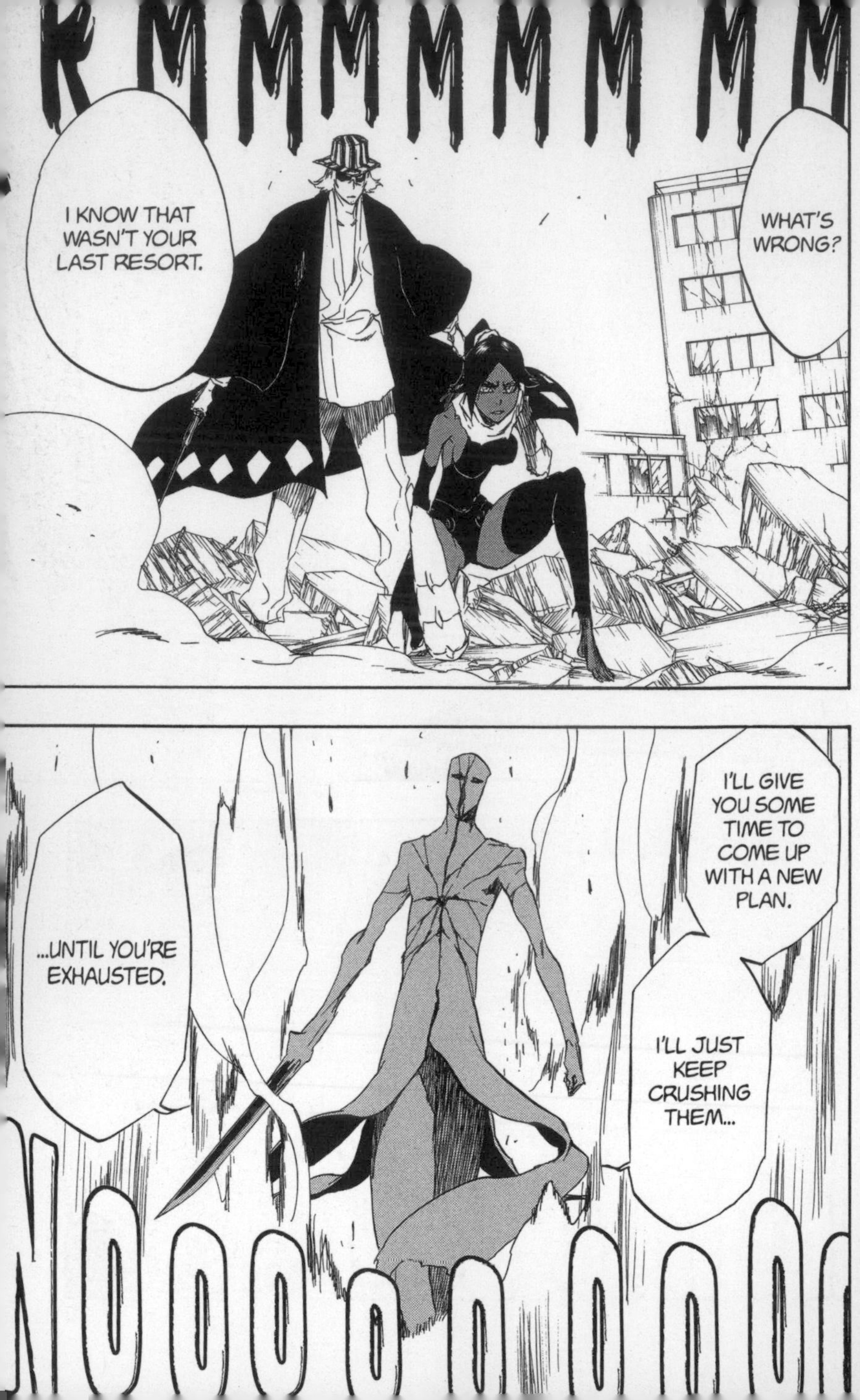
RMMMMMMMM
WHAT'S WRONG?
I KNOW THAT WASN'T YOUR LAST RESORT.
I'LL GIVE YOU SOME TIME TO COME UP WITH A NEW PLAN.
I'LL JUST KEEP CRUSHING THEM...
...UNTIL YOU'RE EXHAUSTED.
NOOOOOOOOOO

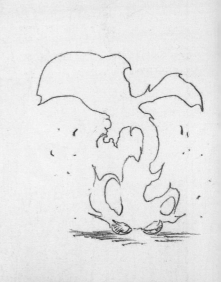

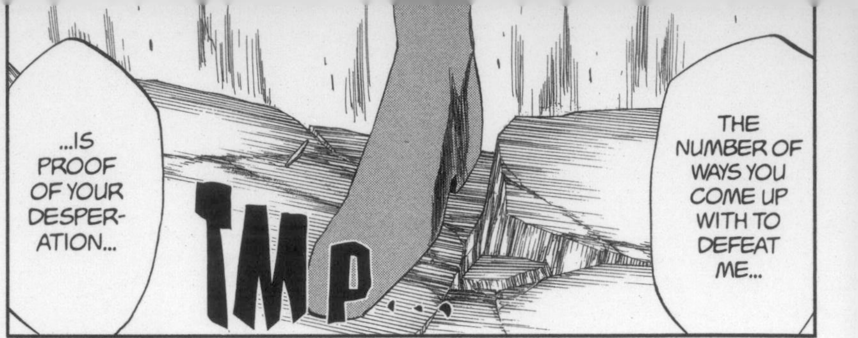
THE NUMBER OF WAYS YOU COME UP WITH TO DEFEAT ME...
...IS PROOF OF YOUR DESPER-ATION...
TMP...

404. DEICIDE 6

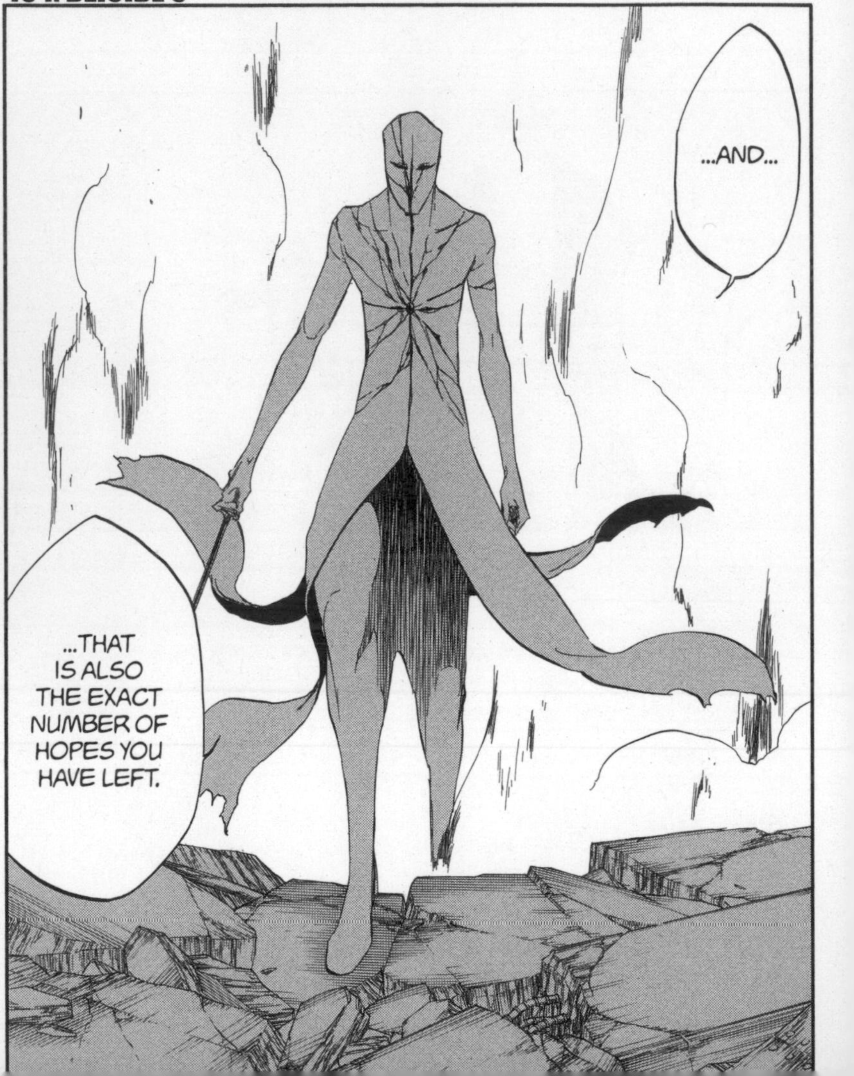
...AND...
...THAT IS ALSO THE EXACT NUMBER OF HOPES YOU HAVE LEFT.

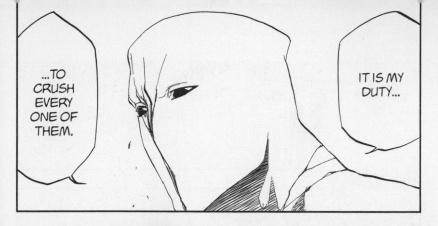

IT IS MY DUTY...
...TO CRUSH EVERY ONE OF THEM.
NOW MAKE YOUR NEXT MOVE...
...KISUKE URAHARA...
...YORUICHI SHIHOIN...
...AND...
...ISSHIN KUROSAKI.

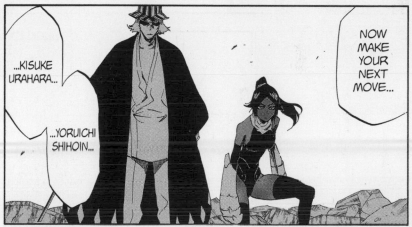

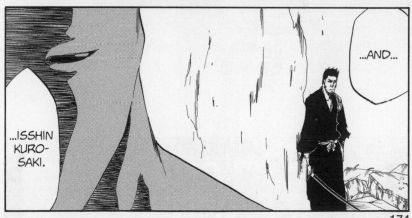

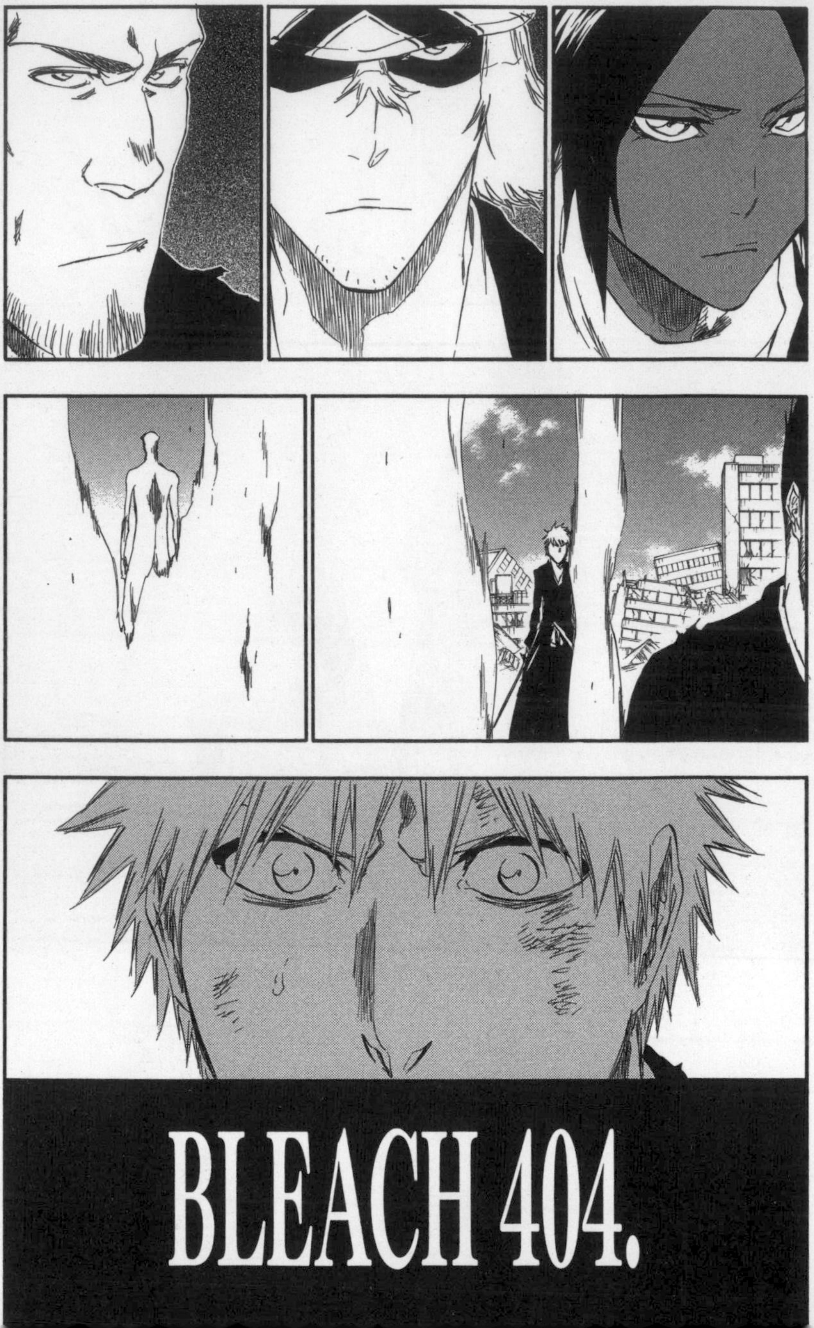
BLEACH 404.

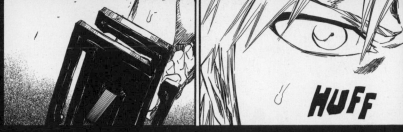

DEICIDE

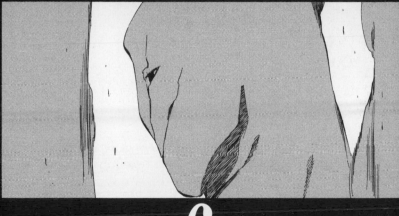

6

THIS IS A
PROBLEM.

WELL
...

READ THIS WAY

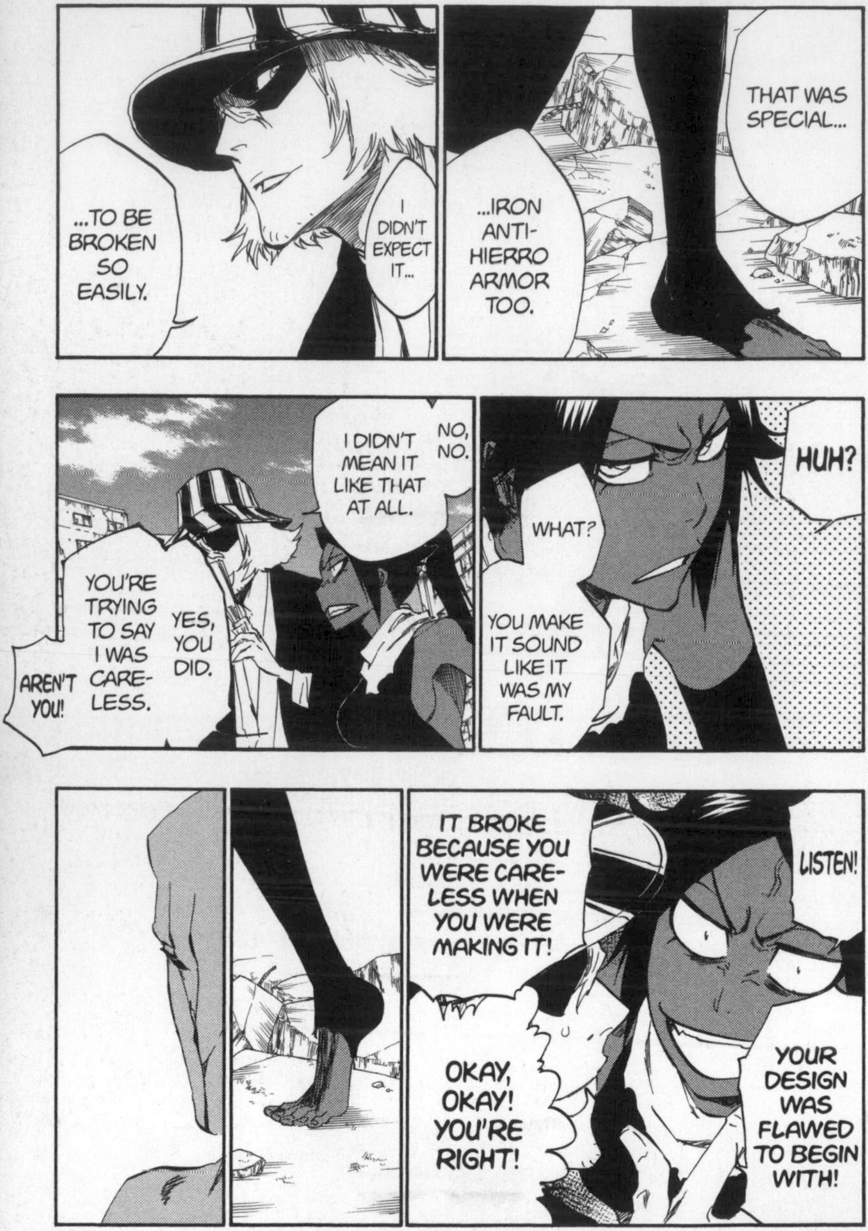
THAT WAS SPECIAL...
...IRON ANTI-HIERRO ARMOR TOO.
I DIDN'T EXPECT IT...
...TO BE BROKEN SO EASILY.
HUH?
WHAT?
YOU MAKE IT SOUND LIKE IT WAS MY FAULT.
NO, NO.
I DIDN'T MEAN IT LIKE THAT AT ALL.
YES, YOU DID.
YOU'RE TRYING TO SAY I WAS CARE-LESS.
AREN'T YOU!
LISTEN!
IT BROKE BECAUSE YOU WERE CARE-LESS WHEN YOU WERE MAKING IT!
YOUR DESIGN WAS FLAWED TO BEGIN WITH!
OKAY, OKAY! YOU'RE RIGHT!

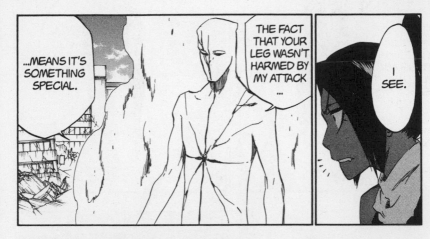

I SEE.
THE FACT THAT YOUR LEG WASN'T HARMED BY MY ATTACK ...
...MEANS IT'S SOMETHING SPECIAL.
YEAH, MY LEG.
BONK
WHAT'S THAT LOOK ON YOUR FACE?!
NOT MY NOSE!!
TMP

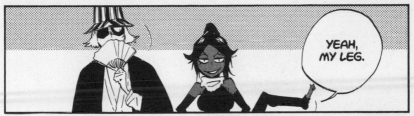

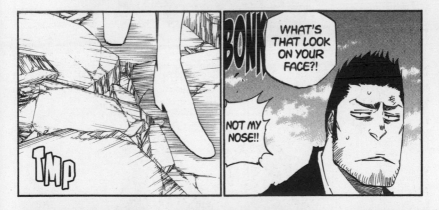

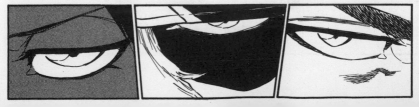

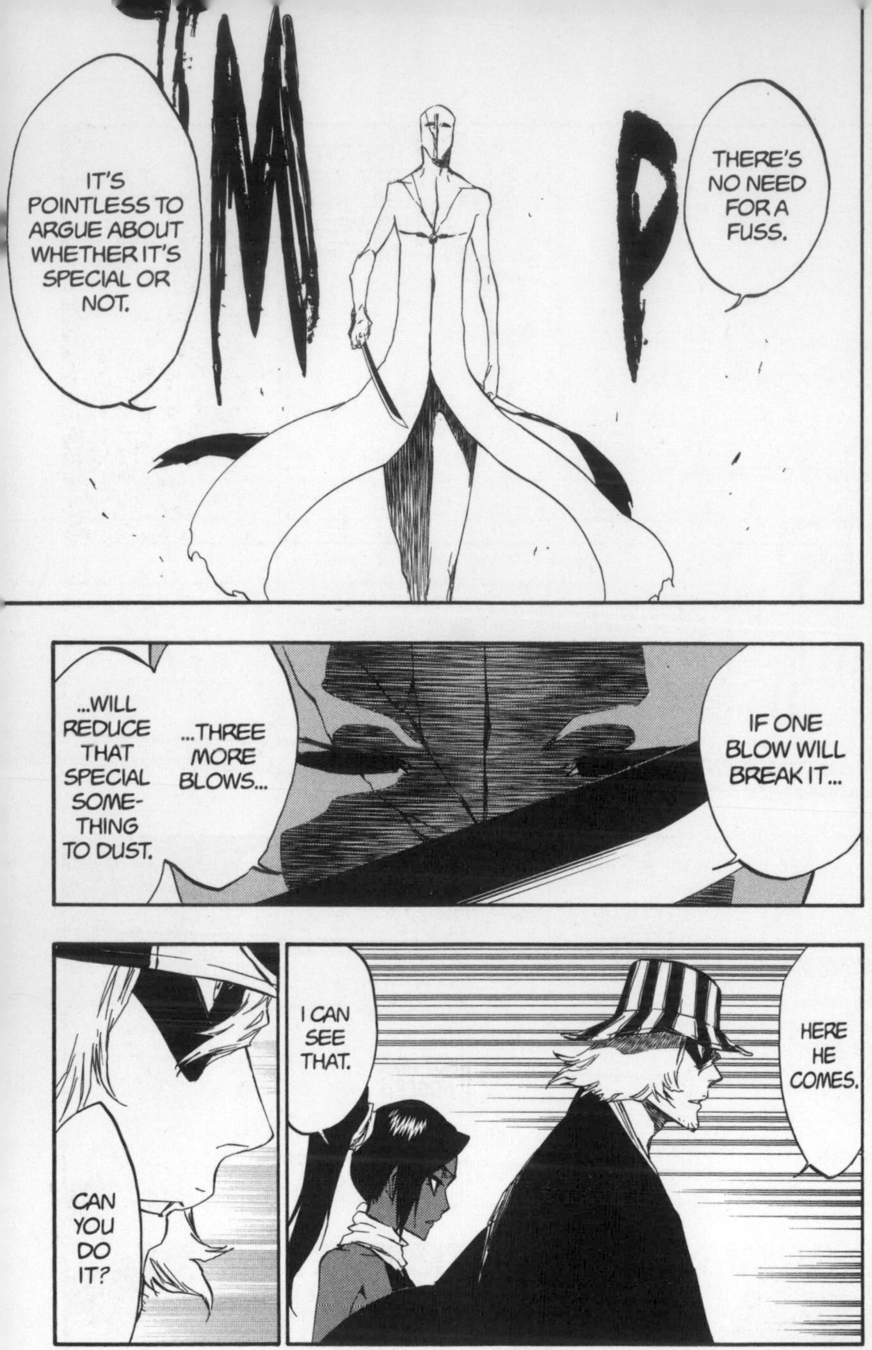
THERE'S NO NEED FOR A FUSS.
IT'S POINTLESS TO ARGUE ABOUT WHETHER IT'S SPECIAL OR NOT.
IF ONE BLOW WILL BREAK IT...
...THREE MORE BLOWS...
...WILL REDUCE THAT SPECIAL SOME-THING TO DUST.
HERE HE COMES.
I CAN SEE THAT.
CAN YOU DO IT?

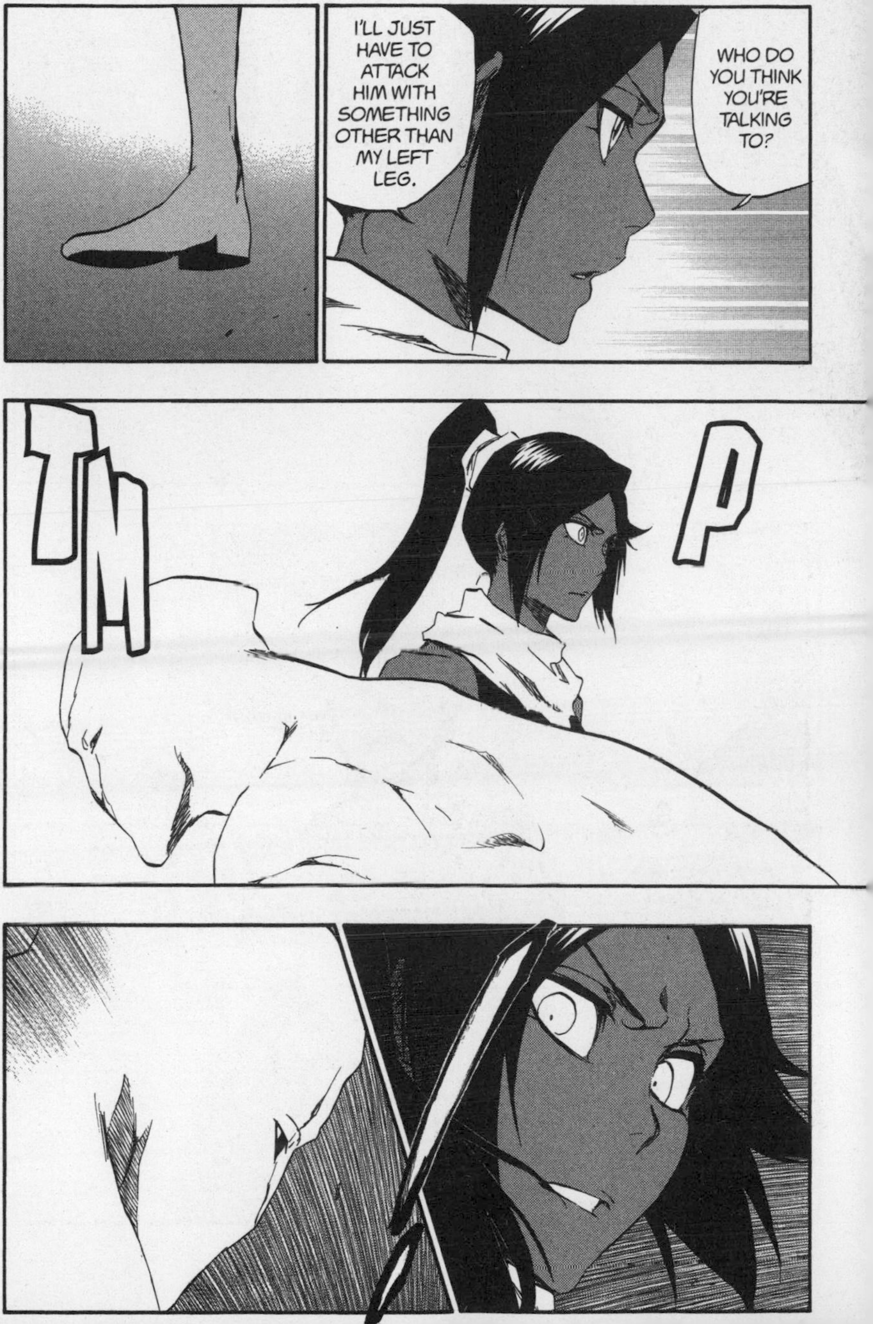
WHO DO YOU THINK YOU'RE TALKING TO?
I'LL JUST HAVE TO ATTACK HIM WITH SOMETHING OTHER THAN MY LEFT LEG.
TMP

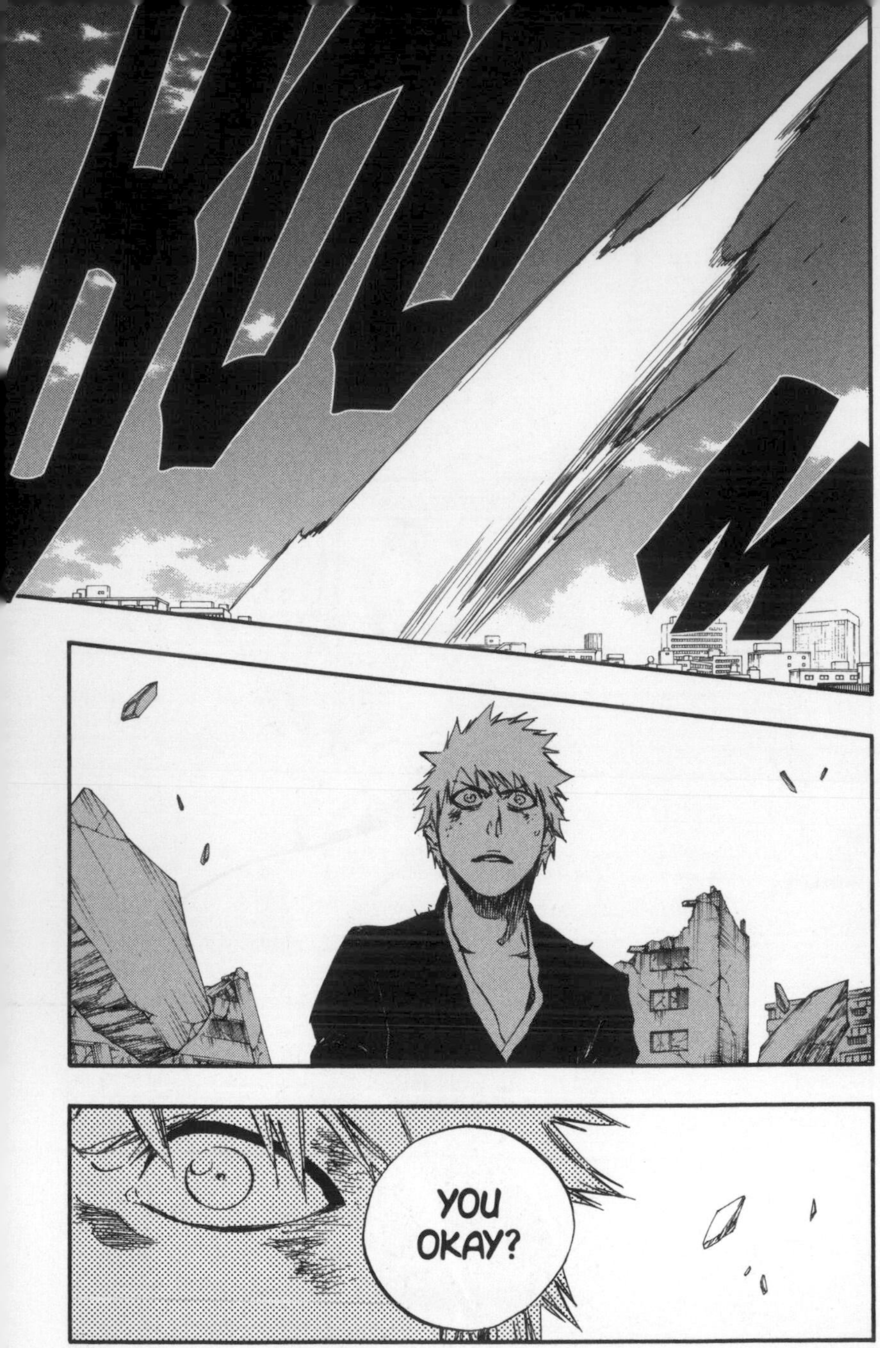
KRUUM
YOU OKAY?

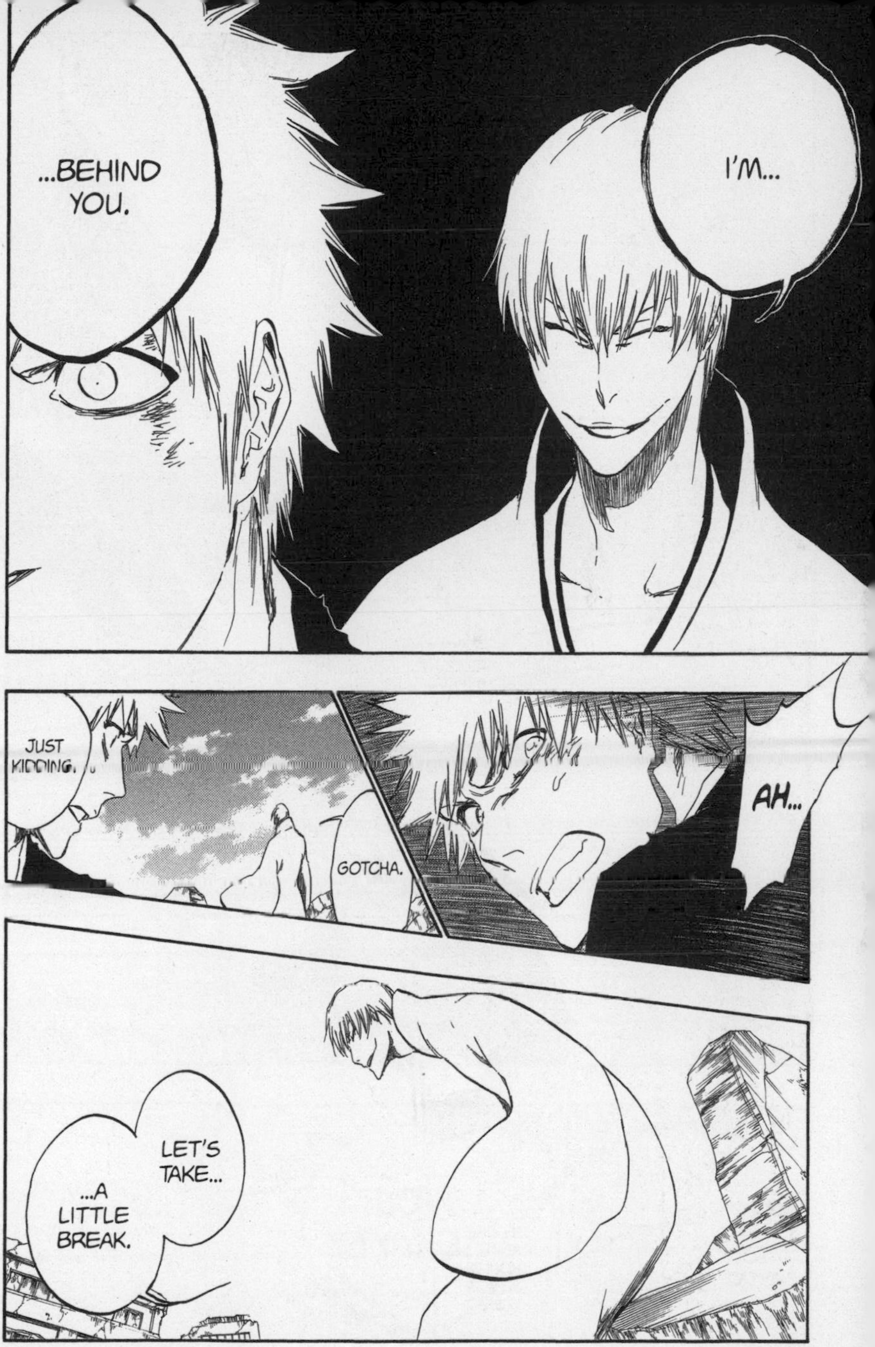
I'M...
...BEHIND YOU.
AH...
GOTCHA.
JUST KIDDING.
LET'S TAKE...
...A LITTLE BREAK.

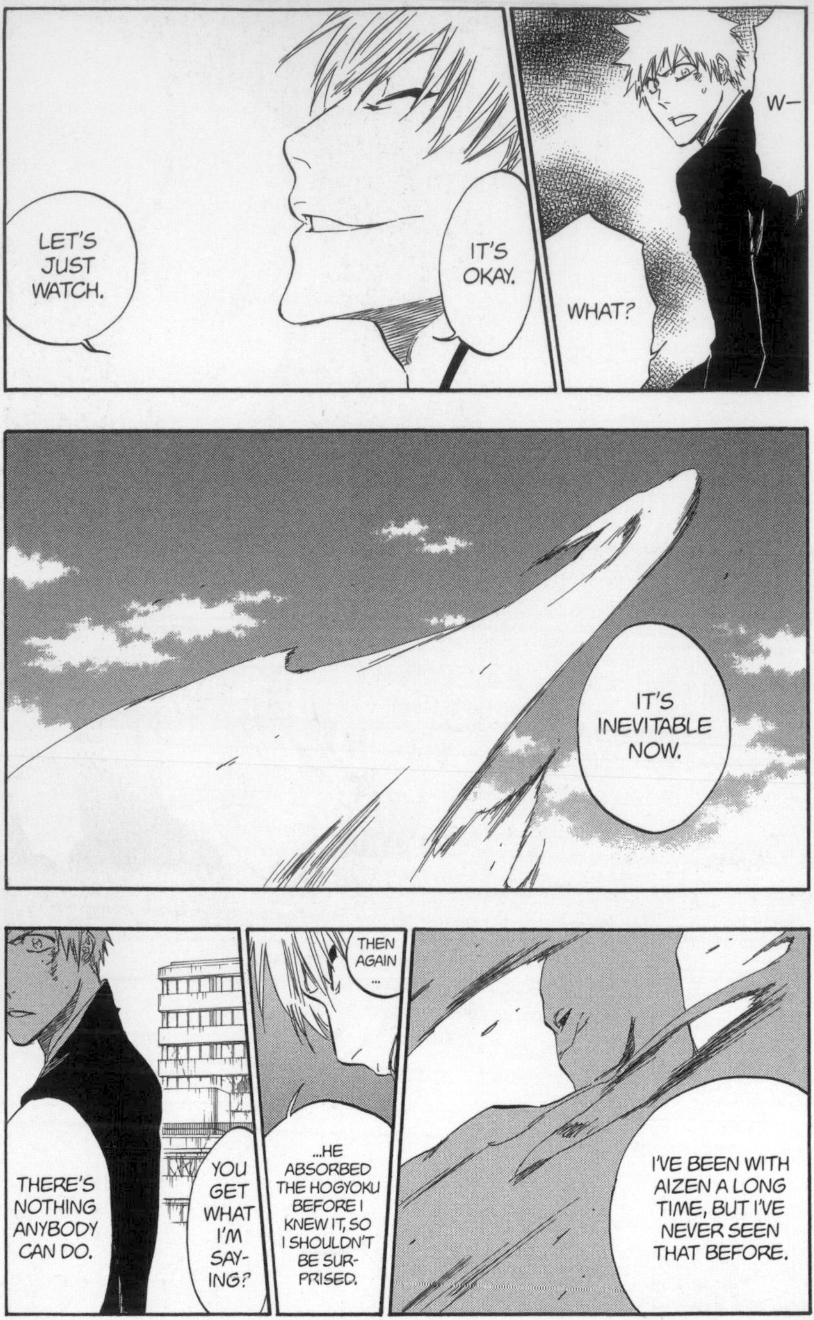
W—
WHAT?
IT'S OKAY.
LET'S JUST WATCH.
IT'S INEVITABLE NOW.
I'VE BEEN WITH AIZEN A LONG TIME, BUT I'VE NEVER SEEN THAT BEFORE.
THEN AGAIN...
...HE ABSORBED THE HOGYOKU BEFORE I KNEW IT, SO I SHOULDN'T BE SURPRISED.
YOU GET WHAT I'M SAYING?
THERE'S NOTHING ANYBODY CAN DO.

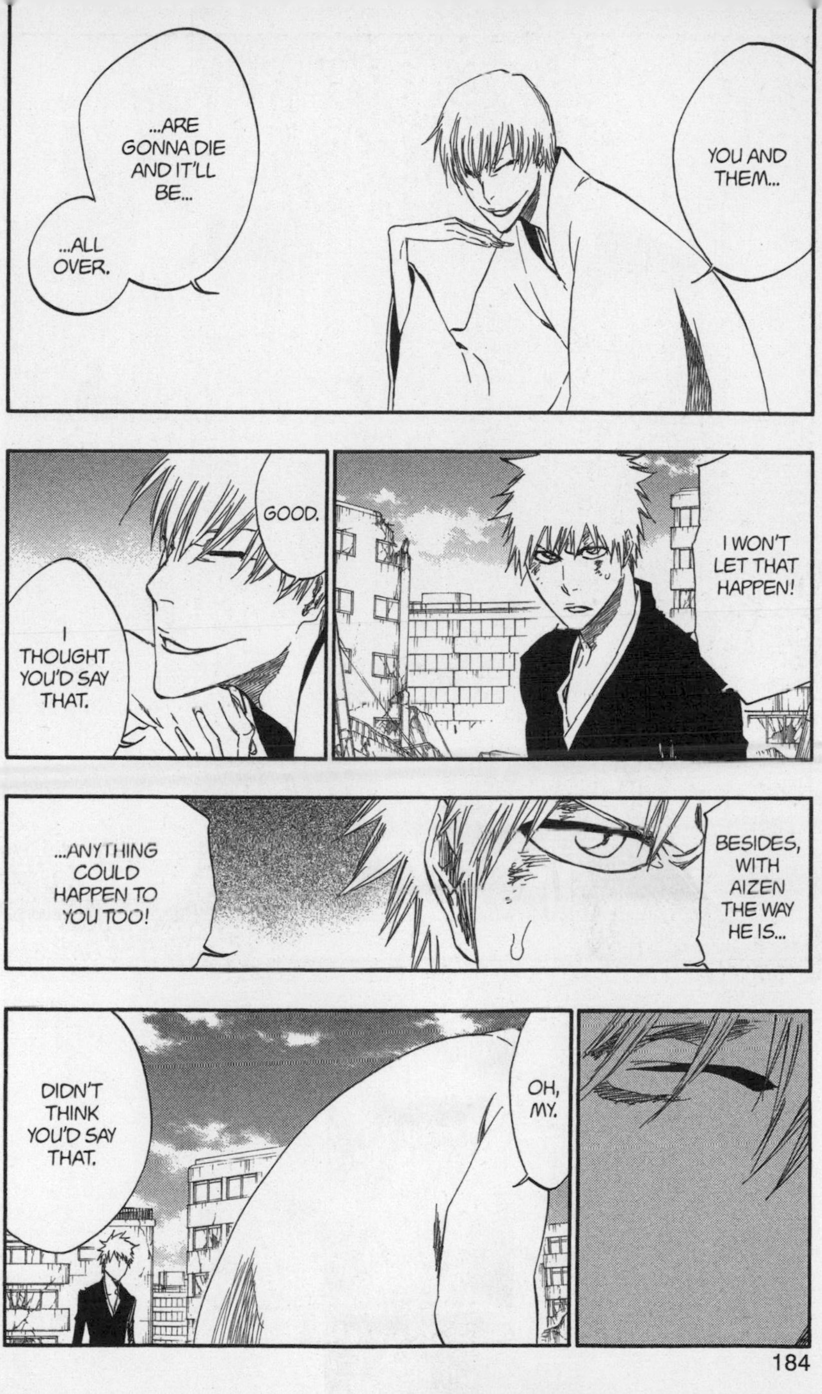
YOU AND THEM...
...ARE GONNA DIE AND IT'LL BE...
...ALL OVER.
I WON'T LET THAT HAPPEN!
GOOD.
I THOUGHT YOU'D SAY THAT.
BESIDES, WITH AIZEN THE WAY HE IS...
...ANYTHING COULD HAPPEN TO YOU TOO!
OH, MY.
DIDN'T THINK YOU'D SAY THAT.

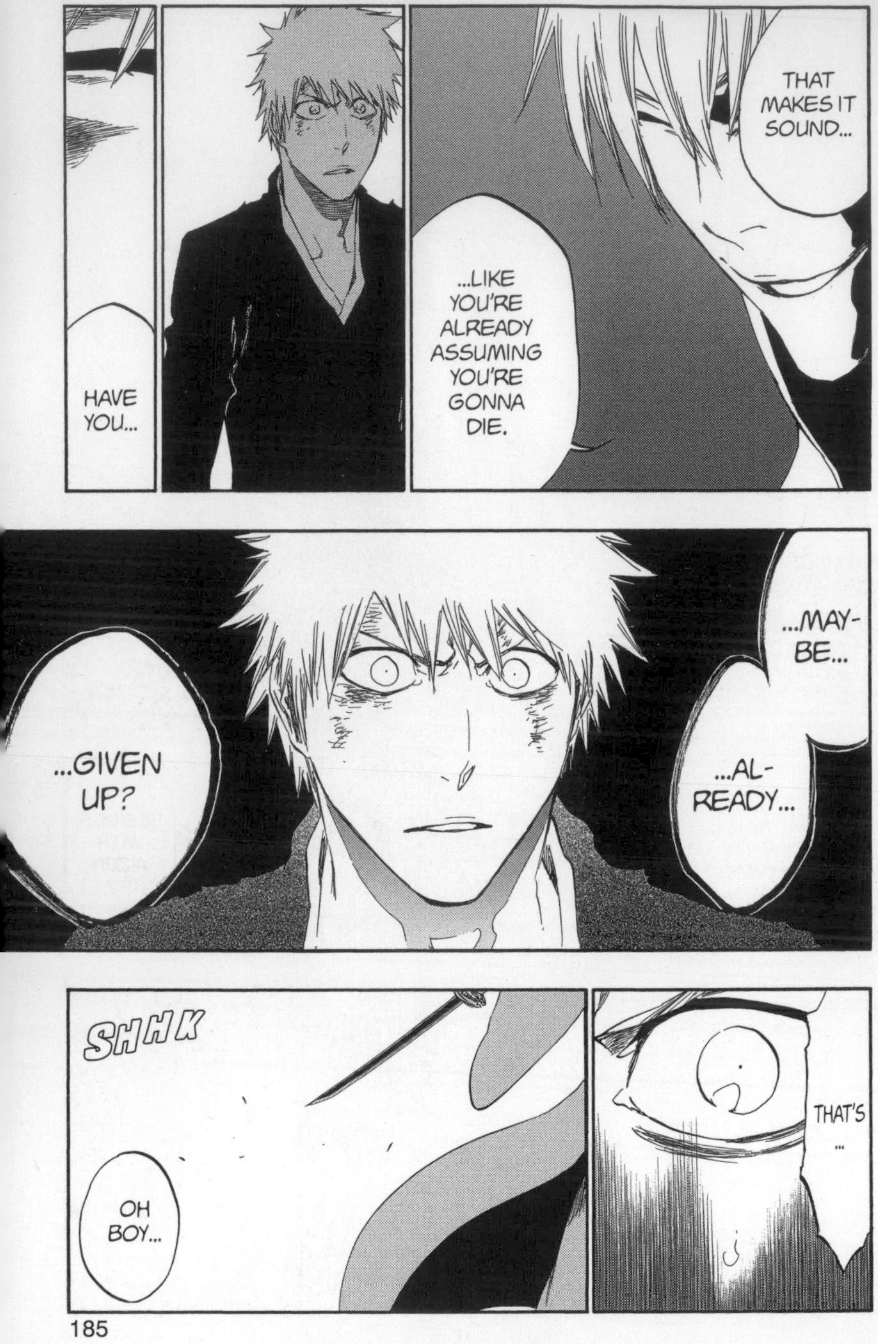
THAT MAKES IT SOUND...
...LIKE YOU'RE ALREADY ASSUMING YOU'RE GONNA DIE.
HAVE YOU...
...MAY-BE...
...AL-READY...
...GIVEN UP?
THAT'S ...
SHHK
OH BOY...

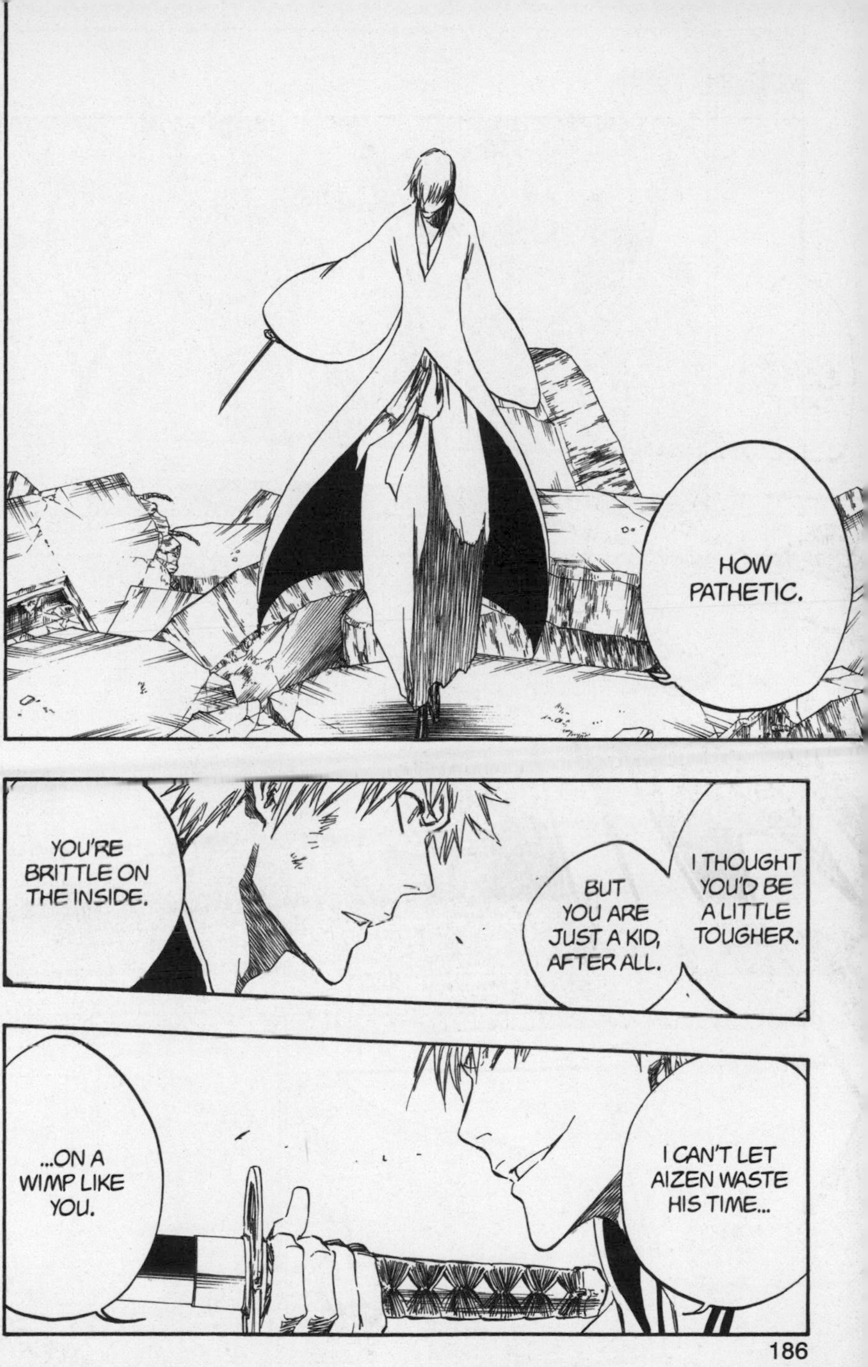
HOW PATHETIC.
I THOUGHT YOU'D BE A LITTLE TOUGHER.
BUT YOU ARE JUST A KID, AFTER ALL.
YOU'RE BRITTLE ON THE INSIDE.
I CAN'T LET AIZEN WASTE HIS TIME...
...ON A WIMP LIKE YOU.

READ THIS WAY

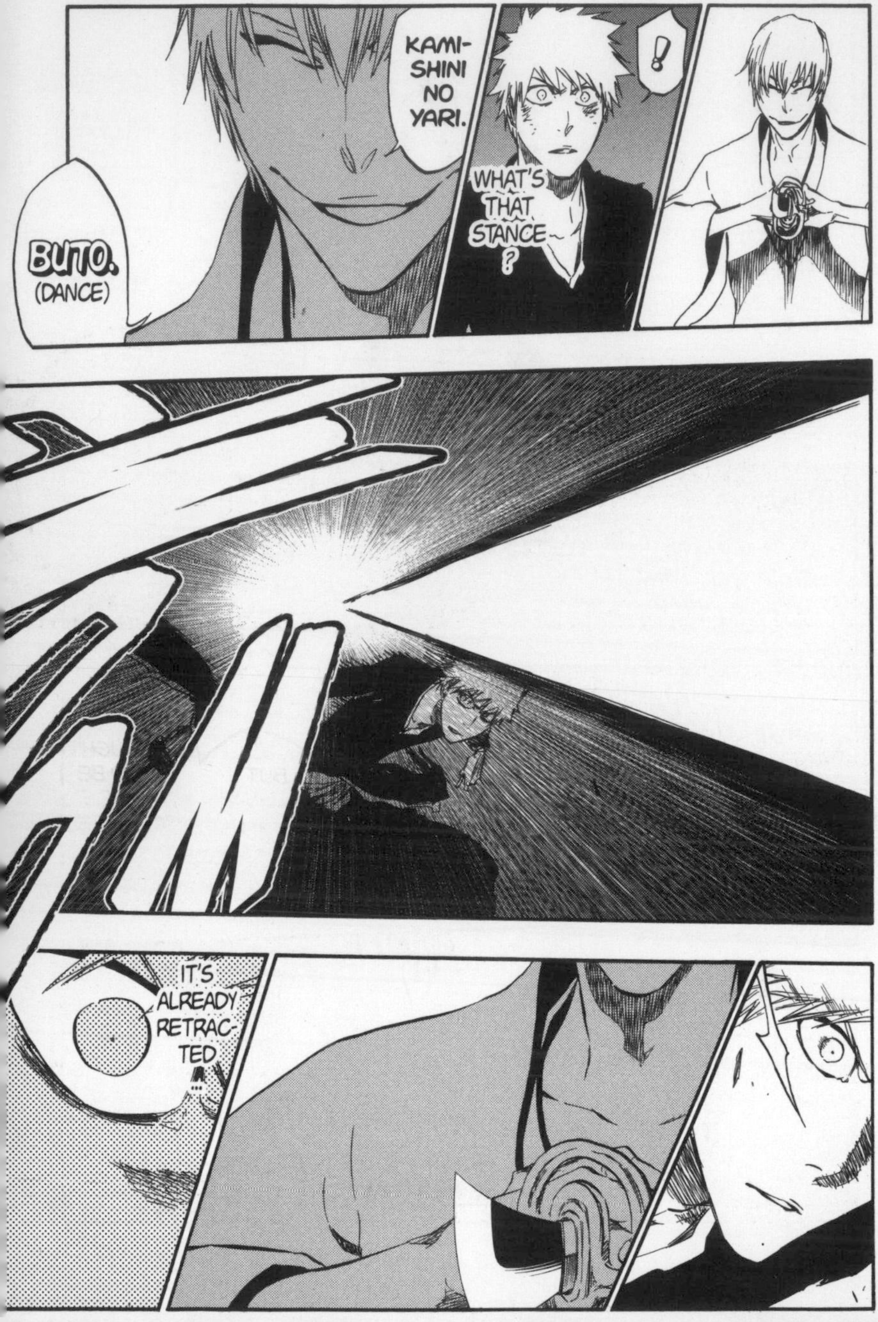
!
WHAT'S THAT STANCE?
KAMI-SHINI NO YARI.
BUTO. (DANCE)
IT'S ALREADY RETRACTED...

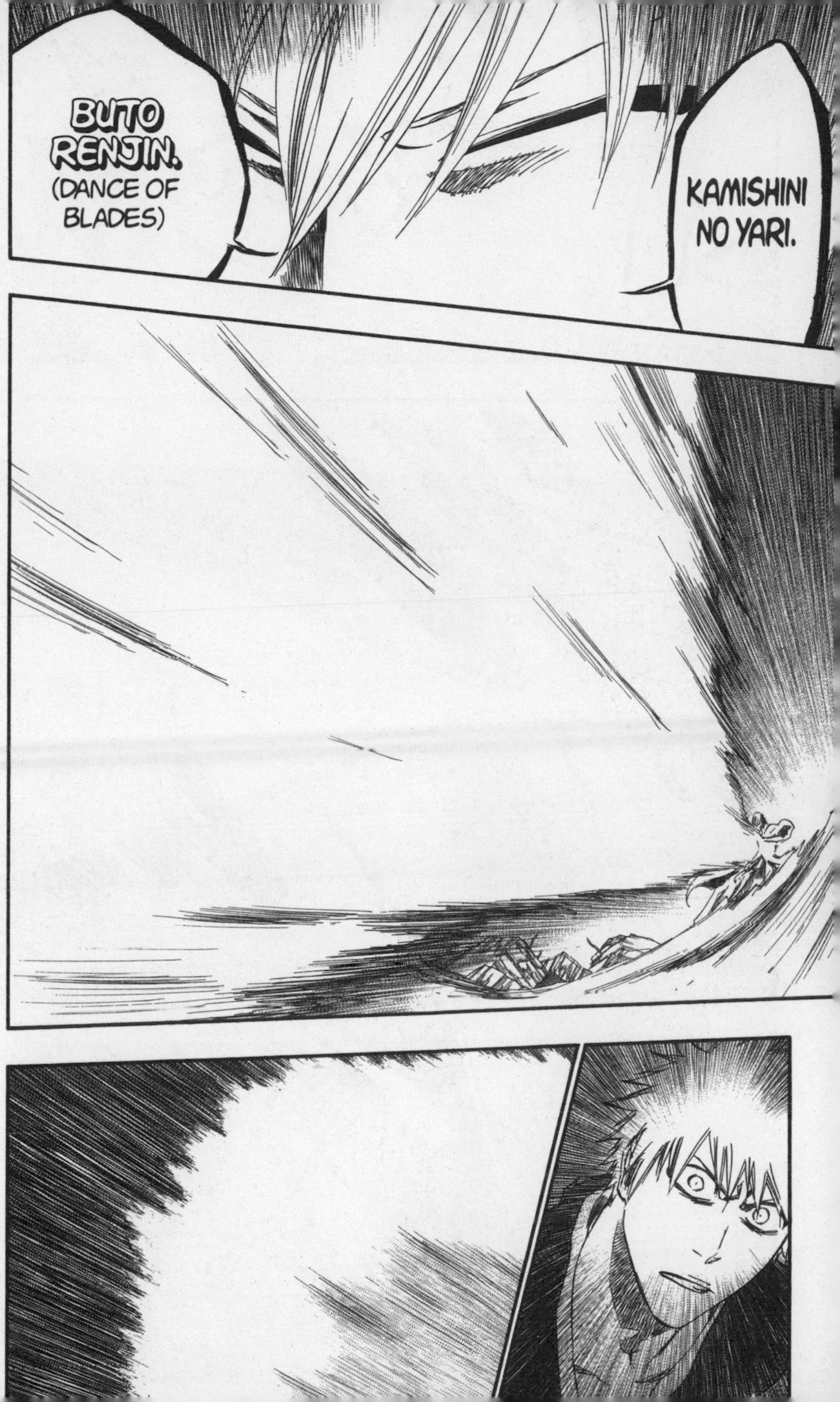
KAMISHINI NO YARI.
BUTO RENJIN. (DANCE OF BLADES)

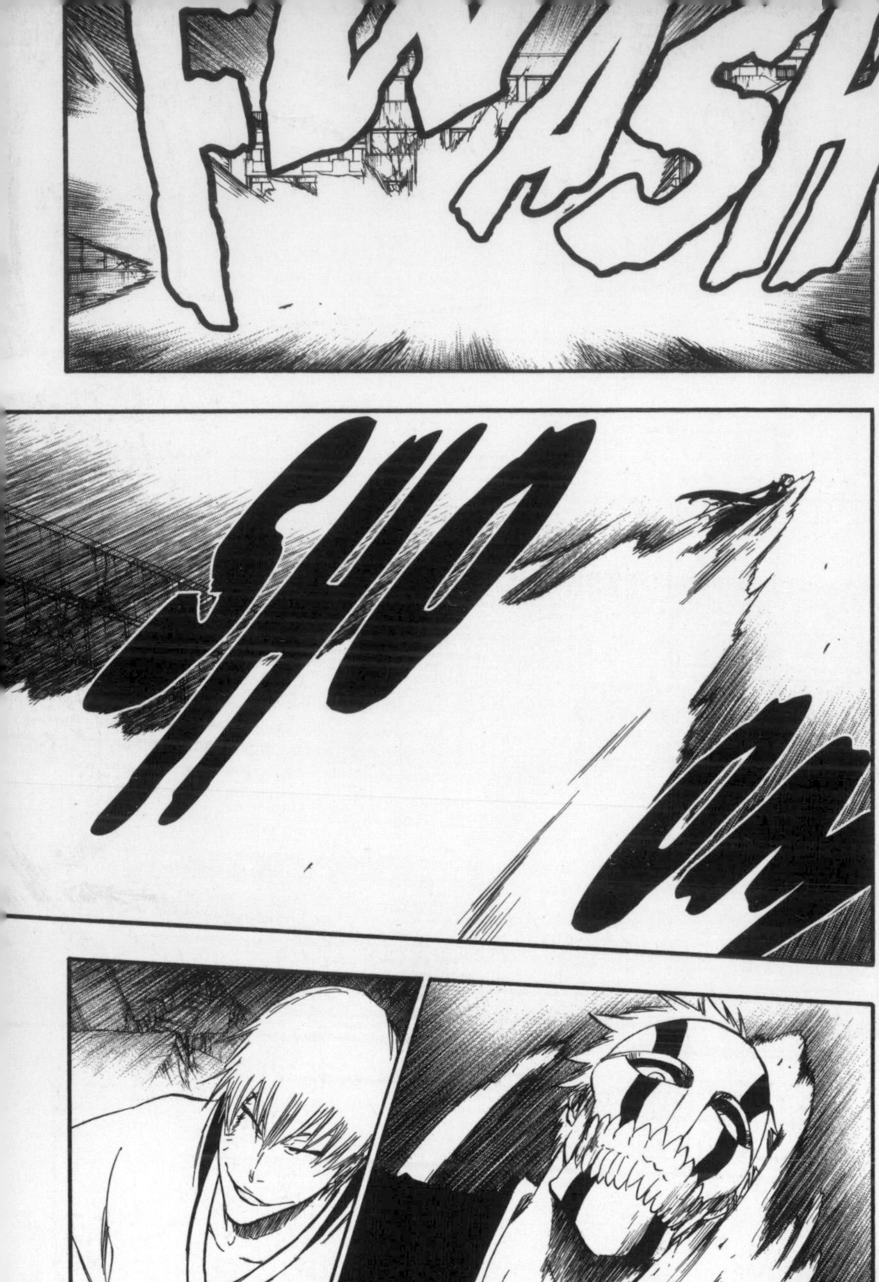
FLASH

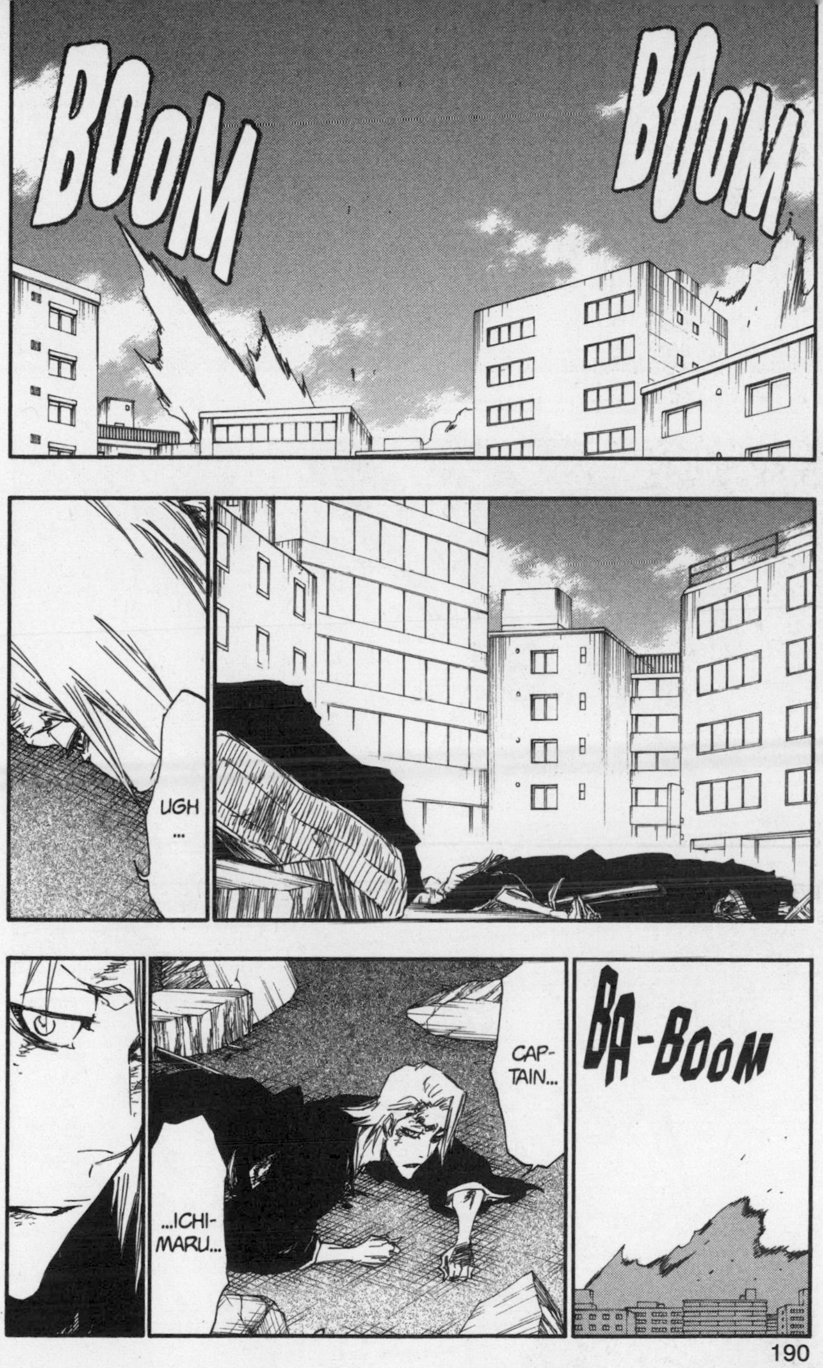
BOOM
BOOM
UGH ...
BA-BOOM
CAP-TAIN...
...ICHI-MARU...

READ THIS WAY

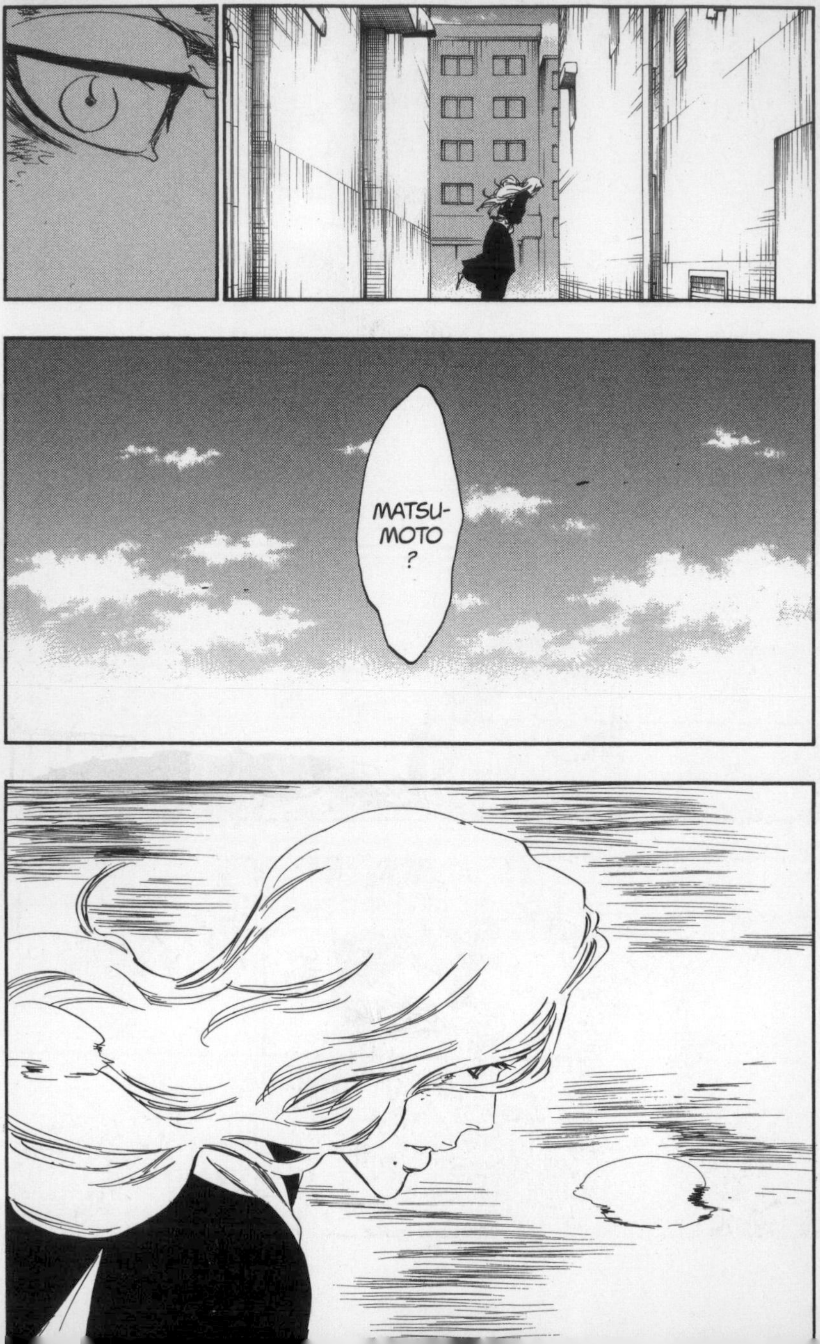
MATSU-MOTO ?

Next Volume Preview

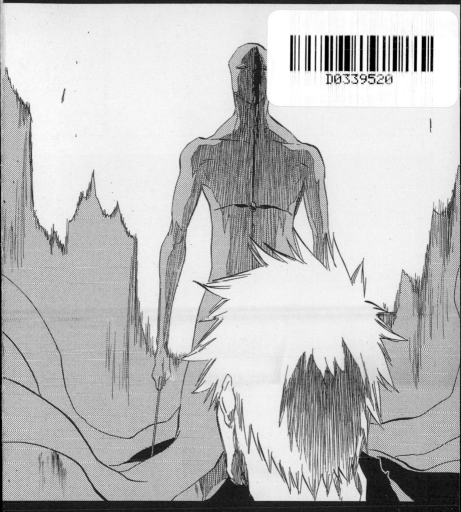

As Ichigo continues his fight against the enigmatic Gin Ichimaru, Aizen completes his terrifying metamorphosis. With his new powers leaving all others in fear, Aizen takes the final steps toward his goals. But what can Ichigo do to stop him...?